M000239796

Richard Pugh

Aimee Gott

Sams **Teach Yourself**

R in 24 Hours

in **24**
Hours

SAMS   800 East 96th Street, Indianapolis, Indiana, 46240 USA

Sams Teach Yourself R in 24 Hours

Copyright © 2016 by Pearson Education, Inc.

ISBN-13: 978-0-672-33848-9
ISBN-10: 0-672-33848-3

Library of Congress Control Number: 2015913320

2   18

Trademarks

All terms mentioned in this book that are known to be trademarks or service marks have been appropriately capitalized. Sams Publishing cannot attest to the accuracy of this information. Use of a term in this book should not be regarded as affecting the validity of any trademark or service mark.

Warning and Disclaimer

Every effort has been made to make this book as complete and as accurate as possible, but no warranty or fitness is implied. The information provided is on an "as is" basis. The authors and the publisher shall have neither liability nor responsibility to any person or entity with respect to any loss or damages arising from the information contained in this book.

Special Sales

For information about buying this title in bulk quantities, or for special sales opportunities (which may include electronic versions; custom cover designs; and content particular to your business, training goals, marketing focus, or branding interests), please contact our corporate sales department at corpsales@pearsoned.com or (800) 382-3419.

For government sales inquiries, please contact governmentsales@pearsoned.com.
For questions about sales outside the U.S., please contact international@pearsoned.com.

Editor-in-Chief
Mark Taub

Acquisitions Editor
Trina MacDonald

Development Editor
Songlin Qiu

Managing Editor
Kristy Hart

Project Editor
Elaine Wiley

Copy Editor
Bart Reed

Indexer
Tim Wright

Proofreader
Katie Matejka

Technical Editor
Stephanie Locke

Editorial Assistant
Olivia Basegio

Cover Designer
Mark Shirar

Compositor
Nonie Ratcliff

Contents at a Glance

Table of Contents

Preface

Mango Solutions has been teaching face-to-face R training courses to business professionals and academics alike for over 13 years. In this time, we've seen R grow from its early days as a low cost alternative to S-PLUS and SAS to become the leading analytical programming language in the world today, with several thousand contributors and somewhere upward of a million users. R is widely used throughout academia and is commercially supported by the likes of Microsoft, Google, HP, and Oracle.

In Mango's face-to-face training program we teach R to statisticians, data scientists, physicists, biologists, chemists, geographers, and psychologists among others. All are looking to R to help improve the way they analyze their data in a professional environment. Our aim with this book was to take tried and tested training material and turn it into a lasting resource for anyone looking to learn R for analysis.

Who Should Read This Book?

This book is designed for professional statisticians, data scientists, and analysts looking to widen the scope of analytical tools available to them by learning R. Although it is expected that you might have some programming knowledge in another analytical application or language for data analysis, such as SAS, Python, or Excel/VBA, this is not a prerequisite. This book is suitable for complete novices in programming. From the start, we do not assume any prior knowledge of R; however, those familiar with the basics may find that they can jump straight to later chapters.

What Should You Expect from This Book?

This book is designed to take you from the basics of the R language through common tasks in data science, including data manipulation, visualization, and modeling, to elements of the language that will allow you to produce high-quality, production-ready code. As with our face-to-face training, this book is structured around simple and easy-to-follow examples, all of which are available to download from the book's website (http://www.mango-solutions.com/wp/teach-yourself-r-in-24-hours-book). Throughout, we introduce good practices for writing code as well as provide tips and tricks from our combined experience in R development.

By the end of this book, you should have a good understanding of the fundamentals of R as well as many of the most commonly used packages. You should have a good understanding of what makes well written R code and how to implement this yourself.

How Is This Book Organized?

This book is designed to guide you through everything you need to know to get started with the R language and then introduce additional elements of the language for specific tasks.

The following is an outline of each of the hours and what to expect:

Hour 1, "The R Community"—In this hour, we start by looking at how R evolved from the S language to become the all-purpose data science programming language that it is today. The R community offers a plethora of help and support options for users. We look at some of the better-known options during this hour.

Hour 2, "The R Environment"—In this hour, we start a new R session via RStudio, type some basic commands, and explore the idea of an R "object." You will be more formally introduced to the concept of an R package.

Hour 3, "Single-Mode Data Structures"—In this hour, we describe the standard types of data found in R and introduce three key structures that can be used to store these data types: vectors, matrices, and arrays. We illustrate the ways in which these structures can be created and manage these data structures with a focus on how we can extract data from them.

Hour 4, "Multi-Mode Data Structures"—The majority of data sources contain a mixture of data types, which we need to store together in a simple, effective format. In this hour, we focus on two key data structures that allow us to store "multi-mode" data: lists and data frames. We illustrate the ways in which these structures can be created and manage these data structures with a focus on how we can extract data from them. We also look at how these two data structures can be effectively used in our day-to-day work.

Hour 5, "Dates, Times, and Factors"—In this hour, you learn more about some of the special data types in R that enable us to work with dates and times and with categorical data.

Hour 6, "Common R Utility Functions"—In this hour, we introduce you to some of the most common utility functions in R that you will find yourself using every day.

Hour 7, "Writing Functions: Part I"—One of the strengths of R is that we can extend it by writing our own functions, allowing us to create utilities that can perform a variety of tasks. In this hour, we look at ways in which we can create our own functions, specify inputs, and return results to the user. We also discuss the "if/else" structure in R and use it to control the flow of code within a function.

Hour 8, "Writing Functions: Part II"—This hour looks at a range of advanced function-writing topics, such as returning error messaging, checking whether inputs are appropriate to our functions, and the use of function "ellipses."

Hour 9, "Loops and Summaries"—In this hour, you see how we can apply simple functions and code in a more "applied" fashion. This allows us to perform tasks repeatedly over sections of our data without the need to produce verbose, repetitive code.

Hour 10, "Importing and Exporting"—In this hour, we introduce common methods for importing and exporting data. By the end of the hour you will have seen how R can be used to read and write flat files and connect to database management systems (DBMSs) as well as Microsoft Excel.

Hour 11, "Data Manipulation and Transformation"—As data scientists and statisticians, we rarely get to control the structure and format of our data. Now we will look a little closer at the structure of our data. Several approaches to data manipulation in R have evolved over time. In this hour, we start by looking at what could be called "traditional" approaches to the data manipulation tasks of sorting, setting, and merging. We then look at the popular packages **reshape**, **reshape2**, and **tidyr** for data restructuring.

Hour 12, "Efficient Data Handling in R"—We begin the hour by looking at the incredibly popular **dplyr** package. The **data.table** package is a standalone package for data manipulation that offers greater efficiency for very large data.

Hour 13, "Graphics"—After all the manipulations to our data, we want to be able to start to do something with it. In this hour, we look at how we can create graphics using the base graphics functionality, including how to send your graphics to devices such as a PDF and the standard graphics functions. We finally look at how to control the layout of graphics on the page.

Hour 14, "The ggplot2 Package for Graphics"—In this hour, we look at the hugely popular **ggplot2** package, developed by Hadley Wickham for creating high-quality graphics.

Hour 15, "Lattice Graphics"—Here we will look at a third way of creating graphics: using the **lattice** package. This graphic system is well suited to graphing highly grouped data, with the code designed to closely resemble the modeling capabilities of R.

Hour 16, "Introduction to R Models and Object Orientation"—In this hour, we see how to fit a simple linear model and assess its performance using a range of textual and graphical methods. Beyond this, we introduce "object orientation" and see how the R statistical modeling framework is built on this concept.

Hour 17, "Common R Models"—In this hour, we extend the ideas of the previous hour to other modeling approaches. Specifically, we look at Generalized Linear Models, nonlinear models, time series models, and survival models.

Hour 18, "Code Efficiency"—In this hour, we look at some of the techniques we can use to improve the efficiency and, importantly, the professionalism of our R code.

Hour 19, "Package Building"—When we put our code into a package, it forces us to ensure that our code is of a high standard and we are adhering to good practices, such as documenting our code. We focus here on making sure our code is well written and documented, the starting point for high-quality, professional code that is easy to share and reuse.

Hour 20, "Advanced Package Building"—There are a number of ways we can extend a package to make it more robust to changes and easier for users to get started with. You learn the most common of these extra components in this hour.

Hour 21, "Writing R Classes"—In this hour, we take a general look at some key features of object-oriented programming before focusing in on R's S3 implementation.

Hour 22, "Formal Class Systems"—During this hour, we look at the more formal S4 and Reference Class systems in R. Along the way, you will be introduced to concepts such as validity checking, multiple dispatch, message-passing object orientation, and mutable objects.

Hour 23, "Dynamic Reporting"—Up to this point we have seen the fundamentals of the R language as well as the aspects of R that allow us to ensure that we write high-quality, well-documented, and easily shareable code. In this hour, we take a look at one of the ways you can extend your use of R, specifically for simplifying the generation of reports that rely heavily on R-generated output.

Hour 24, "Building Web Applications with Shiny"—Although you may initially be put off by the idea of building a web application, we introduce a package that allows you to generate web applications entirely in R, writing only R code. This is currently one of the most popular packages available in R, with more and more packages being added to CRAN that use this framework.

About the Sample Code

Throughout this book, we have included examples of the concepts that are being introduced. You may notice that the code is prefixed with the symbols ">" and "+". These are the

R prompt and continuation characters and do not need to be entered when writing code. We have used the formatting conventions of `function` for a function name and **package** for a package name.

All of the code examples included in this book are available from our web page: http://www.mango-solutions.com/wp/teach-yourself-r-in-24-hours-book/

NOTE

Code-Continuation Arrows and Listing Line NumbersYou might see code-continuation arrows (➥) occasionally in this book to indicate when a line of code is too long to fit on the printed page. Also, some listings have line numbers and some do not. The listings that have line numbers have them so that we can reference code by line; the listings that do not have line numbers are not referenced by line.

Contacting the Authors

If you have any comments or questions about this book, please drop us an email at rin24hours@mango-solutions.com.

About the Authors

Andy Nicholls has a Master of Mathematics degree from the University of Bath and Master of Science in Statistics with Applications in Medicine from the University of Southampton. Andy worked as a Senior Statistician in the pharmaceutical industry for a number of years before joining Mango Solutions as an R consultant in 2011. Since joining Mango, Andy has taught more than 50 on-site R training courses and has been involved in the development of more than 30 R packages. Today, he manages Mango Solution's R consultancy team and continues to be a regular contributor to the quarterly LondonR events, by far the largest R user group in the UK, with over 1,000 meet-up members. Andy lives near the historical city of Bath, UK with his wonderful, tolerant wife and son.

Richard Pugh has a first-class Mathematics degree from the University of Bath. Richard worked as a statistician in the pharmaceutical industry before joining Insightful, the developers of S-PLUS, joining the pre-sales consulting team. Richard's role at Insightful included a variety of activities, providing a range of training and consulting services to blue-chip customers across many sectors. In 2002, Richard co-founded Mango Solutions, developing the company and leading technical efforts around R and other analytic software. Richard is now Mango's Chief Data Scientist and speaks regularly at data science and R events. Richard lives in Bradford on Avon, UK with his wife and two kids, and spends most of his "spare" (ha!) time renovating his house.

Aimee Gott has a PhD in Statistics from Lancaster University where she also completed her undergraduate and master's degrees. As Training Lead, Aimee has delivered over 200 days of training for Mango. She has delivered on-site training courses in Europe and the U.S. in all aspects of R, as well as shorter workshops and online webinars. Aimee oversees Mango's training course development across the data science pipeline, and regularly attends R user groups and meet-ups. In her spare time, Aimee enjoys learning European languages and documenting her travels through photography.

Dedications

This book is dedicated to my wife, for her love and support and for putting up with losing our summer to all the late nights, and to my baby boy who learnt to sit up, eat, crawl, and walk whilst this book was being written! —Andy Nicholls

This book is dedicated to my family for having to put up with me writing the book at weekends. —Richard Pugh

To Stephen, Carol, Richard, and Kirstie. —Aimee Gott

Acknowledgments

Throughout the process of writing, many people have taken time to assist us, guide us, and shape this book. First of all, thanks go to Andy Miskell, Jeff Stagg, Mike K. Smith, and Susan Duke, who took the time to review our initial outline. Thanks also go to the consultancy team at Mango and Stephen Kaluzny of TIBCO who were all able to answer our questions while writing.

We would also like to thank all those who have been involved in the production of this book. In particular we would like to thank Elaine Wiley (production editor), Trina MacDonald (acquisitions editor), Songlin Qiu (development editor), Olivia Basegio (publisher assistant), Stephanie Locke (technical editor), Bart Reed (copyeditor), and Katie Matejka (proofreader).

We Want to Hear from You!

As the reader of this book, you are our most important critic and commentator. We value your opinion and want to know what we're doing right, what we could do better, what areas you'd like to see us publish in, and any other words of wisdom you're willing to pass our way.

We welcome your comments. You can email or write to let us know what you did or didn't like about this book—as well as what we can do to make our books better.

Please note that we cannot help you with technical problems related to the topic of this book.

When you write, please be sure to include this book's title and author as well as your name and email address. We will carefully review your comments and share them with the author and editors who worked on the book.

Email: errata@informit.com

Mail: Addison-Wesley/Prentice Hall Publishing
         ATTN: Reader Feedback
         330 Hudson Street
         7th Floor
         New York, New York, 10013

Reader Services

Register your copy of Teach Yourself R in 24 Hours at informit.com for convenient access to downloads, updates, and corrections as they become available. To start the registration process, go to informit.com/register and log in or create an account.* Enter the product ISBN, 9780672338489, and click Submit. Once the process is complete, you will find any available bonus content under Registered Products.

*Be sure to check the box that you would like to hear from us in order to receive exclusive discounts on future editions of this product.

HOUR 1
The R Community

What You'll Learn in This Hour:

► A brief history of S and R

► An overview of the R community

► The development and release of R versions

In this hour we start by looking at how R evolved from the S language to become the all-purpose data science programming language that it is today. It is important when learning any programming language to understand a little about where it came from and why it functions as it does. This is particularly relevant for R because many of the quirkier aspects of the language have roots in S.

As a free and open-source programming language, R relies strongly on community input. The R community offers a plethora of help and support options for users. We look at some of the better-known options during this hour. Toward the end of the hour we look a little closer at the development and release of R versions.

A Concise History of R

When I first started teaching introductory R courses, I would ask how many people in the room had any experience with S. This was an important question for an R training course because the languages are syntactically similar. If you know S, then what are you doing in an Introduction to R course?! A couple of years ago, the number of raised hands had dropped significantly, and I revised this question to ask, "How many people here have actually heard of S?" Today, very few people have but to begin to understand R, so it helps to know just where it came from, and that means knowing what S is and how it came to be.

The Birth of S

S was initially developed at AT&T Bell Laboratories by John Chambers in the mid-to-late 1970s—a time that predates Google and the need to be able to search for help concerning your programming language! John Chambers' original idea is beautifully portrayed in the now infamous sketch from 1976, shown in Figure 1.1. The essence of Chambers' idea was that his then-unnamed language would provide an accessible interface to lower-level Fortran subroutines, thereby reducing the time a statistician would have to spend coding. Today, languages such as R, SAS, Matlab, and Python all take a similar approach, but at the time this idea was fairly ground-breaking.

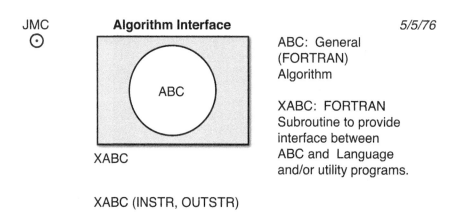

FIGURE 1.1
John Chambers' sketch of the idea that became S

The name "S" stands for "Statistics." It was chosen over other names primarily for consistency (the C language was also born out of Bell Laboratories a few years earlier) and because pretty much every name proposed began with the letter S. One name in particular, SAS (Statistical Analysis Software), had already been taken.

The S language continued to grow and evolve with several key changes that shaped both the S language and eventually R today. These included a gradual transition toward C for internal routines, a switch from macros to functions, and the introduction of the "S3" and then the "S4" class systems, which are described in Hour 21, "Writing R Classes," and Hour 22, "Formal Class Systems."

A particularly important milestone in the life of S was the development and release of the first version of S-PLUS by Statistical Sciences, Inc., in 1988. In the next few years, Statistical Sciences built a new graphical user interface for S and added interactive graphical capabilities by integrating the GUI with their Axum product. They also added connectors to a number of Microsoft products, such as Excel and PowerPoint. However, perhaps most significant of all was that in 1993 Statistical Sciences acquired the exclusive license to market and distribute the S language, closing off the development of S to outsiders. TIBCO acquired the then-owners of S-PLUS, Insightful, in 2008. However, to date, no new versions of S-PLUS have been released since the acquisition, with TIBCO turning their attentions toward R and becoming a founding member of the R Consortium in 2015.

The Birth of R

Earlier in this hour we said that S and R were "syntactically similar." The main R Project website for R, www.r-project.org, does not shy away from the relationship with S, describing R as "similar to the S language and environment" and claiming that "much code written for S runs unaltered under R." It does not go as far as saying that R is a copy or reimplementation of S, but R is widely considered to have evolved from S. The near-identical syntax is no coincidence! The first version of the R language was developed by Robert Gentleman and Ross Ihaka of The University of Aukland in the mid-late 1990s. The name "R" is a play on the names Robert and Ross, though the significance of the position of the letter R next to S in the alphabet should not be downplayed.

Robert and Ross were soon joined by a core group of contributors known as the "R Development Core Team," which is today responsible for the development and release of new R versions. Following the release of R-1.5.0, the core members created "The R Foundation," which, among other things, is responsible for copyright and documentation of R. The R Foundation now contains many of the original S development team, including John Chambers.

R has undergone many iterations of its own since the early days, with minor releases approximately every 3 months. However, much of the functionality, particularly the core statistic routines, resembles the S language of old.

The R Community *(HUGE!)*

Before we install R and begin programming, we would like to highlight some of the available online resources for R. Indeed, there are many online resources, almost all of which can be accessed via the main R project website (see Figure 1.2). From here you can download the latest copy of R, download R packages, find help on R, join several R mailing lists, search for R books such as this, and find events.

A big difference between the open-source R language and commercially supported software such as SAS and SPSS is the large and active online community that has built up around R. Like many open-source communities, the R community is a weird yet wonderful beast that takes some getting used to! However, one of the goals of a group formed in 2015, known as the R Consortium, is to try to make R more accessible for newcomers to the language.

The R Project for Statistical Computing

[Home]

Download

CRAN

R Project

About R
Contributors
What's New?
Mailing Lists
Bug Tracking
Conferences
Search

R Foundation

Foundation
Board
Members
Donors
Donate

Documentation

Manuals

Getting Started

R is a free software environment for statistical computing and graphics. It compiles and runs on a wide variety of UNIX platforms, Windows and MacOS. To download R, please choose your preferred CRAN mirror.

If you have questions about R like how to download and install the software, or what the license terms are, please read our answers to frequently asked questions before you send an email.

News

- The R Journal Volume 7/1 is available.

- R version 3.2.1 (World-Famous Astronaut) has been released on 2015-06-18.

- R version 3.1.3 (Smooth Sidewalk) has been released on 2015-03-09.

- useR! 2015, will take place at the University of Aalborg, Denmark, June 30 - July 3, 2015.

- useR! 2014, took place at the University of California, Los Angeles, USA June 30 - July 3, 2014.

FIGURE 1.2
The main page of the R Project website, www.r-project.org

Mailing Lists

Several mailing lists are dedicated to R, each listed on the R Project website. The first port of call for most new users is the R-help mailing list. My advice to any newcomer is to use the searchable archives on the R Project website (and read the posting guide) before posting any help requests to the community because chances are someone else has had the same issue before. If you do use R-help, what you will first notice is the speed at which users are rushing to help you out; night and day the community is waiting to embrace your R challenge. On the flip side, do beware of making critical remarks about the behavior of a function or quality of the documentation. The chances are the author is reading your post with no sales or marketing team sitting next to him telling you to be kind!

R Manuals

A typical response to an R-help request used to be "read the manuals." Like the language itself, the R manuals, of which there are several, have their roots in S. If you do decide to consult them for help, we can promise you that the information you're looking for will be there. In particular, the "Writing R Extensions" manual is a very handy reference for those wanting to develop and deploy R packages for mass consumption. However, unless you are already very familiar with general programming constructs such as object orientation, and are therefore ready to jump in at the deep end, you may find the manuals hard going. The R Core Team recognizes this, and the "An Introduction to R" manual contains a subsection within the preface titled, "Suggestions to the reader" where the advice for R novices is essentially to skip the first 80 pages and "start with the introductory session in Appendix A"!

Online Resources

Plenty of online resources are available, although they are not always easy to find for the R new-comer. I've been using R for nearly 15 years, yet when I type R and a space into Google, it still thinks I'm looking for R. Kelly! Generally, though, there is enough of a divide between the worlds of R&B and of statistical programming to make Googling for R help fairly straightforward. Besides Google, there are a number of other options for searching for R-based material, some of which are listed on the R Project website. In particular, Sasha Goodman of Stanford University has created Rseek (http://rseek.org/), which searches several known R-related sites.

If you wish to search the manuals for help, you can do so directly using a tool called R Documentation, http://www.rdocumentation.org, developed by DataCamp. R Documentation is a website that pulls together documentation from the main R repositories into a single location. The website also offers the ability to search the Comprehensive R Archive Network's (CRAN's) Task Views for packages of code. We will discuss CRAN and R packages in greater detail during Hour 2, "The R Environment."

The R Consortium

On June 30, 2015, the Linux Foundation launched the R Consortium. The R Consortium consists primarily of data scientists from both industry and academia with the joint goal of trying to advance the R language and support the growth of the R community. The home page for the R Consortium is shown in Figure 1.3. Existing members of the R Foundation were joined by founding members Microsoft and RStudio (Platinum); TIBCO Software, Inc. (Gold); and Alteryx, Google, HP, Mango Solutions, Ketchum Trading, and Oracle (Silver).

The R Consortium is still very much in its infancy, but it is anticipated that its formation will both improve the accessibility of the R language and oversee its next phase of growth. The R Consortium home page may soon replace the R Project home page as the go-to starting point for the R community.

FIGURE 1.3
The home page of the R Consortium, www.r-consortium.org

User Events

Another great plus of the open-source community is the number of user events available to attend globally. New user groups are popping up all the time, and attendance numbers can vary from 5 to 500. Events are typically held in the evening, with participants giving up their own time to attend. Since the very early days of R, these user meetings have been a primary arena for R enthusiasts to meet and share ideas. Many of the more established meetings receive commercial backing.

In addition to the localized R meetings, the main "useR!" conference has been held regularly since 2004, with the number of attendees steadily increasing year over year. The conference is generally focused on developments in the R language and R packages. It is packed with presentations from academia and industry and is now backed by the R Consortium. In 2014, UseR! was joined by the Effective Applications of the R Language (EARL) conference. The primary focus of the EARL conference is the commercial usage of R across a range of industry sectors with the aim of sharing knowledge and applications of the language.

In addition to the cross-sector R conferences, there are also industry-specific R conferences for those working in either the finance or insurance industry. These are, respectively, R/Finance, which has been held annually in Chicago since 2009, and R in Insurance, which has been running annually since 2013.

R Development

Today, the R Development Core Team still controls the write-access to the R source (though as an open-source GNU project, this source code is freely available to download for anyone who wants to see it). However, much of the popularity of the R language today can also be attributed to the many contributors outside of that group who have written one or more of several thousand R "packages," freely available for download from the CRAN repository. CRAN is a network of ftp and web servers mirrored around the world, each of which contains versions of R and the contributed R packages.

The scope and quality of the R packages can vary greatly, but finding and using new R packages is an important part of the life of the modern R user. A proactive statistician or data scientist may have several hundred packages installed on his or her local machine for any particular version of R. R packages are explained in more detail in Hour 2.

Versions of R

The R Core Development Team decides when new versions of R are ready for general public release. Each release comes with a comprehensive description of additional features and fixes since the previous version. R versions follow the Major-Minor-Patch structure (for example, R-3.2.0). The first version of R, R-1.0.0 was released in February 2000, with a steady release pattern of patch, minor and very occasionally major releases, since then. In recent years the rate of release has slowed a little, with minor versions of R released approximately annually. Historically, each new minor release has had two to three associated patch versions.

NOTE   *2022-4.2*

Nicknames

R version 2.15.1 was the first R release to be given a "nickname," Roasted Marshmallows, by the R Core Development Team. Every subsequent R version has been given an interesting but apparently random nickname. This nickname is printed on start-up but can also be accessed by running the line `R.Version()$nickname`.

If you have a background in software such as SAS or Microsoft Excel, you may wonder why R versions are released so frequently. There is often a concern that the high frequency of releases is a sign of instability and that R is very buggy. Actually the opposite is true; however, commercial organizations do tend to be cautious about both the R versions that they adopt and the frequency with which they adopt them. Often companies wait until the second or third patched version of a minor release, such as R-3.1.2, before upgrading their R environment.

If you do ever identify a bug in R, it is very simple and easy to report it by emailing the package maintainer. Unlike most commercially backed closed-source models, the open model allows a direct dialogue with the person developing the code. Once it has been established as a genuine bug, you can work with the maintainer on a solution and in some cases gain recognition as a package author for your efforts. Once a resolution has been established to the issue, your bug-fix is usually implemented in the next patched or minor release. This means you typically never have to wait more than a couple of months for a bug to be fixed.

Summary

During this hour you were presented with a brief history of the evolution of S and then R. Along the way you heard terms such as "S3" and "S4," deriving from S, which will be mentioned at various points throughout the remaining hours and covered specifically during Hours 21 and 22.

You were introduced to the R community and the various groups that support the R language: the R Core Development Team, the R Foundation, and the R Consortium. We looked at a selection of the available online resources and touched on the difficulties of searching for R help. Finally, we discussed the development cycle of R and what it means for bugs in the code.

In the "Activities" section, we install R and the RStudio integrated development environment (IDE). In the next hour, we will begin to use and explore R through the RStudio IDE.

Q&A

Q. With so many versions of R, should I be worried about backward compatibility?

A. If we consider the base R language and ignore the many thousand additional packages available to download from CRAN, it is fair to say that R is pretty backward compatible. Indeed there are many features of R today that exist due to decisions made when the S language was developed. However, the same cannot be said for the thousands of contributed packages residing in the main CRAN repository. Even some of the best known and respected R package authors change their mind from time to time, and package version numbers can make a big difference. Ensuring quality and consistency across R packages is one of the biggest challenges facing the R Foundation today.

Q. A colleague of mine has sent me a bunch of S scripts. Will they run in R?

A. The official line is, "There are some important differences, but much code written for S runs unaltered under R." This is very much the case for day-to-day code, with a few notable exceptions. The function for calculating the standard deviation in S is `stdev` compared with `sd` in R, for example. For slightly more advanced users, functional scoping can become an issue (one of the "important differences"), but in essence the official line is spot on. To the naked eye, S and R code look very similar indeed.

Workshop

The workshop contains quiz questions and exercises to help you solidify your understanding of the material covered. Try to answer all questions before looking at the "Answers" section that follows.

Quiz

1. Which "similar" programming language predated R?

2. What does the acronym CRAN stand for?

3. Which group of R enthusiasts controls the write-access to the R source and is responsible for the distribution of the R language?

    A. The R Core Development Team

    B. The R Foundation

    C. The R Consortium

Answers

1. The S language.

2. Comprehensive R Archive Network.

3. The R Core Development Team is directly responsible, though the resources and support surrounding each release could also be considered the responsibility of the R Foundation or R Consortium.

Activities

1. Refer to the "Installing R" section of this book's Appendix. Download and install the appropriate version of R for your operating system.

2. Refer to the "Installing RStudio" section of this book's Appendix. Download and install the latest version of RStudio Desktop from the RStudio website.

The R Environment

What You'll Learn in This Hour:

▶ Environments for writing R code

▶ Basic R syntax

▶ Elements of the RStudio IDE

▶ The premise of an R object

▶ Working with R packages

▶ Getting internal help

At the end of Hour 1, "The R Community," you installed R and the popular RStudio Desktop IDE. In this hour we start a new R session via RStudio, type some basic commands, and explore the idea of an R "object." You will be more formally introduced to the concept of an R package, and in the "Activities" section you will load an R package from the CRAN repository containing datasets that supplement the book.

Integrated Development Environments

At the end of the previous hour you installed two pieces of software, R and RStudio Desktop. In this hour we focus on RStudio. The R language can be accessed in many different ways, however. For example, when you installed R, you also installed the R GUI, which for a long time was the way most R users interacted with the language. The RStudio Desktop IDE is therefore not necessary in order to use R, but it certainly helps.

The R GUI

The R GUI is installed with R and provides an environment in which you can work with R interactively via the R console. The R GUI contains a small selection of drop-down menus that allow you to quickly install and load R packages, load workspaces, and access the R manuals. There is also a series of quick-access buttons that include a "Run line or selection" button for working with scripts and a Stop Current Computation button to allow users to cancel submitted statements.

Compared with modern IDEs such as RStudio, the R GUI is beginning to look quite dated. It remains very quick to load, however, and can be useful if all you need to do is open R to run one or two commands. Throughout this hour and the remaining hours, we will access the R language via the far richer RStudio IDE. Many of the features we look at in this hour are also available directly through the R language or via the R GUI. They may, however, have a slightly different name within the R GUI or behave slightly differently.

The RStudio IDE

RStudio is a U.S.-based company that builds tools to assist R users. One such tool is their extremely popular integrated development environment (IDE) for R, called RStudio (see Figure 2.1). The first publically available version of the RStudio environment was released in 2011 and was made available in both desktop and server formats, with the server version accessed via a web browser. Since then, development has continued at some pace, and the IDE has surpassed many others to become the de facto standard way of interfacing with R.

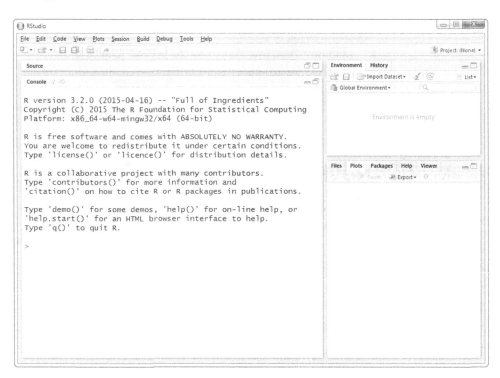

FIGURE 2.1
The RStudio Environment

Today, RStudio is still open source and available as both a desktop and a server product. Commercial versions of both products are now available for those that require additional features such as security or commercial support.

In Hour 1, you installed the latest version of RStudio Desktop appropriate for your operating system. The RStudio environment consists of four primary panels or panes. The size of these panes can easily be adjusted by clicking the dividing line between two panes and moving up/down or left/right accordingly. In order to change the layout of the panes, you need to use the menu options. Select Tools > Global Options... and then click the Pane Layout button on the left. The structured pane layout within RStudio is one of the features that sets RStudio apart from the standard R GUI. Panes such as Packages and Environment provide a user interface to core R functionality that new users are typically not aware of. More generally, the RStudio environment has helped make R more accessible to many new users who might previously have been put off by the rather basic looking R GUI.

The most relevant and useful features within RStudio will be briefly covered within the remainder of this hour. RStudio is an evolving product, and new features are being added all the time. Full documentation is available on the RStudio product website, www.rstudio.com/products/rstudio/, and is accessible via the Help menu within RStudio.

Other Development Environments

The R GUI and RStudio are by no means the only ways to interface with R. Notepad++ is a very popular general-purpose text editor that understands R syntax. You can even use the editor to submit code using the NppToR plug-in available from SourceForge. Similarly, ESS is an add-on package that enhances the Emacs text editor, enabling interaction with R. The highly customizable Vim editor also has an R plug-in.

Eclipse is a very popular development platform maintained by the Eclipse Foundation, which offers support for a number of programming languages. The StatET plug-in enables users to create customized R environments. Eclipse with StatET is particularly useful when working on large projects across multiple languages. Casual users may find it a little too heavyweight for their needs, however. There is also Rattle, an open-source GUI for data mining in R, as well as Tinn-R, an R GUI and development environment for Windows.

The brief list presented here is by no means exhaustive, and you can call R from a number of different applications and environments. For example, you can call R from Excel using a tool called RExcel. Similarly, the major business intelligence vendors all allow users to write extensions in R and provide their own script editors. Oracle, HP, and Teradata all offer the ability to run R within their respective databases. Microsoft announced in May 2015 that they will be offering the same functionality in SQL Server 2016.

R Syntax

Basic R syntax loosely resembles other mathematical/statistical scripting languages such as Matlab and Python. In this section, we take a look at the R console and type a few simple commands to see how an interactive R session functions.

The Console

Within both the R GUI and RStudio, you access your R session via the R Console. The console is essentially equivalent to running a command-line R session. Working directly within the R console, you type an R command, and when you press Enter, the result of that command is displayed on the line(s) below.

When you start an R session, you are greeted with an initial start-up message containing information about the version of R you are using, along with a selection of commands that the R Core Development Team would like you to know about (see Figure 2.2). Following the start-up message is the > symbol. This is commonly referred to as the command prompt.

```
R version 3.2.0 (2015-04-16) -- "Full of Ingredients"
Copyright (C) 2015 The R Foundation for Statistical Computing
Platform: x86_64-w64-mingw32/x64 (64-bit)

R is free software and comes with ABSOLUTELY NO WARRANTY.
You are welcome to redistribute it under certain conditions.
Type 'license()' or 'licence()' for distribution details.

R is a collaborative project with many contributors.
Type 'contributors()' for more information and
'citation()' on how to cite R or R packages in publications.

Type 'demo()' for some demos, 'help()' for on-line help, or
'help.start()' for an HTML browser interface to help.
Type 'q()' to quit R.

>
```

FIGURE 2.2
The R Console

CAUTION

No Warranty!

Note the "ABSOLUTELY NO WARRANTY" comment in the initial startup message. If things go wrong, there is no one you can pick up the phone and complain to!

A flashing cursor to the right of the command prompt is a sign that R is ready for you to submit a new command for processing. An example of the use of the console for a simple mathematical operation can be seen here:

```
> 4*5  # A simple command
[1] 20
>
```

Here, we asked R to evaluate the expression 4*5. The correct answer, 20, was printed on the following line, and we were returned to the command prompt and flashing cursor. The [1] relates to the way R prints vectors. It is something we will look at more closely in Hour 3, "Single-Mode Data Structures." Note the use of the # symbol in order to comment our code. R will ignore anything to the right of the first # symbol of a line.

CAUTION

Comment Blocks

There is no multiline comment capability within R, so comment blocks may only be achieved by starting each line of code with a #.

The command prompt reappears once R has finished processing a complete line of code. If we do not provide a complete line of code, we will get a "continuation" prompt, +, as follows:

```
> 4*  # An incomplete line
+
```

Often this occurs when a closing brace or quotation mark is accidently omitted, though it can also be used deliberately. Because R only processes the statement once the "line" of code is complete, incomplete lines do not necessarily cause syntax errors. If the break was deliberate or if we know what to type to complete the line, we can simply complete the line and press Enter. If we have made a more serious error or are unsure of what mistake we have made, we can press the Esc key to cancel the statement and return to the standard command prompt.

Using the R Console

Let's type a few commands into the console using the following steps:

1. Open RStudio and wait for the command prompt to appear.

2. Type in a mathematical expression to evaluate, such as 20/4.

3. Press Enter.

The correct result should be displayed after a [1] and you should be returned to the command prompt, >.

Scripting

Professional-level code is rarely, if ever, developed directly in a console or command line. Large volumes of well-structured, readable, and well-documented code should be developed within an R script. The RStudio environment provides an enhanced text editor, shown in Figure 2.3, which can be used to develop R scripts. RStudio refers to this as the Source pane. You can open a script window using File > New File > R Script or via the equivalent buttons or keyboard shortcuts within the application.

```
Untitled1* ×
      Source on Save   Q                          Run       Source
 1  # Set working directory
 2  setwd("C:/Users/username/Documents/STY/Hour_2")
 3
 4  # Load required libraries
 5  library(dplyr)
 6  library(ggplot2)
 7
 8  # Create some objects
 9  x <- 5
10  y <- 6
11  z <- x - y
12
```

FIGURE 2.3
The script editor and console windows

During script development, code from the Source pane can be executed in the console by using the Run button at the top of the Source pane. Equivalently, the keyboard shortcut Ctrl+Enter (Windows) or Command+Return (OS X) can be used. By default, submission of code occurs on a line-by-line basis. RStudio will submit the entirety of the line on which the cursor is placed, regardless of where on the line the cursor is placed. By highlighting only part of a line or, for that matter, multiple lines, you can choose exactly what is submitted to the console.

Many of the examples in this book are brief and will therefore use the R Console directly. However, it is thoroughly recommended that you store all of the code you generate when working through the book in your own script or series of scripts. The content of the script editor can be written to a file by selecting File > Save As... or by using the quick access Save button at the top of the Source pane. In Hour 7, "Writing Functions: Part I," we will begin writing functions, and it is almost impossible to do so without using scripts.

R Objects

R is often described as a loosely object-oriented programming language. If you have a background in computer science and have used truly object-oriented languages such as Java, you probably would not consider R to be object-oriented. If, like the authors of this book, you have more of an analytical background, you may find the multiple references to "objects" throughout the R manuals a little off-putting.

We will look closer at object orientation in R during Hour 16, "Introduction to R Models and Object Orientation," and then again in Hour 21, "Writing R Classes," and Hour 22, "Formal Class Systems." To begin with, however, we won't worry too much about the impact of object orientation in R. All it really means is that everything has a name and can be classified into different types of "objects." For example, there are "function" objects, "data" objects, and "statistical model" objects. This book will focus first on "data" objects, then move on to the use of specific "function" objects (such as particular graphic and statistical modelling function objects).

R Packages

Sets of R "objects" are held together in "packages," which are structured elements that store data, functions, and other information. When R is installed, it is distributed with a set of core packages, which can be seen in the "library" subdirectory of the R installation. Only a small subset of the installed packages is actually loaded when you start an R session. This helps reduce the start-up time and avoid a behavior known as masking, which we discuss later in this hour. The Packages pane in RStudio shows you which packages are installed on your machine.

The Search Path

When an R session begins, a set of "default" packages are loaded into the environment, providing immediate access to the most commonly used R functions and other objects. The list of packages included within the environment is called the R "search path," which can be viewed using the search function. The physical location of the packages loaded can be viewed using the searchpaths function. These functions are demonstrated in Listing 2.1.

LISTING 2.1 The Search Path

```
 1: > search()
 2:   [1] ".GlobalEnv"           "tools:rstudio"        "package:stats"
 3:   [4] "package:graphics"     "package:grDevices"    "package:utils"
 4:   [7] "package:datasets"     "package:methods"      "Autoloads"
 5:  [10] "package:base"
 6: > searchpaths()
 7:   [1] ".GlobalEnv"
 8:   [2] "tools:rstudio"
 9:   [3] "C:/Program Files/R/R-3.1.2/library/stats"
10:   [4] "C:/Program Files/R/R-3.1.2/library/graphics"
11:   [5] "C:/Program Files/R/R-3.1.2/library/grDevices"
12:   [6] "C:/Program Files/R/R-3.1.2/library/utils"
```

```
13:    [7] "C:/Program Files/R/R-3.1.2/library/datasets"
14:    [8] "C:/Program Files/R/R-3.1.2/library/methods"
15:    [9] "Autoloads"
16:    [10] "C:/PROGRA~1/R/R-31~1.2/library/base"
```

NOTE

Text Wrapping

In the function call to the search function in Listing 2.1, the output was printed with three elements on each line, whereas the searchpaths output was longer so only one element was printed on each line. The number in square brackets tells us the position in the search path for the first element on the line.

NOTE

RStudio Tools

The "tools:rstudio" item is unique to RStudio. It contains many hidden objects used by the RStudio IDE. The average R user will never touch any of the objects within this item.

Listing Objects

Each package loaded contains (possibly many) R objects that can be accessed. R provides functions to list the objects available in each package. One such function is the objects function. The objects function lists the objects contained in a package. To use the function, you simply call it, specifying the position of the package on the search path from which you wish to list the objects. Alternatively, you can use the "package: [packageName]" syntax produced by running search(). For example, if you want to see the names of the objects contained within the graphics package, you can run either of these lines:

```
objects(4)                   # Assumes that graphics is 4th in the search path
objects("package:graphics")  # Assumes nothing about the search path
```

The ls.str function provides a listing of the objects in a package together with a short view of each object (usually the arguments if the object is a function). You call ls.str in the same way as objects, using either the position of the package in the search path or the text produced by running search().

Find Hidden Objects

When you list package objects in this manner, you list only those objects that the package developer has chosen to expose to the user.

If, however, you wish to view all objects in a package, you can use the `all.names` argument to the `objects` function, setting `all.names = TRUE`.

The R Workspace

Not all the items in the search path refer to R packages. In particular, the first item returned using both `search` and `searchpaths` was `".GlobalEnv"`. This refers to what is known as the "Global Environment," (or "workspace") which is a storage box for objects that you create during your R session. This might be data that you read in to R or functions that you write yourself. To begin with, it is empty, but you can easily create your own objects. The standard method for assigning a name to an object is to use the < and - characters to create an arrow (<-). To the left of the arrow you specify the name of a new object you wish to create. To the right you specify the value that the object will take. Here is an example:

```
> x <- 3*4
> x
[1] 12
```

NOTE

Dynamic Typing

R is a "dynamically typed" programming language. This means that you do not have to specify the type (or class) of an object before you assign it a value. The effect of dynamic typing is that R is quicker to write but slower to run than statically typed languages such as Java and C.

Instead of the left arrow, you can use the = sign. Some would argue that the left arrow makes it clear that a new object is being created, whereas others would argue that the = sign is more consistent with assignment in other programming languages. In most situations, there is very little difference, but experienced R package developers tend to use the left arrow, and this is what we will use for the examples throughout this book.

NOTE

Assigning to the Right

The assignment arrow works both ways. For example, you can create a variable, x, that has the value 9 by typing 9 -> x. Very few people actually use a right arrow to assign, however. It is generally considered good practice to avoid using it.

Object Naming

R object names can be practically any length, and be made up of any combination of letters, numbers, and the . and _ characters. The only real restriction is that it cannot start with a number or "_". Objects beginning with a dot are accessible but hidden objects. It is important to note that R is a case-sensitive language; therefore, an object named myObject is completely different from one named myobject.

NOTE

Naming objects with quotes

Strictly speaking, it is possible to start an object name with a number or underscore. It is also possible to include spaces. However, these forms of naming are generally discouraged. We must use one of three types of quotes to identify the non-standard object name: single quotes, '; double quotes, "; or backticks, `. The standard convention in R is to use backticks if naming objects in this way.

There is no widely adopted object-naming convention among R users. Throughout this book we will predominantly use a convention known as "camelCase," because this is the convention that applies to most cases within the Mango Solutions coding standards. The camelCase convention specifies that each new word within an object's name, excluding the first, should start with a capital letter. A variant of the convention is also discussed within Google's R Style Guide, which is a great starting point for anyone looking for styling tips to help ensure professional-level R code.

TIP

Removing Objects

It is possible to remove objects from the workspace using the rm function—for example rm(x).

The objects and ls functions default to the first item in the search path (that is, the Global Environment). You can therefore delete every object in the Global Environment using rm(list=objects()) or rm(list=ls()).

The Working Directory

In R, the working directory is the default directory from which you import files, and to which you write information. A thorough understanding of how to query and change the working directory is essential in order to collaborate and/or share code effectively. If a codebase is well structured and relative file paths (as opposed to absolute file paths) are used throughout, then setting the working directory need only occur once right at the start of an R session.

TIP

Navigating the File System

The R function `list.files` can also be used to list all the files and folders within a particular directory, returning either file/directory names alone or full file paths.

You can view the current working directory using the `getwd` function, and change the working directory using the `setwd` function. RStudio allows the working directory to be updated via the Session > Set Working Directory menu item. It can also be set via the Files pane.

Note the use of the forward slash (/) in the directory paths specified in Listing 2.2. Every time R reads a backslash (\), it skips onto the next character and tries to evaluate what is known as an "escape sequence." This can be painful when you're copying directory paths from Windows Explorer. The simple solution is to replace every backslash with either a forward slash or a double backslash (\\). This includes paths to servers. For example, a Windows path of \\server would become \\\\server or //server in R.

LISTING 2.2   A Working Direcotry

```
 1: > # Print the current working directory
 2: > getwd()
 3: [1] "C:/Users/username/Desktop/STY"
 4: > # Change the current working directory using an absolute path
 5: > setwd("C:/Users/username/Desktop")
 6: > getwd()
 7: [1] "C:/Users/username/Desktop"
 8: > # Change the current working directory using a relative path
 9: > setwd("STY")
10: > getwd()
11: [1] "C:/Users/username/Desktop/STY"
```

The backslash itself is known as an escape character. An escape character has a special place in programming because it changes the behavior of subsequent characters, assuming the escape sequence is known. The double backslash (\\) is one such use of an escape sequence in R. We will explore some useful escape sequences such as \n and \t in later hours.

Saving Workspace Objects

The collection of objects in the Global Environment that you create during an R session are held in memory during the session. When you close R, you must choose whether to save these objects to disk for use at a later date or to delete them.

When a user decides to quit RStudio (and hence close their R session), they are presented with a dialog box similar to the one shown in Figure 2.4, asking them if they would like to "Save workspace image to ~/.RData." The options presented are Save, Don't Save, and Cancel. Selecting Save will create an .RData file within the current working directory. This is a compressed format that R can use to regenerate the objects within your Global Environment. RStudio automatically saves an .Rhistory file containing a list of all the commands typed during the R session. This file is visible in RStudio via the History pane.

FIGURE 2.4
To save or not save?

TIP

Saving Large Objects

The `save` function can be used at any time during an R session. For example, it can be used to create custom .RData files containing objects you specify directly. The `save` function, along with its counterpart `load`, are great for working with very large datasets because the time to load objects stored as .RData files can be an order of magnitude faster than reading data from a CSV file or other formats.

In a professional environment it is common to work on multiple projects, each with its own directory structure. RStudio allows the creation of projects via a button in the top-right corner of the IDE. When you create a new project within a specified directory, RStudio stores some information within that directory relating to your project. The impact of creating a new project is that the R session restarts and the working directory is set to be the project directory. When you return to a project after closing down RStudio, any files you had open when you closed the program down are reopened, enabling you to continue where you left off. This is not unique to RStudio, and tools such as Eclipse with StatET offer a slightly richer project setup, allowing you to associate a particular version of R with your project.

Using R Packages

The base R distribution consists of approximately 30 R packages classified as either "core" (otherwise known as "base") or "recommended." The packages that make up the base R distribution contain a huge amount of functionality. However, the success of R has largely been due to the contribution of several thousand authors who have chosen to submit new functionality via additional R packages.

The main repository for R packages is CRAN, for which the number of R packages passed 7,000 in 2015. There is also a specialist repository for R developers called R-Forge; however, an increasing number of authors are choosing to share development versions of their packages on the more general-purpose GitHub. In addition to these primary repositories, the field of bioinformatics has its own repository known as Bioconductor, which "provides tools for the analysis and comprehension of high-throughput genomic data." The Bioconductor community is very strong and even maintains its own conference, BioC.

Finding the Right Package

The CRAN repository is growing at an incredible rate. When I began teaching R courses in 2011, there were fewer than 2,000 packages on CRAN. In 2015, the number of packages passed 7,000. The R Core Development Team is constantly looking for ways to limit the number of packages, and the formation of the R Consortium may bring some control to the situation. However, at present, there is no standard way of finding the right package. A good starting point is CRAN's Task Views, shown in Figure 2.5.

At the time of writing, there are 33 Task Views. Each is manually maintained by members of the R community with a special interest in the topic that their Task View covers. There is no higher-level classification of views, so the views themselves are quite diverse and a great deal of overlap occurs between the various Task Views. This is to be expected given that there is no requirement that an R package should focus on a single topic. Conversely, not every package on CRAN appears in a Task View.

A drawback of the open-source nature of CRAN is the duplication of effort that occurs when two independent developers attempt to solve the same problem. This has resulted in several packages that attempt to do the same thing, just in slightly different ways. Ensuring better collaboration on such projects in the future is one of the primary goals of the R Consortium. The aim of CRAN Task Views is to tell you what is available, not to try to rank the packages in any way. Finding the right package via CRAN can therefore be a bit of a challenge!

In 2012, RStudio began maintaining its own CRAN mirror and publish download logs of all the packages downloaded from the mirror. The popularity of the RStudio environment (which defaults to downloading from this mirror) means that if you want to know which packages are the most popular, these download logs can give you a good indication. Gábor Csárdi's

METACRAN (http://www.r-pkg.org/) summarizes the RStudio download logs in a more interactive, user-friendly manner. Alternatively, just search for blog posts discussing the popularity of R packages—there are plenty! Many of the popular general-purpose packages are discussed in this book.

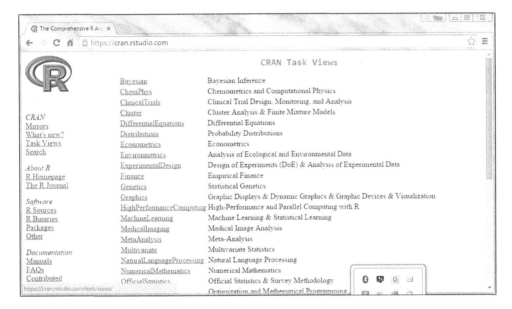

FIGURE 2.5
CRAN Task Views

Installing an R Package

The Packages pane in RStudio provides a user-friendly interface for installing and loading R packages. When you install an R package, you essentially create a directory on your machine. Once installed, the package lives on your machine permanently until such time that you choose to delete it.

TIP

Removing Packages

You can delete packages from your system using the `remove.packages` function.

When you install your first R package, you may be asked if you wish to create your own local library. A library is a just a name for a collection of R packages. Local libraries are particularly useful when you are logged in to your operating system as a standard user and do not have all the necessary admin privileges in order to create new files within your R installation. If you have a local library, you may notice that the Packages pane in RStudio is divided into "User Library" and "System Library" to show where the packages are installed.

The quickest way to install an R package in RStudio is to navigate to the Packages pane and click the Install button. This loads the pop-up shown in Figure 2.6, for installing packages from both CRAN and locally.

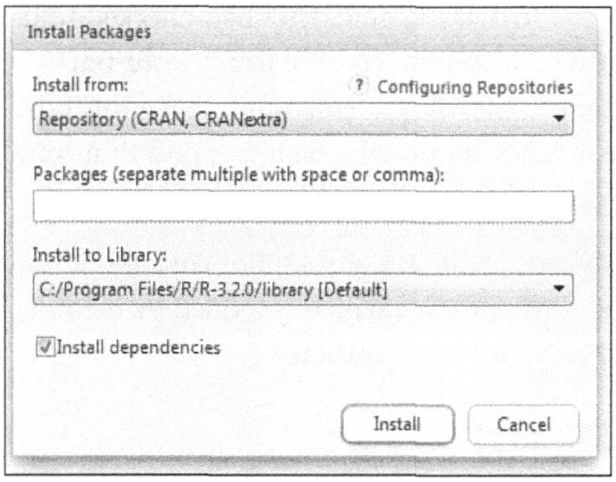

FIGURE 2.6
The Install Packages window

TIP

Local Libraries

You can ask R which libraries it is using with the `.libPaths` function. The same function can also be used to point R at different local libraries. The system library cannot be changed, but you can create as many local libraries as you like.

If you don't specify the package location when loading a package, R will look through each library in turn to try to find a package with the name you specified.

Installing from CRAN

To install from CRAN, you need to ensure the Install From field shown in Figure 2.6 is pointing to CRAN. If you were using R on the command line or through the R GUI, you would first have to choose your CRAN mirror. RStudio does this for you, however, so you don't have to worry about choosing a mirror. If you are connected to the Internet and your firewall allows it, you simply need to start typing the name of the package you wish to install in the Packages field, and RStudio will autocomplete the rest for you. Note that if you have multiple libraries, you can choose which one to install to, though RStudio defaults to a local library if you have one.

CAUTION

Package Quality

A package must pass many checks to make it on to CRAN. It is therefore natural to assume that being on CRAN is a sign of package quality. Although this is partly true, packages downloaded from CRAN have not necessarily been fully tested, or developed in a "valid" environment. Only the "core" and "recommended" packages have been tested by the R Core Development Team.

To save yourself some effort, we recommend leaving the Install Dependencies box checked unless you are concerned about what might be installed onto your system. For one thing, your package will fail to load unless the dependencies are installed. Therefore, if you don't leave this box checked, you will have to manually install each dependency separately. Bear in mind that some of the more popular packages can have 10 or more dependencies.

Note that the Install Packages tool generates a line of code in the R Console that calls the R function `install.packages`. This function resides in the utils package, which is loaded by default when you start R. It is possible to call this function directly in any R session.

Installing from a Package Archive File (Binary)

CRAN is the primary package repository for R users, though it is not the exclusive repository. Many commercial organizations build their own utility packages for internal use and may instead distribute package binaries over an intranet. The term "binary" refers to a package that has been built into an archive (a ".zip" on Windows, a ".tgz" on OS X), ready for installation. When you install a package directly from CRAN, the appropriate package binary is chosen for your operating system; it is downloaded to a temporary location and then "unpacked" and installed. When you install manually from a binary, you are simply skipping the CRAN piece and pointing directly to the binary for R to unpack. It is important to note that binaries are constructed in order to be unpacked by R, and you should never try to install a package that you have unzipped yourself.

Installing from Source

Since R is open source, the source code is always available to use and is distributed as a ".tar.gz" file. In addition to installing from a package binary, we may also install directly from the package source. Linux users have to install from source, though Windows and OS X users usually won't have a need to until they start building their own packages. There are other occasions when it can be useful, but installing from source takes a lot longer than installing from a binary and may require additional tools. For example, Windows users need to install a version of Rtools that is appropriate for their R version. Instructions for installing Rtools can be found in the Appendix.

To install from a source using the RStudio GUI, Linux users simply need to follow the instructions above for installing a package archive file. For those on Windows or OS X we first need download the "tar.gz" file locally. We then install the package as we would a local package binary. Regardless of our operating system, we can install directly from the console by adding the `type = "source"` argument when running the `install.packages` function.

TIP

Installing from GitHub

The package **devtools** contains a function, `install_github`, that facilitates a direct installation from the GitHub repository. You can use `install.packages` to install packages directly from other repositories as well.

Loading an R Package

When you start R, only a subset of your installed packages is actually loaded for use within the R session. This helps reduce the startup time and avoid a behavior called masking. In order to access the functionality of other installed packages, you must load them into the environment. The Packages pane in RStudio lists all the packages that your R session is aware of. To load any of these packages, you simply check the box next to a package name and the packages is loaded. Checking the box calls a line of R code using the `library` function. You can also call the `library` function directly from the R console.

When developing reusable production-level code, it is best to avoid using untraceable "point-and-click" actions as much as possible. It is standard practice to place multiple calls to the `library` function at the top of an R script so that other users can run your code. If R cannot find the specified package library, it will produce an error. The `require` function is an alternative to `library` that returns a warning if a package is not present, allowing more control over the behavior of the script—for example, "do this, but only if package X has successfully been loaded." We will look closer at errors and warnings and control flow when we discuss writing R functions in Hour 7, "Writing Functions: Part I," and Hour 8, "Writing Functions: Part II." In a professional development environment, checking that the right packages are available is only half the battle. Errors may still occur due to differences in package versions or operating systems, but we'll come to that later!

Package Dependencies

When you're developing packages, it is highly unlikely you will need to write every function from scratch. It is likely that you will use one or more functions defined within another package. Rather than copy all the relevant code into your own package, you simply specify a "dependency" on the other package. This avoids duplication and ensures that bugs need only be fixed in a single location. When you load an R package with a dependency, the dependency is also loaded and added to the search path. Note that this means the dependent package must also be installed on your machine.

Masking

Masking occurs when two or more "environments" on the search path contain one or more objects with the same name. Whenever we refer to an object by typing its name, R looks in each of the loaded environments on the search path for that object in turn, starting with the Global Environment. If R finds an object with the name it is looking for, it stops searching. Any objects it doesn't find have been hidden, or "masked."

We can delete objects from our own workspace but we cannot delete objects from R packages, only mask them. If you inadvertently mask an object, you can simply clone your object with a different name and use rm to delete the original object from your workspace, thereby unmasking the hidden object.

TIP

Ensuring the Right Object Is Used

Masking is much less of a problem than most new users perceive it to be. This is largely due to package namespaces, which we will look at more closely in Hour 19, "Package Building," and Hour 20, "Advanced Package Building." To avoid any potential masking issues, it is possible to reference an object within a package directly by using the [packageName]::[objectName] syntax—for example, base::pi.

Internal Help

The help function can be used to display help on a function or indeed any R object. RStudio allows users to navigate R's help files via the Help tab. If the phrase you search for exactly matches the name of an R object available in your current session, then the help file for that object is returned. Otherwise, it searches your package libraries (including packages that are not loaded) for possible help pages.

NOTE

Help from the Console

The RStudio Help pane simply provides wrappers for functionality contained within the utils package. A general search of all help files can be achieved using either the help.search function or the shorthand version, ??. Similarly, if you know the name of the object you require help with, you can use a function help or its shorthand, ?.

The help files can be a little daunting if you are unfamiliar with the standard terminology, as demonstrated in Figure 2.7, which shows the help file for the mean function referring to terms such as "objects," "vectors," and "methods" in several places.

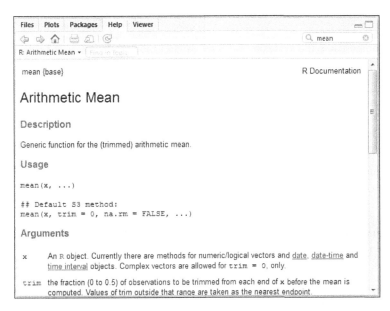

FIGURE 2.7
The help page for the mean function

There is a standard set of fields that package maintainers are encouraged to complete, though few are actually necessary. For example, in order to publish a package on CRAN, you must pass what is known as an "R CMD check." This requires that all your examples in the Examples section of the help file run successfully. However, it is also possible to pass the check by not including the Examples section!

Summary

In this hour we looked at the available development environments for R, focusing on the RStudio environment. We looked closely at the makeup of the language and saw how R is constructed from a number of core and recommended packages that can be extended by downloading additional packages from a repository such as CRAN. In the "Workshop" and "Activities" sections, you will load RStudio, begin using the R console, and install your first R package.

In the next two hours we will look at the standard data objects that are the building blocks of the R language, beginning with vectors and working through to R's data frame structure. You will learn how to create, combine, and subset these structures.

Q&A

Q. I created an object named using the syntax `x <- 5` but when I tried the line `x + 2` I got "Error: object 'X' not found." Is that right?

A. If you have been using a language such as SAS, this may seem odd but it is correct. R is case sensitive, so `x` and `X` are not the same thing.

Q. A colleague sent you an R package via a .zip file but after unzipping the file you found that you could not install the package. Why is this?

A. R packages are commonly distributed as binaries or ".zip" files. Unless you want to build the package from source yourself, you need to provide R with a binary file, which means keeping it zipped up.

Q. Is it possible to install two different versions of the same package to different libraries? If so, what happens when I try to load them?

A. It is entirely possible to install different versions of the same package to different libraries. Unless you specify exactly which one you are loading, R will load the one highest up the library path. Thankfully, you can only load one version of a package at a time. If you do try to load a package that has already been loaded, R does not produce an error or warning, so our advice is to be careful!

Q. Is it possible to have multiple versions of R installed? If so, how are the package libraries affected?

A. You can have as many versions of R installed on your machine as you like, which is great if you work in a heavily regulated environment and need to ensure you can exactly reproduce results from a time when you were working with an earlier version of R. RStudio lets you switch between R versions via the Tools > Global Options... menu, though you will need to restart RStudio for the change to take effect.

The system library is associated with your version of R and therefore this is automatically updated to use the new versions of the core and recommended R packages when you switch to a new version of R. User libraries default to a version-specific location as well, so there is little risk to using packages built for a different version of R. On the flip side, this means that each time you install a new version of R, you will need to install your favorite packages for that R version as well.

Workshop

The workshop contains quiz questions and exercises to help you solidify your understanding of the material covered. Try to answer all questions before looking at the "Answers" section that follows.

Quiz

1. True or false? You must install RStudio in order to work interactively with R.

2. Which of the following is not used for assignment in R?

    A. `<-`

    B. `_`

    C. `->`

    D. `=`

3. What does the line `objects(4)` tell you?

4. What is the difference between installing and loading an R package?

5. What is the difference between an Rhistory and an .RData file?

6. What is masking?

Answers

1. False. There are many ways of working interactively with R, though RStudio is the most popular.

2. The answer is B. However, you might be surprised to learn that prior to R, underscores were used for assignment in S.

3. The line `objects(4)` produces a list of objects that are contained within the fourth item in the search path. In the example used in this hour, this was graphics, though that might not always be the case. As new packages are loaded, the position of packages in the search path can change.

4. Installing an R package creates a permanent directory on your machine. Typically, you only install a package once for a version of R. Loading a package enables you to actually use it within the R session.

5. An .Rhistory file contains a list of commands that were executed during an R session (or sessions). An .RData file stores R objects and can be used to re-create Global Environment objects from a previous R session.

6. Masking occurs when two or more "environments," typically packages, contain an object with the same name. When you type that name into the console, R finds the object that is higher up the search path. Any objects that are not found are hidden, or "masked."

Activities

1. Start an R session by opening RStudio.

2. Print the search path for your R session.

3. List all objects from the "datasets" package using the `objects` function.

4. Use the Packages pane to install the mangoTraining package from CRAN.

5. Load the mangoTraining package into the R session.

6. List the objects the mangoTraining package contains.

HOUR 3
Single-Mode Data Structures

What You'll Learn in This Hour:

▶ The common R data types

▶ What a vector object is

▶ What a matrix object is

▶ What an array object is

R is commonly used to gain insight from data, using graphical or analytic methods. To use R effectively, you must have a good working knowledge of the basic data structures. In this hour, we describe the standard types of data found in R and introduce three key structures that can be used to store these data types: vectors, matrices, and arrays. We will look at the ways in which these structures can be created and managed, with a focus on how to extract data from them.

The R Data Types

Four standard types of data can be used in R. These data types, or "modes" as they are formally known as, are as follows:

▶ Numeric values (integers or continuous values)

▶ Character strings

▶ Logical values (TRUE and FALSE values)

▶ Complex numbers (with real and imaginary parts)

The following code shows examples of each of these data types:

```
> 4 + 5     # numeric
[1] 9
> "Hello"   # character
[1] "Hello"
> 4 > 5     # logical (is 4 greater than 5)
```

```
[1] FALSE
> 3 + 4i     # complex
[1] 3+4i
```

NOTE

Quotation Marks

Note the use of the double quotation marks for specifying character data. You may use either double or single quotation marks (but not both at the same time).

The mode **Function**

In the last section you saw examples of the four "modes" of data within R. You can use the mode function directly to discover the mode of data held in any object, as illustrated in the following example:

```
> X <- 4 + 5      # Assign a (numeric) value to X
> X               # Print the value of X
[1] 9
> mode(X)         # The mode of X
[1] "numeric"

> X < 10          # Logical statement: is X less than 10?
[1] TRUE
> mode(X < 10)    # The mode of this data
[1] "logical"
```

NOTE

Missing Values

In R, any missing value is represented with an "NA" symbol. This can be a "missing" numeric, character, logical, or complex value.

Vectors, Matrices, and Arrays

In R, there are three data structures designed to store a single type of data. These structures are known as "single-mode" data structures:

▶ Vectors—Series of values

▶ Matrices—Rectangular structures with rows and columns

▶ Arrays—Higher dimension structures (for example, 3D and 4D arrays)

Given that these are single-mode structures, they may only hold a single type of data. Therefore, you may have a numeric vector or a character matrix, for example, but you cannot create an array that contains both numeric and logical data.

Vectors

A vector is a series of values of the same mode—it is the basic form of R structure, and most functions in R are ultimately designed to operate on vectors. In this section, we look at the following:

▶ Some ways to create vectors

▶ The attributes of a vector

▶ The ways in which you can extract information from a vector

Creating Vectors

There are many ways to create vectors in the R language, and many functions will return vectors as an output (such as the set of functions that create random samples from statistical distributions, which you'll see later in Hour 6, "Common R Utility Functions"). In this section, we focus on four ways to create simple vectors.

Combining Elements with the c Function

The c function allows you to create simple vectors by combining elements of the same mode. (Note that c is lowercase!) You specify as many elements as you want, separated by commas, optionally saving the results as objects for reuse later. Here's an example:

```
> numericVector <- c(2, 6, 8, 4, 2, 9, 4, 0)  # Vector of numerics
> numericVector           # Print the numeric vector
[1] 2 6 8 4 2 9 4 0
> mode(numericVector)     # What is the mode of "numericVector"?
[1] "numeric"

> c("Hello", "There")     # Vector of characters
[1] "Hello" "There"
> c(F, T, T, F, F, T, F, F)  # Vector of logicals
[1] FALSE  TRUE  TRUE FALSE FALSE  TRUE FALSE FALSE
> c(3+4i, 5+9i, 3+7i)        # Vector complex numbers
[1] 3+4i 5+9i 3+7i
```

NOTE

Logical Values

You specify logical values without quotation marks, using either T and F or TRUE and FALSE, as shown here:

```
> c(T, F, TRUE, FALSE)
[1]   TRUE FALSE   TRUE FALSE
```

You can use the c function to combine single values, or even vectors of values (because a single value is actually a vector of length 1). In this way, you can combine vectors, as illustrated here:

```
> X <- c(1, 2, 3, 4, 5, 6, 7, 8, 9, 10)    # Create a simple vector of numerics
> X                                          # Print the vector
 [1]  1  2  3  4  5  6  7  8  9 10
> c(X, X, X, X, X)                           # Combine vectors
 [1]  1  2  3  4  5  6  7  8  9 10  1  2  3  4  5  6  7  8  9 10  1  2  3  4
[25]  5  6  7  8  9 10  1  2  3  4  5  6  7  8  9 10  1  2  3  4  5  6  7  8
[49]  9 10
```

NOTE

Indexed Printing

When you print vectors in R, you see that the values are prefixed with [1]. This specifies an index for the values in the vector. If you print a vector with many elements, it is clearer to see this indexing behavior. In the preceding example, the first 5 on the second "line" of printing is the 25th value in the vector, as noted by the [25] that precedes it.

Although the horizontal printing of the vector may encourage you to think of a vector as a "row" of data, this is just a printing convention. In fact, a vector has no structure: It is simply a series of values.

TIP

Multi-Mode Structures

Earlier, we stated that vectors are strictly single-mode structures—that is, they contain only values of a single data type. If you try to create vectors containing more than one mode of data, R coerces the vector to a single mode, as shown here:

```
> c(1, 2, 3, "Hello")                # Multiple modes
[1] "1"      "2"      "3"      "Hello"
> c(1, 2, 3, TRUE, FALSE)            # Multiple modes
[1] 1 2 3 1 0
> c(1, 2, 3, TRUE, FALSE, "Hello")   # Multiple modes
[1] "1"      "2"      "3"      "TRUE"   "FALSE" "Hello"
```

Creating a Sequence of "Integers"

In the previous section, we looked at the use of the c function to create vectors. In one of the examples, we created a sequence of integers:

```
> X <- c(1, 2, 3, 4, 5, 6, 7, 8, 9, 10)    # Create a simple vector of numerics
> X                                         # Print the vector
 [1]  1  2  3  4  5  6  7  8  9 10
```

This is a simple line of code that creates a sequence of values from 1 to 10, "by 1." However, if you wanted to create a sequence of integer values from 1 to 100, this would require significantly more typing! If you do wish to create a series of integers, you can use the : symbol, specifying the start and end values, as follows:

```
> 1:100    # Series of values from 1 to 100
  [1]   1   2   3   4   5   6   7   8   9  10  11  12  13  14  15  16  17  18
 [19]  19  20  21  22  23  24  25  26  27  28  29  30  31  32  33  34  35  36
 [37]  37  38  39  40  41  42  43  44  45  46  47  48  49  50  51  52  53  54
 [55]  55  56  57  58  59  60  61  62  63  64  65  66  67  68  69  70  71  72
 [73]  73  74  75  76  77  78  79  80  81  82  83  84  85  86  87  88  89  90
 [91]  91  92  93  94  95  96  97  98  99 100
```

In fact, the : notation can be used to create any sequence of numeric values from one number to another number, "by 1," as shown in the following examples:

```
> 1:5
[1] 1 2 3 4 5
> 5:1
[1] 5 4 3 2 1
> -1:1
[1] -1  0  1
> 1.3:5.3
[1] 1.3 2.3 3.3 4.3 5.3
```

You can combine R statements, such as those in the last two sections, to create more complex vectors. Here is an example of the c function and the : notation used together to create a symmetric pattern of values:

```
> c(0:4, 5, 4:0)
 [1] 0 1 2 3 4 5 4 3 2 1 0
```

You can operate on vectors to create sequences where the "gap" in the sequence is not one. For example, this line of code would create a series of values from 2 to 20, "by 2":

```
> 2*1:10
 [1]  2  4  6  8 10 12 14 16 18 20
```

This works well for simple sequences, such as the one illustrated here. However, for more complex sequences of numeric values (for example, 1.3 to 8.4, by 0.3), you need a more general approach.

NOTE
_____

Letter Sequences

In this section we have looked at regular series of numeric (primarily integer) values. This approach works only for numeric values. For example, you cannot create a series of letters using syntax such as A:Z. You will, however, see how to achieve letter sequences in the "Subscripting Vectors" section, later in this hour.

_____

Creating a Sequence of Numeric Values with the `seq` Function

In the preceding section, we used the : notation to create a series of numeric values, where the "gap" in the sequence is one. A more general way of performing the same operation is with the `seq` function. The first two arguments to `seq` are the starting and ending values, and the default gap is one. Therefore, the following lines are equivalent:

```
> 1:10
 [1]  1  2  3  4  5  6  7  8  9 10
> seq(1, 10)
 [1]  1  2  3  4  5  6  7  8  9 10
```

The advantage of using the `seq` function is that it has an additional argument, by, that allows you to specify the gap between consecutive sequence values, as shown in the following examples:

```
> seq(1, 10, by = 0.5)    # Sequence from 1 to 10 by 0.5
 [1]  1.0  1.5  2.0  2.5  3.0  3.5  4.0  4.5  5.0  5.5  6.0  6.5
[13]  7.0  7.5  8.0  8.5  9.0  9.5 10.0

> seq(2, 20, by = 2)      # Sequence from 2 to 20 by 2
 [1]  2   4   6   8  10 12 14 16 18 20

> seq(5, -5, by = -2)     # Sequence from 5 to -5 by -2
 [1]  5   3   1 -1 -3 -5
```

These examples illustrate some simple sequences of values. However, let's consider the following examples, where we create a sequence of values from 1.3 to 8.4 by 0.3:

```
> seq(1.3, 8.4, by = 0.3)  # Sequence from 1.3 to 8.4 by 0.3
 [1] 1.3 1.6 1.9 2.2 2.5 2.8 3.1 3.4 3.7 4.0 4.3 4.6 4.9 5.2 5.5
[16] 5.8 6.1 6.4 6.7 7.0 7.3 7.6 7.9 8.2
```

In this example, note that the last value in the vector is 8.2, whereas we requested a sequence from 1.3 to 8.4. Of course, the reason that the last value is not precisely 8.4 is that the difference between the start and end of the sequence is not divisible by 0.3 (the specified "gap").

If instead we wanted to create a sequence of values from a start point to a particular end point, we could specify a length of the output vector instead of the gap in consecutive sequence values:

```
> seq(1.3, 8.4, length = 10)   # Sequence of 10 values from 1.3 to 8.4
 [1] 1.300000 2.088889 2.877778 3.666667 4.455556 5.244444
 [7] 6.033333 6.822222 7.611111 8.400000
```

Creating a Sequence of Repeated Values

In the earlier section "Combining Elements with the c Function," we created a repeated sequence of values by combining a created vector a number of times:

```
> X <- c(1, 2, 3, 4, 5, 6, 7, 8, 9, 10)   # Create a simple vector of numerics
> X                                         # Print the vector
 [1]  1  2  3  4  5  6  7  8  9 10

> c(X, X, X, X, X)                          # Combine vectors
 [1]  1  2  3  4  5  6  7  8  9 10  1  2  3  4  5  6  7  8  9 10  1  2  3  4
[25]  5  6  7  8  9 10  1  2  3  4  5  6  7  8  9 10  1  2  3  4  5  6  7  8
[49]  9 10
```

We can use the rep function in R to create a vector containing repeated values. The first two arguments to the rep function are the value(s) to repeat and the number of times to repeat the value(s), as shown here:

```
> rep("Hello", 5)   # Repeat "Hello" 5 times
[1] "Hello" "Hello" "Hello" "Hello" "Hello"
```

In the last example, we are repeating a single value, but the first argument to rep could be a vector of values. In this way, we could re-create the earlier vector of repeated sequences (where we used the c function to combine multiple instances of a vector) using rep, as follows:

```
> X <- c(1, 2, 3, 4, 5, 6, 7, 8, 9, 10)
> rep(X, 5)         # Repeat the X vector 5 times
 [1]  1  2  3  4  5  6  7  8  9 10  1  2  3  4  5  6  7  8  9 10  1  2  3  4
[25]  5  6  7  8  9 10  1  2  3  4  5  6  7  8  9 10  1  2  3  4  5  6  7  8
[49]  9 10
```

You saw in the earlier section "Creating a Sequence of Integers" that you can create a series of integers with the : notation. Therefore, we can further simplify this example as follows:

```
> X <- 1:10
> rep(X, 5)          # Repeat the X vector 5 times
 [1]  1  2  3  4  5  6  7  8  9 10  1  2  3  4  5  6  7  8  9 10  1  2  3  4
[25]  5  6  7  8  9 10  1  2  3  4  5  6  7  8  9 10  1  2  3  4  5  6  7  8
[49]  9 10
```

Or even:

```
> rep(1:10, 5)       # Repeat 1:10 5 times
 [1]  1  2  3  4  5  6  7  8  9 10  1  2  3  4  5  6  7  8  9 10  1  2  3  4
[25]  5  6  7  8  9 10  1  2  3  4  5  6  7  8  9 10  1  2  3  4  5  6  7  8
[49]  9 10
```

In these examples, we repeat a series of values a specific number of times. Alternatively, we can repeat each of the values a specified number of times by supplying a vector value for the second argument the same length as that in the first argument:

```
> rep( c("A", "B", "C"), c(4, 1, 3))
[1] "A" "A" "A" "A" "B" "C" "C" "C"
```

In this example, we repeat "A" four times, "B" once, and "C" three times. Using this same approach, we can replace each value of a vector a specific number of times, as shown here:

```
> rep( c("A", "B", "C"), c(3, 3, 3))
[1] "A" "A" "A" "B" "B" "B" "C" "C" "C"
```

Alternatively, because the second input is a repeated set of values, this could be written as follows:

```
> rep( c("A", "B", "C"), rep(3, 3))
[1] "A" "A" "A" "B" "B" "B" "C" "C" "C"
```

However, an argument to rep called each provides an easy way to achieve the same result:

```
> rep( c("A", "B", "C"), each = 3)
[1] "A" "A" "A" "B" "B" "B" "C" "C" "C"
```

As you can see, the rep function can be used to create a variety of vectors with repeated sequences. Let's quickly recap the three ways of using rep, as illustrated in this section:

```
> rep( c("A", "B", "C"), 3)              # Repeat the vector 3 times
[1] "A" "B" "C" "A" "B" "C" "A" "B" "C"
```

```
> rep( c("A", "B", "C"), c(4, 1, 3))   # Repeat each value a specific number of
                                          times
[1] "A" "A" "A" "A" "B" "C" "C" "C"

> rep( c("A", "B", "C"), each = 3)      # Repeat each value 3 times
[1] "A" "A" "A" "B" "B" "B" "C" "C" "C"
```

CAUTION

Nested Calls

The last section included the following line of code:

```
> rep( c("A", "B", "C"), rep(3, 3))
[1] "A" "A" "A" "B" "B" "B" "C" "C" "C"
```

This is possibly the most complex line of code you've seen so far, and includes nested calls: The inputs to rep are, themselves, derived from calls to functions (c and rep, respectively). This sort of syntax is common in R, but care must be taken not to create overly complex nested calls because this may make your code hard to read and understand later. Where appropriate, consider breaking the code into smaller, commented fragments, as shown here:

```
> theVector <- c("A", "B", "C")   # Vector to repeat
> repTimes <- rep(3, 3)            # Number of times to repeat the vector
> rep(theVector, repTimes)         # Repeat the vector
[1] "A" "A" "A" "B" "B" "B" "C" "C" "C"
```

Vector Attributes

A vector has a number of attributes that you can query using a set of simple functions. Specifically, you can query a vector's length, mode, and element names.

The mode function you saw earlier in this hour takes a vector input and returns the mode of the data it contains. Here's an example:

```
> X <- c(6, 8, 3, 1, 7)   # Create a simple vector
> X                        # Print the vector
[1] 6 8 3 1 7
> mode(X)                  # The mode of the vector
[1] "numeric"
```

If you want to see the number of elements in a vector, you can use the length function:

```
> length(X)                # Number of elements
[1] 5
```

NOTE

Missing Values

If we have a vector that contains one or more missing values, these values will still contribute to the vector's length:

```
> Y <- c(4, 5, NA, 1, NA, 0)
> Y
[1]   4   5 NA   1 NA   0
> length(Y)
[1] 6
```

The third and fifth elements of the preceding vector exist—we just don't know their values.

A vector can also have elements you can query using the names function. (Note that we did not specify names for the vector created earlier.) Here's an example:

```
> X <- c(6, 8, 3, 1, 7)   # Create a simple vector
> X                       # Print the vector
[1] 6 8 3 1 7
> names(X)                # Element names of X
NULL
```

In R, NULL signifies an empty structure. So here, the result of the call to the names function tells us that this vector has no element names. We come across vectors with element names in one of two ways: either as the result of a call to a function or when we assign names directly.

Consider an example where we have created a frequency count of men and women in a set of data. These numbers could be returned as a vector, as shown next:

```
> genderFreq   # Frequency by gender
[1] 165 147
```

Here, we see that the vector contains two values (165 and 147) that relate to the frequency count by gender. However, without labels, we do not know which value refers to which gender. As such, R may return a named vector, as shown here:

```
> genderFreq
Female   Male
   165    147
```

If we want to create a vector with named elements, we can specify names for the elements as we create the vector or assign names using the names function itself:

```
> genderFreq <- c(Female = 165, Male = 147)  # Create a vector with element names
> genderFreq
Female   Male
   165    147

> genderFreq <- c(165, 147)                   # Create a vector with no element
                                                names
> genderFreq
[1] 165 147
> names(genderFreq) <- c("Female", "Male")   # Assign element names
> genderFreq
Female   Male
   165    147
```

When we encounter a "named" vector, we can query it with the names function to return the (character) vector of element names:

```
> genderFreq           # Print the vector
Female   Male
   165    147
> names(genderFreq)    # Return the element names
[1] "Female" "Male"
```

To summarize, the three primary functions used to query vector attributes are listed in Table 3.1.

TABLE 3.1 Functions to Query Vector Attributes

Function	Usage
mode	Returns the (data) mode of the vector
length	Returns the number of elements in the vector
names	Returns the elements' names in a vector (or NULL if there are no names assigned)

Subscripting Vectors

In this section, we look at the ways in which to extract subsets of data from a vector. We can achieve this using square brackets ([ ]) following the name of the vector, as follows:

```
VECTOR [ Input specifying the subset of data to return ]
```

The input itself can be one of a five possible inputs, as shown in Table 3.2.

TABLE 3.2 Possible Vector Subscripting Inputs

Input	Effect
Blank	All values of the vector are returned.
A vector of positive integers	Used as an index of values to return.
A vector of negative integers	Used as an index of values to omit.
A vector of logical values	Only corresponding TRUE values are returned.
A vector of character values	Refers to the element names of values to return.

CAUTION

Square versus Round Brackets

When we call a function, we use round brackets, as shown in our examples of the functions c, seq, and rep. We use square brackets to reference data from an object. If we use the wrong "type" of bracket, R will assume we are trying to call a function instead of reference data:

```
> X      # A vector called X
[1] 6 8 3 1 7
> X[]    # Using square brackets
[1] 6 8 3 1 7
> X()    # Error when using round brackets
Error: could not find function "X"
```

Subscripting Vectors: Blank Inputs

The first (and simplest) input is "blank," which has the result of returning the entire vector of values:

```
> X <- c(6, 8, 3, 1, 7)  # Create a simple vector

> X                      # Print the values
[1] 6 8 3 1 7

> X [ ]                  # Blank input
[1] 6 8 3 1 7
```

TIP

White Space

White space is ignored by R (unless within quotation marks as part of a string). Therefore, in this example, the command x [ ] is equivalent to x[] or even x   [ ]. As a convention, we will use spaces to improve readability where appropriate.

Subscripting Vectors: Positive Integers

If you specify a vector of integers as the input, they are used as an index of values to return:

```
> X                      # Print the values
[1] 6 8 3 1 7
> X [ c(1, 3, 5) ]       # 1st, 3rd and 5th elements
[1] 6 3 7
```

In the preceding example, we used a vector of positive integers within the square brackets as the index. However, we could alternatively create a separate vector with which to reference the data:

```
> index <- c(1, 3, 5)    # Create index vector
> X [ index ]            # 1st, 3rd and 5th elements
[1] 6 3 7
```

Using this approach, we could also specify values to omit from our vector. For example, if we wanted to return all values except the third value, we could achieve that as follows:

```
> X [ c(1:2, 4:5) ]     # Return the 1st, 2nd, 4th and 5th elements
[1] 6 8 1 7
```

Subscripting Vectors: Negative Integers

In the last example, we used a vector of positive integers to remove a value from a vector (that is, to omit one value in the return). However, for larger vectors this is not a scalable solution.

If we provide a vector of negative integers as the input, this refers to an index of values to omit from the vector, as illustrated in this example:

```
> X                      # Original vector of values
[1] 6 8 3 1 7
> X [ c(1:2, 4:5) ]     # Omit 3rd value using positive integers
[1] 6 8 1 7
> X [ -3 ]              # Omit 3rd value using negative integers
[1] 6 8 1 7
```

If we want to omit more than one position, we could either provide a vector of negative integers or place a minus symbol in front of a vector of positive integers. Consequently, the following two lines are equivalent:

```
> X [ c(-2, -4) ]    # Omit 2nd and 4th values
[1] 6 3 7
> X [ -c(2, 4) ]     # Omit 2nd and 4th values
[1] 6 3 7
```

Among other uses, this syntax allows us to exclude values from a vector based on another vector, as shown here:

```
> Y                  # Vector of values to subset
 [1] 6 9 4 3 6 8 1 9 0 3 4 8 7 4 5
> outliers           # Index of values to omit
[1]  4  7  9 11 15
> Y [ -outliers ]    # Omit the values specified in outliers
 [1] 6 9 4 6 8 9 3 8 7 4
```

Subscripting Vectors: Logical Values

Our third possible input is a vector of logical values the same length as the original vector. When we reference a vector in this way, only the corresponding TRUE values are returned, as illustrated here:

```
> X                      # Original vector
[1] 6 8 3 1 7
> c(T, T, F, F, T)        # Vector of logical values
[1]  TRUE  TRUE FALSE FALSE  TRUE
> X [ c(T, T, F, F, T) ]   # Return corresponding TRUE values only
[1] 6 8 7
```

The logical vector has TRUE values in the first, second, and fifth positions, so that is the index of values returned (6, 8, and 7).

Although this example illustrates the "mechanics" of how R returns values when given a logical vector input, in practice this is not useful (in other words, we will not commonly manually enter TRUE and FALSE values into a vector to subscript in this way).

More commonly, we use simple logical statements to create vectors of logical values to use as the input, as shown here:

```
> X              # Original vector
[1] 6 8 3 1 7
> X > 5          # Logical statement: where is X > 5?
[1]  TRUE  TRUE FALSE FALSE  TRUE
> X [ X > 5 ]    # Subset where values of X are greater than 5
[1] 6 8 7
```

This mirrors the previous example, although here we use a logical vector via the statement X > 5. Some other styles of logical statements we can use are listed here:

```
> X > 6            # Greater than 6
[1] FALSE  TRUE FALSE FALSE  TRUE
> X >= 6           # Greater than or equal to 6
[1]  TRUE  TRUE FALSE FALSE  TRUE
> X < 6            # Less than 6
[1] FALSE FALSE  TRUE  TRUE FALSE
> X <= 6           # Less than or equal to 6
[1]  TRUE FALSE  TRUE  TRUE FALSE
> X == 6           # X is equal to 6
[1]  TRUE FALSE FALSE FALSE FALSE
> X != 6           # X is not equal to 6
[1] FALSE  TRUE  TRUE  TRUE  TRUE
> X > 2 & X <= 6   # Between 2 (exclusive) and 6 (inclusive)
[1]  TRUE FALSE  TRUE FALSE FALSE
> X < 2 | X > 6    # Less than 2 or greater than 6
[1] FALSE  TRUE FALSE  TRUE  TRUE
```

Because these statements produce a logical vector that (by definition) is the same length of the input vector, they can all be used to subset the original vector:

```
> X                     # Original vector
[1] 6 8 3 1 7
> X [ X <= 6 ]          # Values less than or equal to 6
[1] 6 3 1
> X [ X != 6 ]          # Values that are not equal to 6
[1] 8 3 1 7
> X [ X >= 3 & X <= 7 ] # Values between 3 and 7
[1] 6 3 7
```

It is important to consider that, for these examples, R performs a two-step process: The input is evaluated, returning the logical vector, which is then used to reference the original vector.

This allows us to reference values of one vector based on a second or third vector, as shown here:

```
> ID          # Vector of ID values
[1] 1001 1002 1003 1004 1005
> AGE         # Vector of ages
[1] 18 35 26 42 22
> GENDER      # Vector of genders
[1] "M" "F" "M" "F" "F"

> AGE [ AGE > 25 ]                # Vectors of AGE that are greater than 25
[1] 35 26 42
> ID [ AGE > 25 ]                 # ID where AGE is greater than 25
[1] 1002 1003 1004
> ID [ AGE > 25 & GENDER == "F" ] # ID where AGE is greater than 25 and GENDER is
                                  #   "F"
[1] 1002 1004
```

Subscripting Vectors: Character Values

When a vector has element names, we can use a vector of characters to refer to the elements to return. First, let's add element names to our vector example:

```
> names(X) <- c("A", "B", "C", "D", "E")      # Add element names

> X                                   # Original vector
A B C D E
6 8 3 1 7

> X[c("A", "C", "E")]                 # Reference based on names
A C E
6 3 7
```

Subscripting Vectors: Summary

At this point, we have looked at referencing data from a vector by specifying one of five possible inputs, as shown earlier in Table 3.2, examples of which are shown here:

```
> X [ ]                  # Blank: all values returned
A B C D E
6 8 3 1 7
> X [ c(1, 3, 5) ]       # Positives: Positions to return
A C E
6 3 7
> X [ -c(1, 3, 5) ]      # Negatives: Positions to omit
B D
8 1
> X [ X > 5 ]            # Logical: TRUE values returned
A B E
6 8 7
> X [ c("A", "C", "E") ] # Character: Named elements returned
A C E
6 3 7
```

TIP

Sequence of Letters

As discussed earlier, you cannot use the : notation to directly create a sequence of letters (for example, A:E). However, there are two in-built R vectors (called `letters` and `LETTERS`) that contain the (lowercase and uppercase) letters of the alphabet:

```
> letters
 [1] "a" "b" "c" "d" "e" "f" "g" "h" "i" "j" "k" "l" "m"
[14] "n" "o" "p" "q" "r" "s" "t" "u" "v" "w" "x" "y" "z"
```

```
> LETTERS
 [1] "A" "B" "C" "D" "E" "F" "G" "H" "I" "J" "K" "L" "M"
[14] "N" "O" "P" "Q" "R" "S" "T" "U" "V" "W" "X" "Y" "Z"
```

Because these are vectors, we can reference them using square brackets with one of the five input types we just discussed. In this way, we can create sequences of lowercase or uppercase letters:

```
> letters [ 1:5 ]  # First 5 (lower case) letters
[1] "a" "b" "c" "d" "e"
> LETTERS [ 1:5 ]  # First 5 (upper case) letters
[1] "A" "B" "C" "D" "E"
```

Matrices

A matrix is a two-dimensional structure containing values of the same mode. Similar to the section "Vectors" earlier in this hour, in this section we look at the following topics:

▶ Some ways to create matrices

▶ The attributes of a matrix

▶ The ways in which we can extract information from a matrix

Creating Matrices

You typically create matrices in two fundamental ways:

▶ By combining a series of vectors to form rows or columns

▶ By reading a single vector into a matrix structure

Combining Vectors to Create a Matrix

You can use the cbind function to combine a series of vectors, thus forming the columns of a matrix. An example, creating a three-row-by-four-column matrix, is shown here:

```
> cbind(1:3, 3:1, c(2, 4, 6), rep(1, 3))
     [,1] [,2] [,3] [,4]
[1,]    1    3    2    1
[2,]    2    2    4    1
[3,]    3    1    6    1
```

Recycling

Note here that we've created a matrix by supplying four vectors of the same length to create our vector. However, if we supply vectors that are not of the same length, R will repeat the shorter-length vectors to the length of the longest vector to create the matrix. That means we can re-create the preceding matrix by specifying a 1 for the fourth column instead of repeating that value:

```
> cbind(1:3, 3:1, c(2, 4, 6), 1)
     [,1] [,2] [,3] [,4]
[1,]    1    3    2    1
[2,]    2    2    4    1
[3,]    3    1    6    1
```

In this example, the shorter-length vector is of length 1, which can easily be repeated to create a vector of length 3. If the shorter-length vectors cannot be recycled to exactly create the required length, a warning is provided. Consider the third column in this example:

```
> cbind(1:3, 3:1, c(2, 4), 1)
     [,1] [,2] [,3] [,4]
[1,]    1    3    2    1
[2,]    2    2    4    1
[3,]    3    1    2    1
Warning message:
In cbind(1:3, 3:1, c(2, 4), 1) :
  number of rows of result is not a multiple of vector length (arg 3)
```

As shown, the two values are repeated but a warning message is produced because the result is not a multiple of the longest-length vector.

Instead of using cbind, we can use the rbind function to specify the rows of a matrix. This time, we will use the same vectors to create a four-row-by-three-column matrix:

```
> rbind(1:3, 3:1, c(2, 4, 6), rep(1, 3))
     [,1] [,2] [,3]
[1,]    1    2    3
[2,]    3    2    1
[3,]    2    4    6
[4,]    1    1    1
```

Transposing Matrices

The t function can be used to transpose a matrix; therefore, the following commands are equivalent:

```
> cbind(1:3, 3:1, c(2, 4, 6), rep(1, 3))
     [,1] [,2] [,3] [,4]
[1,]    1    3    2    1
```

```
[2,]    2    2    4    1
[3,]    3    1    6    1
> t(rbind(1:3, 3:1, c(2, 4, 6), rep(1, 3)))
     [,1] [,2] [,3] [,4]
[1,]    1    3    2    1
[2,]    2    2    4    1
[3,]    3    1    6    1
```

Creating a Matrix with a Single Vector

As you just saw, the rbind and cbind functions can be used to create a matrix by combining vectors as rows or columns. An alternative way is to take a single vector of data and "read" the data into rows and columns of a matrix. You can achieve this using the matrix function, which accepts, as a first argument, the vector of data to be used:

```
> matrix(1:12)
       [,1]
 [1,]    1
 [2,]    2
 [3,]    3
 [4,]    4
 [5,]    5
 [6,]    6
 [7,]    7
 [8,]    8
 [9,]    9
[10,]   10
[11,]   11
[12,]   12
```

The matrix function has two arguments, nrow and ncol, that you can specify to create a matrix with specific "dimensions," as shown here:

```
> matrix(1:12, nrow = 3, ncol = 4)
     [,1] [,2] [,3] [,4]
[1,]    1    4    7   10
[2,]    2    5    8   11
[3,]    3    6    9   12
```

In this example, we have used both nrow and ncol to specify the dimensions of the matrix. When we create a matrix in this way, we need only specify one dimension (nrow or ncol), as shown here:

```
> matrix(1:12, nrow = 3)
     [,1] [,2] [,3] [,4]
[1,]    1    4    7   10
[2,]    2    5    8   11
[3,]    3    6    9   12
```

By default, the values are read in to the matrix in a column-wise manner, resulting in the first column containing the numbers 1 to 3 in this example. This is controlled by an argument to `matrix` called `byrow`, which, by default, is set to `FALSE`:

```
> matrix(1:12, nrow = 3, byrow = F)   # Default behavior - byrow = FALSE
     [,1] [,2] [,3] [,4]
[1,]   1    4    7   10
[2,]   2    5    8   11
[3,]   3    6    9   12
```

We can change this argument to instead read in the values by row, as shown here:

```
> matrix(1:12, nrow = 3, byrow = TRUE)
     [,1] [,2] [,3] [,4]
[1,]   1    2    3    4
[2,]   5    6    7    8
[3,]   9   10   11   12
```

Matrix Attributes

When we have created a matrix, we can query a number of matrix attributes using a set of utility functions. This includes functions to query the following:

▶ The mode of the matrix

▶ The dimensions of the matrix

▶ The row/column names of the matrix

As before, we can query the mode of the matrix using the `mode` function:

```
> aVector <- c(4, 5, 2, 7, 6, 1, 5, 5, 0, 4, 6, 9)   # Create a vector
> X <- matrix(aVector, nrow = 3)                      # Create a matrix
> X                                                   # Print the matrix
     [,1] [,2] [,3] [,4]
[1,]   4    7    5    4
[2,]   5    6    5    6
[3,]   2    1    0    9
> mode(X)                                             # The mode of the matrix
[1] "numeric"
```

Similarly, we can use the `length` function to return the number of elements in the matrix:

```
> length(X)    # Number of elements
[1] 12
```

Although the `length` function returns the total number of elements in the matrix, it does not allow us to directly see the structure (that is, the number of rows and columns) of the matrix.

For this, we can use the dim function, which returns a vector of length 2, specifying the rows (first) and columns of the matrix:

```
> dim(X)       # Dimension of the matrix
[1] 3 4
> dim(X)[1]   # Number of rows
[1] 3
> dim(X)[2]   # Number of columns
[1] 4
```

Here, we use positive integers to reference the position of the vector (returned by dim) to return (1 for rows, 2 for columns). Alternatively, we can use the functions nrow and ncol to directly return the number of rows and columns:

```
> nrow(X)   # Number of rows
[1] 3
> ncol(X)   # Number of columns
[1] 4
```

Earlier you saw that vectors can be associated with element names. With matrices, it is not practical to assign a name for each element (cell) of the matrix. However, you might see matrices that have row and column names.

You'll either create matrices with row and column names (or "dimension names") or, more commonly, come across matrices with dimension names as the result of an operation.

Consider an example where we have created a frequency count of age group versus gender from a set of data. These numbers could be returned as a matrix, as shown next:

```
> freqMatrix  # Frequency by Age Group and Gender
     [,1] [,2]
[1,]   75   68
[2,]   52   49
[3,]   38   30
```

Here, we can see that the matrix contains six values, which relate to the frequency count by age group and gender. However, without labels, we do not know what the values refer to. As such, R may return a matrix with dimension names, as shown here:

```
> freqMatrix
      Female Male
18-35     75   68
26-35     52   49
36+       38   30
```

If we want to create a matrix with dimension names, we can assign names using the dimnames function. It accepts a "list" structure with row and column names. (Note that we will cover lists in Hour 4, "Multi-Mode Data Structures.") Here's an example:

```
> freqMatrix                   # Original matrix - no row/column names
      [,1] [,2]
[1,]   75   68
[2,]   52   49
[3,]   38   30

> dimnames(freqMatrix) <- list(c("18-35", "26-35", "36+"),
+    c("Female", "Male"))      # Assign dimension names

> freqMatrix                   # Resulting matrix
       Female Male
18-35      75   68
26-35      52   49
36+        38   30
```

When we see a matrix that has dimension names, we can query those names using the
dimnames function, which returns a "list" containing two character vectors:

```
> dimnames(freqMatrix)         # Dimension names of freqMatrix
[[1]]
[1] "18-35" "26-35" "36+"

[[2]]
[1] "Female" "Male"
```

Subscripting Matrices

When we covered vectors, you saw that we can use square brackets with one of five input types
to extract data. This included examples such as the following:

▶ Select the first five elements.

▶ Select all but the sixth element.

▶ Select all values greater than 5.

▶ Select the "A", "C", and "E" elements.

With a matrix, which has rows and columns, these selections no longer seem particularly relevant. However, we may wish to select specific rows and columns, which we specify using 2 separate inputs within the square brackets separated by a comma:

```
MATRIX [ Input specifying rows to return, Input specifying columns to return ]
```

Subscripting Matrices: Blanks, Positives, and Negatives

First, let's look at using blank subscripts for both rows and columns. The following returns all rows and all columns:

```
> X [ , ]   # Blank for rows, blank for columns
      [,1] [,2] [,3] [,4]
[1,]    4    7    5    4
[2,]    5    6    5    6
[3,]    2    1    0    9
```

Next, we'll use vectors of positive integers for both the rows and columns:

```
> X [ 1:2 , c(1, 3, 4) ]   # +ives for rows, +ives for columns
      [,1] [,2] [,3]
[1,]    4    5    4
[2,]    5    5    6
```

In this example, we returned the first two rows and the first, third, and fourth columns.

NOTE

Column Index

In this example, note that we selected rows 1 and 2 with columns 1, 3 and 4, and the matrix returned the correct matrix subset. The column index of the new matrix is `[,1]  [,2]  [,3]`.

This is because the subset is a completely new matrix with its own column index, and it has no "memory" of the manner in which it was created (in other words, the index is not "1, 3, 4"). If, however, the matrix we were subsetting had dimension names, the row/column names would be retained in the sub-matrix.

So far, we have used blanks on the rows and columns, then vectors of positive integers for both rows and columns. However, we can also specify different input types for the rows and columns, as shown in this example:

```
> X [ , -2 ]   # Blank for rows, -ives for columns
      [,1] [,2] [,3]
[1,]    4    5    4
[2,]    5    5    6
[3,]    2    0    9
```

Here, we use blank for the rows (so all rows are returned) and a negative integer for the columns (so all but the second column is returned).

Dropping Dimensions

In the preceding example, we referenced data from a 3×4 matrix, but always returned at least two rows/columns. If we instead reference a single row or column, the dimensions of the output matrix are dropped, so a simpler structure (in fact, a vector) is returned:

```
> X [ , 1:2 ]    # First 2 columns - returns a matrix
     [,1] [,2]
[1,]    4    7
[2,]    5    6
[3,]    2    1
> X [ , 1 ]      # First column - returns a vector
[1] 4 5 2
```

Because most R functions work with vectors, the "dropping" of dimensions in this way is often what we want. However, if we want to reference the data but ensure the dimensions are not dropped, we can use an argument called drop within the square brackets, as shown here:

```
> X [ , 1 ]                   # Returns a vector
[1] 4 5 2
> X [ , 1, drop = FALSE ]   # Use drop to maintain dimensions
     [,1]
[1,]    4
[2,]    5
[3,]    2
```

Subscripting Matrices: Logical Values

We can use logical values to reference rows and/or columns of a matrix. To achieve this, we provide a logical vector the same length as the numbers of rows/columns to subscript. A simple example is shown here:

```
> X                    # Original Matrix
     [,1] [,2] [,3] [,4]
[1,]    4    7    5    4
[2,]    5    6    5    6
[3,]    2    1    0    9

> X [ c(T, F, T), ]    # Logical for rows, blank for columns
     [,1] [,2] [,3] [,4]
[1,]    4    7    5    4
[2,]    2    1    0    9
```

In this example, a logical vector is used to subscript the matrix. We provide a logical vector length of 3, and only the rows corresponding to the TRUE values are returned (the first and third rows).

Instead of specifying a vector manually, we could use a logical statement based on one of the other columns to subscript the data. For example, let's consider referencing only rows where the first column is not 5:

```
> X [ , 1 ]                # 1st column
[1] 4 5 2

> X [ , 1 ] != 5           # Where is the 1st column not 5
[1]   TRUE FALSE   TRUE

> X [ X [ , 1 ] != 5 , ]   # Use to subscript the data
     [,1] [,2] [,3] [,4]
[1,]    4    7    5    4
[2,]    2    1    0    9
```

This last line looks particular complex, but relates to syntax that is rarely used. The single-mode nature of matrices means it is not a good structure in which to store our standard rectangular data; there is a more appropriate structure to hold this sort of data (the data.frame structure, covered in Hour 4) that has a simpler syntax for referencing subsets of data.

Subscripting Matrices: Character Values

So far, we have discussed how matrices can be referenced using blank, positive, negative, and logical inputs. If we have a matrix with row and column names, we can also use vectors of characters to refer directly to the rows and columns we wish to return. First, let's add dimension names to our matrix example:

```
> dimnames(X) <- list( letters[1:3], LETTERS[1:4] )
> X
  A B C D
a 4 7 5 4
b 5 6 5 6
c 2 1 0 9
```

Now we can use character vectors to reference the rows and/or columns. For example, let's reference rows "a" and "c" with all the columns:

```
> X [ c("a", "c"), ]   # Characters for rows, blank for columns
  A B C D
a 4 7 5 4
c 2 1 0 9
```

In this next example, we use a character vector to reference the columns we want to return and all the rows:

```
> X [ , c("A", "C", "D") ]    # Blank for rows, Characters for columns
  A C D
a 4 5 4
b 5 5 6
c 2 0 9
```

Arrays

At the start of this hour we introduced vectors as a structure that contains a series of values of the same mode. Next, we looked at matrices as a single-mode structure with rows and columns.

An array is a single-mode structure that can have any number of dimensions (so, in fact, a matrix in R is simply a two-dimensional array).

Similar to the previous sections in this hour on vectors and matrices, in this section we look at the following:

▶ Some ways to create an array

▶ The attributes of an array

▶ The ways in which we can extract information from an array

For the purposes of this hour, we will focus on three-dimensional arrays, but the code works in a similar way for any dimension of array.

Creating Arrays

You create an array by providing a single vector input to the array function along with the dimension of the array you wish to create (as a vector of integers). The following example creates a two-dimensional array (that is, a matrix):

```
> aVector <- c(4, 5, 2, 7, 6, 1, 5, 5, 0, 4, 6, 9)  # Create a vector
> X <- array(aVector, dim = c(3, 4))                 # Create a 2D array (matrix)
> X                                                  # Print the matrix
     [,1] [,2] [,3] [,4]
[1,]    4    7    5    4
[2,]    5    6    5    6
[3,]    2    1    0    9
```

If you want to create a three-dimensional array, you specify a vector of length of 3 for the dim argument, as shown here:

```
> aVector <- c(4, 5, 2, 7, 6, 1, 5, 5, 0, 4, 6, 9)  # Create a vector
> X <- array(rep(aVector, 3), dim = c(3, 4, 3))      # Create a 3D array
> X                                                  # Print the array
, , 1
```

```
       [,1] [,2] [,3] [,4]
[1,]     4    7    5    4
[2,]     5    6    5    6
[3,]     2    1    0    9

, , 2

       [,1] [,2] [,3] [,4]
[1,]     4    7    5    4
[2,]     5    6    5    6
[3,]     2    1    0    9

, , 3

       [,1] [,2] [,3] [,4]
[1,]     4    7    5    4
[2,]     5    6    5    6
[3,]     2    1    0    9
```

Array Attributes

Attributes for arrays can be referenced in exactly the same way as you saw for matrices. Some examples of extracting array attributes can be seen here:

```
> mode(X)          # Mode of array
[1] "numeric"
> length(X)        # Number of elements in array
[1] 36
> dim(X)           # Dimension of array
[1] 3 4 3
```

As with matrices, you specify dimension names using the dimnames function:

```
> dimnames(X) <- list(letters[1:3], LETTERS[1:4], c("X1", "X2", "X3"))
> X
, , X1

  A B C D
a 4 7 5 4
b 5 6 5 6
c 2 1 0 9

, , X2

  A B C D
a 4 7 5 4
b 5 6 5 6
c 2 1 0 9
```

```
, , X3

   A B C D
a 4 7 5 4
b 5 6 5 6
c 2 1 0 9
```

Subscripting Arrays

To extract data from an array, you provide one input per dimension. Therefore, for a three-dimensional array, you need to provide three inputs, each of which can be one of the five types of input (blank, positives, negatives, logicals, or characters).

Some examples of array subscripting with our sample (three-dimensional) array are shown here:

```
> X [ , , 1 ]          # Blank / Blank / Positive
   A B C D
a 4 7 5 4
b 5 6 5 6
c 2 1 0 9
> X [ -1, 1:2, 1:2 ]  # Negative / Positive / Positive
, , X1

   A B
b 5 6
c 2 1


, , X2

   A B
b 5 6
c 2 1
```

Relationship Between Single-Mode Data Objects

So far in this hour we have looked at the three "single-mode" data structures in R: vectors, matrices, and arrays. You have seen how to create these structures, how to query attributes of the structures, and how to extract data from them.

Table 3.3 describes the key aspects of each of these structures.

TABLE 3.3 Comparison of Single-Mode Data Structures

Attribute	Vectors	Matrices	Arrays
Mode	Single mode	Single mode	Single mode
Structure	No structure	Two-dimensional	*N*-dimensional
Length function	Returns # elements	Returns # elements	Returns # elements
Subscripting	X [Input]	X [Input , Input]	X [Input, Input, Input, ...]

During this hour you may have noticed a pattern emerging with the three structures, which is also prevalent in Table 3.3. In fact, these three structures are very closely related because they are all, fundamentally, vectors. The only thing that distinguishes vectors from matrices and arrays is the dimension of the structure, which allows you to print, manage, and reference the data from structures in a particular manner.

This allows you to very easily convert from one structure to another by (re)specifying the dimension with the dim function. Consider the following code, which converts a vector first to a matrix and then to a three-dimensional array:

```
> X <- c(2, 6, 5, 1, 2, 8, 9, 4, 3, 1, 9, 4)     # Create a vector
> X                                               # Print the vector
 [1] 2 6 5 1 2 8 9 4 3 1 9 4
> length(X)                                       # Vector has 12 elements
[1] 12
> dim(X)                                          # Vectors have no "dimension"
NULL

> dim(X) <- c(3, 4)                               # Assign a dimension (3 x 4)
> X                                               # Print X - it is now a matrix
     [,1] [,2] [,3] [,4]
[1,]    2    1    9    1
[2,]    6    2    4    9
[3,]    5    8    3    4

> dim(X) <- c(2, 3, 2)                            # Assign a new dimension (2 x 3 x 2)
> X                                               # Print X - it is now a 3D array
, , 1
```

```
      [,1] [,2] [,3]
[1,]    2    5    2
[2,]    6    1    8


, , 2


      [,1] [,2] [,3]
[1,]    9    3    9
[2,]    4    1    4
```

This also allows you to treat matrices and arrays as vectors for simple functions later, for example:

```
> dim(X)      # X is an array
[1] 2 3 2
> median(X)   # Median of X
[1] 4
```

Summary

In this hour, we have looked at how the four different "modes" of data in R (numeric, character, logical, and complex) can be stored in the three single-mode structures: vectors, matrices, and arrays. We have looked at the ways in which we can create each structure, the attributes each structure has, and how to reference subsets of data from each structure.

Although we have covered matrices and arrays in this section, the majority of the time was spent looking at vectors in some details. This reflects the fact that we typically work with vectors as a primary data structure, so familiarity with how to manage these objects is essential.

Of course, in this hour we have looked only at "single mode" structures (i.e. those structures that only hold a single mode of data). In the next hour, we will look at two data structures that allow us to store data with more than one mode: lists and data frames.

Q&A

Q. Can I mix the five types of subscript input?

A. Not really, because one of two things will happen: either R will convert all elements in the subscript input to a single type or, if you use positives and negatives together, R will return an error.

Q. Why is a matrix not a suitable structure to hold standard rectangular datasets?

A. Because it is a single-mode structure, it isn't capable of storing (say) a numeric column and a character column from a dataset together. In the next hour, you will see a more natural structure for storing this sort of data.

Q. What if I try to reference data outside of the dimensions?

A. Missing values will be returned, as shown in this example:

```
> X <- c(A = 1, B = 2, C = 3)
> X
A B C
1 2 3
> X[2:5]
   B    C <NA> <NA>
   2    3   NA   NA
> X[c("A", "C", "E")]
   A    C <NA>
   1    3   NA
```

Q. How do missing values impact referencing with logical values?

A. If you use a vector of missing values in a logical statement, the return value will also be NA (because you don't know whether the missing value would have met the condition). When you use this to subscript, missing values are returned. Consider the following example:

```
> ID
[1] 1 2 3 4 5
> AGE
[1] 18 35 25 NA 23
> AGE >= 25
[1] FALSE  TRUE  TRUE    NA FALSE
> ID [ AGE >= 25 ]
[1]   2   3 NA
```

Workshop

The workshop contains quiz questions and exercises to help you solidify your understanding of the material covered. Try to answer all questions before looking at the "Answers" section that follows.

Quiz

1. What are the four different "modes" of data in R?

2. Why do we refer to vectors, matrices, and arrays as "single-mode" structures?

3. What function can you use to create a vector of repeated sequences?

4. What are the five different "subscript" inputs you can use to reference a subset of data from a vector?

5. What is the difference between the `cbind` and `rbind` functions?

6. Why do we use a comma within the square brackets when subscripting a matrix (for example, `mat[1:2, -1]`)?

7. What is the difference between a matrix and an array?

Answers

1. The four modes of data are numeric, character, logical, and complex.

2. "Single mode" refers to the fact that these structures can only store data of a single mode (for example, a "numeric" vector or a "character" matrix). Vectors, matrices, and arrays cannot hold data of more than one "mode."

3. You can use the `rep` function to create a vector of repeated sequences.

4. The five "subscript" input types are blanks, vectors of positive integers, vectors of negative integers, vectors of logical values, and vectors of characters.

5. Both functions create a matrix based on a number of vector inputs. The `cbind` function specifies that provided vectors are to be used as the columns of the matrix, whereas `rbind` specifies that the provided vectors should be used to define the rows of the matrix.

6. We use a comma to separate the "row" subscripts from the "column" subscripts. Therefore, the line `mat[1:2, -1]` specifies that we want to return the first two rows, and all but the first column of `mat`.

7. A matrix is strictly a two-dimensional structure (it has rows and columns). An array is a structure with any number of dimensions (that is, we could create a three-, four-, 10-, or 100-dimensional array). A two-dimensional array is exactly equal to a matrix.

Activities

1. There is an object in R called `pi`. What is the length and mode of `pi`?

2. Create the following vectors in R:

```
[1]  6 3 4 8 5 2 7 9 4 5
[1]  TRUE FALSE FALSE TRUE FALSE FALSE TRUE TRUE FALSE FALSE
[1]  -1 0 1 2 3
[1]  5 4 3 2 1
[1]  0.0 0.1 0.2 0.3 0.4 0.5 0.6 0.7 0.8 0.9 1.0
[1]  1 2 3 1 2 3 1 2 3
[1]  "A" "A" "A" "A"
[1]  "A" "A" "A" "A" "B" "B" "B" "C" "C" "D"
```

3. Using the `LETTERS` vector, print the following:

   ▶ The first four letters

   ▶ All but the first four letters

   ▶ The "even" letters (that is, A, C, E, G, ...)

4. Create a numeric vector of length 10 using a selection of integers between 1 and 9. Assign the first 10 elements of the `letters` vector as the element names of your vector. Using this vector, do the following:

  ▶ Select the first and last values of the vector.

  ▶ Select all values of the vector greater than 3.

  ▶ Select all values of the vector between 2 and 7.

  ▶ Select all values of the vector that are not 5.

  ▶ Select the `"D"`, `"E"`, and, `"G"` elements of your vector.

5. Create a 3×4 matrix containing numeric values. Print the first two rows and all but the last column of this matrix.

Multi-Mode Data Structures

What You'll Learn in This Hour:

▶ What a list object is

▶ How to create and manipulate a data frame

▶ How to perform an initial investigation in the structure of our data

The majority of data sources contain a mixture of data types, which we need to store together in a simple, effective format. The "single-mode" structures introduced in the last hour are useful basic data objects, but are not sufficiently sophisticated to store data containing multiple "modes." In this hour, we focus on two key data structures that allow us to store "multi-mode" data: lists and data frames. We will illustrate the ways in which these structures can be created and managed, with a focus on how to extract data from them. We also look at how these two data structures can be effectively used in our day-to-day work.

Multi-Mode Structures

In the last hour, we examined the three structures designed to hold data in R:

▶ Vectors—Series of values

▶ Matrices—Rectangular structures with rows and columns

▶ Arrays—Higher dimension structures (for example, 3D and 4D arrays)

Although these objects provide us with a range of useful functionality, they are restricted in that they can only hold a single "mode" of data. This is illustrated in the following example:

```
> c(1, 2, 3, "Hello")                    # Multiple modes
[1] "1"     "2"     "3"     "Hello"
> c(1, 2, 3, TRUE, FALSE)                # Multiple modes
[1] 1 2 3 1 0
> c(1, 2, 3, TRUE, FALSE, "Hello")       # Multiple modes
[1] "1"     "2"     "3"     "TRUE"  "FALSE" "Hello"
```

As you can see, when we attempt to store more than one mode of data in a single-mode structure, the object (and its contents) will be converted to a single mode.

The preceding example uses a vector to illustrate this behavior, but let's suppose we want to store a rectangular "dataset" using a matrix. For example, we might attempt to create a matrix that contains the forecast temperatures for New York over the next five days:

```
> weather <- cbind(
+    Day  = c("Saturday", "Sunday", "Monday", "Tuesday", "Wednesday"),
+    Date = c("Jul 4", "Jul 5", "Jul 6", "Jul 7", "Jul 8"),
+    TempF = c(75, 86, 83, 83, 87)
+ )
> weather
        Day          Date     TempF
[1,] "Saturday"  "Jul 4" "75"
[2,] "Sunday"    "Jul 5" "86"
[3,] "Monday"    "Jul 6" "83"
[4,] "Tuesday"   "Jul 7" "83"
[5,] "Wednesday" "Jul 8" "87"
```

From the quotation marks, it is clear that R has converted all the data to character values, which can be confirmed by looking at the mode of this matrix structure:

```
> mode(weather)     # The mode of the matrix
[1] "character"
```

This reinforces the need for data structures that allow us to store data of multiple modes. R provides two "multi-mode" data structures:

- ▶ Lists—Containers for any objects
- ▶ Data frames—Rectangular structures with rows and columns

Lists

The list is considered perhaps the most complex data object in R, and many R programmers will go to great lengths to avoid the use of lists in their structures. This perceived complexity, perhaps, stems from a lack of clarity over what a list "looks like." Other structures, such as vectors and matrices, are relatively easy to visualize, and are therefore easier to adopt and manage.

Despite this, lists are simple structures that can be used to perform a number of complex operations.

What Is a List?

Lists are simply containers for other objects. The objects stored in a list can be of any type (for example, "matrix" or "vector") and any mode. Therefore, you can create a list containing the following, for example:

- A character vector
- A numeric matrix
- A logical array
- Another list

When discussing lists, some people use the analogy of a box. For example, you might do the following:

- Create an empty box.
- Put some "things" into the box.
- Look into the box to see what things are in there.
- Take things back out of the box.

In a similar way, in this section, we will look at how to do the following:

- Create an empty list.
- Put objects into the list.
- Look at the number (and names) of objects in the list.
- Extract elements from the list.

Creating an Empty List

You create a list using the `list` function. The simplest list you can create is an empty list, like this:

```
> emptyList <- list()
> emptyList
list()
```

Later, you will see how to add elements to this empty list.

Creating a Non-Empty List

More commonly, you'll create a list and add initial elements to it at the same time. You achieve this by specifying a comma-separated set of objects within the `list` function:

```
> aVector <- c(5, 7, 8, 2, 4, 3, 9, 0, 1, 2)
> aMatrix <- matrix( LETTERS[1:6], nrow = 3)
> unnamedList <- list(aVector, aMatrix)
> unnamedList
[[1]]
 [1] 5 7 8 2 4 3 9 0 1 2

[[2]]
     [,1] [,2]
[1,] "A"  "D"
[2,] "B"  "E"
[3,] "C"  "F"
```

In this example, we created two objects (aVector and aMatrix) and then created a list (unnamedList) containing copies of these objects.

NOTE

Original Objects

When you create lists in this way, you take copies of the objects (aVector and aMatrix in this example). The original objects are not impacted by this action (that is, they are not edited, moved, changed, or deleted).

If you only need the objects within the list, you could create the objects as you specify the list, like this:

```
> unnamedList <- list(c(5, 7, 8, 2, 4, 3, 9, 0, 1, 2),
+                     matrix( LETTERS[1:6], nrow = 3))
> unnamedList
[[1]]
 [1] 5 7 8 2 4 3 9 0 1 2

[[2]]
     [,1] [,2]
[1,] "A"  "D"
[2,] "B"  "E"
[3,] "C"  "F"
```

Creating a List with Element Names

When you create a list, you can optionally assign names to the elements. This helps you when you're referencing elements in the list later.

```
> namedList <- list(VEC = aVector, MAT = aMatrix)
> namedList
$VEC
 [1] 5 7 8 2 4 3 9 0 1 2

$MAT
     [,1] [,2]
[1,] "A"  "D"
[2,] "B"  "E"
[3,] "C"  "F"
```

As before, you can also create the (named) objects as you're creating the list:

```
> namedList <- list(VEC = c(5, 7, 8, 2, 4, 3, 9, 0, 1, 2),
+                   MAT = matrix( LETTERS[1:6], nrow = 3))
> namedList
$VEC
 [1] 5 7 8 2 4 3 9 0 1 2

$MAT
     [,1] [,2]
[1,] "A"  "D"
[2,] "B"  "E"
[3,] "C"  "F"
```

Creating a List: A Summary

You have now seen a few different ways of creating a list. It is worth recapping the ways in which we created the lists with some code examples:

```
> # Create an empty list
> emptyList <- list()

> # 2 Ways of Creating an unnamed list containing a vector and a matrix
> unnamedList <- list(aVector, aMatrix)
> unnamedList <- list(c(5, 7, 8, 2, 4, 3, 9, 0, 1, 2),
+                   matrix( LETTERS[1:6], nrow = 3))

> # 2 Ways of Creating a named list containing a vector and a matrix
> namedList <- list(VEC = aVector, MAT = aMatrix)
> namedList <- list(VEC = c(5, 7, 8, 2, 4, 3, 9, 0, 1, 2),
+                   MAT = matrix( LETTERS[1:6], nrow = 3))
```

In these examples, we created three lists that we will use as examples over the next few sections:

```
> emptyList          # An empty list
list()

> unnamedList        # A list with unnamed elements
[[1]]
 [1] 5 7 8 2 4 3 9 0 1 2

[[2]]
     [,1] [,2]
[1,] "A"  "D"
[2,] "B"  "E"
[3,] "C"  "F"

> namedList          # A list with element names
$VEC
 [1] 5 7 8 2 4 3 9 0 1 2

$MAT
     [,1] [,2]
[1,] "A"  "D"
[2,] "B"  "E"
[3,] "C"  "F"
```

NOTE
_____

Printing Style

Notice the difference in printing when a list has element names versus when there are no element names: Elements are indexed with double square brackets (for example, [[1]]) for "unnamed" lists, and with dollar symbols (for example, $VEC) for "named" lists. This gives you a hint as to how you'll be able to reference the elements of a list later.
_____

List Attributes

As with single-mode structures, a set of functions allows you to query some of the list attributes. Specifically, you can use the length function to query the number of elements in the list, and the names function to return the element names.

The length function returns the number of elements in the list, as shown here:

```
> length(emptyList)
[1] 0
> length(unnamedList)
[1] 2
> length(namedList)
[1] 2
```

The names function returns the names of the elements in the list, or NULL if there are no elements or no element names assigned:

```
> names(emptyList)
NULL
> names(unnamedList)
NULL
> names(namedList)
[1] "VEC" "MAT"
```

With single-mode data structures, we additionally used the mode function to return the type of data they held. Because lists are multi-mode structures, there is no longer a single mode of data being stored, so the word "list" is returned:

```
> mode(emptyList)
[1] "list"
> mode(unnamedList)
[1] "list"
> mode(namedList)
[1] "list"
```

Subscripting Lists

Two types of list subscripting can be performed:

▶ You can create a subset of the list, returning a shorter list.

▶ You can reference a single element within the list.

Subsetting the List

You can use square brackets to select a subset of an existing list. The return object will itself be a list.

```
LIST [ Input specifying the subset of list to return ]
```

As with vectors, you can put one of five input types in the square brackets, as shown in Table 4.1.

TABLE 4.1 Possible List Subscripting Inputs

Input	Effect
Blank	All values of the list are returned.
A vector of positive integers	Used as an index of list elements to return.
A vector of negative integers	Used as an index of list elements to omit.

Input	Effect
A vector of logical values	Only corresponding TRUE elements are returned.
A vector of character values	Refers to the names of elements to return.

To illustrate the subsetting of lists, we will use the namedList object created earlier.

Blank Subscripts

If you use a blank subscript, the whole of the list is returned:

```
> namedList [ ]   # Blank subscript
$VEC
 [1]  5 7 8 2 4 3 9 0 1 2

$MAT
      [,1] [,2]
[1,]  "A"  "D"
[2,]  "B"  "E"
[3,]  "C"  "F"
```

Positive Integer Subscripts

If you use a vector of positive integers, it is used as an index of elements to return:

```
> subList <- namedList [ 1 ]    # Return first element
> subList                       # Print the new object
$VEC
 [1]  5 7 8 2 4 3 9 0 1 2

> length(subList)               # Number of elements in the list
[1] 1
> class(subList)                # Check the "class" of the object
[1] "list"
```

As you can see from this example, the return object (saved as subList here) is itself a list. You can also use the class function to check the type of object, and it confirms subList is a list object.

NOTE

An Object's Class

This is the first time in this book you've seen the class function used. It returns the type of objects, whereas the mode function returns the type of data held in an object. Let's illustrate this distinction with a numeric matrix:

```
> aMatrix <- matrix(1:6, nrow = 2)      # Create a numeric matrix
> aMatrix                               # Print the matrix
     [,1] [,2] [,3]
[1,]    1    3    5
[2,]    2    4    6

> mode(aMatrix)                         # Mode of data held in this object
[1] "numeric"

> class(aMatrix)                        # Type (or "class") of object
[1] "matrix"
```

Negative Integer Subscripts

You can provide a vector of negative integers to specify the index of list elements to omit:

```
> namedList
$VEC
 [1] 5 7 8 2 4 3 9 0 1 2

$MAT
     [,1] [,2]
[1,] "A"  "D"
[2,] "B"  "E"
[3,] "C"  "F"
> namedList [ -1 ]    # Return all but the first element
$MAT
     [,1] [,2]
[1,] "A"  "D"
[2,] "B"  "E"
[3,] "C"  "F"
```

Logical Value Subscripts

You can provide a vector of logical integers to specify the list elements to return and omit:

```
> namedList
$VEC
 [1] 5 7 8 2 4 3 9 0 1 2

$MAT
     [,1] [,2]
[1,] "A"  "D"
[2,] "B"  "E"
[3,] "C"  "F"

> namedList [ c(T, F) ]  # Vector of logical values
$VEC
 [1] 5 7 8 2 4 3 9 0 1 2
```

Character Value Subscripts

If your list has element names, you can provide a vector of character values to identify the (named) elements you wish to return:

```
> namedList
$VEC
 [1] 5 7 8 2 4 3 9 0 1 2

$MAT
     [,1] [,2]
[1,] "A"  "D"
[2,] "B"  "E"
[3,] "C"  "F"

> namedList [ "MAT" ]         # Vector of Character values
$MAT
     [,1] [,2]
[1,] "A"  "D"
[2,] "B"  "E"
[3,] "C"  "F"
```

Reference List Elements

In the last section, you saw that you can reference a list using square brackets to "subset" the list (that is, return a list containing only a subset of the original elements). More commonly, you'll want to reference a specific element within your list.

You can reference elements of a list in two ways:

▶ You can use "double" square brackets.

▶ If there are element names, you can use the $ symbol.

Double Square Bracket Referencing

You can directly reference an element of a list using double square brackets. Although there are a number of uses of the double square brackets, the most common use is to supply a single integer index to refer to the element to extract:

```
> namedList              # The original list
$VEC
 [1] 5 7 8 2 4 3 9 0 1 2

$MAT
     [,1] [,2]
[1,] "A"  "D"
```

```
[2,]  "B"   "E"
[3,]  "C"   "F"

> namedList[[1]]          # The first element
 [1]  5 7 8 2 4 3 9 0 1 2
> namedList[[2]]          # The second element
     [,1] [,2]
[1,]  "A"  "D"
[2,]  "B"  "E"
[3,]  "C"  "F"

> mode(namedList[[2]])   # The mode of the second element
[1] "character"
```

When you use double square brackets in this way, you are directly referencing the objects contained within the list, as supported by the result of the mode function call. This is in contrast to the use of the single square bracket earlier, where we extracted a subset of the list itself:

```
> namedList [1]           # Return a list containing 1 element
$VEC
 [1]  5 7 8 2 4 3 9 0 1 2

> namedList [[1]]         # Return the first element of the list (a vector)
 [1]  5 7 8 2 4 3 9 0 1 2
```

Referencing Named Elements with $

If the elements of your list are named, you can use the $ symbol to directly reference them. As such, the following lines of code are equivalent ways of referencing the first (the "VEC") element of our namedList object:

```
> namedList              # Print the original list
$VEC
 [1]  5 7 8 2 4 3 9 0 1 2

$MAT
     [,1] [,2]
[1,]  "A"  "D"
[2,]  "B"  "E"
[3,]  "C"  "F"

> namedList[[1]]          # Return the first element
 [1]  5 7 8 2 4 3 9 0 1 2
> namedList$VEC           # Return the "VEC" element
 [1]  5 7 8 2 4 3 9 0 1 2
```

Double Square Brackets versus $

The $ symbol provides a more intuitive way of referencing named list elements, which is also more aesthetically pleasing than the use of double square brackets. We tend to use double square brackets when there are no element names assigned, and use $ when names exist. Here's an example:

```
> unnamedList        # List with no element names
[[1]]
 [1] 5 7 8 2 4 3 9 0 1 2

[[2]]
     [,1] [,2]
[1,] "A"  "D"
[2,] "B"  "E"
[3,] "C"  "F"

> unnamedList[[1]]   # First element
 [1] 5 7 8 2 4 3 9 0 1 2

> namedList          # List with element names
$VEC
 [1] 5 7 8 2 4 3 9 0 1 2

$MAT
     [,1] [,2]
[1,] "A"  "D"
[2,] "B"  "E"
[3,] "C"  "F"

> namedList$VEC      # The "VEC" element
 [1] 5 7 8 2 4 3 9 0 1 2
```

TIP

Shortened $ Referencing

When you use the $ symbol, you only need to provide enough of the name so that R understands which element you are referring to. This is illustrated in the following example:

```
> aList <- list( first = 1, second = 2, third = 3, fourth = 4 )
> aList$s    # Returns the second
[1] 2
> aList$fi  # Returns the first
[1] 1
```

```
> aList$fo  # Returns the fourth
[1] 4
```

Although it is possible to use shortened referencing in this way, it can lead to less maintainable and readable code, and should be avoided where possible when creating scripts.

Adding List Elements

You can add elements to a list in one of two ways:

▶ By directly adding an element with a specific name or in a specific position

▶ By combing lists together

Directly Adding a List Element

You can add a single element to a list by assigning it into a specific index or name. The syntax mirrors that of the "Double Square Brackets versus $" section earlier. For example, let's add a single element to our empty list:

```
> emptyList                          # Empty list
[[1]]
[1] "A" "B" "C" "D" "E"

> emptyList[[1]] <- LETTERS[1:5]     # Add an element

> emptyList                          # Updated (non)empty list
[[1]]
[1] "A" "B" "C" "D" "E"
```

Instead of using the double square brackets, we can use the $ symbol to add a "named" element to a list:

```
> emptyList <- list()                # Recreate the empty list
> emptyList                          # Empty list
list()
> emptyList$ABC <- LETTERS[1:5]      # Add an element
> emptyList                          # Updated (non)empty list
$ABC
[1] "A" "B" "C" "D" "E"
```

NOTE

Adding Nonconsecutive Elements

The preceding examples uses either square brackets or the $ symbol to add elements to the "first" position of an empty list. If we add an element to a later index, R interpolates a number of NULL elements to fill any gaps in the list:

```
> emptyList <- list()              # Recreate the empty list
> emptyList                        # Empty list
list()
> emptyList[[3]] <- "Hello"        # Assign to third element
> emptyList
[[1]]
NULL

[[2]]
NULL

[[3]]
[1] "Hello"
```

Combining Lists

You can grow lists by combining them together using the c function, as shown here:

```
> list1 <- list(A = 1, B = 2)     # Create list1
> list2 <- list(C = 3, D = 4)     # Create list2
> c(list1, list2)                 # Combine the lists
$A
[1] 1

$B
[1] 2

$C
[1] 3

$D
[1] 4
```

A Summary of List Syntax

As you have seen so far in this hour, the way we use lists varies slightly based on whether the elements of the list are named. At this point, it is worth reviewing the syntax to create and manage "unnamed" and "named" list structures.

Overview of Unnamed Lists

An overview of the key syntax covered is shown here, using a list without named elements as an example. First, let's create a list and look at the list attributes:

```
> unnamedList <- list(aVector, aMatrix)    # Create the list

> unnamedList                              # Print the list
[[1]]
 [1] 5 7 8 2 4 3 9 0 1 2

[[2]]
     [,1] [,2] [,3]
[1,]    1    3    5
[2,]    2    4    6

> length(unnamedList)                      # Number of elements
[1] 2

> names(unnamedList)                       # No element names
NULL
```

We can subset the list or extract list elements using single/double square brackets:

```
> unnamedList[1]                           # Subset the list
[[1]]
 [1] 5 7 8 2 4 3 9 0 1 2

> unnamedList[[1]]                         # Return the first element
 [1] 5 7 8 2 4 3 9 0 1 2

> unnamedList[[3]] <- 1:5                  # Add a new element

> unnamedList
[[1]]
 [1] 5 7 8 2 4 3 9 0 1 2

[[2]]
     [,1] [,2] [,3]
[1,]    1    3    5
[2,]    2    4    6

[[3]]
[1] 1 2 3 4 5
```

Overview of Named Lists

Let's look at a similar example using a list with element names. First, let's create the list and view the list attributes:

```
> namedList <- list(VEC = aVector, MAT = aMatrix)    # Create the list

> namedList                                          # Print the list
$VEC
 [1] 5 7 8 2 4 3 9 0 1 2

$MAT
     [,1] [,2] [,3]
[1,]    1    3    5
[2,]    2    4    6

> length(namedList)                    # Number of elements
[1] 2

> names(namedList)                     # Element names
[1] "VEC" "MAT"
```

We can subset the list using single square brackets, or reference elements directly with the $ symbol:

```
> namedList[1]                         # Subset the list
$VEC
 [1] 5 7 8 2 4 3 9 0 1 2

> namedList$VEC                        # Return the first element
 [1] 5 7 8 2 4 3 9 0 1 2

> namedList$NEW <- 1:5                 # Add a new element

> namedList
$VEC
 [1] 5 7 8 2 4 3 9 0 1 2

$MAT
     [,1] [,2] [,3]
[1,]    1    3    5
[2,]    2    4    6

$NEW
[1] 1 2 3 4 5
```

Motivation for Lists

A good understanding of lists helps you to accomplish a number of useful tasks in R. To illustrate this, we will briefly look at two use cases that rely on list structures. Note that this section includes syntax that will be covered later in this book, but we include it here to illustrate "the art of the possible" at this stage.

Flexible Simulation

Consider a situation where we want to simulate a number of extreme values (for example, large financial losses by day, or particularly high values of some measure for each patient in a drug study). For each iteration, we may simulate any number of numeric values from a given distribution.

A list provides a flexible structure to hold all the simulated data. Consider the following code example:

```
> nExtremes <- rpois(100, 3)            # Simulate number of extreme values by
                                          day from a Poisson distribution
> nExtremes[1:5]                        # First 5 numbers
[1] 0 3 5 7 3

> # Define function that simulates "N" extreme values
> exFun <- function(N) round(rweibull(N, shape = 5, scale = 1000))
> extremeValues <- lapply(nExtremes, exFun) # Apply the function to our simulated
                                              numbers

> extremeValues[1:5]                    # First 5 simulated outputs
[[1]]
numeric(0)

[[2]]
[1] 1305  948 1077

[[3]]
[1] 676 516 865 614 970

[[4]]
[1]  618 1217  818 1173 1205 1105  519

[[5]]
[1] 1026  933  657
```

From this example, note that the first simulated output generated no "extreme" values, resulting in the output containing an empty numeric vector (signified by numeric(0)). The "unnamed" list structure allows us to hold, in the same structure:

- ▶ This empty vector (indicating no "extreme values" for a particular day)

- ▶ Large vectors holding a number of simulated outputs (for days where many "extreme values" were simulated)

Given that we have stored this information in a list, we can query it to summarize the average number and average of extreme values:

```
> median(sapply(extremeValues, length))     # Average number of simulated extremes
[1] 3
> median(sapply(extremeValues, sum))        # Average extreme value
[1] 2634
```

TIP

The apply Functions

In the preceding examples, we used functions such as `lapply` (which applies a function to each element of a list) and `sapply` (which performs the same action but simplifies the outputs). We cover the apply family of functions later in Hour 9, "Loops and Summaries."

Extracting Elements from Named Lists

In R, most objects are, fundamentally, lists. For example, let's use the `t.test` function to perform a simple T-test. We will take the example straight from the `t.test` help file:

```
> theTest <- t.test(1:10, y = c(7:20))      # Perform a T-Test
> theTest                                    # Print the output

        Welch Two Sample t-test

data:  1:10 and c(7:20)
t = -5.4349, df = 21.982, p-value = 1.855e-05
alternative hypothesis: true difference in means is not equal to 0
95 percent confidence interval:
 -11.052802  -4.947198
sample estimates:
mean of x mean of y
      5.5      13.5
```

The output is printed as a nicely formatted text summary informing us of the significant T-test. But what if we wanted to use one of the elements of this output in further work (for example, the p-value). Consulting the help file, we see the return value is described as follows:

Value

A list with class `htest` containing the following components:

▶ **statistic** The value of the t-statistic.

▶ **parameter** The degrees of freedom for the t-statistic.

▶ **p.value** The p-value for the test.

▶ **conf.int** A confidence interval for the mean appropriate to the specified alternative hypothesis.

- ▶ **estimate** The estimated mean or difference in means, depending on whether it was a one-sample test or a two-sample test.

- ▶ **null.value** The specified hypothesized value of the mean or mean difference, depending on whether it was a one-sample test or a two-sample test.

- ▶ **alternative** A character string describing the alternative hypothesis.

- ▶ **method** A character string indicating what type of t-test was performed.

- ▶ **data.name** A character string giving the name(s) of the data.

The key thing to note here is that the return object is "a list." Given that the output is a list, we can query the named elements of this list and see that the result matches the description of elements in the help file:

```
> names(theTest)          # Names of list elements
[1] "statistic"    "parameter"    "p.value"    "conf.int"    "estimate"
[6] "null.value"   "alternative"  "method"     "data.name"
```

Given that this is a named list, and we know the names of the elements, we can use the $ symbol to directly reference the information we need:

```
> theTest$p.value          # Reference the p-value
[1] 1.855282e-05
```

Using this approach, we can reference a wide range of elements from R outputs.

NOTE

Print Methods

In the preceding example, we created a complex object (fundamentally, a named list) that printed in a neat manner:

```
> theTest                              # Print the output

        Welch Two Sample t-test

data:  1:10 and c(7:20)
t = -5.4349, df = 21.982, p-value = 1.855e-05
alternative hypothesis: true difference in means is not equal to 0
95 percent confidence interval:
 -11.052802  -4.947198
sample estimates:
mean of x mean of y
     5.5       13.5
```

The neat printout is generated by a print "method" associated with outputs from `t.test`. If we want to see the "raw" underlying structure, we can use the `print.default` function, which confirms that the structure is list based:

```
> print.default(theTest)
$statistic
        t
-5.43493

$parameter
       df
21.98221

$p.value
[1] 1.855282e-05
...
```

Data Frames

In the last section, we introduced the "list" structure, which allows you to store a set of objects of any mode. A data frame is, like many R objects, a named list. However, a data frame enforces a number of constraints on this named list structure. In particular, a data frame is constrained to be a named list that can only hold vectors of the same length.

Creating a Data Frame

We create a data frame by specifying a set of named vectors to the `data.frame`. For example, let's create a data frame containing New York temperature forecasts over the next five days:

```
> weather <- data.frame(                 # Create a data frame
+   Day   = c("Saturday", "Sunday", "Monday", "Tuesday", "Wednesday"),
+   Date  = c("Jul 4", "Jul 5", "Jul 6", "Jul 7", "Jul 8"),
+   TempF = c(75, 86, 83, 83, 87)
+ )
> weather                                 # Print the data frame
        Day  Date TempF
1  Saturday Jul 4    75
2    Sunday Jul 5    86
3    Monday Jul 6    83
4   Tuesday Jul 7    83
5 Wednesday Jul 8    87
```

NOTE

Print Methods

As discussed earlier, the neat printing of this object is caused by a print "method" for data frames. We can see the raw structure using `print.default`, which again confirms that a data frame is fundamentally a named list of vectors:

```
> print.default(weather)
$Day
[1] Saturday   Sunday     Monday     Tuesday    Wednesday
Levels: Monday Saturday Sunday Tuesday Wednesday

$Date
[1] Jul 4 Jul 5 Jul 6 Jul 7 Jul 8
Levels: Jul 4 Jul 5 Jul 6 Jul 7 Jul 8

$TempF
[1] 75 86 83 83 87

attr(,"class")
[1] "data.frame"
```

CAUTION

Nonmatching Vector Lengths

If we try to create a data frame using vectors with nonmatching lengths, we get an error message:

```
> data.frame(X = 1:5, Y = 1:2)
Error in data.frame(X = 1:5, Y = 1:2) :
  arguments imply differing number of rows: 5, 2
```

Querying Data Frame Attributes

Because a data frame is simply a named list, the functions we used to query list attributes will work the same way:

▶ The `length` function returns the number of elements of the list (that is, the number of columns).

▶ The `names` function returns the element (column) names.

The following example illustrates the use of these functions:

```
> length(weather)        # Number of columns
[1] 3
> names(weather)         # Column names
[1] "Day"    "Date"   "TempF"
```

Selecting Columns from the Data Frame

As with lists, we can reference a single element (vector) from our data frame using either double squared brackets or the $ symbol:

```
> weather           # The whole data frame
        Day  Date TempF
1   Saturday Jul 4    75
2     Sunday Jul 5    86
3     Monday Jul 6    83
4    Tuesday Jul 7    83
5 Wednesday Jul 8     87

> weather[[3]]     # The "third" column
[1] 75 86 83 83 87
> weather$TempF    # The "TempF" column
[1] 75 86 83 83 87
```

Selecting Columns from the Data Frame

Because we can reference columns in this way, we can also use these approaches to add new columns. For example, let's add a new column called TempC to our data containing the temperature in degrees Celsius:

```
> weather$TempC <- round( (weather$TempF - 32) * 5/9 )
> weather
        Day  Date TempF TempC
1   Saturday Jul 4    75    24
2     Sunday Jul 5    86    30
3     Monday Jul 6    83    28
4    Tuesday Jul 7    83    28
5 Wednesday Jul 8     87    31
```

Subscripting Columns

Because the columns of data frames are vectors, we can subscript them using the approaches from Hour 3, "Single-Mode Data Structures." Specifically, we can subscript the columns using square brackets:

```
DATA$COLUMN [ Input specifying the subset to return ]
```

As before, we can reference using blank, positive, negative, or logical inputs. Character inputs do not make sense for referencing columns because the individual elements within columns are not associated with element names.

Blank, Positive, and Negative Subscripts

If we use a blank subscript, all the values of the vector are returned:

```
> weather
        Day  Date TempF TempC
1  Saturday Jul 4    75    24
2    Sunday Jul 5    86    30
3    Monday Jul 6    83    28
4   Tuesday Jul 7    83    28
5 Wednesday Jul 8    87    31

> weather$TempF [ ]   # All values of TempF column
[1] 75 86 83 83 87
```

If we use a vector of positive integers, it refers to the elements of the column (vector) to return:

```
> weather$TempF [ 1:3 ]   # First 3 values of the TempF column
[1] 75 86 83
```

If we use a vector of negative integers, it refers to the elements of the column (vector) to omit:

```
> weather$TempF [ -(1:3) ]   # Omit the first 3 values of the TempF column
[1] 83 87
```

Logical Subscripts

As you saw in the last hour, we can provide a vector of logical values to reference a vector, and only the corresponding TRUE values are returned. Here's an example:

```
> weather$TempF
[1] 75 86 83 83 87
> weather$TempF [ c(F, T, F, F, T) ]    # Logical subscript
[1] 86 87
```

Of course, we usually generate the logical vector with a logical statement involving a vector. For example, we could return all the TempF values greater than 85 using this statement:

```
> weather$TempF [ weather$TempF > 85 ]   # Logical subscript
[1] 86 87
```

Instead, we could reference a column of a data frame based on logical statements involving one or more other columns (because all columns are constrained to be the same length):

```
> weather$Day [ weather$TempF > 85 ]    # Logical subscript
[1] Sunday    Wednesday
Levels: Monday Saturday Sunday Tuesday Wednesday
```

NOTE

Factor Levels

In the last example, you can see that the days where the forecast is greater than 85°F are Sunday and Wednesday. However, you should note two things about the output:

▶ There are no quotation marks around the returned values (Sunday and Wednesday).

▶ Additional "Levels" information has been printed.

This strange output is produced because, when you create a data frame using character columns, those columns are converted to "factors," which are "category" columns that are automatically derived from character vectors when used in a data frame. You'll see more on factors later in Hour 5, "Dates, Times, and Factors."

Referencing as a Matrix

Although a data frame is structured as a named list, its rectangular output is more similar to the matrix structure you saw earlier. As such, R allows us to reference the data frame as if it was a matrix.

Matrix Dimensions

Because we can treat a data frame as a matrix, we can use the nrow and ncol functions to return the number of rows and columns:

```
> nrow(weather)    # Number of rows
[1] 5
> ncol(weather)    # Number of columns
[1] 4
```

Subscripting as a Matrix

In Hour 3, you saw that you can subscript a matrix using square brackets and two inputs (one for the rows, one for the columns). We can use the same approach to subscript a data frame, where each input can be one of the standard five input types:

```
DATA.FRAME [ Rows to return , Columns to return]
```

Blanks, Positives, and Negatives

We can use blank subscripts to return all rows and columns from a data frame:

```
> weather[ , ]              # Blank, Blank
       Day   Date TempF TempC
1   Saturday Jul 4    75    24
2     Sunday Jul 5    86    30
3     Monday Jul 6    83    28
4    Tuesday Jul 7    83    28
5  Wednesday Jul 8    87    31
```

If we use vectors of positive integers, they are used to provide an index of the rows/columns to return. This example uses positive integers to return the first four rows and the first three columns:

```
> weather[ 1:4, 1:3 ]      # +ive, +ive
        Day   Date TempF
1 Saturday Jul 4    75
2   Sunday Jul 5    86
3   Monday Jul 6    83
4  Tuesday Jul 7    83
```

We can use vectors of negative integers to indicate the rows and columns to omit in the return result, as shown in this example:

```
> weather[ -1, -3 ]        # -ive, -ive
         Day   Date TempC
2    Sunday Jul 5    30
3    Monday Jul 6    28
4   Tuesday Jul 7    28
5 Wednesday Jul 8    31
```

In the preceding examples, we have used the same input type for both rows and columns. However, we can mix up the input types, as illustrated in this example, where we select the first four rows and all the columns:

```
> weather[ 1:4, ]          # +ive, Blank
        Day   Date TempF TempC
1 Saturday Jul 4    75    24
2   Sunday Jul 5    86    30
3   Monday Jul 6    83    28
4  Tuesday Jul 7    83    28
```

Logical Subscripts

We often use logical subscripts to reference specific rows of the data to return. To perform this action, we need to provide a logical value for each row of the data:

```
> weather                          # The original data
         Day   Date TempF TempC
1  Saturday Jul 4    75    24
2    Sunday Jul 5    86    30
3    Monday Jul 6    83    28
4   Tuesday Jul 7    83    28
5 Wednesday Jul 8    87    31

> weather[ c(F, T, F, F, T), ]  # Logical, Blank
         Day   Date TempF TempC
2    Sunday Jul 5    86    30
5 Wednesday Jul 8    87    31
```

As before, we more commonly apply a logical statement to a column (vector) contained in the data frame to generate the logical vector:

```
> weather[ weather$TempF > 85, ]        # Logical, Blank
        Day  Date TempF TempC
2     Sunday Jul 5    86    30
5  Wednesday Jul 8    87    31


> weather[ weather$Day != "Sunday", ]  # Logical, Blank
        Day  Date TempF TempC
1   Saturday Jul 4    75    24
3     Monday Jul 6    83    28
4    Tuesday Jul 7    83    28
5  Wednesday Jul 8    87    31
```

Character Subscripts

We often use vectors of character strings to specify the columns we wish to return. Although a data frame has "row names," we tend not to reference rows using character strings. This example selects the Day and TempC columns from the data, filtering so that only rows with temperatures greater than 85°F are returned:

```
> weather[ weather$TempF > 85, c("Day", "TempC")]  # Logical, Character
        Day TempC
2     Sunday    30
5  Wednesday    31
```

Summary of Subscripting Data Frames

At this point, it is worth a quick review of some of the key syntax used to select subsets of a data frame. In particular, consider the following lines of code:

```
> weather$Day [ weather$TempF > 85 ]               # Days where TempF > 85
[1] Sunday    Wednesday
Levels: Monday Saturday Sunday Tuesday Wednesday

> weather [ weather$TempF > 85 , ]                 # All data where TempF > 85
        Day  Date TempF TempC
2     Sunday Jul 5    86    30
5  Wednesday Jul 8    87    31

> weather [ weather$TempF > 85 , c("Day", "TempF") ] # 2 columns where TempF > 85
        Day TempF
2     Sunday    86
5  Wednesday    87
```

In the first example, we are subscripting `weather$Day`. This is a vector, so we provide a single input (a logical vector in this case). It returns the two values of the `Day` column where the corresponding `TempF` column is greater than 85.

In the second example, we are now referencing data from the whole weather dataset. As such, we need two subscripts (one for rows, one for columns). In this example, we use a logical vector for the rows and blank for the columns, returning all columns but only rows where `TempF` is greater than 85. Attention should be paid to the use of the comma in the first example versus the second example, driven by the fact that we are referencing data from a vector (first example) versus the whole data frame (second example).

The third example extends the second example to pick only columns `Day` and `TempF` using a character vector for the column input.

Exploring Your Data

Later in this book, you'll see a range of functionality for manipulating data frames. For now, it is useful for you to look at a few simple functions that will help you to quickly understand the data stored in a data frame.

The Top and Bottom of Your Data

A function called `head` allows you to return the first few rows of the data. This is particularly useful when you have a large data frame and only want to get a high-level understanding of the structure of the data frame. The `head` function accepts any data frame and will return (by default) only the first six rows. For this example, we use the built-in `iris` data frame (for more information, open the help file for the `iris` data frame using the `?iris` command):

```
> nrow(iris)          # Number of rows in iris
[1] 150
> head(iris)          # Return only the first 6 rows
  Sepal.Length Sepal.Width Petal.Length Petal.Width Species
1          5.1         3.5          1.4         0.2  setosa
2          4.9         3.0          1.4         0.2  setosa
3          4.7         3.2          1.3         0.2  setosa
4          4.6         3.1          1.5         0.2  setosa
5          5.0         3.6          1.4         0.2  setosa
6          5.4         3.9          1.7         0.4  setosa
```

This immediately gives us a view on the structure of the data. We can see that the `iris` data frame has five columns: `Sepal.Length`, `Sepal.Width`, `Petal.Length`, `Petal.Width`, and `Species`. All columns seem to be numeric, except the `Species` column, which appears to be character (or a "factor," as briefly discussed earlier).

The second argument to the head function is the number of rows to return. Therefore, we could look at more or fewer rows if we wish:

```
> head(iris, 2)    # Return only the first 3 rows
  Sepal.Length Sepal.Width Petal.Length Petal.Width Species
1          5.1         3.5          1.4         0.2  setosa
2          4.9         3.0          1.4         0.2  setosa
```

If instead we wanted to look at the last few rows, we could use the tail function. This works in the same way as the head function, with the data frame as the first input and (optionally) the number of rows to return as the second input:

```
> tail(iris)       # Return only the last 6 rows
    Sepal.Length Sepal.Width Petal.Length Petal.Width   Species
145          6.7         3.3          5.7         2.5 virginica
146          6.7         3.0          5.2         2.3 virginica
147          6.3         2.5          5.0         1.9 virginica
148          6.5         3.0          5.2         2.0 virginica
149          6.2         3.4          5.4         2.3 virginica
150          5.9         3.0          5.1         1.8 virginica
> tail(iris, 2)    # Return only the last 2 rows
    Sepal.Length Sepal.Width Petal.Length Petal.Width   Species
149          6.2         3.4          5.4         2.3 virginica
150          5.9         3.0          5.1         1.8 virginica
```

Viewing Your Data

If you are using the RStudio interface, you can use the View function to open the data in a viewing grid. This feature in RStudio is evolving quickly, so readers of this book may find the functionality richer than that presented here (the version of RStudio being used is 0.99.441). See Figure 4.1 for an example.

If we use the View function, our data frame is opened in the data grid viewer in RStudio:

```
> View(iris)       # Open the iris data in the data grid viewer
```

This window allows us to scroll around our data, and tells us the range of data we are viewing (for example, in Figure 4.1 the message at the bottom of the viewer tells us that we are looking at rows "1 to 19 of 150").

The search bar (top right of the window) allows us to input search criteria that will be used to search the entire dataset. This is used to interactively filter the data based on a partial matching of the search term. As a quick example, look at the result of typing **4.5** in the search bar, as shown in Figure 4.2.

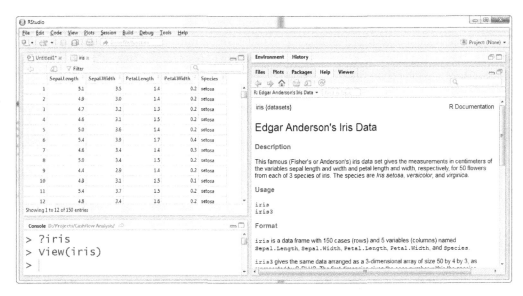

FIGURE 4.1
The iris dataset viewed in the RStudio data grid viewer

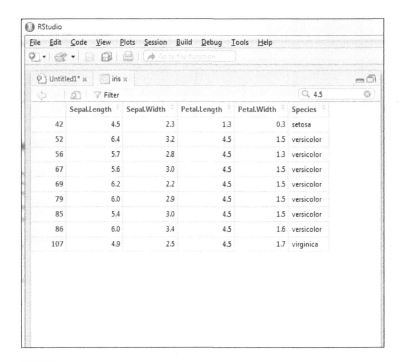

FIGURE 4.2
Using the search bar in the data grid viewer

If we click the Filter icon from the top of the data grid viewer window, we will see a number of filtering fields appear, which we can use to interactively subset the data in a more data-driven manner. This example uses the filter feature to look only at rows for the "setosa" species with Sepal.Length greater than 5.5 (see Figure 4.3).

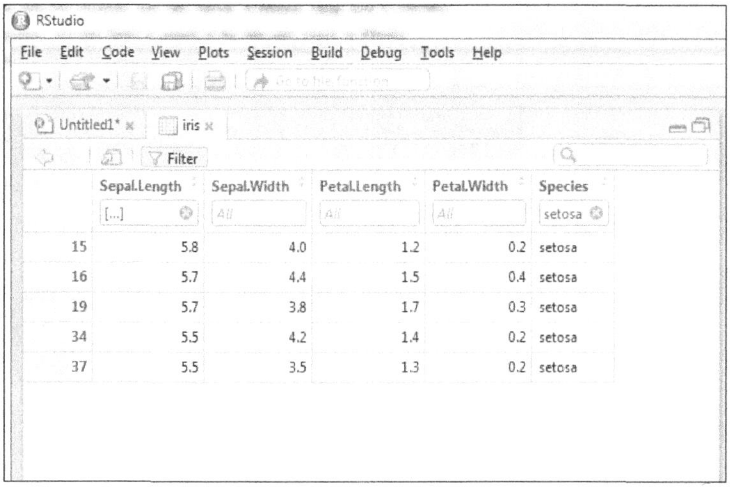

FIGURE 4.3
Filtering data in the data grid viewer

Summarizing Your Data

We can use the summary function to produce a range of statistical summary outputs to summarize our data. The summary function accepts a data frame and produces a textual summary of each column of the data:

```
> summary(iris)      # Produce a textual summary
  Sepal.Length      Sepal.Width      Petal.Length      Petal.Width            Species
 Min.   :4.300    Min.   :2.000    Min.   :1.000    Min.   :0.100    setosa     :50
 1st Qu.:5.100    1st Qu.:2.800    1st Qu.:1.600    1st Qu.:0.300    versicolor:50
 Median :5.800    Median :3.000    Median :4.350    Median :1.300    virginica :50
 Mean   :5.843    Mean   :3.057    Mean   :3.758    Mean   :1.199
 3rd Qu.:6.400    3rd Qu.:3.300    3rd Qu.:5.100    3rd Qu.:1.800
 Max.   :7.900    Max.   :4.400    Max.   :6.900    Max.   :2.500
```

Note that the summaries produced are suitable for each column type (statistical summary for numeric columns, frequency count for factor columns).

Visualizing Your Data

In this book, you will see a number of functions for creating sophisticated graphical outputs. However, let's look at one simple function that creates an immediate visualization of the structure of our data.

We can create a scatter-plot matrix plot of our data frame using the `pairs` function as follows:

```
> pairs(iris)   # Scatter-plot matrix of iris
```

In the graphic shown in Figure 4.4, each variable in the data is plotted against each other. For example, the plot in the top-right corner is a plot of Sepal.Length (y axis) against Species (x axis).

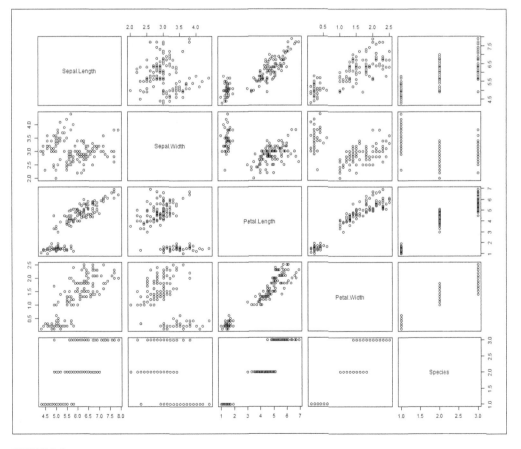

FIGURE 4.4
Scatter-plot Matrix of the iris data frame

From this plot we can quickly identify a number of characteristics of our data:

▶ We see that the data has five columns, whose names are printed on the diagonal of the plot.

▶ We can again see that `Species` is a factor column, whereas the rest are numeric.

▶ If we look at the plots on the right side of the chart, we can see each numeric variable plotted against `Species` and note that the numeric data would seem to vary across each level of `Species`.

▶ Columns `Petal.Length` and `Petal.Width` would seem to be highly correlated.

Summary

In this hour, we focused on two structures that store "multi-mode" data (that is, data containing more than one data type). First, we looked at lists, which allow us to store any number of objects of varying modes. Then, we looked at data frames as a special "type" of list that stores rectangular datasets in an effective manner.

Although lists are very powerful structures, when we import data into R (which you'll see in Hour 10, "Importing and Exporting"), it will be stored as a data frame. Therefore, you need to be very comfortable manipulating this structure in particular. You should practice the syntax relating the subscripting of data frames using square brackets and the $ symbol, because this is a fundamental skill useful across all R tasks.

Q&A

Q. Can we create nested lists?

A. Yes. Because lists can store any type of object, they can themselves store other lists. Here's an example:

```
> nestedList <- list(A = 1, B = list(C = 3, D = 4))  # Create a nested list
> nestedList                                          # Print the nested list
$A
[1] 1

$B
$B$C
[1] 3

$B$D
[1] 4
```

```
> nestedList$B$C                 # Extract the C element within the B element
[1] 3
```

Q. What other inputs can we use within the double square brackets?

A. In the last hour, you saw that you can use integers to directly reference elements of a list. Refer to the help file (opened using `?"[["`) for a complete list of possible inputs. However, it is worth nothing that you can use single-character strings to reference columns. Here's an example:

```
> weather                # The full dataset
        Day  Date TempF TempC
1  Saturday Jul 4    75    24
2    Sunday Jul 5    86    30
3    Monday Jul 6    83    28
4   Tuesday Jul 7    83    28
5 Wednesday Jul 8    87    31
> col <- "TempC"     # The column we want to select
> weather[[col]]     # Return the TempC column
[1] 24 30 28 28 31
```

Q. What is the difference between `DF[ ]` and `DF[ , ]`?

A. As shown previously, you subscript data from a data frame using square brackets. Here's an example:

```
> weather [ , c("Day", "TempC") ]    # All rows, 2 columns
        Day TempC
1  Saturday    24
2    Sunday    30
3    Monday    28
4   Tuesday    28
5 Wednesday    31
```

In this example, we provide two subscripts for the data frame: blank for the rows (so all rows are returned) and a character vector to select two columns. The subscripts are separated by a comma. If we omit the comma, we appear to get the same result:

```
> weather [ c("Day", "TempC") ]     # 2 vector elements
        Day TempC
1  Saturday    24
2    Sunday    30
3    Monday    28
4   Tuesday    28
5 Wednesday    31
```

Here, we are using the fact that a data frame is actually a named list of vectors. In this case, we are creating a "sub-list" containing only the two columns specified.

Q. Why, when I select a single column, is it returned as a vector?

A. When you select a single column via the square brackets approach, it is indeed returned as a vector:

```
> weather [ , c("Day", "TempC") ]    # 2 columns - returns a data frame
        Day TempC
1   Saturday    24
2     Sunday    30
3     Monday    28
4    Tuesday    28
5  Wednesday    31
> weather [ , "TempC" ]                # 1 column - returns a vector
[1] 24 30 28 28 31
```

In this case, the last line is equivalent to `weather$TempC`. When you select a single column of data, R simplifies the output in a way that's similar to how you saw matrix dimensions dropped in Hour 3. If you specifically want to retain the dimensional structure, you can use the argument `drop` within the square brackets, as follows:

```
> weather [ , "TempC", drop = F ]    # 1 column - retain dimensions
   TempC
1     24
2     30
3     28
4     28
5     31
```

As you can see from the output, the use of `drop = F` retains the structure, returning a 5×1 data frame.

Workshop

The workshop contains quiz questions and exercises to help you solidify your understanding of the material covered. Try to answer all questions before looking at the "Answers" section that follows.

Quiz

1. What is a "list" object?

2. How do we reference elements from a list?

3. What is the "mode" of a list?

4. What's the difference between a list and a data frame?

5. Name two ways we can return the number of columns of a data frame.

6. If we run the following code, what would the contents and structure of `result1` and `result2` contain?

```
> myDf <- data.frame(X = -2:2, Y = 1:5)
> result1 <- myDf$Y [ myDf$X > 0 ]
> result2 <- myDf [ myDf$X > 0, ]
```

7. What is the difference between the `head` and `tail` functions?

Answers

1. A "list" is a simple R object that can contain any number of objects of any "class."

2. We can reference elements of a list using the "double square brackets" notation. Most commonly, we provide the index of the element we want to return from the list (for example, `myList[[2]]` for the second element). If a list has element names, we can alternatively use the dollar notation, specifying the name of the list element (for example, `myList$X` to return the X element of `myList`).

3. Because a list is a "multi-mode" object, it has no explicit "mode." If you ask for a list's mode, it simply returns "list."

4. A list can contain any number of objects of any class—its elements may be named or unnamed. A data frame is a "named" list that is restricted to contain only same-length vectors—when printing a data frame, it uses a specific method so the data is presented in a more formatted manner.

5. We can use the `length` function to return the number of columns in a data frame, because this returns the number of vector elements in the underlying "list" structure. Alternatively, because we can treat a data frame as a matrix, we can use the `ncol` function to achieve the same result.

6. The `result1` object will contain a vector of those values from the Y column where the corresponding X column is greater than 0—specifically, this will be a vector containing values 4 and 5. The `result2` object will contain a data frame with two rows, corresponding to the rows where X is greater than 0 (so rows 4 and 5 of the original data frame).

7. The `head` function returns the first six rows (by default) of a data frame. The `tail` function returns the last six rows (by default) of a data frame.

Activities

1. Create a "named" list containing a numeric vector with 10 values (called X) and a character vector with 10 values (called Y) and a sequence of values from 1 to 10 (called Z). Use this list:

   ▶ Print the number of elements and the element names.

   ▶ Select the X element.

   ▶ Select the Y element.

▶ Select values of the X element that are greater than the median of X.

▶ Select values of the Y element where the corresponding X element is greater than the median of X.

2. Adapt your code to instead create a data frame containing two columns (X = a numeric vector with 10 elements, Y = a character column containing 10 elements, Z = integers 1 to 10). Use this structure:

▶ Print the number of columns and the column names.

▶ Select the X column.

▶ Select the Y column.

▶ Select values of the X column that are greater than the median of X.

▶ Select values of the Y column where the corresponding X value is greater than the median of X.

3. Further subset the data in the data frame created in the last exercise as follows:

▶ Select all rows of the data where Z is greater than 5.

▶ Select all rows of the data where Z is greater than 3 and X is greater than the median of X.

▶ Select just the X and Z columns from the data where Z is greater than 5.

4. Print the built-in `mtcars` data frame. Look at the help file for `mtcars` to understand the origin of the data. Use this data frame:

▶ Print only the first five rows.

▶ Print the last five rows.

▶ How many rows and columns does the data have?

▶ Look at the data in the RStudio data viewer (if you are using RStudio).

▶ Print the `mpg` column of the data.

▶ Print the `mpg` column of the data where the corresponding `cyl` column is 6.

▶ Print all rows of the data where `cyl` is 6.

▶ Print all rows of the data where `mpg` is greater than 25, but only for the `mpg` and `cyl` columns.

▶ Create a scatter-plot matrix of your data.

▶ Create a scatter-plot matrix of your data, but only using the first six columns of the data.

HOUR 5
Dates, Times, and Factors

What You'll Learn in This Hour:

▶ How to create a date object
▶ How to create a time object
▶ How to manipulate date and time objects
▶ What a factor is and how to create one
▶ How to manipulate factors

In Hour 3, "Single-Mode Data Structures," and Hour 4, "Multi-Mode Data Structures," you saw how to create the basic data objects in R, objects that allow us to store numeric, logical, and character data.

In this hour, you learn more about some of the special data types in R that enable you to work with dates and times and with categorical data.

Working with Dates and Times

In this section, we look at how to convert date and time data into a format that R will recognize and manipulate.

Creating Date Objects

We can create a date object in R using the function `as.Date`. With this function we can create a vector of dates we can index in the same way we did in Hour 3. Most often our dates will be in the format of a character string, which we will convert to a date using the `format` argument to specify the structure of the date in the character string. You can see all of this in the following example:

```
> myDates <- c("2015-06-21", "2015-09-11", "2015-12-31")
> myDates <- as.Date(myDates, format = "%Y-%m-%d")
> myDates
```

```
[1] "2015-06-21" "2015-09-11" "2015-12-31"
> myDates[2:3]
[1] "2015-09-11" "2015-12-31"
class(myDates)
[1] "Date"
```

As you can see, this creates a special Date type object. When this is printed to the screen, you will see it in the format year-month-day. This is the standard R date format. In actual fact, R has created an object that represents an integer number of days since January 1, 1970:

```
> as.numeric(myDates)
[1] 16607 16689 16800
```

TIP

Date Formats

In these examples we used the `format` argument to `as.Date`. This argument allows us to specify the initial format of our date string. For more details on the specification of the `format` argument, see the help file for the function `strptime`.

If we were to give a numeric value to the function `as.Date`, we would also need to specify the origin, or starting point, for the counting of days. For instance, if we were to pass dates that were generated by Microsoft Excel, which start counting from January 1, 1900, we would need to tell R that this is the origin or date from which the counting should start. Here's an example:

```
> as.Date(42174, origin = "1900-01-01")
[1] "2015-06-21"
```

So what if our date is in a numeric format, such as 20150621? In this instance we first need to convert our date to a character string and then convert to a date as we did previously, using the `format` argument to specify the structure of the dates:

```
> myDates <- c(20150621, 20150911, 20151231)
> myDates <- as.character(myDates)
> myDates <- as.Date(myDates, format = "%Y%m%d")
> myDates
[1] "2015-06-21" "2015-09-11" "2015-12-31"
```

You will see very soon how you can manipulate and work with this type of object further.

Creating Objects That Include Times

When you have data that also includes times, you will need to work with a different class of object to incorporate the additional information. Here, we will use POSIXct and POSIXlt objects to store dates and times down to milliseconds. The two classes are very similar, though POSIXct objects are more suitable for storing data n data frames, whereas `POSIX1t` objects are a more human-readable format.

The functions that we use to create these objects are `as.POSIXct` and `as.POSIX1t`. They work in very much the same way as the `as.Date` function we used in the previous section, but we can now include hours, minutes and seconds. Both functions work in the same way, so here we will only look at `as.POSIXct`. Here is an example:

```
> myTimes <- c("2015-06-21 14:22:00", "2015-09-11 10:23:32", "2015-12-31 23:59:59")
> myTimes <- as.POSIXct(myTimes, format = "%Y-%m-%d %H:%M:%S")
> myTimes
[1] "2015-06-21 14:22:00 BST" "2015-09-11 10:23:32 BST" "2015-12-31 23:59:59 GMT"
> class(myTimes)
[1] "POSIXct" "POSIXt"
```

NOTE

Time Zones

You will have noticed that the preceding example has converted the dates and times into both British Summer Time and Greenwich Mean Time. The default for the POSIX functions is to use the locale of the machine you are working on and account for daylight savings time, but we can control the time zone used with the argument `tz`, for instance:

```
as.POSIXct(myTimes, format = "%Y-%m-%d %H:%M:%S", tz = "US/Pacific")
```

For more information on how to define time zones, take a look at the help pages for "timezones."

As with dates, times are stored as an integer value, though in the instance of times it is the number of seconds starting from 00:00:00 January 1, 1970 UTC.

Manipulating Dates and Times

Once we have converted our dates and times to the appropriate R format, we can do things like

```
> myDates + 1
[1] "2015-06-22" "2015-09-12" "2016-01-01"
```

which makes use of the storage as numeric values to add a day (or second in the case of POSIX objects) to the time we provide. When it comes to adding other amounts of time, you might find the **lubridate** package, which we will see in the next section, useful.

A number of functions allow us to extract information such as weekdays, months, and quarters:

```
> weekdays(myDates)
[1] "Sunday"   "Friday"    "Thursday"
> months(myDates)
[1] "June"        "September" "December"
> quarters(myDates)
[1] "Q2" "Q3" "Q4"
```

However, the more useful functions for working with dates and times are `diff` and `difftime`. These two functions both find the differences between given dates and times but work in a slightly different way. First of all, the `diff` function takes a vector of date-times and returns a vector of the difference between consecutive values. Here's an example:

```
> diff(myDates)
Time differences in days
[1]   82 111
```

The function `difftime`, on the other hand, requires two separate date objects and finds the difference between the two. This is particularly useful if you want to find the difference between a series of dates and a specific date—for instance, the number of days from the start of the new year to the values in a given vector:

```
> difftime(myDates, as.Date("2015-07-04"))
Time differences in days
[1] -13   69 180
```

One useful feature of this function is that you can change the unit used for the difference returned, so you can see the difference in weeks, days, hours, minutes, or seconds:

```
> difftime(myDates, as.Date("2015-07-04"), units = "weeks")
Time differences in weeks
[1] -1.857143   9.857143 25.714286
```

TIP
_____

Date Sequences

You might want to know that you can also create dates and times using a special version of the `seq` function. For instance, try the following:

```
seq (as.Date("2015-01-01"), as.Date("2015-12-01"), by = "week")
```

This will create a sequence of dates from January 1st to December 1st in weekly increments.
_____

The lubridate Package

Instead of using the functions we have seen so far that are in the base R installation, we can use a number of additional packages for working with dates and times. In this section we look at the **lubridate** package, which has been designed to simplify the way in which you work with dates and times, making it easier to read them in to R and easier to manipulate, particularly when it comes to adding a unit of time. Because this package is not available in the standard R installation, you will first need to install and load it. See Hour 2, "The R Environment," for a reminder on installing and loading an R package.

This package includes a number of useful functions, such as now, which gives the current date and time:

```
> now()
```

The equivalent to this in the base functionality of R would be Sys.time. You will notice functions in **lubridate** have been named in what is intended to be a more user-friendly manner. Before we look at some of the other useful functions in this package, let's first look at converting our character strings or numeric values into date formats. There are three main functions in **lubridate** for converting to a date: ymd, mdy, and dmy. The one to use will depend on the order in which the year, month, and day are provided.

```
> myDates <- c("2015-06-21", "2015-09-11", "2015-12-31")
> myDates <- ymd(myDates)
> myDates
[1] "2015-06-21 UTC" "2015-09-11 UTC" "2015-12-31 UTC"
```

You will notice here that we simply provided the vector of dates; we did not need to provide the separator or any other formatting for the dates. Because the **lubridate** package is intended to make reading data easier, it will try to automatically determine the format based on the function we have called. In this example, it assumes the data is in the format year, month, day. In most instances this will be sufficient; however, in the case of mixed separators, it may not be able to determine the format and will return an appropriate warning to inform you of that fact.

You will also notice that the date is in the time zone UTC, or Universal time. As with the usual date function, we can change the time zone that is used when we import our data with the argument tz. Also, the useful functions force_tz and with_tz allow us to change the time zone after converting it.

When it comes to times, we continue to use the three functions from earlier, but now we add on "_hms," or simply use the function hm or hms. Here is an example:

```
myTimes <- c("14:22:00", "10:23:32", "23:59:59")
myTimes <- hms(myTimes)
myTimes
[1] "14H 22M 0S"  "10H 23M 32S" "23H 59M 59S"
```

These functions make it much easier to work with unconventional date-time data—for instance, when you only have the date and hour of an observation rather than data down to the second.

Further useful functions in this package include `year`, `month`, and `day`, which allow us to add a given amount of a specific period, for instance 2 seconds or 3 months, to a date-time:

```
newYearEve <- ymd_hms("2015-12-31 23:59:59")
newYearEve + seconds(2)
[1] "2016-01-01 00:00:01 UTC"
newYearEve + months(3)
[1] "2016-03-31 23:59:59 UTC"
newYearEve - years(1)
[1] "2014-12-31 23:59:59 UTC"
```

Working with Categorical Data

When we work with categorical data in R, we need to use a special data type called a factor. A factor is simply a categorical variable that is made up of levels and labels. In this section you will see how to convert a vector of categorical data into a factor and how to further manipulate these special objects. You will also see how to convert continuous data to a factor using the `cut` function.

Creating Factors

You can convert a vector of numeric values or character strings into a factor using the `factor` function. The default behavior of this function is to use the unique values of the vector as the levels and labels for the factor in alphanumeric order. As an example, consider Listing 5.1.

LISTING 5.1 Creating a Factor

```
 1: > x <- c("B", "B", "C", "A", "A", "A", "B", "C", "C")
 2: > x
 3: [1] "B" "B" "C" "A" "A" "A" "B" "C" "C"
 4: > mode(x)
 5: [1] "character"
 6: > class(x)
 7: [1] "character"
 8: >
 9: > y <- factor(x)
10: > y
11: [1] B B C A A A B C C
12: Levels: A B C
13: > mode(y)
14: [1] "numeric"
15: > class(y)
16: [1] "factor"
```

As you can see in line 9, you can very simply create a factor from a vector of character strings. You will notice in lines 11 and 12 that the output is printed differently when it is converted to a factor, displaying not only the vector but the levels of the factor. There are a few things to take note of in the factor and the mode of the object itself.

Let's first consider the mode, or the way in which a factor is stored. Notice on lines 13 and 14 that the mode of the factor is numeric. A factor in R is actually stored as integer values that match up to the levels. In this example, any elements with the label "A" are in fact stored as 1, "B" stored as 2, and "C" as 3. In general, this will not impact the way in which you work with a factor but is worth noting.

CAUTION

Numeric Factors

When working with factors that have numeric levels, be aware that although the labels will take the values of the individual levels, the factor will be stored as integer values starting from 1. If you want to convert your factor back to numeric values, you first need to convert to character strings and then to numeric values.

The second thing to consider is the way in which factor levels are determined. As mentioned earlier and shown in Listing 5.1, the default behavior is to order levels alphanumerically. In the preceding example, this was not a problem, but consider the following example, where we are using the `sample` function to randomly select 20 values from a vector (see Hour 6, "Common R Utility Functions," for more details on this function):

```
> ratings <- c("Poor", "Average", "Good")
> myRatings <- sample(ratings, 20, replace = TRUE)
> factorRatings <- factor(myRatings)
> factorRatings
 [1] Poor    Average Good    Poor    Good    Good    Good    Poor
 [9] Average Poor    Average Good    Average Average Average Average
[17] Good    Average Poor    Good
Levels: Average Good Poor
```

You can see here that the levels of the factor have been ordered alphabetically, even though there is an ordering that is more sensible for this case. This will have an impact when you want the ordering of a factor to be correct (for instance, when creating graphics). You can control the order of the levels of your factors using the `levels` argument, as shown next:

```
> factorRatings <- factor(myRatings, levels = ratings)
> factorRatings
 [1] Poor    Average Good    Poor    Good    Good    Good    Poor
 [9] Average Poor    Average Good    Average Average Average Average
[17] Good    Average Poor    Good
Levels: Poor Average Good
```

Notice here that the levels are now ordered exactly as we have specified.

TIP

Reordering Factors

You can use the `reorder` function to change the order of the levels of a factor based on another vector. This is particularly useful when creating graphics.

Manipulating Factor Levels

After creating your factor, you can work with it as though it was any other character vector, for instance:

```
> y == "A"
[1] FALSE FALSE FALSE  TRUE  TRUE  TRUE FALSE FALSE FALSE
```

However, if you want to change the levels of the factor, you can't just use standard methods for indexing and changing vector elements. As an example, suppose we want to change the levels in the ratings example from "Poor" to "Negative":

```
> factorRatings[factorRatings == "Poor"] <- "Negative"
Warning message:
In `[<-.factor`(`*tmp*`, factorRatings == "Poor", value = "Negative") :
  invalid factor level, NA generated
```

This is because when we defined the levels of the factor, we restricted the values that the factor could take to these groups, so we can't use the usual manipulation techniques because we have to change the set of allowed values for the factor. Instead, we will need to use the `levels` function:

```
> levels(factorRatings)
[1] "Poor" "Average" "Good"
> levels(factorRatings) <- c("Negative", "Average", "Positive")
> factorRatings
 [1] Negative Average  Positive Negative Positive Positive Positive
 [8] Negative Average  Negative Average  Positive Average  Average
[15] Average  Average  Positive Average  Negative Positive
Levels: Negative Average Positive
```

CAUTION

Missing Values in a Factor

If you have introduced missing values into a factor, you will need to re-create the factor or replace the missing values with the previous value that they took, otherwise you will retain missing values in your factor.

Here, we have only used the `levels` function to change the names of existing levels to unique equivalent levels, but we can also use this function to reduce the set of levels. Suppose that we were only interested in which elements were "Negative" and we were not interested in the distinction between "Average" and "Positive". We might want to combine these elements as one level of the factor:

```
> levels(factorRatings) <- c("Negative", "Other", "Other")
> factorRatings
 [1] Negative Other    Other    Negative Other    Other    Other    Negative
 [9] Other    Negative Other    Other    Other    Other    Other    Other
[17] Other    Other    Negative Other
Levels: Negative Other
```

Creating Factors from Continuous Data

So far you have seen how to create a factor from data that is already categorical, but what about if you want to use a continuous variable as the basis for a factor? In this case, you can use the cut function. The `cut` function has a number of arguments that can help you control exactly how the categories are formed. See Table 5.1 for a list of the main arguments.

TABLE 5.1   Arguments to the `cut` Function

Argument	Description	Default
x	Numeric vector on which to base category.	–
breaks	Either a vector of cut points or a single number giving the number of category bins.	–
labels	Labels for the levels of the resulting category.	NULL (derived)
include.lowest	Logical: Should lowest value be placed in adjacent bin?	FALSE
right	Logical: Should intervals be closed on the right (as opposed to on the left)?	TRUE
dig.lab	Number of digits used in default break labels.	3
ordered_result	Logical: Should result be an ordered factor?	FALSE

The simplest way you can create a factor is by providing the data and the `breaks` argument. Therefore, if you wanted to create three groups, you simply give breaks = 3, like so:

```
> ages <- c(19, 38, 33, 25, 21, 27, 27, 24, 25, 32)
> cut(ages, breaks = 3)
 [1] (19,25.3] (31.7,38] (31.7,38] (19,25.3] (19,25.3] (25.3,31.7]
 [7] (25.3,31.7] (19,25.3] (19,25.3] (31.7,38]
Levels: (19,25.3] (25.3,31.7] (31.7,38]
```

You can see in this example that the data has been split into three equally spaced levels. The levels are based on the range of the data rather than the number of values in each level. The levels here take the names of the ranges. You can have much more control over the ranges by instead specifying the lower and upper limits of each of the levels:

```
> cut(ages, breaks = c(18, 25, 30, Inf))
 [1] (18,25]  (30,Inf] (30,Inf] (18,25]  (18,25]  (25,30]  (25,30]  (18,25]  (18,25]
[10] (30,Inf]
Levels: (18,25] (25,30] (30,Inf]
```

When you do this, you need to keep in mind that if the whole range of your data is not covered by the break points, you will introduce missing values, hence the use of Inf at the upper end. The arguments include.lowest and right let you control exactly where the group break points fall. Finally, you can control the labels that are given to the levels using the labels argument:

```
> cut(data, breaks = c(18, 25, 30, Inf), labels = c("18-25", "25-30", "30+"))
 [1] 18-25 30+   30+   18-25 18-25 25-30 25-30 18-25 18-25 30+
Levels: 18-25 25-30 30+
```

As you can see, you can easily convert your continuous data to categories. You can see from Table 5.1 that there are more arguments that let you control the creation of the factor even further, including whether the groups are closed on the right or left (it defaults to left). We will use factors more when we manipulate data and create graphics, in particular when we use the package ggplot2 in Hour 14, "The ggplot2 Package for Graphics."

Summary

In this hour we looked at some additional data types that allow us to work with dates and times and categorical data. You learned how to convert both numeric and character values into date and/or time objects and then how to manipulate these objects using the base functionality in R. You were also introduced to a useful package that can make these manipulations much simpler. Finally, you saw how R manages categorical data, how you can convert your data into this format, and how you can use continuous data to create your own categorical data. In the next hour, we look at some of the functions that we can use for working with the standard data types.

Q&A

Q. I have tried to convert my data to a Date object but it's just returned a series of NA's. Why doesn't it recognize my data?

A. If you find you have been returned a series of NA's after converting to a date or time, it is most likely because you have specified the wrong format in the format argument. Take a look at the help file for strptime for a full list of format codes, and don't forget to include any spaces, dashes, or slashes in your dates.

Q. Why do I need to bother converting my data to a factor?

A. For general data-manipulation tasks, you will find that it makes very little difference whether your data is a factor or not. It will only be if you want to rename elements that you see a difference in behavior. Converting to a factor type is important when it comes to producing graphics and modeling your data. When you're modeling, if your data is really categorical and you treat it as continuous, you will see a significantly different result. You will also find that if your data is large, then storing it as a factor is more efficient, as it will only store the unique values rather than repeating them a potential large number of times.

Workshop

The workshop contains quiz questions and exercises to help you solidify your understanding of the material covered. Try to answer all questions before looking at the "Answers" section that follows.

Quiz

1. What date does R use as the origin for counting dates and times?

2. What is the default time zone for creating POSIX objects?

3. What is a factor?

4. How are the levels of a factor determined?

5. If you were to use the function `cut` with the argument `"breaks = 3"`, how would the levels be determined?

   A. The data would be split into three equally sized groups based on the number of elements.

   B. The range of the data would be split equally into three.

Answers

1. The origin for dates and times in R is January 1, 1970, 00:00:00 UTC.

2. The default time zone is the locale on your operating system. You can change the time zone using the `tz` argument. This is particularly useful if you are working with people across time zones and want to ensure the correct time zone for the data is used.

3. A factor is the way of storing categorical data in R.

4. If you choose not to give the appropriate levels using the `levels` argument, they will be the alphanumerically ordered unique elements of the data.

5. The answer is B. The range of the data is split equally to create three groups. This may mean, however, that the groups are of uneven size or the break points occur at locations that are not sensible for the data.

Activities

1. Create a vector of character strings that contains today's date as well as the date of your next birthday and New Year's Eve. Convert this character vector to a Date object.

2. Use the vector of dates to work out what day of the week your next birthday and New Year's Eve occur on.

3. How many days are there from now until your next birthday?

4. Using the weather data we created in Hour 4, convert the Day column to a factor, ensuring that all possible days of the week can be used as levels and they are in the correct order, starting with Monday.

5. Change the levels of the Day factor column to be "Weekend" and "Weekday."

6. Using the `cut` function, create a new column in the data, TempFactor, that takes the value "low" for temperatures less than 25, "medium" for temperatures from 25 to 30, and "high" for temperatures including and above 30 where all temperatures are in degrees Celsius.

HOUR 6
Common R Utility Functions

What You'll Learn in This Hour:

▶ Common functions for numeric data

▶ How to simulate data in R

▶ Simple logical summaries

▶ Functions for missing data

▶ Useful function for manipulating character data

So far you have seen how to create objects of different modes and how to work with special types of data—but what about numeric, logical, and character data? How can we handle missing data or even remove it from our data? How can we simulate from statistical distributions? In this hour, we answer these questions by introducing you to some of the most common utility functions in R that you will find yourself using every day.

Using R Functions

You have already used a number of functions in the previous hours, including `seq`, `matrix`, `length`, and `factor`. However, before we look many more useful functions, it is handy to know how to work with functions in R.

When you call a function in R, you use the function name with a number of arguments, which you give inside round brackets, to pass information to that function about how it should run and what data it should use. So how do you know what the arguments to a function are? You can either look in the help file—using `?functionName` or `help("functionName")`—or you can use a function called `args`, which will print the arguments to a function in the console. As an example of using a function, we will look at `sample`. This function allows us to randomly sample a number of values from a vector of given values (this is the R way of selecting balls from an urn). So let's take a look at the arguments to this function:

```
> args(sample)
function (x, size, replace = FALSE, prob = NULL)
NULL
```

You can see that we have four arguments to this function. You will notice that the first two are simply given as x and size, whereas the second two are followed by = value. This indicates that they have a default value, so we don't need to supply an alternative. Because x and size do not have a default, we have to tell R what value we want them to take. To know the purpose of the arguments, you will need to take a look at the help files, which will tell you more. In this case, x is the vector that we want to sample from and size is the number of samples we want to take, whereas replace allows us to put values back, and we can set the probability of each value with prob.

When it comes to calling the function, we can supply the arguments in a number of ways. To start with, we can name all the arguments in full:

```
> sample(x = c("red", "yellow", "green", "blue"), size = 2, replace = FALSE, prob =
NULL)
```

Because replace and size have default values, this is the same as the following:

```
> sample(x = c("red", "yellow", "green", "blue"), size = 2)
```

Using this form of complete naming of arguments, we can actually supply them in any order we like. Therefore, the preceding would do the same as this:

```
> sample(size = 2, x = c("red", "yellow", "green", "blue"))
```

It's worth remembering that when you actually run each of these lines, you will most likely get a different result because the function is randomly sampling from the vector x.

If you provide all the arguments in the same order as the args function gives them, you do not actually need to give the names of the arguments. Therefore, we can also say this:

```
> sample(c("red", "yellow", "green", "blue"), 2)
```

In reality, you will often see, and use, a combination of naming and ordering of arguments because you will tend to remember what should come first but not the order of other arguments. Therefore, you might see something like the following:

```
> sample(c("red", "yellow", "green", "blue"), size = 2, replace = TRUE)
```

Now that you know more about how to call functions, we will look at some useful functions for various types of data.

Functions for Numeric Data

When it comes to working with numeric data, there is a whole host of functions we may want to use—from mathematical functions such as logarithms to simulating from statistical distributions. I won't cover every single function available in R, but we will introduce you to some of the most common.

Mathematical Functions and Operators

You have already, briefly, seen that you can use R for basic arithmetic using functions such as +, -, *, and /. In R, these are known as operators, and other useful operators include ^ (power) and %% (mod). Here's an example:

```
> 3^2
[1] 9
> 5 %% 3
[1] 2
```

Other useful mathematical functions are shown in Table 6.1.

TABLE 6.1   Mathematical Functions

Function	Purpose	Function	Purpose
sqrt	Square root	sin/cos/tan	Sine/cosine/tangent
log	Logarithm	asin/acos/atan	Arc-sine/cosine/tangent
exp	Exponential	abs	Absolute

All these functions are used very simply with an argument, x, with the data of interest, typically a vector or matrix. However, for logarithms, you can also provide the base, which is the exponential base (natural logarithm) by default. As an example, let's create a simple vector of values to pass to some of these functions:

```
> x <- seq(1, 4, by = 0.5)
> x
[1] 1.0 1.5 2.0 2.5 3.0 3.5 4.0
> sqrt(x)
[1] 1.000000 1.224745 1.414214 1.581139 1.732051 1.870829 2.000000
> log(x)
[1] 0.0000000 0.4054651 0.6931472 0.9162907 1.0986123 1.2527630 1.3862944
> sin(x)
[1]  0.8414710  0.9974950  0.9092974  0.5984721  0.1411200 -0.3507832 -0.7568025
```

As you can see, these are very simple functions to use and they follow standard mathematical order of operations (that is, brackets, order, division, multiplication, addition, subtraction).

Statistical Summary Functions

When it comes to statistical summaries, there is a whole host of functions you could choose to use to find out more about your data. Just like the mathematical functions you saw in the previous section, these are all very simple to use, and often you need only provide the data to the function. Table 6.2 shows some of the most common summary functions.

TABLE 6.2 Statistical Summaries

Function	Purpose	Function	Purpose
mean	Mean	min	Minimum
median	Median	max	Maximum
sd	Standard deviation	Range	Range of values (minimum, maximum)
var	Variance	Length	Length of the vector (that is, number of elements)
mad	Median absolute deviation	Sum	Total sum

The first argument to all these functions is the data and should be a single vector of values. Here's an example:

```
> age <- c(38, 20, 44, 41, 46, 49, 43, 23, 28, 32)
> median(age)
[1] 39.5
> mad(age)
[1] 10.3782
> range(age)
[1] 20 49
```

When you are working with missing data, you need to take a little extra care with these functions. Take a look at this example:

```
> age[3] <- NA
> median(age)
[1] NA
```

As you can see, when you have missing values in your data, the median function, and in fact all the statistical summary functions in Table 6.2, will return NA. Although this is a technically correct value to return, you are typically more interested in the value of the summary after removing the missing values. By using the argument na.rm, you can do this easily:

```
> median(age, na.rm = TRUE)
[1] 38
```

You will see before the end of this hour how to remove missing values from a vector without these functions.

Simulation and Statistical Distributions

For working with statistical distributions in R, we have functions for working with all of the common distributions and all the common actions. All the functions follow the same pattern of naming, which starts with a single letter to identify what we want to do and is followed by the R code name for the distribution. Table 6.3 shows some of the most common distributions available in the base R installation. Many other distributions, such as the Pareto distribution, are available in contributed packages.

TABLE 6.3 R Codes for Statistical Distributions

Distribution	R Code	Distribution	R Code
Normal	norm	Poisson	pois
Binomial	binom	Exponential	exp
Uniform	unif	Weibull	weibull
Beta	beta	Gamma	gamma
F	f	Chi-Squared	chisq

The list of distributions in Table 6.3 is by no means an exhaustive list, and many more can be found in the help pages by simply searching the name of the distribution. As stated earlier, you will need to combine this name for the distribution with a letter that determines whether you want to sample or calculate the quantiles. The letters you will need, their purpose, and an example of structuring the function name with the Normal distribution is shown in Table 6.4.

TABLE 6.4 Distribution Functions

Letter	Purpose	First Argument	Example
d	Probability density function	x (quantiles)	dnorm(1.64)
p	Cumulative probability density function	q (quantiles)	pnorm(1.64)
q	Quantile function	p (probabilities)	qnorm(0.95)
r	Random sampling	n (sample size)	rnorm(100)

On top of the first argument shown in Table 6.4, and which is the same for all distribution functions, there will be additional arguments specific to the distribution. For example, the Normal distribution has the arguments mean and sd that are set to the Standard Normal defaults (0 and 1 respectively), whereas the Poisson distribution has the argument lambda, which does not have a default value set. In general the arguments will be set to the "standard" values for that distribution. Where the distribution does not have a standard, default values will not be set. For example, if you wanted to simulate five values from the Normal, Poisson, and Exponential distributions, it may look something like this:

```
> rnorm(5)
[1] -0.23515046 -1.79043043 -0.03287786 -0.24937333 -1.00660505
> rpois(5, lambda = 3)
[1] 4 6 6 3 1
> rexp(5)
[1] 3.2443094 1.1198132 0.9365825 0.2731334 0.4363149
```

Although this allows you to simulate values from a distribution, you may want to generate samples from existing data. You have already seen the function for this: sample. As you have seen, this function allows you to specify the vector you want to sample from, the number of samples you want, whether you want to replace the values or not, and whether you want to change the probability of sampling particular values, which are equal by default. As an example, let's sample from our vector of ages:

```
> sample(age, size = 5)
[1] 28 46 20 49 23
>sample(age, size = 5, replace = TRUE)
[1] 20 20 23 28 41
```

As we saw previously, the replace argument here is allowing values to be sampled again when it is set to TRUE whereas when it is set to FALSE a value cannot be sampled again after it has been sampled once.

NOTE

Re-creating Simulated Values

If you want to be able to re-create the random samples you generated, you will need to set the random seed. You can do this with the function set.seed, which simply takes an integer value to indicate the seed to use. You can also use this function to change the type of random number generator used. See the help documentation for more details.

Logical Data

One of the main ways you will work with logical data is to subset the data as we did in Hour 3, "Single-Mode Data Structures." There are, however, a couple of functions you will find useful for, in particular, counting the number of cases of a condition.

First of all, it is worth knowing how logical data is stored in R. As you have seen, a logical vector contains only values that are TRUE or FALSE. In R, these are in fact stored as the numeric values 0 and 1. You can see this by using the as.numeric function to force the numeric representation of a value, like so:

```
> as.numeric(c(TRUE, FALSE))
[1] 1 0
```

Therefore, when you have a logical vector, you can actually use the numeric functions you have seen to manipulate it. Of course, finding the variance of TRUE and FALSE values is not generally something that you want to do, but the sum function will actually allow you to count the total number of TRUE occurrences. As an example, let's see how many values in the age vector from the previous section are less than 30:

```
> age
[1] 38 20 NA 41 46 49 43 23 28 32
> age < 30
[1] FALSE  TRUE    NA FALSE FALSE FALSE FALSE  TRUE  TRUE FALSE
> sum(age < 30, na.rm = TRUE)
[1] 3
```

Another useful function for counting the TRUE versus FALSE cases is table:

```
> table(age < 30)

FALSE  TRUE
    6     3
> table(age < 30, useNA = "ifany")

FALSE  TRUE  <NA>
    6     3     1
```

You can, in fact, use the table function to display the number of cases for any vector, but as you can see, this is useful for tabulating logical cases. You will also notice that by default the function does not include missing values. However, if you set the argument useNA to "ifany", missing values will be included when they are present.

Missing Data

Many of the statistical summary functions allow you to easily remove your missing data from calculations. As you will see when we look at graphics and model fitting, missing data is simply removed. But what if you want to identify the missing values to, for example, determine how many missing values there are or to replace them in some way?

You saw in the last section that you can easily count the number of missing values using the sum function, if you are able to create a logical vector indicating which values are missing. If you were to simply test for values being equal to the missing value NA, you would in fact just be returned a series of NA's. Here's an example:

```
> age <- c(38, 20, NA, 41, 46, 49, 43, 23, 28, 32)
> age == NA
[1] NA NA NA NA NA NA NA NA NA NA
```

This is because we are asking R whether or not each value in the vector is equal to some value that we don't actually know. In each case, R doesn't know the answer! Therefore, you need to use an alternative function for determining whether a value is missing: is.na. This is actually one of a whole series of is.x functions, some of which you will see throughout this book, that allow you to test whether data is of a particular type. Therefore, in this case, you can say the following:

```
> is.na(age)
[1] FALSE FALSE  TRUE FALSE FALSE FALSE FALSE FALSE FALSE FALSE
```

Thus, you can count the number of cases of missing data or generate a table showing the number of missing and non-missing cases, for example:

```
> sum(is.na(age))
[1] 1
> table(is.na(age))

FALSE  TRUE
    9     1
```

Alternatively, you may want to replace your missing values with the mean of the data, or some other value. A useful function for doing this is the replace function. Although this function is not restricted to working with missing data, this is often what you'll be interested in doing. You need to provide this function with three pieces of information: first, the vector of data; second, a condition that returns TRUE and FALSE values to determine which values should be replaced; third, the value to be inserted. Suppose, for example, we wanted to replace the missing age value in the age vector with the mean of the remainder of the age values:

```
> meanAge <- mean(age, na.rm = TRUE)
> missingObs <- is.na(age)
> age <- replace(age, missingObs, meanAge)
```

```
> age
[1] 38.00000 20.00000 35.55556 41.00000 46.00000 49.00000 43.00000
[8] 23.00000 28.00000 32.00000
```

Of course, if we simply wanted to remove the missing values from our data, we could use `is.na` in combination with the "not" operation (`!`), along with the standard subscripting techniques you saw in Hour 3. Here's how to remove the missing values from our `age` vector:

```
> age[!is.na(age)]
[1] 38 20 41 46 49 43 23 28 32
```

TIP

Missing Data Functions

A number of useful functions for working with missing data can be found in the `zoo` package. This includes functions such as `na.locf` for the last observation carried forward and `na.trim` for trimming leading and trailing missing values.

Character Data

We can often find ourselves having to perform string manipulation tasks in R, including creation of character strings and searching for patterns in character strings. In this section, we look at some of the functions in the base R installation, but if you are particularly interested in manipulating strings, you may be interested in the `stringr` and `stringi` packages.

Simple Character Manipulation

Some of the basic manipulations you'll want to perform are counting characters, extracting substrings, and combining elements to create or update a string. Let's start with counting characters. You do this using the `nchar` function, simply providing the string that you are interested in:

```
> fruits <- "apples, oranges, pears"
> nchar(fruits)
[1] 22
```

Notice that all characters are counted, including the spaces. To extract substrings, you use the `substring` function. Here, you need to give the string along with the start and end points for the substring. You can extract multiple substrings by giving the vectors of the start and end points.

```
> substring(fruits, 1, 6)
[1] "apples"
> fruits <- substring(fruits, c(1, 9, 18), c(6, 15, 22))
> fruits
[1] "apples"  "oranges" "pears"
```

Finally, you can create a character string from a series of strings or numeric values using the `paste` function. You can provide as many strings and objects as you wish to the `paste` function and they will all be converted to character data and pasted together. Like with many R functions, you can pass vectors to the `paste` function. Here's an example:

```
> paste(5, "apples")
[1] "5 apples"
> nfruits <- c(5, 9, 2)
> paste(nfruits, fruits)
[1] "5 apples"  "9 oranges" "2 pears"
```

You can use the argument `sep` to change the separator between the pasted strings, which as you can see in the preceding example is a space by default, like so:

```
> paste(fruits, nfruits, sep = " = ")
[1] "apples = 5"  "oranges = 9" "pears = 2"
```

Searching and Replacing

Two of the most useful functions for working with character data are the functions `grep` and `gsub`. These functions allow you to search elements of a vector for a particular pattern (`grep`) and replace a particular pattern with a given string (`gsub`). You search for patterns using regular expressions (that is, a pattern that describes the character string).

TIP

Regular Expressions

Much more information on regular expressions can be found in the R help pages for the function `regex`. If you are familiar with Perl expressions, you can use these along with the argument `perl = TRUE`.

Let's start by looking at the function `grep`. The first argument that we are going to give is the pattern to search for, which can be as simple as the string `"red"`. The second argument will be the vector to search.

```
> colourStrings <- c("green", "blue", "orange", "red", "yellow",
+                   "lightblue", "navyblue", "indianred")
> grep("red", colourStrings, value = TRUE)
[1] "red"       "indianred"
```

In this example, we have used an additional argument, `value`. This allows us to return the actual values of the vector that include the pattern rather than simply the index of their position in the vector. Some more examples of using the `grep` function, with a variety of regular expressions, are shown in Listing 6.1.

LISTING 6.1 Searching Character Strings

```
 1: > colourStrings <- c("green", "blue", "orange", "red", "yellow",
 2: +                     "lightblue", "navyblue", "indianred")
 3: >
 4: > grep("^red", colourStrings, value = TRUE)
 5: [1] "red"
 6: > grep("red$", colourStrings, value = TRUE)
 7: [1] "indianred"
 8: >
 9: > grep("r+", colourStrings, value = TRUE)
10: [1] "green"    "orange"    "red"       "indianred"
11: >
12: > grep("e{2}", colourStrings, value = TRUE)
13: [1] "green"
```

In lines 4 and 6 you can see how the symbols ^ and $ have been used to mark the start and end of the string. In the example in line 4, we are specifying that immediately following the start of the string is the pattern "red", whereas in line 6 the string ends straight after the pattern "red". The examples in lines 9 and 12 show how to specify that something must appear a given number of times. In line 9, the + indicates that the letter r should appear at least once in the string. In line 12, the {2} following the e indicates that there should be two occurrences of the letter.

The gsub function, which allows you to substitute a pattern for a value, is very similar, because you also use regular expressions to search for the pattern. The only additional information you need to give is what to substitute in its place. Here is an example:

```
> gsub("red", "brown", colourStrings)
[1] "green"     "blue"      "orange"      "brown"      "yellow"
[6] "lightblue" "navyblue"  "indianbrown"
```

As with grep, you can use any regular expression to match the pattern you wish to replace.

Summary

In this hour, you saw a number of useful functions when working with a variety of data types. You saw some of the standard mathematical and statistical functions, as well as simulation functions. You also saw how to manipulate character strings, logical values, and missing data. We will use many of these functions throughout the rest of this book, though this is by no means an exhaustive list of useful functions you will find in R. In the next hour, we will start to look at how to write our own functions for common actions we want to perform.

Q&A

Q. I want to simulate data from a distribution that is not listed here. What do I do?

A. First of all, try searching the help documentation using the name of the distribution. We have not given an exhaustive list of all available distributions in this hour, so there is a good chance we just haven't listed it. If you don't immediately find it in the base R help documentation, it may be that there is a package that includes the distribution functions you need; for example, the Pareto distribution can be found in the package evir, among others.

Q. I am trying to use regular expressions to find a particular value to replace, but I simply get back the original vector. Why isn't it replacing my pattern?

A. If you find that while using `gsub` you are returned the original vector, it is most likely because your pattern or regular expression is not specific enough to find the pattern. Try being even more specific by thinking about what will be at the start of the string, whether there may be spaces, and how many occurrences of a pattern there may be.

Workshop

The workshop contains quiz questions and exercises to help you solidify your understanding of the material covered. Try to answer all questions before looking at the "Answers" section that follows.

Quiz

1. Take a look at the following three function calls. Would they all give the same result?

   A. `matrix(1:9, 3, 3)`

   B. `matrix(nrow = 3, ncol = 3, data = 1:9)`

   C. `matrix(data = 1:9, nrow = 3, ncol = 3)`

2. What function would you need to call to find the 95% quantile of the standard Exponential distribution?

3. How is logical data stored in R?

4. What function would you use to test whether your data is missing?

5. What is the purpose of the function `paste`?

Answers

1. Yes, all three would produce the same matrix. When you name the arguments, it doesn't matter what order you provide them in, and as long as you give the arguments in the correct order there is no need to name them. Typically, you will see a combination of naming and ordering of arguments.

2. For the quantiles, you use the `q*` functions along with the distribution code, which in this case would be `exp`, so you would call

   ```
   > qexp(0.95)
   ```

3. Although you see `TRUE` and `FALSE` in vectors of logical data, they are actually stored as 1 and 0. This is what allows you to take the sum to find the number of `TRUE` cases.

4. You test for missing values using the function `is.na`.

5. The `paste` function allows you to combine character strings and vectors of values. This is particularly useful if you wanted to, for example, create character strings for a plot title from a fixed string and a value in the data.

Activities

1. Using the Normal distribution, simulate 50 values with the same mean and standard deviation as the Ozone variable in the `airquality` data.

2. What is the range of values in your simulated data?

3. How many values in your simulated data are larger than the mean of your data?

4. A function in R called `colors` returns a vector of all colors known by name. Using the `grep` function, create a vector that contains only colors that contain the string `"blue"`.

5. How many colors do you have in your vector of blues?

6. Replace the pattern `"blue"` with `"green"` throughout your vector.

Writing Functions: Part I

So far in this book you have seen many functions being used. For example, in the earlier hour on single-mode data structures you saw that you could create vectors using functions such as c, seq, and rep. One of the strengths of R is that you can extend it by writing your own functions. This allows you to create utilities that can perform a variety of tasks. In this hour, we look at ways to create our own functions, specify inputs, and return results to the user. We also introduce the "if/else" structure in R, and we use this to control the flow of code within a function.

The Motivation for Functions

You have seen that functions in R allow you to perform a number of tasks in a simple command. This approach has parallels in most programmable languages, such as "macros" in Visual Basic and SAS.

Creating your own functions is a powerful aspect of R that allows you to "wrap up" a series of steps into a simple container. This way, you can capture common workflows and utilities and call them when needed instead of producing long, verbose scripts of repeated code snippets that can be difficult to manage.

A Closer Look at an R Function

Before we write our own functions, let's take a closer look at the structure of an existing R function. Consider, for example, the upper.tri function, which allows us to identify values in the upper triangle of a matrix:

```
> myMat                      # A sample matrix
      [,1] [,2] [,3]
[1,]    1    6    3
[2,]    1    3    8
[3,]    5    4    1
> upper.tri(myMat)           # Upper triangle
       [,1]   [,2]   [,3]
[1,] FALSE   TRUE   TRUE
[2,] FALSE  FALSE   TRUE
[3,] FALSE  FALSE  FALSE
> myMat [ upper.tri(myMat) ]  # Values from upper triangle
[1] 6 3 8
```

As seen here, we can call the upper.tri function using round brackets, specifying the matrix as the first input. However, if we simply print the upper.tri function, we can see its contents:

```
> upper.tri        # Print the upper.tri function
function (x, diag = FALSE)
{
    x <- as.matrix(x)
    if (diag) row(x) <= col(x)
    else row(x) < col(x)
}
```

The function is split into two parts:

▶ The top part defines the inputs to the function (in this case, the inputs are x and diag).

▶ The next part, captured within curly brackets, contains the main "body" of the function.

In a similar way, we can create our own functions by specifying a function name, defining the function inputs, and specifying the actions we wish to take in the function body.

Creating a Simple Function

We can create a simple function in R using the function keyword. The curly brackets are used to contain the body of the function. In this simple example, we create a function that accepts a single input:

```
> addOne <- function(x) {
+    x + 1
+ }
```

Our new `addOne` function adds 1 to any input object. Once we've created a function, we can call that function in the usual way:

```
> addOne(x = 1:5)    # Call the addOne function
[1] 2 3 4 5 6
```

Saving Outputs

Here, we see the values 2 to 6 returned from a function. If we want to save the output from a function for later use, we need to assign the output from the function to an object, as shown here:

```
> result <- addOne(1:5)
> result
[1] 2 3 4 5 6
```

The function created is itself an R object. As such, it exists in the R Workspace, and can be managed and reused in future sessions if you save your Workspace objects, as discussed in Hour 2, "The R Environment."

The body of our simple `addOne` function contains only one line of code. If the function body contains only a single line of code, we can omit the curly brackets, as follows:

```
> addOne <- function(x) x + 1
> addOne(x = 1:5)    # Call the addOne function
[1] 2 3 4 5 6
```

Named Arguments

As you saw in Hour 6, "Common R Utility Functions," there are many ways to call functions and define arguments. In the preceding example, `addOne(x = 1:5)` is equivalent to `addOne(1:5)`. In this hour, we will name all arguments when calling the functions to aid clarity, but common convention in R is that the first argument (or arguments) is not directly named.

Continual Prompts

In many of our examples, we see the familiar command prompt for the first line of the function, with plus (+) symbols prefixing the following lines. These signify the "continuation" prompt in R, and are not part of the code itself (in other words, you should not type these symbols when creating your functions).

TIP

Using the Script Window

As mentioned earlier, functions typically contain more than one line of code. As such, the script window (in RStudio or other interface) is preferred to the console window when developing functions.

Naming a Function

A function is an R object, so it can be named like any other R object. Hence, its name

▶ Can be of any length

▶ Can contain any combinations of letters, numbers, underscores, and period characters

▶ Cannot start with a number

One thing to note, however, is that creating a function can cause existing functions to be "masked." Consider the following example:

```
> X <- 1:5                          # Create a vector
> median(X)                         # The median of the vector is 3
[1] 3
> find("median")                    # Where is the "median" function?
[1] "package:stats"

> median <- function(input) "Hello" # Create a new "median" function
> median(X)                         # The median of the vector is "Hello"
[1] "Hello"
> find("median")                    # Where is the "median" function?
[1] ".GlobalEnv"    "package:stats"

> rm(median)                        # Remove the new "median" function from the
                                      workspace
> median(X)                         # The median of the vector is 3
[1] 3
```

Here we have created a new median function in the R Workspace, thus "masking" the original median function, which still exists in the stats package. As such, care should be taken when naming functions to ensure you don't "mask" existing key functions.

Defining Function Arguments

In the previous section, we created a very simple function called addOne, defined as follows:

```
> addOne <- function(x) {
+     x + 1
+ }
```

Note that this function takes a single argument, x. If we wanted to extend this example, we could add a second argument:

```
> addNumber <- function(x, number) {
+ x + number
+ }
> addNumber(x = 1:5, number = 2)
[1] 3 4 5 6 7
```

Our new function (addNumber) now accepts two arguments (x and number) and adds these values together. Note, however, that these are both required arguments because they do not have default values. As such, calling the function without both arguments defined will result in an error:

```
> addNumber()                    # Calling with no arguments
Error in addNumber() : argument "x" is missing, with no default

> addNumber(x = 1:5)             # Calling with only the "x" argument
Error in addNumber(x = 1:5) : argument "number" is missing, with no default

> addNumber(number = 2)          # Calling with only the "number" argument
Error in addNumber(number = 2) : argument "x" is missing, with no default

> addNumber(x = 1:5, number = 2)  # Calling with both arguments
[1] 3 4 5 6 7
```

If we want to assign default values for arguments to a function, we can specify them directly in the argument definition, as follows:

```
> addNumber <- function(x, number = 0) {
+    x + number
+ }
> addNumber(x = 1:5)                    # Call function with default (number = 0)
[1] 1 2 3 4 5
> addNumber(x = 1:5, number = 1)        # Call function with number = 1
[1] 2 3 4 5 6
```

Function Scoping Rules

When we define a function, we can create objects within the function body. This may help to simplify functions or make them generally more readable. For example, we may create an object to be returned:

```
> addNumber <- function(x, number = 0) {
+    theAnswer <- x + number        # Create "theAnswer" by adding "x" and "number"
+    theAnswer                      # Return the value
+ }
```

If we call the function, note that the theAnswer object is not accessible once the function has been executed:

```
> output <- addNumber(x = 1:5, number = 1)    # Call the function creating
                                              "output" object
> output                                      # Look at value of "output"
[1] 2 3 4 5 6

> theAnswer                                   # "theAnswer" object does not exist
Error: object 'theAnswer' not found
```

When we run a function, R loads argument inputs and objectives created into a separate, temporary area of memory (a memory "frame"). Once the execution of the function is complete, the output is returned and the temporary area of memory closed. As such, objects created within a function call should be considered "local" to that function, so any required outputs must be explicitly returned from the function.

Return Objects

In the preceding example, you saw an object created within the function body. Let's extend that example to include the creation of more "local" objects. In this example, we create a function called plusAndMinus, which creates two "local" objects (called PLUS and MINUS) and attempts to return both of them:

```
> plusAndMinus <- function(x, y) {
+     PLUS <- x + y                 # Define "PLUS"
+     MINUS <- x - y                # Define "MINUS"
+     PLUS                          # Return "PLUS"
+     MINUS                         # Return "MINUS"
+ }
> plusAndMinus(x = 1:5, y = 1:5)    # Call function
[1] 0 0 0 0 0
```

As you can see, only the last object (the MINUS object) is returned from the function—the PLUS object value is not returned and, as discussed earlier, is only a local object, so the value cannot be retrieved.

R functions can only return a single object, which is the result of the last line of code in the function. This can be confirmed by swapping the order of the PLUS and MINUS return objects:

```
> plusAndMinus <- function(x, y) {
+     PLUS <- x + y                 # Define "PLUS"
+     MINUS <- x - y                # Define "MINUS"
+     MINUS                         # Return "MINUS"
+     PLUS                          # Return "PLUS"
+ }
> plusAndMinus(x = 1:5, y = 1:5)    # Call function
[1]  2  4  6  8 10
```

If we want to return more than one value from a function (for example, the PLUS and MINUS objects), we need to combine them into a single object. First, let's return the two values in a list:

```
> plusAndMinus <- function(x, y) {
+    PLUS <- x + y              # Define "PLUS"
+    MINUS <- x - y             # Define "MINUS"
+    list(PLUS, MINUS)          # Return "PLUS" and "MINUS" in a list
+ }
> plusAndMinus(x = 1:5, y = 1:5)  # Call function
[[1]]
[1]  2  4  6  8 10

[[2]]
[1]  0  0  0  0  0
```

This returns a single object, a list, containing the two values. When we return a list in this way, we should name the elements so we can more easily reference the values later:

```
> plusAndMinus <- function(x, y) {
+    PLUS <- x + y                    # Define "PLUS"
+    MINUS <- x - y                   # Define "MINUS"
+    list(plus = PLUS, minus = MINUS) # Return "PLUS" and "MINUS" in a list
+ }
> output <- plusAndMinus(x = 1:5, y = 1:5)  # Call function, saving the output
> output                            # Print the output
$plus
[1]  2  4  6  8 10

$minus
[1]  0  0  0  0  0

> output$plus                             # Print the "plus" element
[1]  2  4  6  8 10
```

The list object is an appropriate structure in this example, because we are returning multiple vectors. However, we may be returning a number of single values from a function, in which case a vector may be more suitable. Consider the following example, where we return some summary statistics as a vector:

```
> summaryFun <- function(vec, digits = 3) {
+
+    # Create some summary statistics
+    theMean <- mean(vec)
+    theMedian <- median(vec)
+    theMin <- min(vec)
+    theMax <- max(vec)
+
+    # Combine them into a single vector and round the values
```

```
+    output <- c(Mean = theMean, Median = theMedian, Min = theMin, Max = theMax)
+    round(output, digits = digits)
+ }
>
> X <- rnorm(50)    # Generate 50 samples from a normal distribution
> summaryFun(X)     # Produce summaries of the vector
   Mean Median    Min    Max
 -0.214 -0.051 -2.633  1.764
```

NOTE

Checking Function Inputs

For the preceding functions, we frequently make assumptions about the structure of the inputs. For example, in the summaryFun function we assume the vec input is a numeric object (otherwise functions such as mean make no sense). Later, in Hour 8, "Writing Functions: Part II," we will cover ways of checking function inputs. This includes functions for checking the structure of inputs and for producing error or warning messages when those inputs are not appropriate for the function.

The If/Else Structure

In the function examples you've seen so far in this hour, the "flow" through the body of the function has been completely linear and sequential. However, we may alternatively wish to control the flow based on decisions using an "if/else" statement.

NOTE

What Do We Mean by "If/Else"?

If you are not familiar with programming, the if/else statement is a common structure, where code is executed, or not, based on certain decisions. Consider this pseudo-code example:

```
IF I have enough money, I will buy a can of soda and a candy bar
ELSE I will just buy the can of soda
```

Often, we will only need an "IF" statement. Note that because either option in this example involves buying a can of soda, we can rewrite without the "ELSE" statement:

```
Buy the can of soda
IF I have enough money, I will also buy a candy bar
```

We can also have nested statements, such as this:

```
IF I have enough money, I will buy a can of soda and a candy bar
ELSE {
    IF they have my favorite type of candy bar I will just buy that
```

```
    ELSE I will just buy the can of soda
}
```

We can use a similar structure within our code to control the flow of the function based on specific choices.

The basic structure of an if/else statement in R is as follows:

```
if (something is TRUE) {
  do this
}
else {
  do this instead
}
```

As with functions, we use curly brackets to contain a body of code. However, if these are simple one-line statements, we may omit the curly brackets, as follows:

```
if (something is TRUE) do this
else do this instead
```

The "test" that is performed within the if statement (marked as "something is TRUE" here) is called the "condition," and should take the form of a single TRUE or FALSE value.

A Simple R Example

Let's look at a simple example of this in action. Here, we use the cat function, which prints text to the screen based on whether the number passed to it is positive or negative:

```
> posOrNeg <- function(X) {
+    if (X > 0) {
+      cat("X is Positive")
+    }
+    else {
+      cat("X is Negative")
+    }
+ }
> posOrNeg(1)     # is 1 positive or negative?
X is Positive
> posOrNeg(-1)    # is -1 positive or negative?
X is Negative
> posOrNeg(0)     # is 0 positive or negative?
X is Negative
```

NOTE

If/Else in a Script

Note that the above example of if/else is contained within a function. If, instead, the if/else code was run interactively or as part of a script, it would interpret the `if` part of the statement as a single command and would fail when the `else` statement is encountered:

```
> X <- 1
> if (X > 0) {
+    cat("X is Positive")
+ }
X is Positive
> else {
Error: unexpected 'else' in "else"
>    cat("X is Negative")
X is Negative
> }
Error: unexpected '}' in "}"
```

To guard against this issue, we can rewrite the command positioning the `else` statement immediately following the closing curly bracket of the `if` component as follows:

```
> X <- 1
> if (X > 0) {
+    cat("X is Positive")
+ } else {       # NOTE: "else" on same line as closing } of "if"
+    cat("X is Negative")
+ }
X is Positive
```

Nested Statements

In this example, positive and negative integers are handled and the function will return the correct message. However, when we pass the function a 0, this would be reported as a negative, which isn't true (in the most popular definition 0 is neither positive nor negative).

We can improve our example by using a nested if/else statement:

```
> posOrNeg <- function(X) {
+    if (X > 0) {
+      cat("X is Positive")
+    }
+    else {
+      if (X == 0) cat("X is Zero")
+      else cat("X is Negative")
+    }
+ }
> posOrNeg(1)    # is 1 positive or negative?
```

```
X is Positive
> posOrNeg(0)    # is 0 positive or negative?
X is Zero
```

Using One Condition

Consider the following example:

```
> posOrNeg <- function(X) {
+   if (X > 0) {
+     cat("X is Positive")
+   }
+   else {
+     cat("")
+   }
+ }
> posOrNeg(1)    # is 1 positive or negative?
X is Positive
> posOrNeg(0)    # is 0 positive or negative?
```

In this example, the "else" part of the statement does nothing, so we can drop it and simplify as follows:

```
> posOrNeg <- function(X) {
+   if (X > 0) {
+     cat("X is Positive")
+   }
+ }
> posOrNeg(1)    # is 1 positive or negative?
X is Positive
> posOrNeg(0)    # is 0 positive or negative?
```

Multiple Test Values

In the preceding example, the posOrNeg function accepts an input called X and the condition is X > 0. Running this condition outside the if/else statement shows that it returns a single logical value:

```
> X <- 1  # Set X to 1
> X > 0   # Is X greater than 0?
[1] TRUE

> X <- 0  # Set X to 0
> X > 0   # Is X greater than 0?
[1] FALSE
```

If we instead provide a vector of values to this function, we get the following warning message:

```
> posOrNeg <- function(X) {
+    if (X > 0) cat("X is Positive")
+    else cat("X is Negative")
+ }
> posOrNeg(-2:2)     # is 1 positive or negative?
X is Negative
Warning message:
In if (X > 0) cat("X is Positive") else cat("X is Negative") :
   the condition has length > 1 and only the first element will be used
```

In this case, when running the condition outside the if/else statement, we can see that the result is a vector of logicals:

```
> X <- -2:2  # Set X to -2:2
> X > 0      # Is X greater than 0?
[1] FALSE FALSE FALSE  TRUE  TRUE
```

The if/else structure is looking for a single "choice" (that is, should it run the first "if" section of code or the second "else" section of code?). In this example, the condition has returned five "answers" (FALSE FALSE FALSE TRUE TRUE).

R handles this mismatch by only using the first "answer" (as per the warning message). This is FALSE, hence the result ("X is Negative").

Summarizing to a Single Logical

In the last example, you saw that the condition should be a single TRUE or FALSE value. You also saw that warnings and unexpected behaviors can occur if multiple logical values are generated from the condition.

One way of handling this is to use the all and any functions to collapse a vector of logicals into a single TRUE or FALSE value:

```
> X <- -2:2  # Set X to -2:2
> X > 0      # Is X greater than 0?
[1] FALSE FALSE FALSE  TRUE  TRUE
> all(X > 0) # Are all values of X greater than 0?
[1] FALSE
> any(X > 0) # Are any values of X greater than 0?
[1] TRUE
```

We can use these functions directly in the condition as follows:

```
> posOrNeg <- function(X) {
+    if (all(X > 0)) cat("All values of X are > 0")
+    else {
```

```
+      if (any(X > 0)) cat("At least 1 value of X is > 0")
+      else cat("No values are > 0")
+    }
+ }
> posOrNeg(-2:2)
At least 1 value of X is > 0
> posOrNeg(1:5)
All values of X are > 0
> posOrNeg(-(1:5))
No values are > 0
```

Switching with Logical Input

Sometimes we may want the person calling the function to choose the flow of the function. In this case, we can provide a logical argument that the function passes directly to the condition in the if/else statement:

```
> logVector <- function(vec, logIt = FALSE) {
+    if (logIt == TRUE) vec <- log(vec)
+    else vec <- vec
+    vec
+ }
> logVector(1:5)
[1] 1 2 3 4 5
> logVector(1:5, logIt = TRUE) # Call the function with logIt = TRUE
[1] 0.0000000 0.6931472 1.0986123 1.3862944 1.6094379
```

Again, the "else" portion of this statement changes nothing, so we can drop it:

```
> logVector <- function(vec, logIt = FALSE) {
+    if (logIt == TRUE) vec <- log(vec)
+    vec
+ }
> logVector(1:5)
[1] 1 2 3 4 5
> logVector(1:5, logIt = TRUE) # Call the function with logIt = TRUE
[1] 0.0000000 0.6931472 1.0986123 1.3862944 1.6094379
```

There is one more simplification we can make. Consider the possible outcomes from the condition:

▶ If logIt is TRUE, then logIt == TRUE will be TRUE.

▶ If logIt is FALSE, then logIt == TRUE will be FALSE.

So, regardless of the result, `logIt == TRUE` will always return the same value as `logIt`. Therefore, we can simplify the condition as follows:

```
> logVector <- function(vec, logIt = FALSE) {
+    if (logIt) vec <- log(vec)
+    vec
+ }
> logVector(1:5)
[1] 1 2 3 4 5
> logVector(1:5, logIt = TRUE)  # Call the function with logIt = TRUE
[1] 0.0000000 0.6931472 1.0986123 1.3862944 1.6094379
```

Reversing Logical Values

Using `all` and `any`, we can summarize logical vectors as follows:

```
> X <- -2:2  # Set X to -2:2
> X > 0      # Is X greater than 0?
[1] FALSE FALSE FALSE  TRUE  TRUE
> all(X > 0) # Are all values of X greater than 0?
[1] FALSE
> any(X > 0) # Are any values of X greater than 0?
[1] TRUE
```

We can introduce the `!` notation before any logical statement to convert `TRUE` values to `FALSE` values and `FALSE` values to `TRUE` values. This can be seen here:

```
> X <- -2:2  # Set X to -2:2
> X > 0      # Is X greater than 0?
[1] FALSE FALSE FALSE  TRUE  TRUE
> !(X > 0)   # Reverse logical values
[1]  TRUE  TRUE  TRUE FALSE FALSE
```

We can also use the `!` notation before the `all` and `any` functions to reverse the meanings of the conditions as follows:

```
> posOrNeg <- function(X) {
+    if (all(X > 0)) cat("\nAll values of X are greater than 0")
+    if (!all(X > 0)) cat("\nNot all values of X are greater than 0")
+    if (any(X > 0)) cat("\nAt least 1 value of X is greater than 0")
+    if (!any(X > 0)) cat("\nNo values of X are greater than 0")
+ }
> posOrNeg(1:5)        # All > 0

All values of X are greater than 0
At least 1 value of X is greater than 0
> posOrNeg(-2:2)       # Some > 0, Some <= 0
```

```
Not all values of X are greater than 0
At least 1 value of X is greater than 0
> posOrNeg(-(1:5))    # All <= 0

Not all values of X are greater than 0
No values of X are greater than 0
```

NOTE

New Line Characters

Note the use of the `\n` character in the call to `cat` in the preceding example. The `\n` character specifies that a new line is written, which is why each statement printed is on a separate line. This can be further seen in this example:

```
> cat("Hello\nthere")
Hello
there
```

Mixing Conditions

In all our examples so far, there has been a single condition. If we have more than one condition, we can use the `&` or `|` notation to combine conditions. Here is a rather contrived example to show the use of these operators:

```
> betweenValues <- function(X, Min = 1, Max = 10) {
+     if (X >= Min & X <= Max) cat(paste("X is between", Min, "and", Max))
+     if (X < Min | X > Max) cat(paste("X is NOT between", Min, "and", Max))
+ }
> betweenValues(5)
X is between 1 and 10
> betweenValues(5, Min = -2, Max = 2)
X is NOT between -2 and 2
```

We may also mix conditions that come from different sources. Consider the following example that mixes a condition passed from the user with one derived within the function:

```
> logVector <- function(vec, logIt = FALSE) {
+     if (all(vec > 0) & logIt) vec <- log(vec)
+     vec
+ }
> logVector(1:5, logIt = TRUE)   # Logs the data
[1] 0.0000000 0.6931472 1.0986123 1.3862944 1.6094379
> logVector(-5:5, logIt = TRUE) # Doesn't log the data because first condition not
➥met
 [1] -5 -4 -3 -2 -1  0  1  2  3  4  5
```

Control And/Or Statements

When multiple conditions are combined with & and/or | conditions, each condition is evaluated separately, and the each result is compared. To illustrate this, consider the following example:

```
> logVector <- function(vec) {
+    if (all(vec > 0) & all(log(vec) <= 2)) cat("Numbers in range")
+    else cat("Numbers not in range")
+ }
> logVector(1:10)     # Some logged values are greater than 2
Numbers not in range
> logVector(1:5)      # All values are in range
Numbers in range
```

Let's consider the way in which the condition from the last call is evaluated:

▸ The all(vec > 0) statement is evaluated, resulting in a TRUE value.

▸ The all(log(vec) <= 2) statement is evaluated, also resulting in a TRUE value.

▸ The results of the two statements are compared: TRUE & TRUE = TRUE.

Now consider the following example:

```
> logVector(-2:2)
Numbers not in range
Warning message:
In log(vec) : NaNs produced
```

In this example, we see a return value ("Numbers not in range") and also a warning message. This message occurs because both conditions are evaluated and compared. The first condition returns a FALSE value, but the second condition generates a warning message because the function is attempting to calculate logs of negative numbers (which is not mathematically possible).

To remedy these issues, we can use the "control" versions of the & and | operators. This changes the flow so that the second condition is only evaluated if the result of the first is inconclusive. To use the "control" and/or statement, we use double notation (&& or ||). Let's update our logVector function with "control" notation:

```
> logVector <- function(vec) {
+    if (all(vec > 0) && all(log(vec) <= 2)) cat("Numbers in range")
+    else cat("Numbers not in range")
+ }
> logVector(-2:2)
Numbers not in range
```

You can see that the earlier message has been avoided because we specified a "control and" using the && notation. Now, the flow of the condition is as follows:

▶ The all(vec > 0) statement is evaluated, resulting in a FALSE value.

▶ Because the first condition is FALSE, the whole statement must be FALSE, so a FALSE value is returned without evaluating the second condition.

Returning Early

Earlier in this hour, in the "Return Objects" section, you saw that the last evaluated line of code within a function generates the return value. Consider this example:

```
> verboseFunction <- function(X) {
+    if (all(X > 0)) output <- X    # if all values of X > 0, set output to X
+    else {
+       X [ X <= 0 ] <- 0.1         # Set all values <≈0 to 0.1
+       output <- log(X)            # Take logs of the X input data, set as output
+    }
+    output                         # Return the value of output
+ }
> verboseFunction(-2:2)            # Call our function
[1] -2.3025851 -2.3025851 -2.3025851  0.0000000  0.6931472
```

If all the values of X are greater than 0, we set the output to 0. At this point in the function (that is, the first line of the body of the function) we already know the value we want to return from the function. If we wish to return the result of the function early, we can force this to happen using the return function. This way, we can rewrite our function as follows:

```
> verboseFunction <- function(X) {
+    if (all(X > 0)) return(X)      # Return early if all values of X are > 0
+
+    # Carry on if not returned already
+    X [ X <= 0 ] <- 0.1            # Set all values <≈0 to 0.1
+    log(X)                         # Return the logged X values
+ }
> verboseFunction(-2:2)
[1] -2.3025851 -2.3025851 -2.3025851  0.0000000  0.6931472
```

This provides a clear, readable behavior where results are returned earlier in the function when certain conditions are met.

A Worked Example

So far in this hour, all our examples have been very simple (and, often, rather useless). This has been done to ensure we focus on the basic syntax of R functions, but at this point it is worth exploring a more complete and useful worked example to see the various components discussed in this hour in action.

The following function summarizes a numeric object, calculating a variety of statistics:

```
> summaryFun <- function(vec, digits = 3) {
+   N <- length(vec)                      # Calculate the number of values in "vec"
+   if (N == 0) return(NULL)              # Return NULL if "vec" is empty
+
+   testMissing <- is.na(vec)             # Look for missing values
+   if (all(testMissing)) {
+     output <- c( N = N, nMissing = N, pMissing = 100)
+     return(output)                      # Return simple summary if all missing
                                            values
+   }
+
+   nMiss <- sum(testMissing)             # Calculate the number of missing values
+   pMiss <- 100 * nMiss / N              # Calculate the percentage of missing
values
+   vec <- vec [ !testMissing ]           # Remove missing values from the vector
+   someStats <- c(Mean = mean(vec), Median = median(vec), SD = sd(vec),
+       Min = min(vec), Max = max(vec))   # Calculate a number of statistics
+
+   output <- c(someStats, N = N, nMissing = nMiss, pMissing = pMiss)
+   round(output, digits = digits)
+ }

> summaryFun(c())                         # Empty Vector
NULL
> summaryFun(rep(NA, 10))                  # Vector of missing values
        N nMissing pMissing
       10       10      100
> summaryFun(1:10)                         # Basic numeric vector
    Mean    Median       SD      Min      Max        N nMissing pMissing
   5.500     5.500    3.028    1.000   10.000   10.000    0.000    0.000
> summaryFun(airquality$Ozone)            # Vector containing missings
    Mean    Median       SD      Min      Max        N nMissing pMissing
  42.129    31.500   32.988    1.000  168.000  153.000   37.000   24.183
```

Summary

In this hour, we have covered the basic structure of an R function, and you have seen how to create simple functions of your own. In particular, you saw how to specify the function inputs, define what your functions "do" with those inputs, and how results are returned from your functions. Beyond this, we covered the if/else structure, which allows you to control the overall flow through a function.

In the next hour, we will use the skills you learned here to create more complex functions, including the use of error messaging and the checking of function inputs.

Q&A

Q. Is there a convention for naming functions in R?

A. During the history of R, a number of naming conventions have come and gone. The current convention (which I've followed in this hour) is to use camel-case starting with a lower case letter (e.g. `myFunction`). However, there are no specific rules as to how functions should be named.

Q. How do I load and share my functions?

A. Functions are R objects so, when created, they exist in the workspace of the current session. If you save that workspace and restart in the same working directory, your function (and other) objects should still exist. If you want to share with other users, or reuse your functions in other projects, we can do the following:

> ▶ Save the function definitions as scripts, then open and re-execute them in other sessions.

> ▶ Save your functions together in your own "package," which can be shared and loaded into R (you'll see how to do this in Hour 19, "Package Building").

Q. Can I "globally assign" local objects so they can be seen later?

A. Yes, this can be achieved with the `assign` function. However, this practice is discouraged, and we recommend that any required results are passed back to the user in the manner discussed in this hour.

Q. What is the difference between the `cat` and `print` functions?

A. In this section, we make heavy use of the `cat` function to demonstrate the flow of a function when using if/else statements. The `cat` function simply prints the value of an object without printing the structure of that object. The `print` function also returns the structure of the object. This can be seen with a simple example:

```
> cat("Hello")
Hello
> print("Hello")
[1] "Hello"
```

Q. How do missing values impact "conditions"?

A. If the condition results in a single missing value, then an error is returned:

```
> testMissing <- function(X) {
+    if (X > 0) cat("Success")
+ }
> testMissing(NA)
Error in if (X > 0) cat("Success") :
  missing value where TRUE/FALSE needed
```

If you use the `all` function with a condition that contains any missing values, the result is missing, which will also result in an error (because you do not know if "all" the conditions are met):

```
> allMissings <- rep(NA, 5)    # All missing values
> someMissings <- c(NA, 1:4)   # Some missing values
> all(allMissings > 0)
[1] NA
> all(someMissings > 0)
[1] NA
```

If you use the `any` function with a condition that contains all missing values, the result is a missing value. If, however, you use the `any` function with a vector where not all values are missing, some conditions may be met:

```
> any(allMissings > 0)
[1] NA
> any(someMissings > 0)
[1] TRUE
```

Workshop

The workshop contains quiz questions and exercises to help you solidify your understanding of the material covered. Try to answer all questions before looking at the "Answers" section that follows.

Quiz

1. How do you specify default inputs to a function?

2. What value will be held in the `result1` object when the following code is executed?

```
> qaFun <- function(X) {
+     addOne <- X + 1
+     minusOne <- X - 1
+     addOne
+     minusOne
+ }
> result1 <- qaFun(1)
```

3. What value will be held in the `result2` object when the following code is executed?

```
> qaFun <- function(X) {
+     addOne <- X + 1
+     minusOne <- X - 1
+     c(ADD = addOne, MINUS = minusOne)
+ }
> result2 <- qaFun(1)
```

4. When you specify an if/else statement, what object should the "condition" (that is, the statement within the `if` call) return?

5. What is the difference between `all(X > 0)` and `!all(X > 0)`?

6. What is the difference between `&` and `&&` when used in a condition?

7. What function can you use to return an object early (that is, before the last line of the function)?

Answers

1. You specify default values directly in the input statement with "equals" (for example, `function(x = 1)`).

2. The `result1` object will contain a `0`, because only the last line is returned (the value of `minusOne`, created as `X - 1 = 0`).

3. The `result2` object will contain a vector of length 2, containing the values `2` and `0`. The elements of the vector will be named `ADD` and `MINUS`.

4. The condition should return a single logical value. If multiple logical values are returned, unexpected behaviors can occur.

5. The `all` function returns a `TRUE` value if all the values of `X` are greater than 0 (and non-missing). The `!` prefix in `!all` reverses the logical values, so this would return a `TRUE` if "not all" values of `X` are greater than 0 (that is, at least one is less than or equal to 0).

6. When you use a single `&`, the conditions each side of the `&` are evaluated and the outputs compared to see whether both conditions are met. Therefore, if you have `test1 & test2`, both `test1` and `test2` are evaluated, then they are compared. If instead you use the "control" `&&` (for example, in `test1 && test2`), then the first condition (`test1`) is evaluated, and the second condition (`test2`) is only evaluated if the first condition is `TRUE`.

7. You can use the `return` function to return a result earlier in the function call.

Activities

1. Create a function that accepts two inputs (X and Y) and returns the value of X + Y. Test your function by calling it with X and Y inputs.

2. Update your function so that Y has a default value. Test your function by calling it with only an X input, then try specifying a value for Y.

3. Create a function called `firstLast` that accepts a vector and returns the first and last values. Test your function.

4. Update your `firstLast` function so that, if the vector input only has a single value (that is, it is of length 1), only that single value is returned.

5. Update your `firstLast` function so that, if all values of the vector are less than zero, a message is printed to the user informing him or her of this fact.

6. Update your `firstLast` function so that, if any values of the vector are missing, the first value, last value, and the number of missing values are returned to the user.

HOUR 8
Writing Functions: Part II

What You'll Learn in This Hour:

▶ How to check the appropriateness of function inputs
▶ How to return errors and warnings from a function
▶ How to use function "ellipsis"

In the last hour, you saw how to create a number of simple R functions. This included the definition of function inputs, the creation of the function body, and the management of results back to the user. You also saw how to control the overall "flow" through a function with the if/else structure. This hour will look at a range of advanced function writing topics, such as returning error messaging, checking whether inputs are appropriate to our functions, and the use of function "ellipsis."

Errors and Warnings

On occasion, we may wish to return errors or warnings to the users of our functions. This allows us to inform our users of unexpected behavior and communicate the resulting impact on the execution of the functions (for example, stop processing or continue with some assumption).

First, let's consider a simple function. Here's an example that causes unexpected behavior:

```
> logRange <- function(X) {
+    logX <- log(X)            # Takes logs of X
+    round(range(logX), 2)     # Return (rounded) range of values
+ }
> logRange(1:5)  # Only positive integers
[1] 0.00 1.61
> logRange(-2:2) # Positive and negative integers
[1] NaN NaN
Warning message:
In log(X) : NaNs produced
```

When we execute our `logRange` function with a vector of positive integers, the function executes correctly. However, when we introduce negative integers, the function produces unexpected results: two `NaN` values are returned, and a warning message is produced.

NOTE

Adding the `na.rm` Argument

We could, of course, fix this function by removing missing values (with `is.na`) or calculating the range without missing values (using the `na.rm` argument to `range`). However, we'll instead use error and warning messages to illustrate the behavior of these features.

Error Messages

It could be that we want to return an error message when we find negative integers in the input data and halt the execution of the function. We can achieve this with the `stop` function, which accepts an error message to return:

```
> logRange <- function(X) {
+    stop("Negative Values found!")   # Return an error message
+    logX <- log(X)                   # Takes logs of X
+    round(range(logX), 2)            # Return (rounded) range of values
+ }
> logRange(1:5)  # Only positive integers
Error in logRange(1:5) : Negative Values found!
> logRange(-2:2) # Positive and negative integers
Error in logRange(-2:2) : Negative Values found!
```

In this case, we can see that an error message is returned to the user. However, the error message is returned regardless of whether negative values are found. Let's update our function to return an error only when a particular condition is met, using the `if/else` structure from the last hour:

```
> logRange <- function(X) {
+    if (any(X <= 0))  stop("Negative Values found!")
+    logX <- log(X)                   # Takes logs of X
+    round(range(logX), 2)            # Return (rounded) range of values
+ }
> logRange(1:5)  # Only positive integers
[1] 0.00 1.61
> logRange(-2:2) # Positive and negative integers
Error in logRange(-2:2) : Negative Values found!
```

Now the error message is only returned if there are any values of X less than or equal to 0, and we've provided a (slightly) more informative error message to the user. Note that the function stops executing at this point and no value is returned. This can be further illustrated by introducing an artificial message using `cat`:

```
> logRange <- function(X) {
+   if (any(X <= 0))  stop("Negative Values found!")
+   cat("Made it this far!!\n")
+   logX <- log(X)                    # Takes logs of X
+   round(range(logX), 2)             # Return (rounded) range of values
+ }
> logRange(1:5)  # Only positive integers
Made it this far!!
[1] 0.00 1.61
> logRange(-2:2) # Positive and negative integers
Error in logRange(-2:2) : Negative Values found!
```

Warning Messages

In the last example, we halted the flow of the function under a specific condition (that is, if any negative values exist). We sometimes want to warn the user that something has happened, inform them of how we're going to continue, and then execute the rest of the function. For example, we may want to check for any negative values, and if there are any, we want to do the following:

▶ Remove the negative values.

▶ Inform the user that we're continuing without these values.

We can achieve this using the warning function, which, as with the stop function, accepts a message to display to the user:

```
> logRange <- function(X) {
+   if (any(X <= 0)) {
+     warning("Some values were <= 0. We will remove them")
+     X <- X [ X > 0 ]
+   }
+   logX <- log(X)                    # Takes logs of X
+   round(range(logX), 2)             # Return (rounded) range of values
+ }
> logRange(1:5)  # Only positive integers
[1] 0.00 1.61
> logRange(-2:2) # Positive and negative integers
[1] 0.00 0.69
Warning message:
In logRange(-2:2) : Some values were <= 0. We will remove them
```

Note that, in both instances, the function continues and a result is provided. However, when negative integers are found, the user is warned.

We could extend this further to inform the user of the number of values we have removed:

```
> logRange <- function(X) {
+   lessTest <- X <= 0                  # Test for values <= 0
+   if (any(lessTest)) {
+     nLess <- sum(lessTest)            # How many values
+     outMessage <- paste(nLess, "values were <= 0. We will remove them")
+     warning(outMessage)
+     X <- X [ X > 0 ]
+   }
+   logX <- log(X)                      # Takes logs of X
+   round(range(logX), 2)              # Return (rounded) range of values
+ }
> logRange(1:5)  # Only positive integers
[1] 0.00 1.61
> logRange(-2:2) # Positive and negative integers
[1] 0.00 0.69
Warning message:
In logRange(-2:2) : 3 values were <= 0. We will remove them
```

Of course, if we removed all of the negatives there may not be any left, so perhaps we should mix both the "error" and "warn" approaches:

```
> logRange <- function(X) {
+   lessTest <- X <= 0                                    # Test for values <= 0
+   if (all(lessTest)) stop("All values are <= 0")  # Stop if all <= 0
+   if (any(lessTest)) {
+     nLess <- sum(lessTest)            # How many values
+     outMessage <- paste(nLess, "values were <= 0. We will remove them")
+     warning(outMessage)
+     X <- X [ X > 0 ]
+   }
+   logX <- log(X)                      # Takes logs of X
+   round(range(logX), 2)              # Return (rounded) range of values
+ }
> logRange(1:5)     # Only positive integers
[1] 0.00 1.61
> logRange(-2:2)    # Positive and negative integers
[1] 0.00 0.69
Warning message:
In logRange(-2:2) : 3 values were <= 0. We will remove them
> logRange(-(1:5)) # All negative integers
Error in logRange(-(1:5)) : All values are <= 0
```

Missing Values

We should also consider missing values in the preceding example, but we will leave it at this now.

Checking Inputs

In the last example, we checked whether the values of X were less than or equal to 0, and informed the user of the impact (with either an error or warning message). However, in this case, we are assuming the input to the function is a numeric object. Consider, instead, if we pass a character vector to the logRange function:

```
> logRange <- function(X) {
+    if (any(X <= 0))  stop("Negative Values found!")
+    logX <- log(X)                  # Takes logs of X
+    round(range(logX), 2)           # Return (rounded) range of values
+ }
> logRange(LETTERS)  # A Character vector
Error in log(X) : non-numeric argument to mathematical function
```

Because we often write functions to expect a particular type of data structure, we commonly want to check whether these assumptions hold at the start of the function. To achieve this, R contains a large suite of functions that start with "is.":

```
> apropos("^is\\.") # Show all objects starting with "is."
 [1] "is.array"        "is.atomic"        "is.call"
 [4] "is.character"    "is.complex"       "is.data.frame"
 [7] "is.double"       "is.element"       "is.empty.model"
[10] "is.environment"  "is.expression"    "is.factor"
[13] "is.finite"       "is.function"      "is.infinite"
[16] "is.integer"      "is.language"      "is.leaf"
[19] "is.list"         "is.loaded"        "is.logical"
[22] "is.matrix"       "is.mts"           "is.na"
...
```

The "is." functions take an object and return a TRUE or FALSE value, depending on whether the object matches the mode or class we're testing for. Let's look at some examples:

```
> letters         # The letters vector
 [1] "a" "b" "c" "d" "e" "f" "g" "h" "i" "j" "k" "l" "m" "n" "o"
[16] "p" "q" "r" "s" "t" "u" "v" "w" "x" "y" "z"
> mode(letters)   # It's a character vector
[1] "character"
```

```
> is.vector(letters)    # Is it a vector?
[1] TRUE
> is.character(letters)  # Is it a character?
[1] TRUE
> is.matrix(letters)    # Is it a matrix?
[1] FALSE
> is.numeric(letters)   # Is it numeric?
[1] FALSE
```

We can introduce these functions to check the mode and class of our inputs before continuing:

```
> logRange <- function(X) {
+   if (!is.numeric(X) | !is.vector(X)) stop("Need a numeric vector!")
+   if (any(X <= 0)) stop("Negative Values found!")
+   logX <- log(X)                    # Takes logs of X
+   round(range(logX), 2)            # Return (rounded) range of values
+ }
> logRange(1:10)        # A Numeric vector
[1] 0.0 2.3
> logRange(LETTERS)     # A Character vector
Error in logRange(LETTERS) : Need a numeric vector!
> logRange(airquality) # A Data Frame
Error in logRange(airquality) : Need a numeric vector!
```

NOTE

Converting Objects

In addition to the suite of "is." functions to check our object's mode and class, there is an equivalent suite of "as." functions, which will (attempt to) convert an object from one mode/class to another. Here is an example:

```
> charNums <- c("1.65", "2.03", "9.88", "3.51")  # Create character vector
> charNums
[1] "1.65" "2.03" "9.88" "3.51"
> is.numeric(charNums)                          # Is it numeric?
[1] FALSE
> convertNums <- as.numeric(charNums)           # Convert to numeric
> is.numeric(convertNums)                       # Is it numeric now?
[1] TRUE
> is.matrix(convertNums)                        # Is it a matrix?
[1] FALSE
> matNums <- as.matrix(convertNums)             # Convert to matrix
> is.matrix(matNums)                            # Is it a matrix now?
[1] TRUE
> matNums                                       # Print the matrix
     [,1]
```

```
[1,]  1.65
[2,]  2.03
[3,]  9.88
[4,]  3.51
```

The Ellipsis

As discussed in Hour 6, "Common R Utility Functions," we can use the `args` function to check the inputs to a function. Let's consider two examples: the `runif` function (which creates samples from a Uniform distribution) and the `paste` function (which concatenates strings). First, let's use the `runif` function:

```
> args(runif)                            # Arguments of runif
function (n, min = 0, max = 1)
NULL
> runif(n = 10, min = 1, max = 100)      # Call runif
 [1] 84.95420 51.39096 66.54084 91.43757 88.51552 66.70264 45.44668
 [8] 19.76205 82.41349 36.74277
```

As you can see, we've specified the n, `min`, and `max` inputs to generate some random numbers. Now let's consider an example using the `paste` function:

```
> fruits <- c("apples", "bananas", "pears", "peaches")
> paste("I like", fruits[1])
[1] "I like apples"
> paste("I like", fruits[1], "and", fruits[2])
[1] "I like apples and bananas"
> paste("I like", fruits[1], "and", fruits[2], "and", fruits[3])
[1] "I like apples and bananas and pears"
> paste("I like", fruits[1], "and", fruits[2], "and", fruits[3], "and", fruits[4])
[1] "I like apples and bananas and pears and peaches"
```

You can see that the `paste` function accepts any number of inputs that are simply "pasted" together. Given that we can pass "any number of inputs," what do the arguments of `paste` look like? Let's find out:

```
> args(paste)
function (..., sep = " ", collapse = NULL)
NULL
```

The first argument for `paste` is "...", which is referred to as an "ellipsis." The ellipsis here refers to "one or more inputs," and the help file describes what the function will do with these inputs. In the case of the `paste` function, the inputs are described as follows:

```
...      one or more R objects, to be converted to character vectors.
sep         a character string to separate the terms. Not NA_character_.
collapse    an optional character string to separate the results. Not
⇒NA_character_.
```

Therefore, we can pass "one or more R objects" as the ellipsis.

Using the Ellipsis

We can use the ellipsis in our function definitions by specifying them in the arguments and then specifying where in the function body the inputs should be passed. Consider the following example, which allows the user to generate random samples from one of three different distributions:

```
> genRandoms <- function(N, dist, mean = 0, sd = 1, lambda, min, max) {
+    switch(dist,
+        "norm" = rnorm(N, mean = mean, sd = sd),
+        "pois" = rpois(N, lambda = lambda),
+        "unif" = runif(N, min = min, max = max))
+ }
> genRandoms(10, "norm", mean = 5)
 [1] 4.071533 5.212119 5.610405 6.527552 4.519315 4.333632 4.518676
 [8] 5.242985 3.050987 5.969838
> genRandoms(10, "unif", min = 1, max = 10)
 [1] 2.830932 8.213797 5.294915 1.089826 4.190719 9.482410 2.877680
 [8] 1.398005 9.294324 9.313718
```

Here, we define many arguments that are parameters to the distribution functions (mean, sd, lambda, min, and max) and then pass them directly into function calls with syntax such as mean = mean, sd = sd.

Instead of defining the inputs in this way, we could use the ellipsis, as follows:

```
> genRandoms <- function(N, dist, ...) {
+    switch(dist,
+            "norm" = rnorm(N, ...),
+            "pois" = rpois(N, ...),
+            "unif" = runif(N, ...))
+ }
> genRandoms(10, "norm", mean = 5)
 [1] 4.812319 4.330495 5.369091 4.205875 5.072567 4.029603 5.116522
 [8] 4.163062 6.231766 5.481158
> genRandoms(10, "unif", min = 1, max = 10)
 [1] 2.141485 5.552706 5.114769 2.800839 9.396432 8.006636 3.249285
 [8] 7.320116 4.525931 9.238757
```

Switching Flow

Note the use of the `switch` function in the preceding example. This function allows for a number of alternative flows to be executed, depending on the outcome of an initial expression. See the help file (`?switch`) for more details.

Passing Graphical Parameters Using the Ellipsis

We see many examples of the ellipsis with graphic functions. Consider the `hist` function, which (as you'll see later) produces a simple histogram. The `col` and `main` arguments to the `hist` function control the color of the plot and the main title, respectively. Let's see an example of producing a histogram with 1,000 samples from a Normal distribution. The output is seen in Figure 8.1.

```
> hist(rnorm(1000), main = "Nice Red Histogram", col = "red")
```

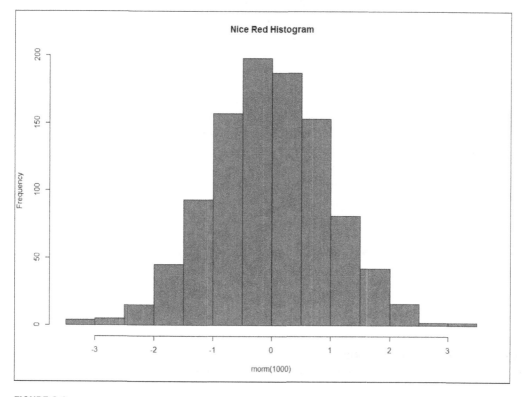

FIGURE 8.1
Histogram of samples from a normal distribution

Graphics

We will cover the use of functions such as `hist` to create graphics in Hour 13, "Graphics," but they are useful to illustrate the ellipsis at this point. As such, in this section, do not worry too much about the uses of graphic functions, but look at the way in which the ellipsis is used.

Now let's see the inputs to the `hist` function using `args`:

```
> args(hist)
function (x, ...)
NULL
```

From the help file, we can see that the `col` and `main` inputs are passed via the ellipsis, and are considered "further arguments and graphical parameters passed to `plot.histogram`."

If we wanted to create a function that draws a specific graphic, we could also use the ellipsis to pass graphical parameters in the same way. Consider the following example, where we define a function `histFun` which creates a histogram and (optionally) adds a vertical line at the median. The output from this function can be seen in Figure 8.2.

```
> histFun <- function(X, addLine = TRUE, col = "lightblue", main = "Histogram") {
+    hist(X, col = col, main = main)
+    if (addLine) abline(v = median(X), lwd = 2)
+ }
> histFun(rnorm(1000), main = "New Title")
```

We could represent many graphic parameters in this way, but we would need to specify them as inputs before our users can control those aspects of the graphic. This is another case where the ellipsis can add value. In this example, we've updated the `histFun` function with the ellipsis, then passed those inputs directly to the call to `hist`. The output from this example can be seen in Figure 8.3.

```
> histFun <- function(X, addLine = TRUE, ...) {
+    hist(X, ...)
+    if (addLine) abline(v = median(X), lwd = 2)
+ }
> histFun(rnorm(1000), col = "plum", xlab = "X AXIS LABEL")
```

Shortened Argument Calling

Earlier you saw that we can shorten the name of the input when calling a function as follows:

```
> aFunction <- function(x, inputWithLongName) {
+    x + inputWithLongName
```

```
+ }
> aFunction(x = 1, i = 2)
[1] 3
```

When there is an ellipsis in the argument definition, we can only use this approach for inputs defined before the ellipsis, as shown here:

```
> aFunction <- function(x, inputWithLongName, ...) {
+    x + inputWithLongName
+ }
> aFunction(x = 1, i = 2)
[1] 3
> aFunction <- function(..., x, inputWithLongName) {
+    x + inputWithLongName
+ }
> aFunction(x = 1, i = 2)
Error in aFunction(x = 1, i = 2) :
  argument "inputWithLongName" is missing, with no default
```

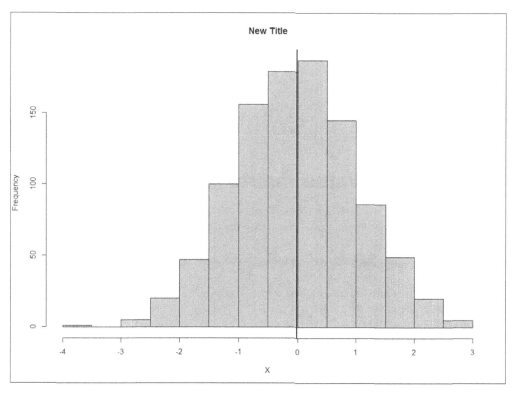

FIGURE 8.2
Output from histFun: a histogram of samples from a normal distribution

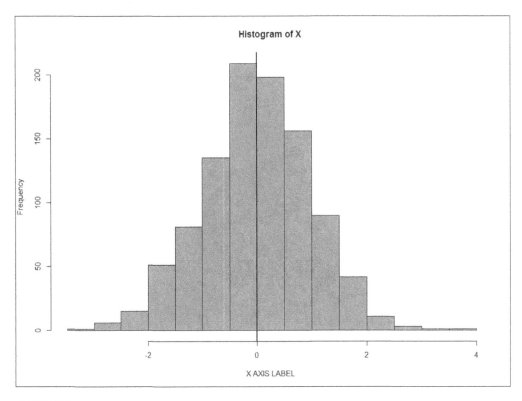

FIGURE 8.3
Plum-colored histogram created with `histFun`

Checking Multivalue Inputs

In the previous section we defined a function called genRandoms that generates random numbers based on three possible distributions. We specify the distribution using the dist argument as follows:

```
> genRandoms <- function(N, dist, ...) {
+    switch(dist,
+          "norm" = rnorm(N, ...),
+          "pois" = rpois(N, ...),
+          "unif" = runif(N, ...))
+ }
> genRandoms(10, "norm", mean = 5)
 [1] 4.152562 4.330108 6.580539 5.708272 5.872492 4.533635 4.295672
 [8] 5.654961 3.838976 4.474047
> genRandoms(10, "Normal", mean = 5)
```

Note that, for the last example, we specified the distribution as "Normal," which isn't an option in the switch function. As such, no tasks are performed—but this isn't very intuitive.

We could improve the messaging to the users by specifying a last, unnamed option to the switch function:

```
> genRandoms <- function(N, dist, ...) {
+    switch(dist,
+          "norm" = rnorm(N, ...),
+          "pois" = rpois(N, ...),
+          "unif" = runif(N, ...),
+          stop(paste0("Distribution \"", dist, "\" not recognized")))
+ }
> genRandoms(10, "norm", mean = 5)
 [1] 3.213303 5.564620 4.029048 6.004051 4.965648 3.395951 5.754919
 [8] 5.019788 5.627128 4.528970
> genRandoms(10, "Normal", mean = 5)
Error in genRandoms(10, "Normal", mean = 5) :
  Distribution "Normal" not recognized
```

This produces an error message stating that the input "Normal" is not recognized. Alternatively, we could use the match.arg function, which provides a neat mechanism for checking that an input is one of a list of "valid" inputs. The simplest way to use match.arg is to place a value in a first argument to be matched against a vector of possible values as the second argument:

```
> match.arg("norm", choices = c("norm", "pois", "unif"))
[1] "norm"
> match.arg("NORM", choices = c("norm", "pois", "unif"))
Error in match.arg("NORM", choices = c("norm", "pois", "unif")) :
  'arg' should be one of "norm", "pois", "unif"
```

We could include this approach to check whether an input is valid:

```
> genRandoms <- function(N, dist, ...) {
+    dist <- match.arg(dist, choices = c("norm", "pois", "unif"))  # Check dist
+    switch(dist,
+          "norm" = rnorm(N, ...),
+          "pois" = rpois(N, ...),
+          "unif" = runif(N, ...))
+ }
> genRandoms(10, "norm", mean = 5)
 [1] 4.503535 4.971087 3.758512 4.580493 6.297477 2.688116 5.637076
 [8] 4.921771 4.408372 4.484797
> genRandoms(10, "Normal", mean = 5)
Error in match.arg(dist, choices = c("norm", "pois", "unif")) :
  'arg' should be one of "norm", "pois", "unif"
```

We can alternatively use match.arg in "one-argument form," which matches our input against choices set in the argument statement:

```
> genRandoms <- function(N, dist = c("norm", "pois", "unif"), ...) {
+    dist <- match.arg(dist)   # Check validity if "dist" input
+    switch(dist,
+           "norm" = rnorm(N, ...),
+           "pois" = rpois(N, ...),
+           "unif" = runif(N, ...))
+ }
> genRandoms(10, "norm", mean = 5)
 [1] 6.243477 4.173172 6.449329 3.768405 5.283295 4.849446 5.190646
 [8] 4.464281 6.497654 3.584767
> genRandoms(10, "Normal", mean = 5)
Error in match.arg(dist) : 'arg' should be one of "norm", "pois", "unif"
```

TIP

Getting a Function

If we wanted to, we could write this function more concisely using the get function, which returns a function, given its name as a character string. Therefore, the function could be rewritten as follows:

```
> genRandoms <- function(N, dist = c("norm", "pois", "unif"), ...) {
+    dist <- match.arg(dist)              # Check validity if "dist" input
+    randFun <- get(paste0("r", dist))    # Get the function
+    randFun(N, ...)                      # Run the function
+ }
> genRandoms(10, "norm", mean = 5)
 [1] 5.698743 5.463239 6.596608 4.385926 5.288524 6.200866 5.537720
 [8] 3.854999 4.781841 5.588260
> genRandoms(10, "pois", lambda = 3)
 [1] 5 3 1 1 2 2 3 2 2 1
```

Using Input Definition

Consider the following code, which plots two variables as a scatter plot. The output can be seen in Figure 8.4.

```
> Day <- 1:7
> Sales <- c(100, 120, 150, 130, 160, 210, 120)
> plot(Day, Sales, type = "o")
```

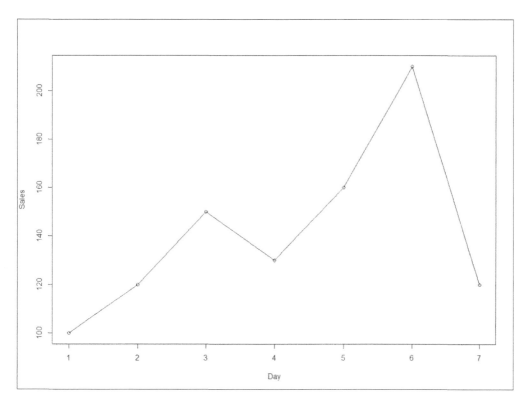

FIGURE 8.4
Simple line plot of Sales versus Day

Note that the X axis is labeled "Day" and the Y axis is labeled "Sales." This occurs because R is able to access the argument definitions and use them as the labels. This can be further illustrated using a modified example, the result of which can be seen in Figure 8.5.

```
> plot(Day - 1, log(Sales), type = "o")
```

As you can see, the labels reflect the modified inputs. This ability to capture not just the input values but also the definition that was used can be very useful. Consider, for example, if we create a function based on this plot, and use it to create a graph of our Sales data, shown in Figure 8.6.

```
> nicePlot <- function(X, Y) {
+    plot(X, Y, type = "o")
+ }
> nicePlot(Day, Sales)
```

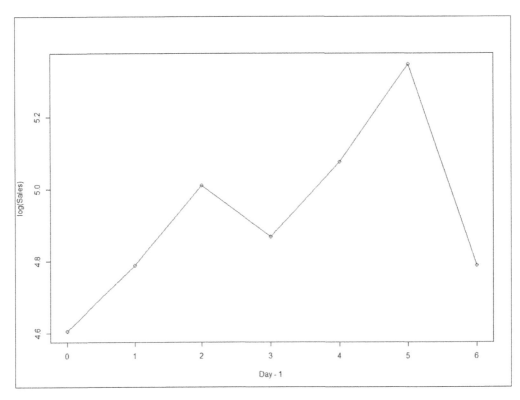

FIGURE 8.5
Simple line plot of log(Sales) versus "Day − 1"

In this example, the `plot` function uses the calling inputs X and Y for the axes. What if we instead want to capture the input definitions (Day and Sales) and use those for the axis labels?

To do this we use two functions together: `substitute` and `deparse`. The `substitute` function performs the action of capturing the definition, and the `deparse` function then converts this to characters:

```
> x <- 1 + 2                          # Add 2 numbers
> substitute(x <- 1 + 2)              # Capture the call
x <- 1 + 2
> deparse(substitute(x <- 1 + 2))     # Convert this to character
[1] "x <- 1 + 2"
```

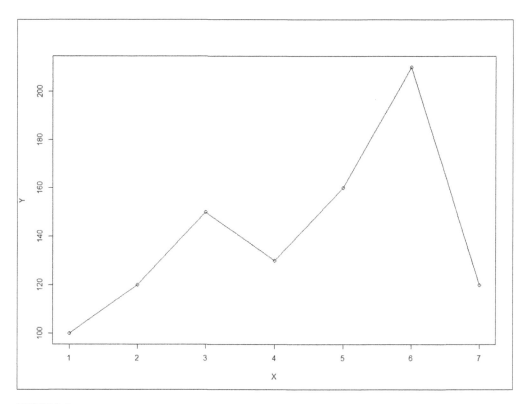

FIGURE 8.6
Simple line plot of Y versus X

We can use this approach to capture the inputs to our functions, then use the inputs to provide better labels to our plots. An example of this can be seen here, with the output seen in Figure 8.7.

```
> nicePlot <- function(X, Y) {
+    xLab <- deparse(substitute(X))    # Capture X input
+    yLab <- deparse(substitute(Y))    # Capture Y input
+    plot(X, Y, type = "o", xlab = xLab, ylab = yLab)
+ }
> nicePlot(Day, Sales)
```

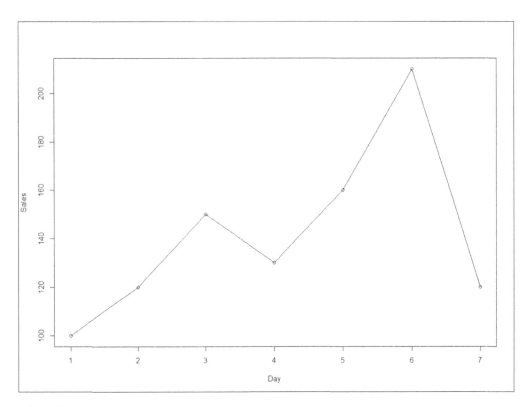

FIGURE 8.7
Simple line plot of Sales versus Day, with correct axis labels

Summary

In this hour, we looked at some more approaches that can enrich our R functions. In particular, we focused on ways in which we can check the inputs to a function, providing feedback to the function user if the inputs are not appropriate. In the next hour, we'll look at how to perform tasks in a repetitive manner using loop structures, and how to extend into frameworks that allow us to apply functions to structures in more complex ways.

Q&A

Q. Is it possible to simplify the error messages by removing the "call"?

A. By default, the call made is included in the error message. See the inclusion of "in logFun(-2:2)" in the following error message:

```
> logFun <- function(X) stop("Your Error Message here!")
> logFun(-2:2)
Error in logFun(-2:2) : Your Error Message here!
```

You can remove the call itself from the error using the `call.` argument, which accepts a single logical value. (Note the period character in this argument name!) This argument can be used in both `stop` and `warning` functions.

```
> logFun <- function(X) stop("Your Error Message here!", call.=F)
> logFun(-2:2)
Error: Your Error Message here!
```

Q. What is the "environment" tag I see when I print out (some) functions?

A. Every function (with the exception of low-level "primitive" functions) has an "environment," which is the active environment when the function was created.

Q. When is a warning message printed?

A. By default, a warning message is printed after a function completes; therefore, warnings are collated on the last line(s) of output:

```
> addFun <- function(x, y) {
+   warning("This is a warning!")
+   x + y
+ }
> addFun(1, 2)
[1] 3
Warning message:
In addFun(1, 2) : This is a warning!
```

We could, instead, issue warnings immediately using the `immediate.` argument to `warning`:

```
> addFun <- function(x, y) {
+   warning("This is a warning!", immediate. = T)
+   x + y
+ }
> addFun(1, 2)
Warning in addFun(1, 2) : This is a warning!
[1] 3
```

For more control over the behavior of warning messages, see the details for the `warn` option in the `getOption` function help file.

Q. Can the ellipsis be used in multiple places within the function body?

A. Yes, although care has to be taken to ensure the inputs in the ellipsis are applicable to all the functions we pass the ellipsis to.

Q. Can I capture the inputs contained in the ellipsis?

A. Yes, you can directly capture the input values using a line such as `X <- list(...)` and then process them in any manner you wish. Here's an example:

```
> getDots <- function(...) {
+    list(...)
+ }
> getDots(1, 2)
[[1]]
[1] 1

[[2]]
[1] 2

> getDots(x = 1, y = 2)
$x
[1] 1

$y
[1] 2
```

Workshop

The workshop contains quiz questions and exercises to help you solidify your understanding of the material covered. Try to answer all questions before looking at the "Answers" section that follows.

Quiz

1. What's the difference between `stop` and `warning`?

2. How would you check whether an input to a function is a character matrix?

3. What is the difference between `is.data.frame` and `as.data.frame`?

4. How many dots make up the ellipsis?

5. What are the two ways you've seen for using `match.arg`?

6. What do the `deparse` and `substitute` functions do?

Answers

1. The `stop` and `warning` functions both issue messages to the user. The primary difference is that the `stop` function causes the execution of the function to halt, whereas the `warning` function continues to execute after a warning is reported—unless controlled explicitly with `getOption("warn")`.

2. You can use `is.character` & `is.matrix` as a condition.

3. The `is.data.frame` function takes an object and returns a `TRUE` value if the object is a data frame. The `as.data.frame` function takes an object and attempts to convert to a data frame.

4. The ellipsis is represented by exactly three dots.

5. You can call `match.arg` with the input as the first argument and a vector of possible "choices" as the second argument. Alternatively, you can use `match.arg` in one-argument mode, where you pass only an input to the function with the "choices" defined in the input definition. Here's an example:

```
> genRandoms <- function(N, dist = c("norm", "pois", "unif"), ...) {
+    dist <- match.arg(dist)  # Check validity if "dist" input
+    dist
+ }
```

6. The `substitute` function returns the call that was made to create an input. The `deparse` function converts the output from `substitute` to character format. By using them together, you can access the call made to define an argument in a suitable (character) format:

```
> theCall <- function(x) {
+    deparse(substitute(x))
+ }
> theCall(x = mean(Sales))
[1] "mean(Sales)"
```

Activities

1. Create a function that accepts a vector input, `x`, and returns the mean and median of `x`.

2. Update your function so that a warning is issued if any missing values exist in `x`.

3. Update your function so that an error is returned if all values of `x` are missing.

4. Update your function to ensure that `x` is, actually, a numeric vector, and return an error if not.

5. Add an argument to your function called `funs`, and ensure the input is either `mean`, `median`, `sd`, `min`, or `max`. When called, the selected function defined in `funs` should be used to summarize `x`.

6. Look at the `several.ok` argument to `match.arg`. Update your function so that multiple summaries (that is, multiple values of `funs`) are returned from the function.

7. Update your function so the input definition of `x` (that is, the call used to define the `x` input) is printed (via a called to `cat`) before the summaries are returned.

HOUR 9
Loops and Summaries

What You'll Learn in This Hour:

▶ How to perform iterative "looping" techniques in R

▶ How to apply functions to complex data structures

▶ How to calculate metrics "by" one or more variables

Throughout this book you have seen how to use, and even create, simple R functions. In this hour, we are going to use simple functions and code in a more "applied" fashion. This allows us to perform tasks repeatedly over sections of our data without the need to produce verbose, repetitive code.

Repetitive Tasks

Imagine we want to perform the same task multiple times—for example, on each row of some dataset, df. We might first create a simple function, performAction, and then write a verbose R script such as this:

```
> performAction(df[1,])   # Perform action on first row
> performAction(df[2,])   # Perform action on second row
> performAction(df[3,])   # Perform action on third row
> performAction(df[4,])   # Perform action on fourth row
...
```

Writing code in this way can lead to large scripts that can be very difficult to manage; for example, if you need to change the name of the function, you need to do it in a variety of places. This code is also not overtly reusable because we'll need to specify a call for each row in our data—if we try to apply this code to a different data structure, it may not have the same number of rows.

Instead of writing scripts in this manner, we can use a "loop."

What Is a Loop?

A *loop* is a programming structure that allows us to perform the same task in a repetitive manner. Two types of loops are supported by R: the "for" loop and the "while" loop.

What Is a For Loop?

A "for" loop will perform the same action on each of a pre-specified set of inputs. For example, imagine we have a bag containing 100 potato chips and we have decided we're going to eat every one. In this case, our "for" loop may be structured as follows:

```
For each of our 100 chips:
    Reach into the bag
    Remove a single potato chip
    Eat the potato chip
```

This is a simple repetitive pattern. However, we do need to pre-specify the inputs over which we're going to iterate. For example, if we didn't know exactly how many potato chips were in the bag, we cannot use this approach.

What Is a While Loop?

By contrast, a "while" loop allows us to perform the same action in a repeated manner until a condition is met. For example, if we had a bag of potato chips and we wanted to eat the contents, we may write a "while" loop as follows:

```
While there are still chips left in the bag:
    Reach into the bag
    Remove a single potato chip
    Eat the potato chip
```

Again, this is a simple structure and will work well in our case. However, we need to be sure no one hands us a bag with an infinite number of potato chips, in which case we'll never "leave" the loop and just keep on eating.

The `for` Function

The `for` function in R allows us to implement a "for" loop. The structure of the loop is as follows:

```
for (variable in set_of_values) {
  # do this
}
```

The `variable` defined will iteratively take each value of the `set_of_values`, and the body of the "for" loop will then be executed. Here's an example:

```
> for (i in 1:5) {
```

```
+    cat("\n Hello")  # Say Hello
+ }

 Hello
 Hello
 Hello
 Hello
 Hello
```

In this very simple example, i is iteratively set to each value in vector 1:5 and then the body of the loop is executed—the result is to print the message "Hello" five times.

NOTE
_____

Using Curly Brackets

In this example, we are using curly brackets to encapsulate the body of code. As with writing functions, we can omit these if the body of code is a single line; therefore, this example could be rewritten as follows:

```
> for (i in 1:10) cat("\n Hello")  # Say Hello
```

As a convention, and as good practice, we will use curly brackets throughout this hour.
_____

Using the Loop Variable

In the last example, we set i to each value in vector 1:5. If we use i in the body of the loop, we can more easily see this process:

```
> for (i in 1:5) {
+    cat("\n i has been set to the value of", i)
+ }

 i has been set to the value of 1
 i has been set to the value of 2
 i has been set to the value of 3
 i has been set to the value of 4
 i has been set to the value of 5
```

Let's look at a slightly different example, this time involving a set of character values over which to iterate:

```
> for (let in LETTERS[1:5]) {
+    cat("\n The Letter", let)
+ }

 The Letter A
 The Letter B
```

```
The Letter C
The Letter D
The Letter E
```

Referencing Data with Loops

For loops are often used to iterate over data sources, performing actions on groupings within that data. Let's use the internal `airquality` dataset for this example, which contains air quality measurements for New York from May to September 1973:

```
> head(airquality)
  Ozone Solar.R Wind Temp Month Day
1    41     190  7.4   67     5   1
2    36     118  8.0   72     5   2
3    12     149 12.6   74     5   3
4    18     313 11.5   62     5   4
5    NA      NA 14.3   56     5   5
6    28      NA 14.9   66     5   6
```

The `Month` column stores the month number (May = 5 to September = 9). We can generate a vector of unique month values using the `unique` function as follows:

```
> unique(airquality$Month)
[1] 5 6 7 8 9
```

What if we wanted to report the average `Ozone` value for each month? Without a loop, we might write code like this:

```
> # Perform summary for Month 5
> ozoneValues <- airquality$Ozone [ airquality$Month == 5 ] # Subset the data
> theMean <- round(mean(ozoneValues, na.rm = TRUE), 2)      # Calculate the mean
> cat("\n Average Ozone for month 5 =", theMean)            # Print the message

 Average Ozone for month 5 = 23.62
>
> # Perform summary for Month 6
> ozoneValues <- airquality$Ozone [ airquality$Month == 6 ] # Subset the data
> theMean <- round(mean(ozoneValues, na.rm = TRUE), 2)      # Calculate the mean
> cat("\n Average Ozone for month 6 =", theMean)            # Print the message

 Average Ozone for month 6 = 29.44
>
> # Perform summary for Month 7
> ozoneValues <- airquality$Ozone [ airquality$Month == 7 ] # Subset the data
> theMean <- round(mean(ozoneValues, na.rm = TRUE), 2)      # Calculate the mean
> cat("\n Average Ozone for month 7 =", theMean)            # Print the message

 Average Ozone for month 7 = 59.12
```

Note that the only varying aspect between these sections of code is the Month value itself. Using a for loop, we could iterate over each (unique) month value, calculating summaries specific to that month, as follows:

```
> for (M in unique(airquality$Month)) {
+    ozoneValues <- airquality$Ozone [ airquality$Month == M ] # Subset the data
+    theMean <- round(mean(ozoneValues, na.rm = TRUE), 2)       # Calculate and round
                                                                   the mean
+    cat("\n Average Ozone for month", M, "=", theMean)        # Print the message
+ }

 Average Ozone for month 5 = 23.62
 Average Ozone for month 6 = 29.44
 Average Ozone for month 7 = 59.12
 Average Ozone for month 8 = 59.96
 Average Ozone for month 9 = 31.45
```

In this example, we are iterating over the unique values of Month. We use the iterator variable M to subset the data, saving the result each time as ozoneValues. We then calculate the mean based on this vector and report the result.

Nested Loops

It is possible to perform "nested" loop operations, where we iterate over more than one set of values. For example, let's again loop through sections of the airquality dataset, but this time report the average values of the Ozone, Wind, and Solar.R columns. We could extend the last loop as follows:

```
> for (M in unique(airquality$Month)) {
+
+    cat("\n\n Month =", M, "\n =========")              # Write Month Number
+    subData <- airquality [ airquality$Month == M, ]    # Subset the data
+
+    theMean <- round(mean(subData$Ozone, na.rm = TRUE), 2)     # Calculate the mean
+    cat("\n   Average Ozone =\t", theMean)                     # Print the message
+
+    theMean <- round(mean(subData$Wind, na.rm = TRUE), 2)      # Calculate the mean
+    cat("\n   Average Wind =\t", theMean)                      # Print the message
+
+    theMean <- round(mean(subData$Solar.R, na.rm = TRUE), 2)   # Calculate the mean
+    cat("\n   Average Solar.R =\t", theMean)                   # Print the message
+
+ }
```

```
Month = 5
=========
  Average Ozone =        23.62
  Average Wind =         11.62
  Average Solar.R =      181.3

Month = 6
=========
  Average Ozone =        29.44
  Average Wind =         10.27
  Average Solar.R =      190.17

Month = 7
=========
  Average Ozone =        59.12
  Average Wind =          8.94
  Average Solar.R =      216.48

Month = 8
=========
  Average Ozone =        59.96
  Average Wind =          8.79
  Average Solar.R =      171.86

Month = 9
=========
  Average Ozone =        31.45
  Average Wind =         10.18
  Average Solar.R =      167.43
```

TIP

Tab Characters

Note the use \t in the preceding example. This allows us to insert a "tab" symbol when printing text in this way. For this example, it left-aligns the numeric mean values produced. If we wanted to (more correctly) right-align these numeric values, we could additionally call the format function to convert the numeric values to a nicely formatted character output.

We could instead iterate over values of Month and then iterate over the columns within Month using a nested loop, as follows:

```
> for (M in unique(airquality$Month)) {
+
+    cat("\n\n Month =", M, "\n =========")          # Write Month Number
+    subData <- airquality [ airquality$Month == M, ] # Subset the data
+
```

```
+    for (column in c("Ozone", "Wind", "Solar.R")) {        # Iterate over columns
+        theMean <- round(mean(subData[[column]], na.rm = TRUE), 2)   # Calculate the
                                                                        mean
+        cat("\n  Average", column, "=\t", theMean          # Print the message
+    }
+
+ }


Month = 5
=========
  Average Ozone =          23.62
  Average Wind =    11.62
  Average Solar.R =        181.3

Month = 6
=========
  Average Ozone =          29.44
  Average Wind =    10.27
  Average Solar.R =        190.17

Month = 7
=========
  Average Ozone =          59.12
  Average Wind =    8.94
  Average Solar.R =        216.48

Month = 8
=========
  Average Ozone =          59.96
  Average Wind =    8.79
  Average Solar.R =        171.86

Month = 9
=========
  Average Ozone =          31.45
  Average Wind =    10.18
  Average Solar.R =        167.43
```

NOTE

Referencing Columns

Note that we used the double square brackets notation here as opposed to the $ syntax in the more verbose example. This is because we can't parameterize values used by $, as shown in this example:

```
> airquality$Wind[1:5]    # The Wind column
```

```
[1]   7.4  8.0 12.6 11.5 14.3
> airquality$"Wind"[1:5]  # Also works
[1]   7.4  8.0 12.6 11.5 14.3
> whichColumn <- "Wind"   # set value of whichColumn
> airquality$whichColumn  # Reference using whichColumn
NULL
```

We must therefore use a double square bracket notation (or alternatively the [, whichColumn] notation) that was introduced in Hour 4, "Multi-Mode Data Structures".

NOTE

Loop Performance

Later, in Hour 18, "Code Efficiency," we will look again at loops and discuss performance and efficiency gains.

Looping through data frames in this way is generally not recommended. As we will see shortly, and again in Hour 12, "Efficient Data Handling in R," there are many simpler, faster ways to loop through columns or rows in a data frame. However the concept of a for loop is a much more widely applicable programming concept that can help clean up repetitive, unmaintainable code.

The while **Function**

The while function in R allows us to implement a "while" loop. The structure of the "while" loop is as follows:

```
while (condition) {
  # do this
}
```

The result is that the loop will iterate constantly until the condition is no longer TRUE. Of course, if the condition is always TRUE, the loop will never stop iterating, so we need to exercise caution.

Let's look at a simple example:

```
> index <- 1             # Set value of index to 1
> while(index < 6) {
+    cat("\n Hello")      # Write a message
+    index <- index + 1   # Update the value of index
+ }
```

```
Hello
Hello
Hello
Hello
Hello
```

Here, we initially set the value of index to 1. Then, we iteratively write a simple message and increment index. The loop continues to iterate until the condition (index < 6) is no longer true.

We can see this more clearly by improving the message produced:

```
> index <- 1                                      # Set value of index to 1
> while(index < 6) {
+    cat("\n Setting the value of index from", index)   # Write a message
+    index <- index + 1                           # Update the value of index
+    cat(" to", index)                            # Write a message
+ }

 Setting the value of index from 1 to 2
 Setting the value of index from 2 to 3
 Setting the value of index from 3 to 4
 Setting the value of index from 4 to 5
 Setting the value of index from 5 to 6
```

The "apply" Family of Functions

The majority of functions in R are relatively simple and designed to work with single-mode structures. Consider, for example, the median function, which can be used to calculate the median of a numeric data object (typically a vector). Let's have a look at the arguments of the function and a simple example:

```
> args(median)
function (x, na.rm = FALSE)
NULL
> median( airquality$Wind )   # Median of Wind column
[1] 9.7
```

We can see that median has two arguments (x and na.rm), which can be used to specify the values for which the median is to be calculated, and a logical value specifying whether missing values should be removed before calculating the median.

What if we wanted to apply this function in a more sophisticated way? Here are some examples:

▶ The median of rows or columns of a matrix

▶ The median of each element of a list

▶ The median of some variable for each level of one or more grouping variables (for example, median sales by age group)

As you have seen earlier in this hour, the loop structure provides a way to iteratively call a function (for example, on subsections of a data object). Although we could apply a function using loops, much of our code would be needed just to reference the subsections of the data we need given the values over which we're iterating (as you saw previously).

Instead, R provides a set of functions (the "apply" family of functions) that offer a more natural structure for applying simple functions to data structures in a more sophisticated way.

The Set of "apply" Functions

In R, many functions could be considered part of the "apply" family of functions. Let's start by looking at the set of functions in R of the form "*x*apply," where *x* is an optional letter, using the apropos function:

```
> apropos("^[a-z]?apply$") # Find all objects ending in "apply"
[1] "apply"  "eapply" "lapply" "mapply" "rapply"
[6] "sapply" "tapply" "vapply"
```

NOTE

Other Functions in the "apply" Family

We could conceivably include functions such as by and aggregate in the "apply" family given their aims and usage. We'll cover aggregate in Hour 11, "Data Manipulation and Transformation," but will not cover by in this book given the numerous better ways of performing the tasks by enables.

TIP

Regular Expressions

As seen in the apropos call, the regular expression capabilities of R are very useful for looking for patterns in vectors of characters.

The call to apropos returns eight functions, which are listed in Table 9.1.

TABLE 9.1 Set of "apply" Functions

Function	Usage
apply	Applies functions over dimensions of an array
lapply	Applies functions over elements of a list or vector

Function	Usage
sapply	Applies functions over elements of a list or vector, then simplifies the output
tapply	Applies functions to a vector for each level of one or more factors
mapply	Multivariate version of sapply
rapply	Recursive version of lapply
eapply	Applies functions over named elements of an "environment"
vapply	Similar to sapply with a pre-specified type of return value

For now, let's focus on the first four functions listed in Table 9.1 (apply, lapply, sapply and tapply).

The apply Function

The apply function allows us to apply a function over dimensions of a data object. Acceptable inputs to apply include any object that has a "dimension"—for example, matrices, data frames, and arrays. The arguments to the apply function are as follows:

```
> args(apply)
function (X, MARGIN, FUN, ...)
NULL
```

Table 9.2 details the arguments of the apply function.

TABLE 9.2 Arguments to the apply Function

Argument	Description
X	A data object with dimensions to which we will apply the functions
MARGIN	The "Margin" over which to apply the function (see next)
FUN	The function to apply
. . .	Other arguments to the function

The "Margin"

The second argument, the "Margin," specifies the "dimension number" over which to apply the function, as described in Table 9.3.

TABLE 9.3 Margin Values

Margin	Description
1	Rows of a structure
2	Columns of a structure
3	Third dimension (if our structure has at least three dimensions)
4	Fourth dimension (if our structure has at least four dimensions)
...	...

We typically specify the margin as a single integer value or vector of integer values.

NOTE

Named Dimensions

If your structure has dimension names assigned, a character vector can be provided instead of the (more commonly used) vector of integers.

A Simple `apply` Example

The `apply` function is best described with a simple example. First, let's create a structure that has dimensions:

```
> myMat <- matrix(rpois(20, 3), nrow = 4)   # Create a simple matrix
> myMat                                      # Print myMat
     [,1] [,2] [,3] [,4] [,5]
[1,]    5    6    4    2    2
[2,]    1    7    3    1    6
[3,]    2    3    0    3    4
[4,]    2    2    4    3    4
> dim(myMat)                                 # Dimensions of myMat
[1] 4 5
```

Now let's use our first call to `apply`. In this example, we'll calculate the maximum of each column (dimension 2) of our matrix:

```
> apply(myMat, 2, max)    # Column Maxima
[1] 5 7 4 3 6
```

The result is a vector that holds the maximum of each column (for example, we see that the maximum of the values in the second column is 7).

NOTE

The Use of Random Numbers

In this and the following sections I use functions such as `rpois` to generate random samples. Since these are random draws, they will not necessarily match your results if you run the same code.

The `apply` function operates by "breaking apart" the structure based on the margin(s) provided and then applying the function to each "piece" of the partitioned structure. In this example, the matrix is split into separate columns with the `max` function applied to each column, as illustrated in Figure 9.1.

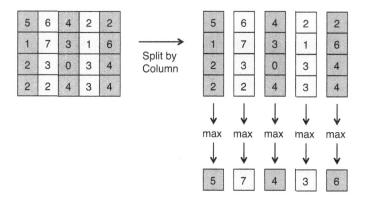

FIGURE 9.1
A visual demonstration of the `apply` function calculating column maxima

Now let's look at another simple example—this time we'll calculate the minimum of each row (dimension 1) of our matrix:

```
> apply(myMat, 1, min)    # Row Minima
[1] 2 1 0 2
```

Again, the result is a vector, this time containing the minimum of each row of the matrix (so the minimum value in row 3 is 0). This time, the `apply` function "breaks apart" the structure by rows and applies the `min` function to each "piece" of the structure, as illustrated in Figure 9.2.

Using Multiple Margins

In these simple examples, we specified a single margin in each call (1 for rows or 2 for columns). We can, instead, use multiple margins, as shown here:

```
> myMat
     [,1] [,2] [,3] [,4] [,5]
[1,]    5    6    4    2    2
```

```
[2,]    1    7    3    1    6
[3,]    2    3    0    3    4
[4,]    2    2    4    3    4

> apply(myMat, c(1, 2), median)    # Median by row AND column
       [,1] [,2] [,3] [,4] [,5]
[1,]    5    6    4    2    2
[2,]    1    7    3    1    6
[3,]    2    3    0    3    4
[4,]    2    2    4    3    4
```

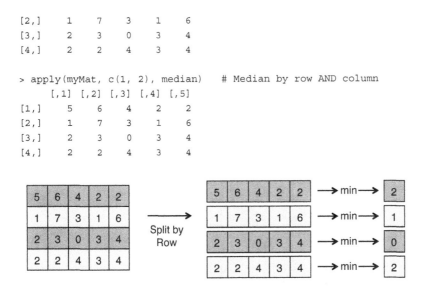

FIGURE 9.2
A visual demonstration of the `apply` function calculating row minima

In this example, we've calculated the median value by row and column by specifying two values for the margin (1 and 2). This calculates the median of each cell of the matrix (that is, the median of "5" is "5") and thus returns exactly the same matrix that we started with. This process is visualized in Figure 9.3.

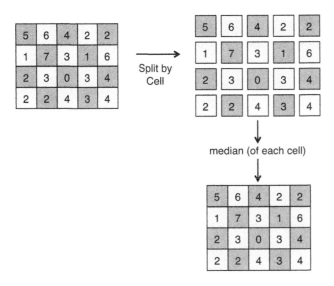

FIGURE 9.3
A visual demonstration of the `apply` function performing cell calculations

Although this is not of any practical use, it does further illustrate the way the `apply` function works.

Using `apply` with Higher Dimension Structures

Although using multiple margins may not be useful for two-dimensional structures (that is, matrices or data frames), when we deal with structures with a higher number of dimensions it can be useful. To illustrate this, let's create a three-dimensional array:

```
> myArray <- array( rpois(18, 3), dim = c(3, 3, 2)) # Create array
> myArray                                            # Print myArray
, , 1

     [,1] [,2] [,3]
[1,]    2    2    4
[2,]    4    3    1
[3,]    4    1    1

, , 2

     [,1] [,2] [,3]
[1,]    0    6    3
[2,]    4    3    1
[3,]    1    5    1

> dim(myArray)                                       # Dimensions of myArray
[1] 3 3 2
```

Now, there are three dimensions over which we could apply our functions. Let's try to apply a function over dimension 3 of the array:

```
> apply(myArray, 3, min)
[1] 1 0
```

Here, the array is first broken apart based on dimension 3, resulting in 2×2-dimensional structures. The `min` function is then applied to each of the two structures, as illustrated in Figure 9.4.

Instead, we could provide multiple margins. For example, let's apply the `max` function, this time over dimensions 1 and 2:

```
> apply(myArray, c(1, 2), max)
     [,1] [,2] [,3]
[1,]    2    6    4
[2,]    4    3    1
[3,]    4    5    1
```

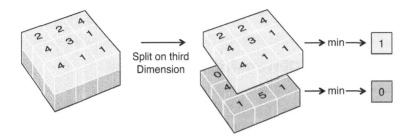

FIGURE 9.4
The `apply` function operating over the third dimension of an array

This time the structure is "collapsed" over the third dimension, producing a matrix of outputs. This process is illustrated in the Figure 9.5.

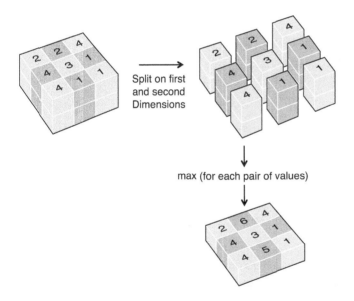

FIGURE 9.5
The `apply` function operating over the first and second dimensions of an array

Passing Extra Arguments to the "applied" Function

Let's return to our matrix example, but this time insert a missing value:

```
> myMat[2, 2] <- NA    # Add a missing value in cell 2, 2
> myMat                # Print the matrix
    [,1] [,2] [,3] [,4] [,5]
```

```
[1,]    5    6    4    2    2
[2,]    1   NA    3    1    6
[3,]    2    3    0    3    4
[4,]    2    2    4    3    4
```

Now, let's once again apply a function. For example, let's calculate the maximum of each column (dimension 2) of the matrix:

```
> apply(myMat, 2, max)   # Maximum of each column
[1]   5 NA  4  3  6
```

This time, our output contains a missing value. The reason for this is that when the second column is passed into the max function, the missing value causes the max function to return an NA value. This is illustrated in Figure 9.6.

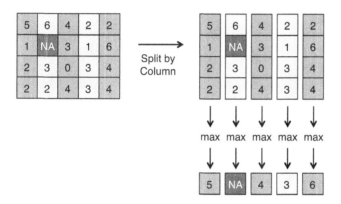

FIGURE 9.6
The use of apply with missing values

We can also see this behavior directly by calculating the maximum of the second column:

```
> max(myMat[,2])   # Maximum of 2nd column
[1] NA
```

As you saw earlier, functions such as max have a na.rm argument, which allows us to specify that missing values are removed before performing the calculation:

```
> max(myMat[,2], na.rm = TRUE)   # Maximum of 2nd column
[1] 6
```

If we want to call a function but also pass additional arguments, we can take advantage of the ellipsis argument to apply, as follows:

```
> args(apply)                          # Ellipsis is 4th argument
function (X, MARGIN, FUN, ...)
NULL
> apply(myMat, 2, max, na.rm = TRUE)    # Maximum of each column
[1] 5 6 4 3 6
```

As you can see, the max function is now called with the argument na.rm set to TRUE, so the maximum of the (nonmissing) values of column 2 is now reported.

We can pass as many additional arguments as we need. For example, let's calculate the quantiles of a slightly larger matrix using the quantile function:

```
> biggerMat <- matrix( rpois(300, 3), ncol = 3)    # Create a 100 x 3 matrix

> head(biggerMat)                                  # First few rows
     [,1] [,2] [,3]
[1,]    4    2    3
[2,]    5    3    5
[3,]    4    7    1
[4,]    5    3    3
[5,]    3    3    4
[6,]    1    5    4

> apply(biggerMat, 2, quantile)                    # Column quantiles
     [,1] [,2] [,3]
0%      0    0    0
25%     2    2    2
50%     3    3    3
75%     4    4    4
100%    8    8    8
```

Now, let's artificially add a number of missing values; therefore, we need to pass the extra na.rm argument to quantile:

```
> biggerMat [ sample( 1:300, 50) ] <- NA            # Randomly add some missings

> head(biggerMat)                                   # First few rows
     [,1] [,2] [,3]
[1,]    4    2   NA
[2,]    5    3   NA
[3,]    4    7    1
[4,]    5    3    3
[5,]   NA   NA    4
[6,]    1   NA    4

> apply(biggerMat, 2, quantile, na.rm = TRUE)       # Column quantiles
     [,1] [,2] [,3]
0%      0    0    0
```

```
25%     2    2    1
50%     3    3    3
75%     4    4    4
100%    8    8    8
```

The quantile function has an argument, probs, that allows us to specify that a different set of quantiles are returned. Let's additionally pass the probs argument to specify some new quantiles:

```
> apply(biggerMat, 2, quantile,
+    probs = c(0, .05, .5, .95, 1), na.rm = TRUE)      # Column quantiles
      [,1] [,2] [,3]
0%       0 0.00    0
5%       0 1.00    1
50%      3 3.00    3
95%      6 6.15    6
100%     8 8.00    8
```

Using apply with Our Own Functions

So far in this hour, we have used simple functions to illustrate the use of the apply function (for example, row minima, column maxima). There are in fact several utility functions designed for this very purpose, for example rowMeans, colMeans, rowSums, and colSums. However, we can also create our own functions and "apply" those over dimensions instead.

Consider the matrix we created earlier:

```
> myMat
     [,1] [,2] [,3] [,4] [,5]
[1,]    5    6    4    2    2
[2,]    1    7    3    1    6
[3,]    2    3    0    3    4
[4,]    2    2    4    3    4
```

Let's imagine we want to count the number of values in each column that are greater than 3. There isn't currently a function in R that will return "the number of values greater than 3," so let's create one:

```
> above3 <- function(vec) {
+    sum(vec > 3)
+ }
> above3( c(1, 6, 5, 1, 2, 3) )  # Try out our function
[1] 2
```

In the same way as before, we can now "apply" this function across dimensions of our matrix. So to calculate the number of values in each column that are greater than 3, we use the following code:

```
> apply(myMat, 2, above3)    # Number of values > 3 in each column
[1] 1 2 2 0 3
```

In this example, we created the function above3 and "applied" it to our structure. If we wanted to use above3 for other uses, this is fine. However, if this is only something we want to do once, we can define the function directly in the apply call (so it is never created as an R object in our session). To achieve this, we replace the function object with the definition as follows:

```
> apply(myMat, 2, function(vec) {
+    sum(vec > 3)
+ })
[1] 1 2 2 0 3
```

TIP

One-Line Function Definitions

As before, we can omit the {} (curly brackets) if our function can be defined on a single line. As such, the preceding code could be rewritten as follows:

```
> apply(myMat, 2, function(vec) sum(vec > 3))
[1] 1 2 2 0 3
```

As a convention, we will use the curly brackets consistently throughout this hour.

Passing Extra Arguments to Our Functions

As shown earlier, if we want to pass additional arguments, we can list them after the function call. We can do the same for the functions we write. For example, let's update our function with a second argument to control the threshold value for counting:

```
> aboveN <- function(vec, N) {
+    sum(vec > N)
+ }
> someValues <- c(1, 6, 5, 1, 2, 3)
> aboveN( someValues, N = 3 )         # Number > 3
[1] 2
> aboveN( someValues, N = 5 )         # Number > 4
[1] 1
```

If we "apply" this function to columns of our matrix, we need to additionally pass the N argument:

```
> myMat                             # Print the matrix
     [,1] [,2] [,3] [,4] [,5]
[1,]    5    6    4    2    2
[2,]    1    7    3    1    6
[3,]    2    3    0    3    4
[4,]    2    2    4    3    4
> apply(myMat, 2, aboveN, N = 3)    # Number > 3
[1] 1 2 2 0 3
> apply(myMat, 2, aboveN, N = 4)    # Number > 4
[1] 1 2 0 0 1
```

If, instead, we want to define the function directly in the `apply` call, we would need to list the additional arguments after the definition itself:

```
> apply(myMat, 2, function(vec, N) {
+    sum(vec > N)
+ }, N = 3)
[1] 1 2 2 0 3
```

Applying to Data Frames

Throughout this hour, we have used single-mode structures (matrices and arrays) as sample inputs to the `apply` function. However, because we can use any structure that has a dimension, we could also use `apply` with data frames. As an example, let's "apply" the median function to columns of the `airquality` data frame:

```
> head(airquality)                    # First few rows
  Ozone Solar.R Wind Temp Month Day
1    41     190  7.4   67     5   1
2    36     118  8.0   72     5   2
3    12     149 12.6   74     5   3
4    18     313 11.5   62     5   4
5    NA      NA 14.3   56     5   5
6    28      NA 14.9   66     5   6

> apply(airquality, 2, median, na.rm = TRUE)    # Median of each column
  Ozone Solar.R    Wind    Temp   Month     Day
   31.5   205.0     9.7    79.0     7.0    16.0
```

This command returns the median of each column (although, perhaps the "median `Month`" and "median `Day`" are not that useful). Now let's consider a second example, this time using the `iris` data frame:

```
> head(iris)
  Sepal.Length Sepal.Width Petal.Length Petal.Width Species
1          5.1         3.5          1.4         0.2  setosa
2          4.9         3.0          1.4         0.2  setosa
```

3	4.7	3.2	1.3	0.2	setosa
4	4.6	3.1	1.5	0.2	setosa
5	5.0	3.6	1.4	0.2	setosa
6	5.4	3.9	1.7	0.4	setosa

```
> apply(iris, 2, median, na.rm = TRUE)
Sepal.Length  Sepal.Width Petal.Length  Petal.Width       Species
          NA           NA           NA           NA            NA
Warning messages:
1: In mean.default(sort(x, partial = half + 0L:1L)[half + 0L:1L])  :
    argument is not numeric or logical: returning NA
2: In mean.default(sort(x, partial = half + 0L:1L)[half + 0L:1L])  :
    argument is not numeric or logical: returning NA
3: In mean.default(sort(x, partial = half + 0L:1L)[half + 0L:1L])  :
    argument is not numeric or logical: returning NA
4: In mean.default(sort(x, partial = half + 0L:1L)[half + 0L:1L])  :
    argument is not numeric or logical: returning NA
5: In mean.default(sort(x, partial = half + 0L:1L)[half + 0L:1L])  :
    argument is not numeric or logical: returning NA
```

This time, the output returns missing values along with a number of warning messages—but why is this?

When we apply functions over dimensions of single-mode structures (for example, matrices and arrays), we know the "mode" of data being passed to our function is the same each time it is called (that is, if we have a numeric matrix, we know that each column will necessarily be numeric).

By comparison, a data frame is a multi-mode structure, so each column may (or may not) be of the same mode. When we call "apply," R will first break the data and store it in a single-mode structure—at this point, all the data is coerced to a single mode, which may or may not be a suitable input to the function.

With the `airquality` example, the `apply` function first structures the data into a single-mode (numeric) object and then applies the `median` function to each (numeric) column. With the `iris` data frame, the `Species` column is not a numeric column, so when the data is structured into a single-mode object, the resulting data is no longer numeric. We can see this in the following call, where we query the `class` of each column of the data:

```
> apply(iris, 2, class)
Sepal.Length  Sepal.Width Petal.Length  Petal.Width       Species
 "character"  "character"  "character"  "character"   "character"
```

So, when R then attempts to apply the `median` function to each column, the missing values and warning messages are produced.

So, in summary, we can use `apply` with data frames, but we have to take care that data over which we're "applying" can be adequately combined into a single mode. For example, if we wanted to calculate the mean of all numeric columns of `iris`, we could use this approach:

```
> # Apply median function over the first 4 columns of iris
> apply(iris[,-5], 2, median, na.rm = TRUE)
Sepal.Length  Sepal.Width Petal.Length  Petal.Width
        5.80         3.00         4.35         1.30
```

The `lapply` Function

The `lapply` function applies functions to each element of a list and always returns a list structure as its output. For example, let's create a list of numeric vectors and calculate the median of each element. First, we'll create the list:

```
> myList <- list(P1 = rpois(10, 1), P3 = rpois(10, 3), P5 = rpois(10, 5))
> myList
$P1
 [1] 1 2 2 2 1 0 0 1 1 4

$P3
 [1] 0 1 4 0 2 3 2 2 1 6

$P5
 [1] 5 4 9 6 6 4 6 5 3 5
```

To use the `lapply` function, we simply pass the list and the function to apply (there is no "margin" here because the data is already "split" into list elements):

```
> lapply(myList, median)
$P1
[1] 1

$P3
[1] 2

$P5
[1] 5
```

The `split` Function

In the preceding example, the `lapply` call itself was actually a lot simpler (and more concise) than the code used to create the sample list. In a slight departure, let's quickly look at a simple function that creates lists (which we could then use as examples in `lapply`). This function is called `split`.

The split function divides a data structure into separate parts based on one or more grouping variables. The output from a split is a list. As a first example, let's split the Wind column from airquality based on levels of Month. We can achieve that by calling split with the Wind column as the first input and the "grouping" column (Month) as the second argument. Note that the output is a list:

```
> spWind <- split(airquality$Wind, airquality$Month)
> $`5`
 [1]  7.4  8.0 12.6 11.5 14.3 14.9  8.6 13.8 20.1  8.6  6.9  9.7  9.2
[14] 10.9 13.2 11.5 12.0 18.4 11.5  9.7  9.7 16.6  9.7 12.0 16.6 14.9
[27]  8.0 12.0 14.9  5.7  7.4

$`6`
 [1]  8.6  9.7 16.1  9.2  8.6 14.3  9.7  6.9 13.8 11.5 10.9  9.2  8.0
[14] 13.8 11.5 14.9 20.7  9.2 11.5 10.3  6.3  1.7  4.6  6.3  8.0  8.0
[27] 10.3 11.5 14.9  8.0

$`7`
 [1]  4.1  9.2  9.2 10.9  4.6 10.9  5.1  6.3  5.7  7.4  8.6 14.3 14.9
[14] 14.9 14.3  6.9 10.3  6.3  5.1 11.5  6.9  9.7 11.5  8.6  8.0  8.6
[27] 12.0  7.4  7.4  7.4  9.2
```

Given that this structure is a list, it is a suitable input to the lapply function. Let's calculate the median value of each element of spWind:

```
> lapply(spWind, median)
$`5`
[1] 11.5

$`6`
[1] 9.7

$`7`
[1] 8.6

$`8`
[1] 8.6

$`9`
[1] 10.3
```

This result is, therefore, the median Wind value for each level of Month, or the "median Wind by Month."

Nested Calls to `lapply` **and** `split`

In the preceding example, we separated the `split` and `lapply` calls for clarity. We could, of course, combine them into a single call, as follows:

```
> lapply(split(airquality$Wind, airquality$Month), median)
```

Or

```
> with(airquality, lapply(split(Wind, Month), median))
```

Splitting Data Frames

In the preceding example, we split a vector based on levels specified in another vector. The `split` function can also be used to divide data frames. For example, let's split our `airquality` data based on `Month`:

```
> spAir <- split(airquality, airquality$Month)   # Split the data

> length(spAir)                                   # Length of list
[1] 5
> names(spAir)                                    # Element names
[1] "5" "6" "7" "8" "9"

> head(spAir[[1]])                                # First element
  Ozone Solar.R Wind Temp Month Day
1    41     190  7.4   67     5   1
2    36     118  8.0   72     5   2
3    12     149 12.6   74     5   3
4    18     313 11.5   62     5   4
5    NA      NA 14.3   56     5   5
6    28      NA 14.9   66     5   6
```

As you can see, this creates a list of length 5 where each element contains a data frame containing data for only one month. Now let's use `lapply` to apply a function to each data frame stored in this list. We need to apply a function that will perform an operation on a data frame, so let's return the first three rows in each element of the list using `head`:

```
> lapply(spAir, head, n = 3)
$`5`
  Ozone Solar.R Wind Temp Month Day
1    41     190  7.4   67     5   1
2    36     118  8.0   72     5   2
3    12     149 12.6   74     5   3
```

```
$`6`
   Ozone Solar.R Wind Temp Month Day
32    NA     286  8.6   78     6   1
33    NA     287  9.7   74     6   2
34    NA     242 16.1   67     6   3

$`7`
   Ozone Solar.R Wind Temp Month Day
62   135     269  4.1   84     7   1
63    49     248  9.2   85     7   2
64    32     236  9.2   81     7   3

$`8`
   Ozone Solar.R Wind Temp Month Day
93    39      83  6.9   81     8   1
94     9      24 13.8   81     8   2
95    16      77  7.4   82     8   3

$`9`
    Ozone Solar.R Wind Temp Month Day
124    96     167  6.9   91     9   1
125    78     197  5.1   92     9   2
126    73     183  2.8   93     9   3
```

Perhaps instead we could `lapply` our own function to each data frame. For example, let's create a function that calculates column means for the `Ozone`, `Solar.R`, `Wind`, and `Temp` variables:

```
> lapply(spAir, function(df) {
+   apply(df[,1:4], 2, median, na.rm = TRUE)
+ })
$`5`
  Ozone Solar.R    Wind    Temp
   18.0   194.0    11.5    66.0

$`6`
  Ozone Solar.R    Wind    Temp
   23.0   188.5     9.7    78.0

$`7`
  Ozone Solar.R    Wind    Temp
   60.0   253.0     8.6    84.0

$`8`
  Ozone Solar.R    Wind    Temp
   52.0   197.5     8.6    82.0

$`9`
  Ozone Solar.R    Wind    Temp
   23.0   192.0    10.3    76.0
```

Here, each element of spAir is passed into the function we defined as input: df. Then, for each df, we calculate the column means of the first four columns.

NOTE

Splitting on Multiple Variables

You've seen that the split function can be used to divide data structures (such as vectors or data frames) into elements of a list based on values of another vector. We can split by more than one variable by passing a list of factors:

```
> split(airquality$Wind, list(airquality$Month, cut(airquality$Temp, 3)))
$`5.(56,69.7]`
 [1]  7.4 11.5 14.3 14.9  8.6 13.8 20.1  8.6  9.7  9.2 10.9 13.2 11.5 12.0 18.4
11.5  9.7
[18]  9.7  9.7 12.0 16.6 14.9  8.0 12.0

$`6.(56,69.7]`
[1] 16.1  9.2

$`7.(56,69.7]`
numeric(0)

...
```

This could then be passed to lapply to calculate summaries by more than one grouping variable.

Using lapply with Vectors

At the start of this section, we said that the lapply function will apply a function to each element of a list. However, if we instead pass a vector to the lapply function, it will convert it to a list using the as.list function as follows:

```
> as.list(1:5)
[[1]]
[1] 1

[[2]]
[1] 2

[[3]]
[1] 3

[[4]]
[1] 4

[[5]]
[1] 5
```

That means we can use `lapply` to apply a function to each element of a vector. Let's consider a simple example, where we apply the `rnorm` function to values 1 to 5:

```
> lapply(1:5, rnorm)
[[1]]
[1] 0.8168998

[[2]]
[1] -0.8863575 -0.3315776

[[3]]
[1] 1.1207127 0.2987237 0.7796219

[[4]]
[1]  1.4557851 -0.6443284 -1.5531374 -1.5977095

[[5]]
[1]  1.8050975 -0.4816474  0.6203798  0.6121235 -0.1623110
```

This is equivalent to the following:

```
> list(
+    rnorm(1),
+    rnorm(2),
+    rnorm(3),
+    rnorm(4),
+    rnorm(5)
+ )
[[1]]
[1] 0.8118732

[[2]]
[1] 2.196834 2.049190

[[3]]
[1] 1.6324456 0.2542712 0.4911883

[[4]]
[1] -0.32408658 -1.66205024  1.76773385  0.02580105

[[5]]
[1]  1.1285108 -2.3803581 -1.0602656  0.9371405  0.8544517
```

Let's add a second argument to `rnorm`. For example, let's specify a mean for the Normal distribution:

```
> lapply(1:5, rnorm, mean = 10)
[[1]]
[1] 11.46073
```

```
[[2]]
[1]   8.586901 10.567403

[[3]]
[1] 10.583188   8.693201   9.459614

[[4]]
[1] 11.947693 10.053590 10.351663   9.329023

[[5]]
[1] 10.277954 10.691171 10.823795 12.145065   7.653056
```

The Order of "apply" Inputs

When the lapply function (like all "apply" functions) passes the data to the function, the data is passed as the first input and is not named. So, the last example is equivalent to this:

```
> list(
+    rnorm(1, mean = 10),
+    rnorm(2, mean = 10),
+    rnorm(3, mean = 10),
+    rnorm(4, mean = 10),
+    rnorm(5, mean = 10)
+ )
[[1]]
[1] 10.14959

[[2]]
[1]   8.657469 10.553303

[[3]]
[1] 11.589963   9.413120   8.167623

[[4]]
[1] 10.888139 11.593488 10.516855   8.704328

[[5]]
[1] 10.054616   9.215351   8.950647 12.330512 11.402705
```

Let's quickly remind ourselves of the arguments of rnorm:

```
> args(rnorm)
function (n, mean = 0, sd = 1)
NULL
```

The first argument to rnorm, the number of values to sample, is called n. Although the lapply function is not "naming" the first input, the order-based method for specifying arguments in a function means that it is this "n" input that accepts each of the values, 1 to 5. What if we, instead, specify the first argument (n) as an extra parameter?

```
> lapply(1:5, rnorm, n = 5)
[[1]]
[1] 1.9426009 1.8262583 0.1884595 1.4762483 2.0212584

[[2]]
[1] 2.645383 3.043144 1.695631 4.477111 2.971221

[[3]]
[1] 4.867099 3.672042 2.692047 3.536524 3.824870

[[4]]
[1] 3.036099 3.144917 5.886947 3.608181 3.019367

[[5]]
[1] 5.687332 4.494956 7.157720 4.400202 4.305453
```

This produces a slightly different output, where each element of the list is a sample of five values from a Normal distribution. Here, the lapply call is equivalent to the following:

```
> list(
+    rnorm(1, n = 5),
+    rnorm(2, n = 5),
+    rnorm(3, n = 5),
+    rnorm(4, n = 5),
+    rnorm(5, n = 5)
+ )
[[1]]
[1]  1.2239254 -0.1562233  1.4224185 -0.3247553  1.1410843

[[2]]
[1] 1.463952 1.688394 3.556110 1.551967 2.321124

[[3]]
[1] 1.769828 1.675941 4.261242 4.319232 2.919246

[[4]]
[1] 3.494910 3.947846 4.628861 6.180002 3.930983

[[5]]
[1] 6.544864 6.321452 5.322152 6.530955 4.578760
```

In this case, we are explicitly naming the "n" input and setting it to 5, which explains why five samples are being returned in each list element. Therefore, the values we pass to the function (1 to 5) are instead used as the second input: the mean of the distribution from which to sample. In other words, this code returns the following:

- ► Five samples from a Normal distribution with mean 1
- ► Five samples from a Normal distribution with mean 2
- ► Five samples from a Normal distribution with mean 3
- ► Five samples from a Normal distribution with mean 4
- ► Five samples from a Normal distribution with mean 5

As a natural extension, if we specify the n and mean inputs, then each value of 1 to 5 will move to the third argument (the standard deviation).

Using `lapply` with Data Frames

As you saw in Hour 4, data frames are structured as lists of vectors. Therefore, we can use lapply to apply functions to each column of a data frame as follows:

```
> lapply(airquality, median, na.rm = TRUE)
$Ozone
[1] 31.5

$Solar.R
[1] 205

$Wind
[1] 9.7

$Temp
[1] 79

$Month
[1] 7

$Day
[1] 16
```

This is a similar process to using apply to apply functions over columns of a data frame. The two primary differences are as follows:

- ► The `lapply` function always returns a list.
- ► When using `apply`, the structures are first put into a single-mode structure before processing, whereas the `lapply` function does not attempt to combine columns between processing.

The last point here can be illustrated by the following example, where we look at the `class` of each column in our data frame:

```
> apply(airquality, 2, class)
    Ozone   Solar.R      Wind      Temp     Month       Day
"numeric" "numeric" "numeric" "numeric" "numeric" "numeric"
> lapply(airquality, class)
$Ozone
[1] "integer"

$Solar.R
[1] "integer"

$Wind
[1] "numeric"

$Temp
[1] "integer"

$Month
[1] "integer"

$Day
[1] "integer"
```

Note that, by the time the `class` function is applied in our first example, the `apply` function has already structured the data into a single-mode structure (so all data is forced to be of the same mode). With `lapply`, this coercion is not done, so we see instances of "numeric" (the "Wind" column) and "integer" column classes reported.

The `sapply` Function

The `sapply` function is a simple wrapper for the `lapply` function. In fact, the call to `lapply` can be clearly seen on the second line of the `sapply` function body:

```
> sapply
function (X, FUN, ..., simplify = TRUE, USE.NAMES = TRUE)
{
    FUN <- match.fun(FUN)
    answer <- lapply(X = X, FUN = FUN, ...)
    if (USE.NAMES && is.character(X) && is.null(names(answer))) names(answer) <- X
    if (!identical(simplify, FALSE) && length(answer))
        simplify2array(answer, higher = (simplify == "array"))
    else answer
}
```

Therefore, as with `lapply`, the `sapply` function allows us to apply functions to elements of a list (or vector). The primary difference is that, whereas `lapply` always returns a list, `sapply` will (by default) attempt to simplify the return object using the `simplify2array` function.

To illustrate this, let's look back at an earlier example where we use `lapply` and `split` to calculate the median values of `Wind` by `Month`:

```
> lapply(split(airquality$Wind, airquality$Month), median)
$`5`
[1] 11.5

$`6`
[1] 9.7

$`7`
[1] 8.6

$`8`
[1] 8.6

$`9`
[1] 10.3
```

If we replace the `lapply` function with the `sapply` function, we get a simpler output (in this case, a named vector):

```
> sapply(split(airquality$Wind, airquality$Month), median)
    5    6    7    8    9
 11.5  9.7  8.6  8.6 10.3
```

For another example, let's use `sapply` to see the class of each column of the `iris` data frame:

```
> sapply(iris, class)
Sepal.Length  Sepal.Width Petal.Length  Petal.Width      Species
   "numeric"    "numeric"    "numeric"    "numeric"     "factor"
```

Returns from `sapply`

The return values from `sapply` can sometimes be rather unpredictable. That is because `sapply` will attempt to simplify the return structure (which may result in a nicely formatted structure) but is often not able to simplify the return (in which case it stays as a list). Table 9.4 summarizes the return values, which depend on the number of values returned from the "applied" function.

TABLE 9.4 Return Values from `sapply`

Number of Return Values from Function	Return Structure
Always 1 value	A vector (with element names if the list elements were named).
Always returns the same number of values (> 1)	A matrix with output corresponding to each element in the columns (with column names specified by the list element names, if they exist) and the multiple return values from the function across rows (with row names specified by the named outputs from the function, if they exist).
Returns a variable number of values	It depends. If the function returns a variable number of values across the summaries, a list will be returned (that is, no simplification is performed). If it so happens that the return values are the same, then `sapply` will simplify the return structure as described previously.

Some examples showing the various return objects are provided here:

```
> myList <- list(P1 = rpois(5, 1), P3 = rpois(5, 3), P5 = rpois(5, 5))
>
> # Function that (always) returns a single value > vector output
> sapply(myList, median)
P1 P3 P5
 1  3  4

> # Function that (always) returns 2 values > matrix output
> sapply(myList, range)
     P1 P3 P5
[1,]  0  1  3
[2,]  3  4  6

> # Function that (always) returns 5 values > matrix output
> sapply(myList, quantile)
     P1 P3 P5
0%    0  1  3
25%   0  3  4
50%   1  3  4
75%   2  3  5
100%  3  4  6

> # Function that can return a variable number of values > list output
> sapply(myList, function(X) X [ X > 2 ])
```

```
$P1
[1] 3

$P3
[1] 3 3 3 4

$P5
[1] 3 5 4 4 6

> # Function that can return a variable number of values
> # BUT it happens that the return values are of the same
> # length in this instance > simplification occurs
> sapply(myList, function(X) min(X):max(X))
      P1 P3 P5
[1,]   0  1  3
[2,]   1  2  4
[3,]   2  3  5
[4,]   3  4  6
```

Why Not Just Stick with `sapply`?

At this point, you may be wondering why we'd ever need to use `lapply` given that `sapply` returns a "simpler" output.

The key reason for using `lapply` instead of `sapply` is that you always know a list will be returned, whereas the returns from `sapply` can be unpredictable, particularly when the function applied can return a variable number of values (as seen previously). When we write code, we need to be sure of the structure returned so we can write code to deal with that structure—for example, imagine writing a script where you expect the return output from an `sapply` call to be a list, but then it is unexpectedly simplified to an array (as seen in the last example).

More generally, there may be times when you explicitly don't want to try and simplify the output. Consider a situation where we have a list containing two matrices:

```
> matList <- list(
+    P3 = matrix( rpois(8, 3), nrow = 2),
+    P5 = matrix( rpois(8, 5), nrow = 2)
+ )
> matList
$P3
     [,1] [,2] [,3] [,4]
[1,]    8    1    1    4
[2,]    4    2    8    2

$P5
     [,1] [,2] [,3] [,4]
[1,]    5    4    3    2
[2,]    1    7    7    1
```

Now let's use our `lapply` and `sapply` functions to extract the first row of each matrix:

```
> lapply(matList, head, 1)
$P3
     [,1] [,2] [,3] [,4]
[1,]    8    1    1    4

$P5
     [,1] [,2] [,3] [,4]
[1,]    5    4    3    2

> sapply(matList, head, 1)
     P3 P5
[1,]  8  5
[2,]  1  4
[3,]  1  3
[4,]  4  2
```

As you can see, the `lapply` function has returned a list, whereas the `sapply` function has simplified the output by combining the results into a single (matrix) structure. If these two matrices were measurements on two different systems, we may want to ensure the results are analyzed separately, so combining them into a single structure is not desirable.

The `tapply` Function

The `tapply` function allows us to apply a function to elements of a vector, grouped by levels of one or more other variables. The primary arguments to `tapply` are described in Table 9.5.

TABLE 9.5 The Primary Arguments of `tapply`

Margin	Description
X	The data to summarize, typically a vector
INDEX	A factor, or list of factors, by which to apply the function to X
FUN	The function to be applied to X
. . .	Other arguments to FUN

Let's look at a simple example of `tapply` used to calculate the median `Wind` by `Month` using the `airquality` data:

```
> tapply(airquality$Wind, airquality$Month, median)
    5    6    7    8    9
 11.5  9.7  8.6  8.6 10.3
```

As you can see, in this case `tapply` returns a named vector of values, containing the median `Wind` values by `Month`.

NOTE

Similarity to `split` + `sapply`

This is very similar to an earlier example using `sapply` and `split`:

```
> sapply(split(airquality$Wind, airquality$Month), median)
   5    6    7    8    9
11.5  9.7  8.6  8.6 10.3
```

In fact, `tapply` is primarily a wrapper for a call to the `split` and `sapply` (technically, `lapply` with a simplify step) functions.

Multiple Grouping Variables

We can specify more than one grouping variable by which to process the data—this is achieved by providing a list of factors instead of a single factor. Let's calculate the median `Wind` by `Month` and grouped `Temp` (which we'll create using the `cut` function):

```
> tapply(airquality$Wind,
+        list(airquality$Month, cut(airquality$Temp, 3)), median)
  (56,69.7] (69.7,83.3] (83.3,97]
5     11.50         8.0        NA
6     12.65         9.7       9.2
7        NA         9.2       7.4
8        NA        10.3       7.4
9     12.05        10.3       6.0
```

The return from this function is a matrix with the levels of the first grouping variable (`Month`) set as the rows (dimension 1) and the levels of the second grouping variable (`Temp`) in columns (dimension 2).

CAUTION

Missing Values in Return Structure

In the preceding example, a number of missing values have been returned. Usually when we see a missing value, it presents a value that "exists" but one we do not know. Consider the missing value for high temperature values in Month 5 in this example. It is difficult to know whether this value is generated because

▶ There were `Wind` values in Month 5 for high temperatures, but they contained missing values so we do now know the median value.

▶ There were actually no values in Month 5 for high temperatures (that is, there is no data).

In fact, in this case, the latter is true—there were no days in Month 5 when the temperature went above 83.3 degrees Fahrenheit. So, this missing value represents a "lack" of data. However, care should be taken when interpreting the results.

Let's extend this example a little further, calculating the median `Wind` by `Month` levels of `Temp` and levels of `Solar.R`:

```
> tapply(airquality$Wind,
+        list(airquality$Month, cut(airquality$Temp, 3), cut(airquality$Solar.R,
➥2)),
+        median)
, , (6.67,170]

   (56,69.7] (69.7,83.3] (83.3,97]
5     12.60        10.3        NA
6      9.20         8.0        NA
7        NA         8.6     11.45
8        NA         9.7      8.60
9     13.45        10.3      7.40

, , (170,334]

   (56,69.7] (69.7,83.3] (83.3,97]
5     10.90       11.15        NA
6     16.10       12.65       9.2
7        NA        9.70       7.4
8        NA       10.90       8.0
9     12.05       10.30       4.6
```

This now creates a three-dimensional array of output, where each of our three grouping variables is aligned to a dimension.

Multiple Returns

In the preceding example, we used the `median` function to illustrate the use of `tapply`, which will always return a single value. If, instead, our function returns multiple values, the outputs from `tapply` can be unexpected and, occasionally, highly complex. Let's start with a simple example, this time calculating quantiles of `Wind` values by `Month`:

```
> tapply(airquality$Wind, airquality$Month, quantile)
$`5`
  0%   25%   50%   75%  100%
5.70  8.90 11.50 14.05 20.10

$`6`
 0%  25%  50%  75% 100%
1.7  8.0  9.7 11.5 20.7
```

```
$`7`
  0%  25%  50%  75% 100%
  4.1  6.9  8.6 10.9 14.9

$`8`
  0%  25%  50%  75% 100%
  2.3  6.6  8.6 11.2 15.5

$`9`
    0%     25%     50%     75%    100%
  2.800   7.550 10.300 12.325 16.600
```

We can see that, with multiple return values, no simplification is performed and a list is returned. This is the equivalent of the following:

```
> lapply(split(airquality$Wind, airquality$Month), quantile)
$`5`
    0%    25%    50%    75%   100%
  5.70   8.90  11.50  14.05  20.10

$`6`
  0%  25%  50%  75% 100%
  1.7  8.0  9.7 11.5 20.7

$`7`
  0%  25%  50%  75% 100%
  4.1  6.9  8.6 10.9 14.9

$`8`
  0%  25%  50%  75% 100%
  2.3  6.6  8.6 11.2 15.5

$`9`
    0%     25%     50%     75%    100%
  2.800   7.550 10.300 12.325 16.600
```

Now let's extend this example to calculate the quantiles by Month and (grouped) Temp:

```
> tapply(airquality$Wind,
+        list(airquality$Month, cut(airquality$Temp, 3)), quantile)
  (56,69.7]   (69.7,83.3]  (83.3,97]
5 Numeric,5  Numeric,5    NULL
6 Numeric,5  Numeric,5    Numeric,5
7 NULL       Numeric,5    Numeric,5
8 NULL       Numeric,5    Numeric,5
9 Numeric,5  Numeric,5    Numeric,5
```

The "simplification" process has now forced the outputs into a matrix, creating a "matrix of lists," which is a particularly complex and unhelpful structure:

```
> X <- tapply(airquality$Wind,
+         list(airquality$Month, cut(airquality$Temp, 3)), quantile)
> class(X)
[1] "matrix"
> X
  (56,69.7] (69.7,83.3] (83.3,97]
5 Numeric,5 Numeric,5   NULL
6 Numeric,5 Numeric,5   Numeric,5
7 NULL      Numeric,5   Numeric,5
8 NULL      Numeric,5   Numeric,5
9 Numeric,5 Numeric,5   Numeric,5
> X[1,1]
[[1]]
    0%    25%    50%    75%   100%
 7.400  9.700 11.500 13.925 20.100
```

Return Values from `tapply`

As with `sapply`, the returns from `tapply` can sometimes be difficult to predict. Table 9.6 summarizes the return objects from `tapply` based on the number of return values from a function and the number of grouping variables.

TABLE 9.6 Return Values from `tapply`

Number of Return values from Function	Number of Grouping Variables		
	1	2	>2
Always one value	A vector	A matrix	An array
Always returns the same number of values (> 1)	A list	A "matrix of lists"	An "array of lists"
Returns a variable number of values	A list or, if the function happens to return all single values, a vector	A "matrix of lists" or, if the function happens to return all single values, a matrix	An "array of lists" or, if the function happens to return all single values, an array

Given that `tapply` may return unexpected (and/or highly complex) values, we recommend the use of `lapply` and `split` instead of `tapply`, unless we can guarantee the number of return values from the function (so we can rely on the outputs).

TIP

The *plyr* Package

The **plyr** package was developed and is maintained by popular R package author, Hadley Wickham. It was first released to CRAN in 2008 and is still one of the most popular R packages on CRAN, with a huge number of packages depending on **plyr** functionality. The **plyr** package offers a more consistent "apply" syntax based on the input and output structures to which we apply a function. Functions follow the form *[i] [o]*ply, where i and o represent the input and output format respectively. For example the function llply expects a list input and produces a list output:

```
> air <- split(airquality, airquality$Month)
> llply(air, dim)
```

In addition to providing an alternative apply framework **plyr** offers data manipulation functionality such as merging and aggregation. However, for those working with data frames, the **dplyr** package that you will be introduced to in Hour 12 provides a much more user-friendly approach to data manipulation and aggregation.

Summary

In this hour, we have looked at a number of ways we can apply simple functions to data structures in a more sophisticated way. Specifically, we've look at

▶ The use of loops to iterate over data objects

▶ The rich set of "apply" functions

Together, this provides a range of capabilities of summarizing data and performing tasks in a repetitive manner. In later hours, we'll extend this to cover higher-level mechanisms for processing and aggregating data, with a focus on summarizing data frames. In Hour 18, we'll also look again at loops and "apply" functions with respect to coding efficiency and performance.

Q&A

Q. How can I stop a "for" loop if a certain condition is met?

A. You can stop the for loop using the break construct, as follows:

```
> for (i in 1:100) {
+    cat("\n Hello")              # Writing a message
+    if (runif(1) > .9) {
+      cat(" - STOP!!")
+      break  # 90% chance of stopping each time
+    }
+ }
```

```
Hello
Hello
Hello
Hello
Hello
Hello
Hello
Hello
Hello - STOP!!
```

Q. **How do I stop the process if I get stuck in an infinite "while" loop?**

A. You can use the Esc key (in interactive mode) to stop the process.

Q. **How could I apply a function over multiple lists at the same time?**

A. The `mapply` function is a multivariate version of `sapply`, which allows us to apply functions over multiple lists at the same time. For example, let's apply the `rpois` function over elements `1:5` (for the number of values to sample) and `5:1` (for the lambda values to use):

```
> mapply(rpois, n = 1:5, lambda = 5:1)
[[1]]
[1] 2

[[2]]
[1] 7 3

[[3]]
[1] 4 1 1

[[4]]
[1] 1 0 2 4

[[5]]
[1] 3 0 1 0 2
```

Q. **How performant is a "for" loop compared to, say, an "apply" function?**

A. Generally, the R language is optimized for vectorized operations, and it is quite possible to write very underperforming code using (nested) for loops. The "apply" family of functions can add some gains in terms of both performance and code maintenance. This will be discussed further in Hour 18.

Workshop

The workshop contains quiz questions and exercises to help you solidify your understanding of the material covered. Try to answer all questions before looking at the "Answers" section that follows.

Quiz

1. What is the difference between a "for" and a "while" loop?

2. If you use a for loop to iterate over a vector of (character) column names, how would you use each value to reference a column in a data frame?

3. When using the `apply` function, what does the `MARGIN` argument control?

4. How do you pass additional arguments to a function you wish to "apply"?

5. What is the difference between `sapply` and `lapply`?

6. What does the `split` function do, and how can you use it in conjunction with `lapply/sapply`?

7. When using `tapply`, how do you specify that a summary is to be performed "by" more than one variable?

Answers

1. A "for" loop will iterative for a predefined set of values. A "while" loop instead iterates until a specified condition is no longer true.

2. If the condition results in a single missing value, then an error is returned:

```
> testMissing <- function(X) {
+    if (X > 0) cat("Success")
+ }
> testMissing(NA)
Error in if (X > 0) cat("Success") :
  missing value where TRUE/FALSE needed
```

If you use the `all` function with a condition that contains any missing values, the result is missing and therefore will also result in an error (since you do not know if "all" the conditions are met):

```
> allMissings <- rep(NA, 5)    # All missing values
> someMissings <- c(NA, 1:4)   # Some missing values
> all(allMissings > 0)
[1] NA
> all(someMissings > 0)
[1] NA
```

If we use the `any` function with a condition that contains all missing values, the result is a missing value. If, however, you use the `any` function with a vector where not all values are missing, some conditions may be met:

```
> any(allMissings > 0)
[1] NA
> any(someMissings > 0)
[1] TRUE
```

3. The `MARGIN` argument controls the dimension over which you want to apply your function (for example, 1 for rows, 2 for columns).

4. Each "apply" function has an ellipsis argument where you list additional arguments—for example, `apply(Y, X min, na.rm = TRUE)`.

5. The `lapply` function applies a function to elements of a list (or vector) and (always) returns its results in a list. The `sapply` function performs exactly the same actions but, where possible, will try to simplify the output (for example, as a vector or array).

6. The `split` function will take a data object (typically a vector or data frame) and break it into parts based on one or more grouping variables, storing the results as a list. When the results are "broken" into a list structure, we can use `lapply` or `sapply` to apply a function to each element—for example, you can calculate the mean Y by levels of X using the following:

```
sapply(split(Y, X), mean)
```

7. You can specify multiple "by" variables using a list as follows:

```
tapply(Y, list(X1, X2), mean)
```

Activities

1. Create a "for" loop that iteratively prints each element of `LETTERS` on a new line.

2. Create a "for" loop that prints the mean `mpg` value (from the `mtcars` dataset) for each unique level of the `carb` variable.

3. Look at the provided `WorldPhones` matrix, which contains the total number of phones in different regions of the world between 1951 and 1961. Use the `apply` function to calculate the total number of phones by year and the maximum number of phones by region.

4. Create a list containing three numeric vectors. Use `lapply` or `sapply` to print the median value from each element of the list.

5. Use `split` together with `sapply` to calculate the median value of `mpg` (from the `mtcars` data) by levels of `carb`.

6. Use `split` together with `lapply` to calculate a summary (`?summary`) of the `iris` data by levels of `Species`.

HOUR 10
Importing and Exporting

What You'll Learn in This Hour:

▶ Storage of data in R
▶ Working with flat files
▶ Connecting to databases
▶ Working with Microsoft Excel

In Hours 3 through 6, we looked at the various mechanisms for storing data in R and some useful functions for manipulating modes of R data. In this hour, you are introduced to the common methods for importing and exporting data. By the end of the hour you will have seen how R can be used to read and write flat files and connect to database management systems (DBMSs) as well as Microsoft Excel.

Working with Text Files

Everyday R users tend to prefer importing and exporting Comma Separated Value (CSV) and other text-based ("flat file") formats. Text files are, of course, completely open and can easily be generated from any analysis tool. Reading flat files in to R (and exporting them) is very straightforward.

TIP

File Navigation

The `file.choose` function allows us to browse and select a file to import using our operating system's standard file browsing interface.

Perhaps the easiest way to import a text file in RStudio is via the menu system. The Import Wizard can be started by navigating to Tools > Import Dataset > From Text File and then navigating to the file you wish to import. The wizard looks at the file and tries to evaluate whether your dataset has headers and which character separates columns. In most cases the defaults are correct, and you simply need to click the Import button when you are ready to import your data.

Reading in Text Files

The RStudio import feature is, of course, unique to RStudio. However, if you try it, you will notice that, like many of the menu features in RStudio, it produces the line of R code required to read in the data, which is great if you work in a heavily regulated industry where reproducible code is a necessity. We will now look at the functions `read.table` and `read.csv` used by the Import Wizard.

The `read.table` function reads tabular information from a text file and returns a data frame. An example of using `read.table` to read in djiData.csv, embedded within the **mangoTraining** package, is shown in Listing 10.1. In the example, we assume that the data has been copied to our current working directory for simplified file referencing. Note that when we call `read.table`, we create a named R object. This is how we will refer to the dataset once we have read it into R. If we don't do this, R will just print the dataset to the screen and we won't be able to access it.

LISTING 10.1   Reading in Text Files

```
1: > djiData <- read.table("djiData.csv", header= TRUE, sep = ",")
2: > head(djiData,3)
3:         Date DJI.Open DJI.High  DJI.Low DJI.Close DJI.Volume DJI.Adj.Close
4: 1 12/31/2014 17987.66 18043.22 17820.88  17823.07   82840000      17823.07
5: 2 12/30/2014 18035.02 18035.02 17959.70  17983.07   47490000      17983.07
6: 3 12/29/2014 18046.58 18073.04 18021.57  18038.23   53870000      18038.23
```

The first line in Listing 10.1 only works because we first copy djiData.csv to our working directory. R then uses relative paths to find and import the data. If we instead place the file within a "data" directory within our working directory then we can import using the line:

```
> djiData <- read.table("data/djiData.csv", header= TRUE, sep = ",")
```

Alternatively, we can provide the full file path to the file; however, this makes our code less transferable, particularly when importing multiple files because we would have to change the file path for each dataset that we import. As we discussed in Hour 2, "The R Environment," it is important to remember to use forward slashes when referencing file paths.

TIP

Package Data

In Listing 10.1, we copy the data from the **mangoTraining** package to our working directory in order to read it in. This highlights the ease with which data can be imported from our working directory.

We normally extract data from an R package using the `package` argument contained within the `system.file` function:

```
> system.file(package = "mangoTraining", "extdata/djiData.csv")
[1] "C:/Program Files/R/R-3.1.2/library/mangoTraining/extdata/djiData.csv"
```

Using the `package` argument contained within the `system.file` function allows us to write code that is independent of our own operating system and therefore more transferrable.

CAUTION

Case-Sensitivity for File Paths

The import and export functions within R work directly with the operating system. If you use an operating system such as Windows that is not case-sensitive, then there is no need to match case for the file path. In other words, djiData.csv is equivalent to djidata.csv. However, if you use an operating system such as Linux, which is case-sensitive, then this case-sensitivity must be respected in file paths.

The `read.table` function is a generic function for reading in text data, and it makes several assumptions about your data. The important assumptions (or defaults) are that the dataset does not have a row of column headings, that `header = FALSE`, and that elements are separated using a space (`sep = " "`). There are also function arguments to specify the symbol that represents missing data and the characters used for marking character data. In addition, we can choose which rows to start and stop reading the data from, which is particularly useful for text output where the first few lines are meta-information before the data actually begins.

TIP

The Windows Clipboard

In Windows you can copy and paste your data into R by taking advantage of the "clipboard." Simply set the `file` argument in `read.table` to be `file="clipboard"`. Setting `sep="\t"` specifies a tab separator and allows you to copy and paste directly from Excel. However, this practice is generally discouraged as it is not reproducible.

TIP

Troublesome Factors

As you saw in Hour 5, "Dates, Times, and Factors," when R creates a data frame, the default behavior is to convert anything nonnumeric into factors. This means that you have to carefully handle dates and other columns that have been turned into factors, as well as reorder or relabel factor levels for the factors you do want. If this becomes a major part of your workflow, you might consider the `stringsAsFactors` argument to `read.table`. Setting `stringsAsFactors=FALSE` will prevent any columns being turned into factors, giving you more control over how your data is represented in R.

Reading in CSV Files

If you work with CSV files, sooner or later you will become tired of typing `header=TRUE`, `sep=","` each time you read in a dataset. The `read.csv` function is simply a wrapper for `read.table` that assumes your dataset has headers and that the separator is a comma. Note that we are still required to provide the ".CSV" file extension when specifying the file we want to read in, assuming that file has the correct extension.

```
> djiData <- read.csv("djiData.csv", header= TRUE, sep = ",")
```

NOTE

Comma Used as a Decimal Point?

In some European countries and other countries throughout the world, a comma is used as a decimal point instead of a period, and data elements are instead separated by semicolons. If you work with such data or have colleagues that do, then the `read.csv2` function is designed specifically for such data.

Exporting Text Files

We can write data frames to CSV or other simple text formats using the `write.csv` or `write.table` function, respectively. As with `read.csv` and `read.table`, the `write.csv` function is simply a wrapper for `write.table` that reduces the number of required arguments when exporting .CSV files. Both functions expect the data frame that you want to export as the first argument and the name of the file that you want to create as the second.

As with the `read.*` functions, there are a number of other useful arguments that can assist with writing out data. In particular, the argument `row.names = FALSE` prevents the row names (which are often numbers) from being written to the output file. We can also control whether quotes are placed around character data as well as the character used to represent missing data. Here, we write out the internal `airquality` dataset to our working directory:

```
> write.csv(airquality, "airquality.csv", row.names = FALSE)
```

Faster Imports and Exports

The package **data.table** has a function called `fread` that is much faster for large files. The `fread` function is also generally easier to use than `read.table` because it guesses the separator and can interpret common column types that are known to cause trouble for R users. We will look closer at **data.table** and `fread` in Hour 12, "Efficient Data Handling in R."

Another alternative for flat files is **readr**, released to CRAN by popular R package author Hadley Wickham in 2015. As with `fread`, the aim of the functions within **readr** is to improve the speed at which (large) CSV and other flat files can be read into R as well as to interpret common column types to save post-processing effort on the part of the user. The package also produces data frames in a "`tbl_df`" format, ready for use with the **dplyr** package, which we will look at in Hour 11, "Data Manipulation and Transformation," and Hour 12. The main function in **readr** for reading .CSV files into R is the `read_csv` function.

Neither **data.table** nor **readr** are installed as part of the base R distribution and must therefore be installed separately.

Efficient Data Storage

As you saw in Hour 2, when we close R (or RStudio) we have the option of saving our workspace. By saving the objects in our workspace, we are moving them from memory to a single ".RData" file stored on disc. When we start a new R session, our workspace is restored to the same state as when we closed R down.

CAUTION

Restoring Sessions

When we start a new session using an .RData file, it restores all of the objects but it does not reload all of the packages we were using. Clearly this will cause some problems if any of our objects rely on functionality within the packages that were loaded. Be sure to reload any necessary packages when starting a new session from an .RData file.

To avoid errors and ensure reproducible code, it is generally better to work with a clean environment than rely on a saved workspace. The .RData format is exclusive to R and is therefore not a suitable means of transferring data between applications. However, it can be used as an efficient means of storing large interim datasets during an analysis. A similar .rds format can be used for saving individual datasets.

To illustrate the efficiency of the .RData and .rds formats, let's create a data frame with 10 million rows and write it out to.CSV, .RData, and .rds formats:

```
> longData <- data.frame(ID = 1:10000000, Value = rnorm(10000000))
> write.csv(longData, "longData.csv", row.names = F)
> save(longData, file = "longData.RData")
> saveRDS(longData, file = "longData.rds")
```

We start by deleting the `longData` object from our session. Now let's read in the .CSV file and time the operation with a function called `system.time`:

```
> rm(longData)
> system.time(longData <- read.csv("longData.csv"))
   user  system elapsed
 118.04    1.03  119.31
```

I'm using a decent machine here with 8GB RAM running 64-bit R, so nearly 2 minutes of elapsed time is pretty slow. So how does `load` perform with the .RData and .rds file types?

```
> rm(longData)
> system.time(load("longData.RData"))
   user  system elapsed
   0.78    0.03    0.81
> rm(longData)
> system.time(load("longData.RData"))
   user  system elapsed
   0.81    0.03    0.84
```

Using the R formats, we are down to less than a second, which is a huge difference. Incidentally, the `read_csv` function from **readr** and `fread` from **data.table** both managed the same .CSV import in less than 10 seconds. We will look more closely at some R packages that can generally improve R's speed and efficiency when handling large data during Hour 11 and Hour 12. We will also look at code efficiency in Hour 18, "Code Efficiency."

Proprietary and Other Formats

If you have previously been using another statistical analysis language such as SAS or SPSS, then you will probably find yourself needing to read .SAS7BDAT or .SAV files into R. One solution would be to use SAS or SPSS to write out a CSV file, which can easily be read into R; however, this is not always possible, and you may find yourself needing to read in data from SAS, SPSS, Stata, Minitab, and so on into R. Such data can (mostly) be read into R using the **foreign** package, which is a "recommended" R package and therefore distributed with each new version of R.

The **foreign** package is a small collection of functions to read and write data to some well-known data formats. The package functions very well; however, it is limited by proprietary formats. For example, in order to write to SAS, the package actually generates an intermediary text file and corresponding SAS script that it tries to call from your SAS installation in order to read the text into SAS.

NOTE

SAS Users

If you are a SAS user, you may find the package **sas7bdat** useful for reading and writing .SAS7BDAT files. However, you should be aware that the package is documented as being experimental in places and does not work in all cases. If you are working with transport files, the **SASxport** package provides tools for writing SAS transport files from R.

The **haven** package provides a wrapper for Evan Miller's ReadStat C library and offers an alternative to **foreign**. The package is still in its infancy and limited to SAS, SPSS, and STATA, but unlike **foreign** it can read the proprietary .SAS7BDAT format, and like **readr** it can correctly interpret some date formats and generate data that is ready for **dplyr**.

Relational Databases

Unfortunately there is no "one-size-fits-all" solution to working with relational databases in R. There are a few general-purpose packages for working with databases, but for the best results you are better off looking for the package that has been built specifically for the database that you are using.

The approach that the various database packages take in R is very much the same. There are typically one or more functions to assist with making a connection to the database, plus a number of utility functions that wrap up common tasks that you might perform in SQL. If you are familiar with SQL, though, you may prefer to write SQL directly, which all the main packages allow you to do.

RODBC

The **RODBC** package is probably the most well established method for connecting to a database from R. Note that the package is not installed by default; it must first be installed and loaded. As the name suggests, it implements standard ODBC database connectivity. You can therefore use **RODBC** to connect to all the popular DBMSs: Oracle, MySQL, Microsoft Access as well as SQL Server, PostgreSQL, and SQLite. You can even use **RODBC** to connect to Excel spreadsheets!

Let's look at an example of an **RODBC** workflow using the well-known training database distributed with Microsoft Access: Northwind.mdb. The package is available online via the book's website or within the **mangoTraining** package. To find the file within **mangoTraining** we can use the following line:

```
> system.file(package = "mangoTraining", "extdata/Northwind.mbd")
```

The **RODBC** package contains a general-purpose `odbcConnect` function for connecting to any database, though for Access we can use a "convenience wrapper," `odbcConnectAccess`. As always, when importing or connecting to external data from R it is important that we name the connection in order to be able to refer to it. If a username and password is required, these can be entered using the arguments `uid` and `pwd`. We start by loading the **RODBC** package and making a connection to the database. In the following example, it is assumed that the database has been placed in our current working directory. We therefore provide the file name only. Alternatively, a full file path can be specified.

```
> library(RODBC)
> nWind <- odbcConnectAccess("Northwind.mdb")
```

CAUTION

Windows Architecture

The `odbcConnectAccess` function only works with 32-bit versions of the Microsoft drivers. These cannot be used when working in 64-bit R. For Access 2007 and beyond, there is the option to install 64-bit drivers, though the drivers cannot be installed with 32-bit Office. These compatibility issues can make **RODBC** difficult (but not impossible) to set up in a managed IT environment. If you run into problems, a sensible first step is to check whether you are running 32-bit or 64-bit R using `Sys.getenv("R_ARCH")`.

The RODBC package contains a number of utility functions, such as `sqlTables`, that can be used to explore the database. The first each of the utility functions is always the name of the connection:

```
> nwTableData <- sqlTables(nWind)
> nwTableData[1:3, c("TABLE_NAME", "TABLE_TYPE")]     # Preview main information
        TABLE_NAME    TABLE_TYPE
1 MSysAccessObjects SYSTEM TABLE
2          MSysACEs SYSTEM TABLE
3       MSysCmdbars SYSTEM TABLE
```

Another useful function is `sqlColumns`, which returns information about the columns within a specific table:

```
> sqlColumns(nWind, "Orders")
```

In order to extract data from the database, we can use wrappers such as `sqlFetch` to import an entire table or subsets of rows, or we can use SQL commands directly via `sqlQuery`:

```
> orderQuery <- "SELECT OrderID, EmployeeID, OrderDate, ShipCountry FROM Orders"
> keyOrderInfo <- sqlQuery(nWind, orderQuery)
> head(keyOrderInfo, 3)
  OrderID EmployeeID  OrderDate ShipCountry
```

1	10248	5 1996-07-04	France
2	10249	6 1996-07-05	Germany
3	10250	4 1996-07-08	Brazil

Further utility functions exist in order to clear the rows of a table (sqlClear), drop the table entirely (sqlDrop), and add new tables (sqlSave). When we have finished working with the database, it is important to remember to close the connection, like so:

```
> odbcClose(nWind)
```

If making multiple connections, we can use the odbcCloseAll function to close all of them in a single command.

DBI

The **RODBC** package is an extremely popular, well-tested package, but it is certainly not the only option available. Away from **RODBC**, the vast majority of R packages available for connecting to databases implement a standard database interface (DBI). Packages such as **ROracle**, **RJDBC**, **RPostgreSQL**, **RMySQL**, **RMySQLite**, and many more use the interface, which is wrapped in an R package, **DBI**.

The aim of the DBI is to ensure consistency when working with databases. Each of the packages that uses the interface contains a common set of functions that behave in the same way regardless of which package you are using or which database you are connecting to. The only difference is the connection itself. The standard set of functions follow the format db* (for example, dbReadTable). This standardization makes it incredibly easy to switch between packages because, once you've learned how to use one, you can essentially use them all. Alternatively, you can use **DBI** directly, as Listing 10.2 demonstrates, via **RSQLite**. Note how similar the approach is to the **RODBC** package, despite the fact that **RODBC** does not follow **DBI**.

LISTING 10.2   Using DBI Directly

```
 1: > library(DBI)
 2: > library(RSQLite)     # We create a SQLite DB
 3: > # Create a new SQLite database in-memory
 4: > dbiCon <- dbConnect(SQLite(), dbname = ":memory:")
 5: >
 6: > # Write airquality to the DB as a new table
 7: > dbWriteTable(dbiCon, "airquality", airquality)
 8: [1] TRUE
 9: >
10: > # Check what columns (fields) are in the airquality table
11: > dbListFields(dbiCon, "airquality")
12: [1] "Ozone"   "Solar.R" "Wind"    "Temp"    "Month"   "Day"
13: >
14: > # Send a query and return the result
```

```
15: > aQuery <- "SELECT * FROM airquality WHERE Month = 5 AND Wind > 15"
16: > dbiQuery <- dbSendQuery(dbiCon, aQuery)
17: > dbFetch(dbiQuery)
18:    Ozone Solar.R Wind Temp Month Day
19: 1     8      19 20.1   61    5   9
20: 2     6      78 18.4   57    5  18
21: 3    11     320 16.6   73    5  22
22: 4    NA      66 16.6   57    5  25
23: >
24: > dbClearResult(dbiQuery) # Be tidy!
25: [1] TRUE
```

Working with Microsoft Excel

If you are reading this book, there is an extremely high likelihood that either you or one of your close colleagues has been using Excel for day-to-day analysis. And why not?! So long as it's not pushed beyond its limits, it's a fantastic, easy-to-use tool for generating simple summary statistics. It's also a tool that very few analysts are willing to throw away, even after they have seen what R is capable of. You won't be surprised to learn, therefore, that there are a million and one R packages available for connecting R and Excel (well, more than 10 anyway). It probably also won't surprise you that they all do it in a slightly different way.

Connecting to R from Excel

If you want to link R and Excel, you can either call R from Excel or call Excel from R. Those who want to call R from Excel usually do so because they have a large number of colleagues who are extremely comfortable in Excel and want any analysis to start and end in there. This approach is particularly common in the insurance industry, where the underwriters typically consume advanced algorithms that actuaries have developed in R but via an Excel front end.

There are a number of ways of calling R from Excel, depending on the level of sophistication you require. At some point, a Microsoft language such as VBA or C# will be required to call to R either via command line or using a technology such as RServe. The focus of this book is on R, however, so we will look at the methods for connecting to Excel from R.

Reading Structured Data from Excel

If you have structured data—that is, data that is neatly laid out such that each tab of your workbook contains just a single table of data, usually stored in the top-left corner of the sheet—then there are some very efficient options available to you for reading in data from Excel. One such package is **RODBC**, which you have just seen in the context of databases. Using **RODBC**, we connect to a workbook using the odbcConnectExcel function for .XLS files or odbcConnectExcel2007 for .XLSX files. We then treat the workbook like a mini database, where each tab is a separate table. All of the standard SQL wrappers work in the same way as for other types of database. The **RJDBC** package can similarly be used with Excel.

An alternative solution designed specifically to work with structured data in Excel is Hadley Wickham's **readxl** package. This package was released in 2015 and, in a similar vein to **readr**, aims to improve the speed at which data can be read from Excel. Likewise, it also produces tbl_df output for use with **dplyr**.

Let's start with a simple example using the airquality.xlsx workbook. This workbook can be found in the **mangoTraining** package. As with other examples in this hour, we can use the following line to locate the file within the package:

```
> system.file(package = "mangoTraining", "extdata/airquality.xlsx")
```

The workbook consists of a single sheet named "data" containing a copy of the internal airquality data frame. We start by loading the package and using the excel_sheets function to return the sheet names.

```
> library(readxl)
>
> # What sheets does the workbook contain?
> excel_sheets("airquality.xlsx")
[1] "data"
```

Next we use the primary read_excel function to read the airquality.xlsx file. We pass the name of the sheet we want to read as the second argument. As an alternative, we can provide the sheet position, in this case 1. Since 1 is also the default sheet number, we could also leave out the argument altogether in the following example:

```
> # Read in the "data" sheet
> air <- read_excel("airquality.xlsx", sheet = "data")
> head(air, 3)
  Ozone Solar.R Wind Temp Month Day
1    41     190  7.4   67     5   1
2    36     118  8.0   72     5   2
3    12     149 12.6   74     5   3
```

The function automatically ignores blank rows and columns until it finds a cell containing data; however, we can control the row and column that it starts reading from using the arguments skip and col_names respectively. We can use the col_types argument to specify a vector of types of data contained within each column, including date ("date") type. The **readxl** package also works with the older .xls format. It cannot be used to write to Excel workbooks, however. For that we need one of four "all-rounder" packages.

Connecting to Excel from R

At the time of writing there are four "all-rounder" packages that can both read and write to Excel from R. Two of these four, **XLConnect** and **xlsx**, are very similar in their approach and use Java with the **rJava** package underneath to make the connection. The other two are the **openxlsx** package and the **excel.link** package, the most different of the four in terms of approach.

Each of the first three packages mentioned implements a similar workflow idea, albeit implemented in slightly different ways using functions with slightly different names. That workflow involves creating an image of the workbook in R that can be manipulated before saving any changes back to the workbook or to a new file. The **excel.link** package uses the **RDCOMClient** package to open an Excel workbook and edit it live using R code.

The XLConnect Package

Let's walk through an example of a typical analysis workflow using **XLConnect**. In this workflow we will take the following steps:

1. Connect to a workbook.

2. Import data from one of the tabs.

3. Generate some statistical summaries of the key columns.

4. Create a simple plot (using the `plot` function from the **graphics** package, which is covered in Hour 13, "Graphics.")

5. Write the summary data and graphic back to new tabs in the workbook.

6. Save the workbook with a new filename.

Making the connection results in a named R object that we must reference when using any of the other functions within the package. Note that, strictly speaking, we are not actually making a connection but a copy of the workbook, which is held in memory: The workbook can still be opened and edited from Excel while we are making changes in R. The `loadWorkbook` function can also be used to create new workbooks.

```
> airWB <- loadWorkbook("airquality.xlsx")
```

CAUTION

Java Dependency

Loading the **XLConnect** package is not as straightforward as for other packages due to the reliance on the **rJava** package, which itself has a reliance on the Java SE Development Kit, better known as JDK. If JDK is not installed, R cannot find `JAVA_HOME` and the **XLConnect** package fails to load. In most cases, simply installing the appropriate version of JDK (greater than 1.4 is required for **rJava**) for your operating system and architecture (that is, the 32-bit or the 64-bit version) and accepting all defaults fixes the issue. Instructions for installing JDK versions and the required executable can be found at http://www.oracle.com.

Once we have made our connection, we can use a function such as getSheets or getDefinedNames to explore the workbook:

```
> getSheets(airWB)
[1] "data"
```

Once we're done exploring, we can use a function such as readWorksheet, readNamedRegion, or readTable to read in data from the workbook. In this case we use readWorksheet. The function automatically ignores blank rows and columns until it finds a cell containing data. Otherwise, we can use the arguments startRow, endRow, startCol, and endCol to specify the exact location of the data within the sheet. Note the use of the sheet name in the second argument. We could also have used the sheet index.

```
> air <- readWorksheet(airWB, "data")
> head(air)
  Ozone Solar.R Wind Temp Month Day
1    41     190  7.4   67     5   1
2    36     118  8.0   72     5   2
3    12     149 12.6   74     5   3
4    18     313 11.5   62     5   4
5    NA      NA 14.3   56     5   5
6    28      NA 14.9   66     5   6
```

TIP

Indexing Columns

In Excel, rows can be referenced numerically, whereas columns are referenced alphabetically. In R, we tend to work with numerical referencing for both, and the **XLConnect** package is no different. The col2idx function is a useful function for converting columns such as AA into their equivalent numeric position:

```
> col2idx("AA")
[1] 27
```

Next, we summarize the data using the aggregate function that we discuss in Hour 11 and create a plot in our working directory using the plot function from the **graphics** package, which we will explore fully in Hour 13.

```
> # Summary Data
> averageOzone <- aggregate(data = air, Ozone ~ Month, mean, na.rm = T)
>
```

```
> # Graphic as png
> png("Ozone_Levels.png")
> hist(air$Ozone, col = "lightblue",
+       main = "Histogram of Ozone Levels in New York\nMay to September 1973",
+       xlab = "Ozone (ppb)")
> dev.off()
```

In this next-to-last step, we create a new sheet and load it with the summary data and graphic we just created. Note the use of createName to create a new named region within the workbook, which is then used to place the graphic. Note also the use of the argument originalSize = TRUE. This ensures that the image dimensions are retained and that it is not resized to fit the named region.

```
> # New tab
> createSheet(airWB, "Summary")
>
> # Write summary data
> writeWorksheet(airWB, averageOzone, "Summary", startRow = 2, startCol = 2)
>
> # Add graphic
> createName(airWB, "PlotGoesHere", "Summary!$E$2")
> addImage(airWB, filename = "Ozone_Levels.png", name = "PlotGoesHere",
+          originalSize = TRUE)
```

Finally, we set the Summary tab to be the current active tab so that when we next open the workbook, this is the tab we see and then save the workbook. A screenshot of the final workbook open in Excel is show in Figure 10.1.

```
> # Set active sheet and close
> setActiveSheet(airWB, "Summary")
> saveWorkbook(airWB, "air_summary.xlsx")
```

XLConnect has many more features, many of which are replicated using similarly named functions in **xlsx** and **openxlsx**. Such features include formatting, writing Excel formulas, and merging cells.

In our experience, the biggest restriction of **XLConnect** (and **xlsx**) is the large amount of memory required when working with Excel workbooks. There are options for dealing with memory issues, but eventually you will reach a limit and may need to explore one of the other options.

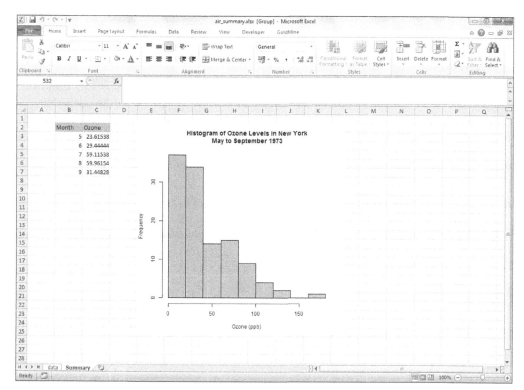

FIGURE 10.1
Writing data and graphics to Excel from R

Summary

In this hour, we looked at some of the primary methods for importing data into R for analysis. You saw how to easily read and write text files using read.table and read.csv, and if your data is large you can use faster alternatives within the **data.table** and **readr** packages. You also saw how R's .RData format can be used as an efficient means for storing data on disk.

You also saw how to use either the **RODBC** or **DBI** syntax to connect to and edit a DBMS from R and how to connect to an Excel spreadsheet using **XLConnect**. The "Activities" section provides an opportunity for you to try these tools yourself. In the next hour, we will continue with the data workflow and look at manipulation and transformation in R.

Q&A

Q. A colleague of mine is using xlsx to connect to Excel. Should I encourage them to switch to XLConnect?

A. After installation there really is very little difference between the two packages (or **openxlsx** for that matter). In certain circumstances you may experience limitations with one or the other, but if your colleague is using **xlsx** and your only experience of **XLConnect** to date is what you've read in this hour, then you may as well begin learning **xlsx**.

Q. You say that RODBC can be used to read structured data from Excel. Can it be used to write data to Excel as well?

A. Absolutely. For reasons of efficiency this is not the default behavior, but if you specify `readOnly = FALSE` when calling `odbcConnectExcel` or `odbcConnectExcel2007`, you can override the default and write tables back to the spreadsheet.

Workshop

The workshop contains quiz questions and exercises to help you solidify your understanding of the material covered. Try to answer all questions before looking at the "Answers" section that follows.

Quiz

1. What argument prevents row numbers or names being written to a CSV file when using `write.csv`?

2. In which R packages would you find the functions `read.csv`, `read_csv`, and `fread`?

3. What binary format can you use to store R objects on disk?

4. Is it possible to use a 32-bit ODBC driver to connect to Excel from 64-bit R?

5. Which **RMySQL** function can be used to read tables from a database?

6. Name three packages that can be used to connect to Excel from R.

Answers

1. To prevent R's default behavior of writing out what are known as "row names," you specify `row.names = FALSE`.

2. The `read.csv` function is in the **utils** package that is distributed with R. The `read_csv` and `fread` functions can be found in **reader** and **data.table**, respectively.

3. You use the .RData format to save any number of objects from your workspace to disk. This facilitates easy loading later on.

4. No. You need to ensure that the R architecture matches the ODBC driver architecture to use **RODBC**.

5. We didn't explicitly cover **RMySQL**, but it is a DBI package and therefore the `dbReadTable` function can be used.

6. In this hour, we mentioned several, including **XLConnect**, **xlsx**, **openxlsx**, **excel.link**, **RODBC**, and **readxl**. There is also the **gdata** package, which offers general programming tools for data manipulation.

Activities

1. Read the NST-EST2014-01.csv data containing annual estimates of the resident population for the United States, Regions, States, and Puerto Rico from April 1, 2010 to July 1, 2014, taken from the U.S. Census Bureau.

2. Write out R's internal `quakes` dataset to a .CSV file. Ensure that row numbers are not written to the file.

3. Simulate a million records of a demographic data frame containing columns ID, Age, Sex, Weight, and Height and then save the data to an .RData file.

4. Make a connection to the Northwind database:
   ▶ Create data tables from the Order Details and Orders tables.
   ▶ Merge the two tables based on the Order ID.
   ▶ Calculate the mean unit price by Customer ID.
   ▶ Save this data back to the Northwind database.

5. Use the **XLConnect** package to create an Excel workbook containing R's internal `mtcars` data:
   ▶ Install JDK from http://www.oracle.com.
   ▶ Install and load the **XLConnect** package.
   ▶ Use `loadWorkbook` to create a new file.
   ▶ Write the `mtcars` dataset to this file.
   ▶ Save the workbook.

HOUR 11
Data Manipulation and Transformation

What You'll Learn in This Hour:

- ▶ Sorting
- ▶ Setting and merging
- ▶ Handling duplicate values
- ▶ Restructuring data frames
- ▶ Data Aggregation

In the previous hour, we walked through a variety of methods for reading data into R as well as exporting it. This included working with flat files, R's .RData format, databases, and Microsoft Excel. However, reading data into R is only the start of the data analysis workflow. As data scientists and statisticians, we rarely get to control the structure and format of our data. In Hour 5, "Dates, Times, and Factors," and Hour 6, "Common R Utility Functions," you saw some useful functions for working with the format of your data. We looked at dates, times, factors, and missing data. We also looked at common functions for working with numeric and character data. Now we will look a little closer at the structure of our data.

Analysts will tend to quote all kinds of numbers for the proportion of a data analysis workflow that is taken up with data manipulation, or "data munging" as it is increasingly being referred to. However, one thing that most people agree on is that it takes more time than it should—and takes up significantly more time than the interesting analysis piece at the end! These days you can make a career out of being an expert data wrangler!

Several approaches to data manipulation in R have evolved over time. In this hour, we start by looking at what could be called "traditional" approaches to the data manipulation tasks of sorting, setting, and merging. We will then look at the popular packages **reshape**, **reshape2**, and **tidyr** for data restructuring. We will then continue the data manipulation theme into Hour 12, "Efficient Data Handling in R," where we will look deeper at two of the most popular packages for data manipulation and aggregation, **data.table** and **dplyr**.

Sorting

In R we are rarely required to sort our data in order to use a particular function. Most functions do it for us if it's needed. However, if we are calculating cumulative sums, analyzing time series, or if we just want to view our data in a way that makes sense to us, then we will need to sort the data ourselves. Base R contains a function named `sort` that enables us to easily sort vectors. By default, the function sorts vectors from low to high, though we can sort in descending order by specifying `decreasing = TRUE`.

```
> sort(airquality$Wind)[1:10]
 [1] 1.7 2.3 2.8 3.4 4.0 4.1 4.6 4.6 4.6 4.6
```

Unfortunately, the `sort` function only works with vectors, and it is useless to us if we want to sort data frames. To do so, we need to use the `order` function.

Sorting Data Frames

The `order` function returns a vector of positions or indices corresponding to the elements we would select *if* we were to order our data. Let's create a simple numeric vector, `myVec`, and examine the output when we feed it to the `order` function:

```
> myVec <- c(63, 31, 48, 82, 51, 20, 72, 99, 84, 53)
> order(myVec)
 [1]  6  2  3  5 10  1  7  4  9  8
```

The first value of the output vector is 6. This tells us that if we were to sort our data from low to high, the first value in the `myVec` vector that we should select is the sixth value (in this case, the number 20). Next, we should select the second value, which is 31, and so on. The sort order that the `order` function produces can be used to sort vectors; however, the real benefit is felt when working with data frames. In Listing 11.1 we use `order` to sort the entire `airquality` data frame based on the `Wind` column. The `order` function is used to select rows in the subscript.

LISTING 11.1 Sorting Data Frames

```
 1: > sortedByWind <- airquality[order(airquality$Wind), ]
 2: > head(sortedByWind, 10)
 3:      Ozone Solar.R Wind Temp Month Day
 4: 53      NA      59  1.7   76     6  22
 5: 121    118     225  2.3   94     8  29
 6: 126     73     183  2.8   93     9   3
 7: 117    168     238  3.4   81     8  25
 8: 99     122     255  4.0   89     8   7
 9: 62     135     269  4.1   84     7   1
10: 54      NA      91  4.6   76     6  23
11: 66      64     175  4.6   83     7   5
12: 98      66      NA  4.6   87     8   6
13: 127     91     189  4.6   93     9   4
```

Another benefit of the order function is that it allows us to order data by more than one variable. Looking again at Listing 11.1 we can see that each of the last four printed rows has a Wind value of 4.6. Where two or more values match like this, R uses the original order of the data for the sorting. To instead specify a second ordering variable, we simply have to add the variable as the second argument to order. We can continue to add as many ordering variables as we like in this way.

Descending Sorts

The order function has an argument, decreasing, which if set to TRUE, can be used to sort from high to low instead of the default low to high. However, this only really helps us if we are sorting a single variable or if we want to specify that all the order variables should be sorted from high to low. If we want to be specific about which variables will be ascending and which are descending, then we accept the default decreasing = FALSE and place a minus sign (-) in front of any variables that require a descending sort. An example of this is shown in Listing 11.2, where the airquality data is sorted by Wind and then by descending values of Temp.

LISTING 11.2   **Descending Sorts**

```
 1: > sortedByWindandDescTemp <- airquality[order(airquality$Wind, -airquality$Temp), ]
 2: > head(sortedByWindandDescTemp, 10)
 3:       Ozone Solar.R Wind Temp Month Day
 4: 53       NA      59  1.7   76     6  22
 5: 121     118     225  2.3   94     8  29
 6: 126      73     183  2.8   93     9   3
 7: 117     168     238  3.4   81     8  25
 8: 99      122     255  4.0   89     8   7
 9: 62      135     269  4.1   84     7   1
10: 127      91     189  4.6   93     9   4
11: 98       66      NA  4.6   87     8   6
12: 66       64     175  4.6   83     7   5
13: 54       NA      91  4.6   76     6  23
```

Appending

Appending, also commonly referred to as combining or setting, normally occurs when data are arriving to us in chunks over a time period. Each dataset we receive is structurally identical to the last but contains one or more new rows of data. All we therefore need to do is append the new rows to our existing data. In R this can be achieved using the rbind function, which you first saw in action with data frames in Hour 4, "Multi-Mode Data Structures." To use rbind with data frames, we need to ensure that the column names and the type of data contained within the columns matches between the two data frames. The `rbind` function is clever enough to resolve any potential issues with factor levels.

```
> # New data arrives each month
> jan <- data.frame(Month = "Jan", Value = 46.4)
> feb <- data.frame(Month = "Feb", Value = 55.2)
> rbind(jan, feb)
  Month Value
1   Jan  46.4
2   Feb  55.2
```

Merging

For some reason R tends not to be compared favorably with languages such as SAS when it comes to merging, though as a user of both R and SAS I actually find it slightly easier to merge data in R than in SAS, and it certainly beats Excel! In R, there is no need to sort before a merge. In many cases, you can also get away without specifying the variable(s) you want to merge by, though it's generally considered bad practice not to do so explicitly. The function that we use is the `merge` function.

The `merge` function allows us to merge two datasets by one or more common variables. The function has a number of arguments that can be used to control the "by" variables and match the rows in each dataset. These arguments are listed in Table 11.1.

TABLE 11.1 Arguments to the `merge` Function

Argument	Usage
x	First dataset to merge
y	Second dataset to merge
by	Character vector of columns to merge by
by.x	The columns in x to merge by
by.y	The columns in y to merge by
all	Logical flag—include all rows
all.x	Logical flag—include all rows from x
all.y	Logical flag—include all rows from y
suffixes	Column name suffix for matching column names

A Merge Example

In order to see the `merge` function in action, let's walk through an example using two of the datasets contained within the **mangoTraining** package, `demoData` and `pkData`. The data frames contain data from a fictitious clinical trial in which 33 subjects were given doses of a drug and then monitored over time. First of all, let's preview the data frames:

```
> head(demoData, 3)
  Subject Sex Age Weight Height  BMI Smokes
1       1   M  43     57    166 20.7     No
2       2   M  22     71    179 22.2     No
3       3   F  23     72    170 25.1     No
> head(pkData, 7)
  Subject Dose Time    Conc
1       1   25    0    0.00
2       1   25    1  660.13
3       1   25    6  178.92
4       1   25   12   88.99
5       1   25   24   42.71
6       2   25    0    0.00
7       2   25    1  445.55
```

For each of the 33 subjects in `demoData` there are five corresponding records in `pkData` representing times at which blood samples were taken during the fictitious study. In order to model drug concentration, `Conc`, as a response to `Dose` and each subject's demographic information, we would need to create a single data frame containing all relevant information. We do this by merging the two data frames together by the `Subject` column:

```
> fullPk <- merge(x = demoData, y = pkData, by = "Subject")
```

The `merge` function requires at least an `x` and a `y` argument to specify the two data frames that we want to merge by. Here, we specified `by = "Subject"` to illustrate that we were merging by the common variable `Subject`. However, because this is a common variable, we could just as easily have omitted the argument and let R find the common variables to merge by:

```
> fullPk <- merge(x = demoData, y = pkData)
```

The arguments `by.x` and `by.y` come into play when the name of the variable(s) that we want to merge by differs within the two data frames. The `x` and `y` refer to the first two arguments of the function. Therefore, if `Subject` had been labeled `ID` in the `pkData` data frame (our "y" data frame), we would have specified `by.x = "Subject"`, `by.y = "ID"`.

Missing Data

The `all`, `all.x`, and `all.y` arguments control the way in which records are merged when a value of the `by` variable only appears in one of the two data frames. By default, each of these arguments is set to FALSE, meaning that records will only be merged if the value of the by variable appears in both data frames. In database terminology, this is commonly referred to as an inner join. This is probably best illustrated with an example. Suppose we take tiny subsets of demoData and pkData, keeping only data for the first two subjects in demoData and subjects 2 and 3 in pkData.

```
> demo1and2 <- demoData[demoData$Subject %in% 1:2, ]
> pk2and3 <- pkData[pkData$Subject %in% 2:3, ]
>
> demo1and2
  Subject Sex Age Weight Height  BMI Smokes
1       1   M  43     57    166 20.7     No
2       2   M  22     71    179 22.2     No
> pk2and3
   Subject Dose Time    Conc
6        2   25    0    0.00
7        2   25    1  445.55
8        2   25    6  129.31
9        2   25   12   93.33
10       2   25   24   46.11
11       3   25    0    0.00
12       3   25    1  500.65
13       3   25    6  146.04
14       3   25   12  116.93
15       3   25   24   68.25
```

The default behavior of merge only merges data for subject 2 because this is the only subject that appears in both data frames:

```
> merge(demo1and2, pk2and3)
  Subject Sex Age Weight Height  BMI Smokes Dose Time    Conc
1       2   M  22     71    179 22.2     No   25    0    0.00
2       2   M  22     71    179 22.2     No   25    6  129.31
3       2   M  22     71    179 22.2     No   25   12   93.33
4       2   M  22     71    179 22.2     No   25   24   46.11
5       2   M  22     71    179 22.2     No   25    1  445.55
```

Specifying all.x = TRUE retains all records in our "x" data (that is, demo1and2), regardless of whether they appear in pk2and3 (a.k.a. a "left join"). Specifying all.y = TRUE does likewise for pk2and3 (a "right join"). An "outer join," where all records in each data frame are merged regardless of whether there is a matching value to merge by in the other data frame is achieved by specifying all = TRUE. An example of an outer join is provided next. Notice that in cases where the merge by variable only has records in the "x" data frame, values for all other variables in the "y"" data frame are set to NA, and vice versa.

```
> merge(demo1and2, pk2and3, all = TRUE)
   Subject  Sex Age Weight Height  BMI Smokes Dose Time    Conc
1        1    M  43     57    166 20.7     No   NA   NA      NA
2        2    M  22     71    179 22.2     No   25    0    0.00
3        2    M  22     71    179 22.2     No   25    6  129.31
4        2    M  22     71    179 22.2     No   25   12   93.33
5        2    M  22     71    179 22.2     No   25   24   46.11
6        2    M  22     71    179 22.2     No   25    1  445.55
7        3 <NA>  NA     NA     NA   NA   <NA>   25   12  116.93
8        3 <NA>  NA     NA     NA   NA   <NA>   25    0    0.00
9        3 <NA>  NA     NA     NA   NA   <NA>   25    1  500.65
10       3 <NA>  NA     NA     NA   NA   <NA>   25    6  146.04
11       3 <NA>  NA     NA     NA   NA   <NA>   25   24   68.25
```

NOTE

Naming Common Variables

If our two datasets have common variables that we do not wish to merge by, then R will append ".x" and ".y" to the column names in the resulting data frame. The `suffixes` argument can be used to create an alternative suffix.

Duplicate Values

The `duplicated` function finds duplicate values. It does so by asking the question, "Have I seen this before?" For example, take the `Month` column from the `airquality` data frame. The `airquality` data frame contains daily records for five months (May through September). In total there are therefore 153 individual values in the `Month` column but most are repeats. Calling `duplicated` on the column yields the following:

```
> isMonthValueADuplicate <- duplicated(airquality$Month)
> isMonthValueADuplicate[1:10]    # View first 10 records
 [1] FALSE  TRUE  TRUE  TRUE  TRUE  TRUE  TRUE  TRUE  TRUE  TRUE
```

The fact that we can generate these TRUE and FALSE values like this is very useful. By placing `!` in front of the call to `duplicated`, we switch the TRUE and FALSE values around. The corresponding logical vector can then be used to remove duplicate values and hence subset our data to leave only the first instance of a value occurring. Here, we use this to extract the first record for each month in the `airquality` dataset:

```
> airquality[!duplicated(airquality$Month), ]
   Ozone Solar.R Wind Temp Month Day
1     41     190  7.4   67     5   1
32    NA     286  8.6   78     6   1
```

```
62     135    269  4.1  84    7  1
93      39     83  6.9  81    8  1
124     96    167  6.9  91    9  1
```

Perhaps a more standard use of the duplicated function is to find and remove duplicated records. To achieve this, we can call duplicated directly on a data frame:

```
> # Create data with a duplicate record for ID==2
> duplicateData <- data.frame(ID = c(1,2,2,3,4), Score = c(57, 45, 45, 63, 54))
> duplicateData
  ID Score
1  1    57
2  2    45
3  2    45
4  3    63
5  4    54
> # Remove the duplicate record
> duplicateData[!duplicated(duplicateData),]
  ID Score
1  1    57
2  2    45
4  3    63
5  4    54
```

TIP
_____

Unique Values

If we just want to identify the unique values within a vector, the unique function removes all dupli-cates within a vector and returns a smaller subset containing the unique values.

_____

Restructuring

Before we can begin to fit models or even plot our data, we need to ensure that it is in a suitable structure. If it is not, we will need to restructure the data. SAS users would call this transposing the data. Excel users might call it pivoting. Others might call it reshaping or tidying. In R, the best known and most used packages for restructuring data are **reshape**, **reshape2**, and recently **tidyr**. Each of the packages has been written by Hadley Wickham and is based around the notion of what he now refers to as "tidy" data. We can think of the packages as an evolution (beginning with **reshape** and ending with **tidyr**). The terminology and usability have improved slightly with each, though the scope of these packages has actually decreased. We will therefore take a little time to look at the packages in turn.

Although the term "tidy data" might be unfamiliar, the concept is nothing new. If you are familiar with relational databases, the basic aim is to structure the data as you would in a database table. In other words, we structure the data such that

▶ Each variable forms a column.

▶ Each observation forms a row.

This differs from Excel, for which it is common to spread values that we want to compare across multiple columns in order to treat them as separate series when working with Excel's plotting wizards. The tidy structure is, however, very standard in R, and most of the graphical and analytical packages in R expect a data frame in the tidy format.

Restructuring with reshape

The **reshape** and **reshape2** packages offer essentially the same functionality for restructuring our data. We will work through an example using **reshape** and highlight differences within **reshape2**. There are several utility functions contained within the **reshape** package, but the main restructuring functions are `melt`, `cast`, and `recast`. The basic idea is to "melt" a data frame (using the `melt` function) into a very long and thin structure and then, if necessary, "cast" it (using the `cast` function in **reshape** or `dcast` in **reshape2**) into a new structure.

TIP

Getting to Grips with reshape via reshapeGUI

Reshaping data can be hard! The `melt` and `cast` functions in **reshape** are great but can take some getting used to. The **reshapeGUI** package provides an interactive graphical user interface for practicing using the `melt` and `cast` functions. When we use the GUI to select ID and measurement variables, it builds up the equivalent line of R code for us. The GUI also allows us to preview the results before we submit to the R console.

Melting

The trick to understand the `melt` function is to be able to identify what are referred to as ID and measurement ("measured") variables within the package. ID variables represent fixed information about the data collected; this is usually IDs or names, geographic information about where the data was collected, the date and time the data was collected, and so on. The measurement variables contain the data we have collected. If you consider fitting a model to the data, then as a rough guide the measurement variables would be the response variables and the ID variables would be the explanatory variables.

Once we've decided what our ID variables are and what our measurement variables are, we feed them into the respective `id.vars` and `measure.vars` arguments. Any variables we are not interested in can be ignored and are excluded from the restructuring. To save some typing, we need only specify one of `id.vars` and one of `measure.vars`. R will assume that the rest of our variables fall into the unused category.

The `melt` function is best seen through an example. Listing 11.3 shows a simple example using the `french_fries` data contained within the **reshape** package. The data was originally collected from a sensory experiment to investigate fryer oils conducted at Iowa State University in 2004.

LISTING 11.3   Melting the `french_fries` Data

```
 1: > # Let's begin by loading the package and looking at the data
 2: > library(reshape)
 3: > head(french_fries, 3)
 4:    time treatment subject rep potato buttery grassy rancid painty
 5: 61    1         1       3   1    2.9     0.0      0    0.0    5.5
 6: 25    1         1       3   2   14.0     0.0      0    1.1    0.0
 7: 62    1         1      10   1   11.0     6.4      0    0.0    0.0
 8: > tail(french_fries, 3)
 9:     time treatment subject rep potato buttery grassy rancid painty
10: 695   10         3      78   2    3.3       0      0    2.5    1.4
11: 666   10         3      86   1    2.5       0      0    7.0   10.5
12: 696   10         3      86   2    2.5       0      0    8.2    9.4
13:
14: # Now we 'melt' having identified the ID variables
15: > fryMelt <- melt(french_fries,
16: +      id.vars = c("time", "treatment", "subject", "rep"))
17:
18: # Our new data is long and thin
19: > head(fryMelt, 3)
20:    time treatment subject rep variable value
21: 1     1         1       3   1   potato   2.9
22: 2     1         1       3   2   potato  14.0
23: 3     1         1      10   1   potato  11.0
24: > tail(fryMelt, 3)
25:      time treatment subject rep variable value
26: 3478   10         3      78   2   painty   1.4
27: 3479   10         3      86   1   painty  10.5
28: 3480   10         3      86   2   painty   9.4
```

Lines 1 to 11 of the listing show the basic structure of our data. We can deduce from the data that at each time point, a subject was given two French fries to taste that had undergone one of three treatments. The subject rated each of the fries using the criteria defined in the remaining columns. These remaining columns are therefore our measurement variables. The variables time, treatment, subject, and rep are our ID variables. Once we have identified the ID and measurement variables, the code is fairly straightforward; we call the melt function and specify the ID variables using id.vars. As can be seen from line 17 onward in the listing, the resulting data is very long and thin. The column names for the measurement variables have been stacked into a single column named variable, and the ID variables have been repeated accordingly. The associated values for the measurement variables have been stacked into a column named value.

Casting

Calling the melt function on a data frame will normally produce a data frame in the desired format. However, more often than not some further work is required in order to "cast" the data into a new structure. The cast function in **reshape** (or dcast in **reshape2**) accepts a formula that describes the shape of the output format. It has the following basic form:

```
untouched_column_1 + untouched_column_2 ~ column_to_split_1 + column_to_split_2
```

On the left side we specify the columns that are to remain as they are. On the right side we specify columns that are to be split apart into new columns. A new column will be created for each unique combination of values contained within the variables on the right side of the equation. We never reference the value column because this represents our content or measured data. The behavior is best seen using an example. In Listing 11.4 we create two new columns from the fryMelt data we created in Listing 11.3 based on the rep variable. The "..." notation is used to mean "all other columns." A single period can also be used to represent "no variable" in the casting formula.

LISTING 11.4   Casting the french_fries Data

```
1: > # Create two new columns based on the rep variable
2: > fryReCast <- cast(fryMelt, ... ~ rep)
3: > head(fryReCast, 3)
4:    time treatment subject variable    1   2
5: 1    1         1       1        potato 2.9 14
6: 2    1         1       1       buttery 0.0  0
7: 3    1         1       1        grassy 0.0  0
```

NOTE

Differences Between reshape and reshape2

In **reshape2** the distinction is made between casting to data frames and casting to arrays. Instead of the cast function, we have two new functions: acast for arrays and dcast for data frames.

Using `melt` and then `cast` (or `dcast`) helps break up the reshaping process. For more complicated examples, it can be really useful to check that the intermediate "melted" data frame is as expected before casting into a new shape. However, this is not actually a necessary step. The entire transformation can be performed in a single step using the `recast` function. The only difference when using `recast` is that instead of the `id.vars` and `measure.vars` arguments that we used in `melt`, we drop the "s" and use `id.var` and `measure.var` instead.

```
> recast(french_fries,
+       id.var = c("time", "treatment", "subject", "rep"),
+       formula = ... ~ rep)
  time treatment subject variable   1    2
1    1           1       3   potato 2.9 14.0
2    1           1       3  buttery 0.0  0.0
3    1           1       3    grassy 0.0  0.0
...
```

NOTE

Aggregation Using reshape

The `fun.aggregate` argument to `cast` (and `dcast` in **reshape2**) provides the ability to aggregate the data using summary functions such as `mean`.

```
> # Mean across replicates
> replicateMeans <-
+   cast(fryMelt, time + treatment + subject + variable ~ ., mean)
> head(replicateMeans, 3)
  time treatment subject variable (all)
1    1           1       3   potato  8.45
2    1           1       3  buttery  0.00
3    1           1       3    grassy  0.00
```

Although it is possible to aggregate data using `reshape`, we will look at more straightforward aggregation techniques later in the hour and then again in Hour 12.

Restructuring with tidyr

The main difference between the **reshape** approach to restructuring and **tidyr** is the terminology. The functions `melt` and `cast` (or `dcast`) become `gather` and `spread`. Otherwise, the idea is very much the same. In **tidyr** we also have a third option, `separate`, that comes in handy when multiple pieces of information are stored together in a single variable.

Gather

When the values of a particular variable are spread over several columns, we look to "gather" the data into a single column. We do this using `gather`. The required arguments to the `gather` function are shown in Table 11.2.

TABLE 11.2 Arguments to the `gather` Function

Argument	Usage
data	The name of the dataset, a data frame object
key	The key column to create in the output (that is, the new column name of the variable)
value	The value column to create in the output (that is, the new column name for the observed value)
...	The columns that will be used for the gathering

Let's look at how we would use `gather` with some real data. For this example, we will use the `djiData` stock data contained within the **mangoTraining** package. To simplify the example, we will first subset the data to obtain a data frame with three columns; the date, and the low and high values for the DJI for each date:

```
> djiHighLow <- djiData[, c("Date", "DJI.High", "DJI.Low")]
> head(djiHighLow, 3)
        Date DJI.High  DJI.Low
1 12/31/2014 18043.22 17820.88
2 12/30/2014 18035.02 17959.70
3 12/29/2014 18073.04 18021.57
```

Suppose that we want to create a single graphic of the high and low DJI values using one of the packages described in Hours 13–15. We need one column containing the values to plot and another column specifying whether each value was a high or a low value. We do this using the `gather` function.

Having loaded the package, we next specify each of the columns we wish to gather, separated by a comma, referencing each by name directly and without wrapping in quotes. As highlighted in Table 12, we must also specify names for the `key` and `value` columns in the gathered data frame. In this example, we gather two columns, `DJI.High` and `DJI.Low`, but in general we can specify as many columns as we like:

```
> gatheredDJI <- gather(djiHighLow, key="DJI", value="Value", DJI.High, DJI.Low)
> head(gatheredDJI, 4)
        Date      DJI    Value
1 2014-12-31 DJI.High 18043.22
```

```
2 2014-12-30 DJI.High 18035.02
3 2014-12-29 DJI.High 18073.04
4 2014-12-26 DJI.High 18103.45
```

Variables that are not listed, such as Date in the preceding example, are unaffected by the gathering process. If we find the need to gather the majority of columns within our data, then instead of specifying what to gather we can specify what *not* to gather. We do so by listing columns that we are not interested in and placing a minus sign in front of each one.

TIP

Lots to Gather?

The **tidyr** package allows a special use of the : operator for sequencing. The operator allows us to specify a "from" and a "to" in terms of column names. Therefore, a:z would be interpreted as start gathering at column "a" and gather all columns up to column "z."

Spread

The term "spread" is similar to "cast" in **reshape**. It enables us to take a column of values and a column label for these values (the "key") and "spread" the contents over several columns. The primary arguments to spread are again key and value. A new column is created for each label in the key column. This can be useful if we need to calculate, say, changes over time. We take a column of values, value, and a column of times, key, at which these values occurred. We then spread the information, creating a new column for each time point. In the following example, we undo the process of gathering the low and high DJI values into a single column, spreading back into the two original columns:

```
> backToOriginal <- spread(gatheredDJI, key = DJI, value = Value)
> head(backToOriginal, 3)
        Date DJI.High  DJI.Low
1 01/02/2014 16573.07 16416.49
2 01/03/2014 16518.74 16439.30
3 01/06/2014 16532.99 16405.52
```

TIP

Piping Commands

The **tidyr** package has been designed to work with **magrittr**'s pipe operator. This allows us to chain commands together, thus avoiding intermediate data frames. You will learn more about the pipe operator in Hour 12.

Separate

Occasionally we may find ourselves in a situation where two separate pieces of information are joined together in a single variable. R packages provide a nice example of this. An R package source name is made up of a package name and version number. An example of this is shown here:

```
> Packages <- data.frame(Source=c("reshape_0.8.5", "tidyr_0.2.0"))
> Packages
         Source
1 reshape_0.8.5
2    tidyr_0.2.0
```

We can use the `separate` function to split the package names from the version numbers. Further arguments such as `sep` are used to specify the splitting character:

```
> separate(Packages, Source, into = c("Package", "Version"), sep = "_")
  Package Version
1 reshape   0.8.5
2   tidyr   0.2.0
```

By default, the original variable is deleted. We override this behavior, however, by specifying `remove = FALSE`.

Data Aggregation

In Hour 9, "Loops and Summaries," you saw two ways of applying simple functions to more complex data structures:

- ▶ Iterate over sections of data with a loop.

- ▶ Use one of the apply family of functions.

Let's consider if we want to add a new column to `airquality`, containing the difference between the `Wind` speed for a particular day and the median `Wind` speed for that `Month`. To achieve this, we need to perform three tasks:

- ▶ Calculate the median `Wind` speed by `Month`.

- ▶ Align the median `Wind` speed value calculated with the daily `Wind` speed data.

- ▶ Calculate the difference between the daily `Wind` speed and the "median" data.

Using a "for" Loop

If we choose to use loops, we could do the following, for example:

- ▶ Create an empty column in our data.
- ▶ For each row in the data:
    - ▶ Look at the Month value for this row.
    - ▶ Calculate the median Wind for all data with that Month value.
    - ▶ Calculate the difference between the daily Wind value and this median.
    - ▶ Insert this value in the cell.

This approach is very inefficient. For example, it involves calculating a median repeatedly (once per row). Instead, we could calculate the medians using one loop and then reference the values in a second loop, using an approach like this:

- ▶ Create an empty column in our data.
- ▶ For each unique Month value, calculate and store the mean Wind.
- ▶ For each row in the data:
    - ▶ Look at the Month value for this row.
    - ▶ Reference the correct median Wind for that Month value (from previous loop).
    - ▶ Calculate the difference between the daily Wind value and this median.
    - ▶ Insert this value in the cell.

Again, this isn't ideal. Let's instead consider (and see) an approach using the "apply" functions that we saw in Hour 9.

Using an "apply" Function

The first thing we have to decide is which "apply" function to use. Let's first use the tapply function (or split and sapply) to return the median Wind by Month:

```
> head(airquality)   # Print airquality
  Ozone Solar.R Wind Temp Month Day
1    41     190  7.4   67     5   1
2    36     118  8.0   72     5   2
3    12     149 12.6   74     5   3
4    18     313 11.5   62     5   4
5    NA      NA 14.3   56     5   5
6    28      NA 14.9   66     5   6
```

```
> windMedians <- tapply(airquality$Wind, airquality$Month, median)
> windMedians
    5    6    7    8    9
 11.5  9.7  8.6  8.6 10.3
```

This is straightforward and calculates the median `Wind` speed by `Month`, storing the results in a named vector. The next step is to align the daily values with the corresponding `windMedians` values so we can calculate the differences. This is, perhaps, the most complex part of this process.

As you saw in Hour 3, "Single-Mode Data Structures," we can reference values from a vector using square brackets and specifying with blank, positive, negative, logical, or character inputs. In this case, we have a vector of `Month` values to use to reference values from the `windMedians` vector. Let's convert our `Month` values to characters and then use those values to reference the (named) elements of `windMedians`:

```
> charMonths <- as.character(airquality$Month)        # Converted character values of
                                                        Month
> # Use character values to reference named elements
> head(windMedians [ charMonths ])
    5    5    5    5    5    5
 11.5 11.5 11.5 11.5 11.5 11.5
```

Now we can create a column of means in our dataset and calculate differences from those. Of course, we don't have to create the column of intermediate values, but we included it here to help illustrate the process:

```
> airquality$MedianWind <- windMedians [ charMonths ]         # Add Median Wind
                                                                column
> airquality$DiffWind <- airquality$Wind - airquality$MedianWind  # Calculate
                                                                    differences
> head(airquality, 3)                                         # First few rows
   Ozone Solar.R Wind Temp Month Day MeanWind DiffWind MedianWind
1    41     190  7.4   67     5   1     11.5     -4.1       11.5
2    36     118  8.0   72     5   2     11.5     -3.5       11.5
3    12     149 12.6   74     5   3     11.5      1.1       11.5
> tail(airquality, 3)                                         # Last few rows
    Ozone Solar.R Wind Temp Month Day MeanWind DiffWind MedianWind
151    14     191 14.3   75     9  28     10.3      4.0       10.3
152    18     131  8.0   76     9  29     10.3     -2.3       10.3
153    20     223 11.5   68     9  30     10.3      1.2       10.3
```

This approach works, but the second step (aligning the means with the daily values) was perhaps a little complex. If we decide later that we want to perform the same process for a number of columns, the solution would become more verbose/complex. We can simplify this approach using the `aggregate` function.

The aggregate Function

The aggregate function allows us apply functions over sections of a data frame, returning a data frame as the output. We can use aggregate using two different methods:

▶ We can supply a "formula" to describe the data over which to apply.

▶ We can specify a set of variables to summarize and a set of variables by which to summarize separately.

Let's first see an example using a formula to define the structure of the data.

Using aggregate with a Formula

We can use a formula with aggregate to specify the variables to summarize and the variables by which to perform the summary. A basic formula is of the form Y ~ X, where Y is the variable to summarize and X is the variable by which to summarize. The aggregate function additionally accepts a data argument (specifying the data frame containing the data) and a FUN argument (specifying the function to apply). Let's look at a simple example where we again calculate the median Wind by Month:

```
> aggregate(Wind ~ Month, data = airquality, FUN = median)
  Month Wind
1     5 11.5
2     6  9.7
3     7  8.6
4     8  8.6
5     9 10.3
```

As you can see, the return structure is a data frame, which is a very simple and useable structure.

Summarizing by Multiple Variables

If we want to apply the function by more than one variable, we can add the names of the variables to the set of variables in the formula:

```
> aggregate(Wind ~ Month + cut(Temp, 2), data = airquality, FUN = median)
  Month cut(Temp, 2) Wind
1     5   (56,76.5] 11.5
2     6   (56,76.5]  9.7
3     7   (56,76.5] 10.6
4     8   (56,76.5] 12.6
5     9   (56,76.5] 10.9
6     5   (76.5,97] 10.3
7     6   (76.5,97]  9.7
```

```
8      7     (76.5,97]  8.6
9      8     (76.5,97]  8.3
10     9     (76.5,97]  7.7
```

Again, the return structure is a data frame.

Summarizing Multiple Columns

If we want to perform the same summary on a number of variables at the same time, we can combine the summary variables in a call to cbind. For example, let's calculate the median Wind and Ozone values by Month:

```
> aggregate(cbind(Wind, Ozone) ~ Month, data = airquality, FUN = median, na.rm =
➡TRUE)
  Month Wind Ozone
1     5 11.5    18
2     6 11.5    23
3     7  7.7    60
4     8  8.0    52
5     9 10.3    23
```

Multiple Return Values

In the preceding examples, we used the median function, which returns a single value. If, instead, we used a function that returned multiple values, these would be returned as separate columns. To illustrate this behavior, let's repeat the last three examples with the range function:

```
> # Range of Wind values by Month
> aggregate(Wind ~ Month, data = airquality, FUN = range, na.rm = TRUE)
  Month Wind.1 Wind.2
1     5    5.7   20.1
2     6    1.7   20.7
3     7    4.1   14.9
4     8    2.3   15.5
5     9    2.8   16.6

> # Range of Wind AND Ozone values by Month
> aggregate(cbind(Wind, Ozone) ~ Month, data = airquality, FUN = range, na.rm =
➡TRUE)
  Month Wind.1 Wind.2 Ozone.1 Ozone.2
1     5    5.7   20.1       1     115
2     6    8.0   20.7      12      71
3     7    4.1   14.9       7     135
4     8    2.3   15.5       9     168
5     9    2.8   16.6       7      96
```

```
> # Range of Wind AND Ozone values by Month AND grouped Temp
> aggregate(cbind(Wind, Ozone) ~ Month + cut(Temp, 2), data = airquality,
+          FUN = range, na.rm = TRUE)
   Month cut(Temp, 2) Wind.1 Wind.2 Ozone.1 Ozone.2
1      5   (56,76.5]    6.9   20.1       1      41
2      6   (56,76.5]    9.2   20.7      12      37
3      7   (56,76.5]    6.9   14.3      10      16
4      8   (56,76.5]    7.4   14.3       9      23
5      9   (56,76.5]    6.9   16.6       7      30
6      5   (76.5,97]    5.7   14.9      45     115
7      6   (76.5,97]    8.0   14.9      21      71
8      7   (76.5,97]    4.1   14.9       7     135
9      8   (76.5,97]    2.3   15.5       9     168
10     9   (76.5,97]    2.8   15.5      16      96
```

In these examples, the values returned are named based on the column that was summarized and an index of the return value. If, instead, the function returned "named" elements, these names would be appended to the summarized column names:

```
> aggregate(Wind ~ Month, data = airquality,
+   FUN = function(X) {
+     c(MIN = min(X), MAX = max(X))
+   })
   Month Wind.MIN Wind.MAX
1      5      5.7     20.1
2      6      1.7     20.7
3      7      4.1     14.9
4      8      2.3     15.5
5      9      2.8     16.6
```

Using aggregate by Specifying Columns

Instead of the formula, we can use aggregate by specifying variables separately in the function call. Specifically, we specify lists of variables, which we can rename when specifying the variables if we want to control the names of the resulting summary variables:

▶ The first input specifies the variable(s) to summarize.

▶ The second input specifies the grouping variable(s).

▶ The third input is the function to apply.

Let's again calculate the median Wind by Month, this time specifying the inputs as described earlier:

```
> aggregate(list(aveWind = airquality$Wind), list(Month = airquality$Month),
➥median)
  Month aveWind
1     5    11.5
2     6     9.7
3     7     8.6
4     8     8.6
5     9    10.3
```

The output is a data frame, with the variables named as specified in the input lists.

Summarizing by Multiple Variables

If we want to apply the function by more than one variable, we can add these variables to the list, as follows:

```
> aggregate(list(aveWind = airquality$Wind),
+    list(Month = airquality$Month, TempGroup = cut(airquality$Temp, 2)), median)
   Month TempGroup aveWind
1      5 (56,76.5]    11.5
2      6 (56,76.5]     9.7
3      7 (56,76.5]    10.6
4      8 (56,76.5]    12.6
5      9 (56,76.5]    10.9
6      5 (76.5,97]    10.3
7      6 (76.5,97]     9.7
8      7 (76.5,97]     8.6
9      8 (76.5,97]     8.3
10     9 (76.5,97]     7.7
```

Again, this approach allows us to easily control the names of the resulting variables (for example, naming the TempGroup and aveWind columns).

Summarizing Multiple Columns

If we want to perform the same summary on a number of variables at the same time, we can provide multiple variables in the first input list, as follows:

```
> aggregate(list(aveWind = airquality$Wind, aveOzone = airquality$Ozone),
+          list(Month = airquality$Month), median, na.rm = TRUE)
  Month aveWind aveOzone
1     5    11.5       18
2     6     9.7       23
3     7     8.6       60
4     8     8.6       52
5     9    10.3       23
```

TIP

Specifying Inputs as Data Frames

Because a data frame is, structurally, a list of vectors, we can supply data frame inputs directly instead of lists, if preferred. This is most useful when there are multiple variables being specified. For example, we could rewrite the last example as follows:

```
> aggregate(airquality[,c("Wind", "Ozone")],
+           list(Month = airquality$Month), median, na.rm = TRUE)
  Month Wind Ozone
1     5 11.5    18
2     6  9.7    23
3     7  8.6    60
4     8  8.6    52
5     9 10.3    23
```

Although this is far more concise, we do lose the ability to directly rename the variables (for example, to aveWind and aveOzone as per the previous example).

Multiple Return Values

As with the example where we specified formulas, we can apply functions that return multiple values. In this case, the index of values is appended to the summarized variable name:

```
> aggregate(list(Wind = airquality$Wind),
+   list(Month = airquality$Month), range)
  Month Wind.1 Wind.2
1     5    5.7   20.1
2     6    1.7   20.7
3     7    4.1   14.9
4     8    2.3   15.5
5     9    2.8   16.6
```

Again, if our function returns named elements, these are appended instead of the index values:

```
> aggregate(list(Wind = airquality$Wind),
+           list(Month = airquality$Month),
+           function(X) {
+             c(MIN = min(X), MAX = max(X))
+           })
  Month Wind.MIN Wind.MAX
1     5      5.7     20.1
2     6      1.7     20.7
3     7      4.1     14.9
4     8      2.3     15.5
5     9      2.8     16.6
```

Calculating Differences from Baseline

At the start of the Data Aggregation section, we introduced a task that we were aiming to complete and discussed how the previous approaches (for loops and apply functions) could be used to achieve that task. To recap, we are aiming to add a new column to `airquality`, containing the difference between the `Wind` speed for a particular day and the median `Wind` speed for that `Month`.

To achieve this, we need to perform three tasks:

▶ Calculate the median `Wind` speed by `Month`.

▶ Align the median `Wind` speed value calculated with the daily `Wind` speed data.

▶ Calculate the difference between the daily `Wind` speed and the "median" data.

Using the `aggregate` function, we can calculate the median `Wind` by `Month`, returning our results as a data frame:

```
> windMedians <- aggregate(list(MedianWind = airquality$Wind),
+                          list(Month = airquality$Month), median)
> windMedians
  Month MedianWind
1     5       11.5
2     6        9.7
3     7        8.6
4     8        8.6
5     9       10.3
```

NOTE

Using List Inputs to Aggregate

In this example, I'm specifying the inputs to aggregate as list elements, instead of a formula, so I can explicitly control the naming of the summary (that is, the `MedianWind` column). If I used a formula, I'd need to rename the column to `MedianWind` as a second step.

Now that we have our median `Wind` values in a data frame, we can merge this onto our original dataset to create the `MedianWind` column:

```
> airquality <- merge(airquality, windMedians)
> head(airquality)
  Month Ozone Solar.R Wind Temp Day MedianWind
1     5    41     190  7.4   67   1       11.5
2     5    36     118  8.0   72   2       11.5
3     5    12     149 12.6   74   3       11.5
```

4	5	18	313	11.5	62	4	11.5
5	5	NA	NA	14.3	56	5	11.5
6	5	28	NA	14.9	66	6	11.5

Summary

In this hour, you saw how to sort, set, and merge data using traditional R functions. We looked at the popular **reshape (reshape2)** and **tidyr** packages for restructuring our data, ready for plotting and modeling. We also looked at various options for aggregating data including the powerful `aggregate` function.

In the next hour, we will look closer at two packages that are changing the way people manipulate and summarize data with R. The **data.table** and **dplyr** packages offer speed and efficiency, borrowing approaches from the database world.

Q&A

Q. I tried to sort the `airquality` data using `airquality[sort(airquality$Wind),]` but got strange results. What happened?

A. To sort a data frame in this way, you need to know which rows to select. The sort order is returned by the `order` function, not `sort`.

Q. I have two data frames, each containing data for specified locations at specified times. Can I merge by both variables?

A. Absolutely. You can specify as many merge-by-variable operations as you like using `merge`. Pass the names to `merge` as a character vector.

Q. Is it possible to merge three data frames at once using `merge`?

A. Unfortunately, no. However, the `merge_recurse` function in **reshape** provides this functionality.

Q. Should I be using reshape2 instead of reshape?

A. Development of **reshape** ceased in 2011. However, it depends on what you want to do. In some sense, **reshape2** supersedes **reshape**; however, there is arguably more functionality contained within **reshape**. If you want to use **reshape/reshape2** for data aggregation, it is worth noting that the `cast` function can handle summary functions such as `range` that produce a vector of multiple values, whereas `dcast` cannot and fails with an error.

Workshop

The workshop contains quiz questions and exercises to help you solidify your understanding of the material covered. Try to answer all questions before looking at the "Answers" section that follows.

Quiz

1. What is the difference between `sort` and `order`?

2. Which function can be used to return the unique values in a vector?

3. What function would you use to append rows to a data frame?

4. What does the "d" represent in the `dcast` function?

Answers

1. The `sort` function is used to sort vectors. It cannot be used to sort data frames. The `order` function provides a sort order that can be used to sort vectors or data frames.

2. The `unique` function directly returns the unique values. Alternatively, `duplicated` could be used as a means to subscript and obtain the same result.

3. The `rbind` function is a simple means of appending new rows to a data frame.

4. The "d" stands for "data frame." In **reshape2**, the more generic cast was replaced with `acast` and `dcast` functions to allow casting to both arrays and data frames via separate functions.

Activities

1. Sort the `mtcars` data frame by the number of cylinders and then descending by miles per gallon.

2. Extract the "Employees" and "Orders" tables from the Northwind.mdb file contained within the **mangoTraining** package using **RODBC**. Merge the two data frames by EmployeeID.

3. Use `melt` and `dcast` to find the average tip size by the sex and smoking habit of the bill payer using the `tips` data contained within the **reshape2** package.

4. Separate the `Date` column within `djiData` into three new columns: Month, Day, and Year. Ensure that you keep the original `Date` column.

Efficient Data Handling in R

What You'll Learn in This Hour:

- ► The **dplyr** package
- ► Piping commands together
- ► The **data.table** package
- ► Options for improving efficiency

In Hour 11, "Data Manipulation and Transformation," we looked at some standard methods for processing data in R. In particular, you saw how to sort and merge data. In previous hours we discussed how to subscript and summarize data using the "apply" family of functions. Now we will look at two packages, **dplyr** and **data.table**, that enable us to do all of these tasks for data frames within consistent, highly efficient frameworks.

We will begin the hour by looking at Hadley Wickham's incredibly popular **dplyr** package. Although **dplyr** is actually the more recent of the two packages we'll discuss in this hour, it fits in with packages such as **readr** and **tidyr** from the previous two hours. The **data.table** package is a standalone package for data manipulation that offers greater efficiency for very large data.

dplyr: A New Way of Handling Data

The **dplyr** package is another Hadley Wickham package that is revolutionizing the way people work with data in R. The package, which was first released in January 2014, fits into an analysis workflow that Hadley Wickham has helped define. In Hour 10, "Importing and Exporting," you saw how packages such as **readr**, **haven**, and **readxl** can be used to import data into R. In Hour 11, you saw how the **tidyr** package can be used to transform data into a new shape. We will now look at how **dplyr** can be used to sort, subset, merge and summarize data.

The **dplyr** package can be thought of as an evolution of the popular **plyr** package, although it focuses solely on the manipulation of rectangular data structures, whereas **plyr** provides a more general framework. The focus of **dplyr** is very much on usability; however, there has also been considerable effort to ensure that **dplyr** is fast and efficient.

Creating a dplyr (tbl_df) Object

The **dplyr** package is intended to be used in a data analysis workflow in which data is imported using packages such as **readr**, **haven**, and **readxl** and then (possibly) transformed using **tidyr**. Each of these packages contains functions that produce an object of the tbl_df class. A tbl_df object is a **dplyr** construct that extends a data frame, affecting the way it prints.

The tbl_df class extension does not affect standard data frame operations; however, each of the data-manipulation functions within **dplyr** returns a tbl_df object and so it is worth us spending a little time to see what a tbl_df actually looks like. We can create a tbl_df object directly from a data.frame using the tbl_df function. An example of this is shown in Listing 12.1.

LISTING 12.1   Creating tbl_df Objects

```
 1 : > library(dplyr)
 2 : >
 3 : > # Create a tbl_df object from mtcars
 4 : > head(mtcars)
 5 :                    mpg cyl disp  hp drat    wt  qsec vs am gear carb
 6 : Mazda RX4         21.0   6  160 110 3.90 2.620 16.46  0  1    4    4
 7 : Mazda RX4 Wag     21.0   6  160 110 3.90 2.875 17.02  0  1    4    4
 8 : Datsun 710        22.8   4  108  93 3.85 2.320 18.61  1  1    4    1
 9 : Hornet 4 Drive    21.4   6  258 110 3.08 3.215 19.44  1  0    3    1
10 : Hornet Sportabout 18.7   8  360 175 3.15 3.440 17.02  0  0    3    2
11 : Valiant           18.1   6  225 105 2.76 3.460 20.22  1  0    3    1
12 : >
13 : > carData <- tbl_df(mtcars)
14 : > carData
15 : Source: local data frame [32 x 11]
16 :
17 :     mpg cyl  disp  hp drat    wt  qsec vs am gear carb
18 : 1  21.0   6 160.0 110 3.90 2.620 16.46  0  1    4    4
19 : 2  21.0   6 160.0 110 3.90 2.875 17.02  0  1    4    4
20 : 3  22.8   4 108.0  93 3.85 2.320 18.61  1  1    4    1
21 : 4  21.4   6 258.0 110 3.08 3.215 19.44  1  0    3    1
22 : 5  18.7   8 360.0 175 3.15 3.440 17.02  0  0    3    2
23 : 6  18.1   6 225.0 105 2.76 3.460 20.22  1  0    3    1
24 : 7  14.3   8 360.0 245 3.21 3.570 15.84  0  0    3    4
25 : 8  24.4   4 146.7  62 3.69 3.190 20.00  1  0    4    2
26 : 9  22.8   4 140.8  95 3.92 3.150 22.90  1  0    4    2
27 : 10 19.2   6 167.6 123 3.92 3.440 18.30  1  0    4    4
28 :.. ...  ...   ...  ...  ...   ...   ... .. ..  ...  ...
29 : >
30 : > class(carData)    # A dbl_df object is just an extension to a data.frame
➥object
31 : [1] "tbl_df"    "tbl"       "data.frame"
```

In addition to changing the way in which data frames print, the creation of a `tbl_df` object also removes row names. In Listing 12.1 we can see how the creation of the carData "tbl_df" removes the row names from the original `mtcars` data. This is intentional and enforces the tidy data principle that all meaningful information should be stored in the same way (in columns). However, it can of course be a little frustrating if you have meaningful row names! The terms "tbl_df" and "data frame" will be used interchangeably throughout the remainder of this hour.

NOTE
___

Working with Data Tables

The **dplyr** package allows us to work with data table objects via the `tbl_dt` function, which extends the `data.table` class to create a `tbl_dt` object. A `tbl_dt` object behaves just like a `tbl_df` object.
___

Sorting

In **dplyr** we sort data using the `arrange` function. The `arrange` function expects a data frame (or a `tbl_df`) as the first argument. We can then list any number of columns as the subsequent arguments. The data is sorted by the first column we provide, then by the second, and so on. By default, an ascending sort is used. In the example below, we sort the carData data by `carb` and then by `cyl`:

```
> arrange(carData, carb, cyl)
Source: local data frame [32 x 11]

    mpg cyl  disp  hp drat    wt  qsec vs am gear carb
1  22.8   4 108.0  93 3.85 2.320 18.61  1  1    4    1
2  32.4   4  78.7  66 4.08 2.200 19.47  1  1    4    1
3  33.9   4  71.1  65 4.22 1.835 19.90  1  1    4    1
4  21.5   4 120.1  97 3.70 2.465 20.01  1  0    3    1
5  27.3   4  79.0  66 4.08 1.935 18.90  1  1    4    1
6  21.4   6 258.0 110 3.08 3.215 19.44  1  0    3    1
7  18.1   6 225.0 105 2.76 3.460 20.22  1  0    3    1
8  24.4   4 146.7  62 3.69 3.190 20.00  1  0    4    2
9  22.8   4 140.8  95 3.92 3.150 22.90  1  0    4    2
10 30.4   4  75.7  52 4.93 1.615 18.52  1  1    4    2
.. ....  .. ..... ... ....  ....  ....  . ..  ...  ...
```

If we want to sort by descending values for any of our sort columns, we can wrap the column name in a call to the `desc` function; for example, to sort by `carb` and then descending values of `cyl` we would write `arrange(carData, carb, desc(cyl))`. Alternatively, we can simply place a minus sign in front of the column name, as shown here:

```
arrange(carData, carb, -cyl)
```

Subscripting

The **dplyr** package defines subscripting as two distinct operations: choosing rows and choosing columns. These are defined respectively as `filter` and `select`. As with all of the **dplyr** functions we are discussing in this hour, each function expects a data frame (or `tbl_df` object) as the first argument. This allows us to reference variables directly in subsequent arguments without using dollar signs or square brackets. In the second argument, we choose how we wish to "filter" the rows or "select" the columns. Let's start by using the `filter` function to create a subset of `carData` containing only four-cylinder cars:

```
> cyl4 <- filter(carData, cyl == 4)
> cyl4
Source: local data frame [11 x 11]

      mpg cyl  disp  hp drat    wt  qsec vs am gear carb
1   22.8   4 108.0  93 3.85 2.320 18.61  1  1    4    1
2   24.4   4 146.7  62 3.69 3.190 20.00  1  0    4    2
3   22.8   4 140.8  95 3.92 3.150 22.90  1  0    4    2
4   32.4   4  78.7  66 4.08 2.200 19.47  1  1    4    1
5   30.4   4  75.7  52 4.93 1.615 18.52  1  1    4    2
6   33.9   4  71.1  65 4.22 1.835 19.90  1  1    4    1
7   21.5   4 120.1  97 3.70 2.465 20.01  1  0    3    1
8   27.3   4  79.0  66 4.08 1.935 18.90  1  1    4    1
9   26.0   4 120.3  91 4.43 2.140 16.70  0  1    5    2
10  30.4   4  95.1 113 3.77 1.513 16.90  1  1    5    2
11  21.4   4 121.0 109 4.11 2.780 18.60  1  1    4    2
```

We can use any standard logical operations to filter our data. In addition to the standard ampersand (&), **dplyr** also permits us to separate "and" operations with a comma:

```
> filter(carData, cyl == 4, gear == 5)    # equivalent to cyl == 4 & gear == 5
Source: local data frame [2 x 11]

    mpg cyl  disp  hp drat    wt qsec vs am gear carb
1 26.0   4 120.3  91 4.43 2.140 16.7  0  1    5    2
2 30.4   4  95.1 113 3.77 1.513 16.9  1  1    5    2
```

The `select` function operates in much the same way as `filter`. We can either use column names or column numbers to select which columns to keep or drop, much like the `select` option in the `subset` function. The standard way to select multiple columns is to separate each column with a comma. Note again that we do not use quotes to specify columns.

```
> select(carData, mpg, wt, cyl)    # Return just these columns
Source: local data frame [32 x 3]

    mpg    wt cyl
1  21.0 2.620   6
2  21.0 2.875   6
```

```
3   22.8 2.320    4
4   21.4 3.215    6
5   18.7 3.440    8
6   18.1 3.460    6
7   14.3 3.570    8
8   24.4 3.190    4
9   22.8 3.150    4
10 19.2 3.440    6
..  ...   ... ...
> select(carData, -vs, -am)    # Return everything except these columns
Source: local data frame [32 x 9]

   mpg cyl  disp  hp drat    wt  qsec gear carb
1   21.0   6 160.0 110 3.90 2.620 16.46    4    4
2   21.0   6 160.0 110 3.90 2.875 17.02    4    4
3   22.8   4 108.0  93 3.85 2.320 18.61    4    1
4   21.4   6 258.0 110 3.08 3.215 19.44    3    1
5   18.7   8 360.0 175 3.15 3.440 17.02    3    2
6   18.1   6 225.0 105 2.76 3.460 20.22    3    1
7   14.3   8 360.0 245 3.21 3.570 15.84    3    4
8   24.4   4 146.7  62 3.69 3.190 20.00    4    2
9   22.8   4 140.8  95 3.92 3.150 22.90    4    2
10 19.2   6 167.6 123 3.92 3.440 18.30    4    4
..  ...  ...   ...  ...   ...    ...   ... ...  ...
```

Another nice property of the `select` function is that we can choose a sequence of columns using the column names in addition to the column numbers. For example, we could specify `select(carData, mpg:wt)`. Choosing the columns that we want is simplified via a number of additional utility functions, as listed in Table 12.1.

TABLE 12.1   Utility Functions for Selecting Columns

Function	Description	Usage
starts_with	Names starting with x	starts_with(x, ignore.case = TRUE)
ends_with	Names ending in x	ends_with(x, ignore.case = TRUE)
contains	Contains string x	contains(x, ignore.case = TRUE)
matches	Regular expression matching	matches(x, ignore.case = TRUE)
num_range	Variables numerically from x1 to xn	num_range("x", 1:n, width = 2)
one_of	Variables provided in a vector	one_of("x", "y", "z")
everything	Selects all variables	everything()

CAUTION

Specialist functions within select

The functions described in Table 12.1 *only* work inside the `select` function and cannot be used to find patterns in standard character vectors.

Adding New Columns

The `mutate` function enables us to easily add new columns to our data. We can either provide a vector of values in the same way we would with a standard data frame or we can create new columns from existing variables. In the following example, we create a new column containing the original row names from the `mtcars` data frame. We then use the information contained with the `hp` and `wt` columns to create a second new column containing the power-to-weight ratio.

```
> fullCarData <- mutate(carData, type = rownames(mtcars), pwr2wt = hp/wt)
> fullCarData
Source: local data frame [32 x 13]

      mpg cyl  disp  hp drat    wt  qsec vs am gear carb           type  pwr2wt
1    21.0   6 160.0 110 3.90 2.620 16.46  0  1    4    4       Mazda RX4 41.98473
2    21.0   6 160.0 110 3.90 2.875 17.02  0  1    4    4   Mazda RX4 Wag 38.26087
3    22.8   4 108.0  93 3.85 2.320 18.61  1  1    4    1      Datsun 710 40.08621
4    21.4   6 258.0 110 3.08 3.215 19.44  1  0    3    1  Hornet 4 Drive 34.21462
5    18.7   8 360.0 175 3.15 3.440 17.02  0  0    3    2 Hornet Sportabout 50.87209
6    18.1   6 225.0 105 2.76 3.460 20.22  1  0    3    1         Valiant 30.34682
7    14.3   8 360.0 245 3.21 3.570 15.84  0  0    3    4      Duster 360 68.62745
8    24.4   4 146.7  62 3.69 3.190 20.00  1  0    4    2       Merc 240D 19.43574
9    22.8   4 140.8  95 3.92 3.150 22.90  1  0    4    2        Merc 230 30.15873
10   19.2   6 167.6 123 3.92 3.440 18.30  1  0    4    4        Merc 280 35.75581
..    ... ...   ...  ... ...   ...   ... .. ..  ...  ...            ...     ...
```

We can also drop columns by assigning existing names to `NULL`. The `mutate` function is similar to the base R function `transform`. However, unlike `transform`, the `mutate` function creates variables in the order in which we specify them, allowing variables that we create to themselves create new variables.

```
> fullCarData <- mutate(carData, type = rownames(mtcars),
+                       drat = NULL, qsec = NULL,
+                       pwr2wt = hp/wt, pwr2wt.Sq = pwr2wt^2)
> head(fullCarData,3)
Source: local data frame [3 x 12]

    mpg cyl disp  hp    wt vs am gear carb          type  pwr2wt pwr2wt.Sq
1  21.0   6  160 110 2.620  0  1    4    4     Mazda RX4 41.98473  1762.718
2  21.0   6  160 110 2.875  0  1    4    4 Mazda RX4 Wag 38.26087  1463.894
3  22.8   4  108  93 2.320  1  1    4    1    Datsun 710 40.08621  1606.904
```

Merging

In Hour 11, you saw how the merge function can be used to merge data frames. The merge function allows us to specify arguments such as all.x in order to achieve what is also commonly known as a "left join." In contrast, **dplyr** splits these arguments out into separate functions. These can be seen in Table 12.2. As with merge, we refer to our two datasets as x and y.

TABLE 12.2 Functions for Merging Data in dplyr

Function	Description
inner_join	Inner join, only matching rows retained
left_join	Left join; retains all rows from x and matching rows from y
right_join	Right join; retains all rows from y and matching rows from x
full_join	Full join; retains all rows from both x and y
semi_join	Find rows of x that have a matching row in y
anti_join	Find rows of x that do not have a matching row in y

The first four functions listed in Table 12.2 operate in the same way as the merge function. For example, inner_join(demoData, pkData) provides an equivalent to merge(demoData, pkData). In addition, **dplyr** offers us the concepts of a semi-join and an anti-join. The semi_join function does not actually perform a merge. Instead, it returns rows in x that would be retained *if* we were to merge x with y. Conversely, the anti_join function returns rows of x that would *not* be retained if we were to merge with y. Listing 12.2 illustrates a semi-join and an anti-join using two (fabricated) sample data frames.

LISTING 12.2 Sample Joins

```
 1 : > # Fabricate two datasets to merge
 2 : > beerData <- data.frame(ID = c(1, 2, 3), Beer = c(75, 64, 92))
 3 : > diaperData <- data.frame(ID = c(1, 3, 4), Diapers = c(51, 68, 32))
 4 : > beerData
 5 :    ID Beer
 6 : 1  1   75
 7 : 2  2   64
 8 : 3  3   92
 9 : > diaperData
10 :    ID Diapers
11 : 1  1      51
12 : 2  3      68
13 : 3  4      32
14 : >
15 : > # Rows of beerData that have a corresponding "ID" in diaperData
```

```
16 : > semi_join(beerData, diaperData, by = "ID")
17 :    ID Beer
18 : 1  1   75
19 : 2  3   92
20 : > # Rows of beerData that do not have a corresponding "ID" in diaperData
21 : > anti_join(beerData, diaperData, by = "ID")
22 :    ID Beer
23 : 1  2   64
24 : > # An inner join of the two datasets
25 : > inner_join(beerData, diaperData, by = "ID")
26 :    ID Beer Diapers
27 : 1  1   75      51
28 : 2  3   92      68
```

Note that in each case we specified the "by" variable for the merge as "ID" but we did not have to. Like merge, each of the **dplyr** *join functions will automatically determine the merge by variables for us if we do not specify it. Because we stated that the data in the example is to be merged by the ID variable, the semi-join looks for ID values in beerData that also appear in diaperData. These are the rows that would be merged using either inner_join (as in lines 25 to 28) or left_join. Accordingly, anti_join returns the remaining rows that would not be merged.

Aggregation

In addition to facilitating data manipulation, **dplyr** also provides an easy-to-use syntax for data aggregation that is a marked improvement upon the more generic predecessor, the **plyr** package. In **dplyr** terminology, data aggregation is referred to as a data *summary*. We therefore use a function called summarize to obtain numeric summaries of our data. As always, when using **dplyr** we pass the data as the first argument. In the subsequent arguments we can use standard summary functions to summarize columns in the data. In the following example, we use the mean function to summarize the mpg column within carData:

```
> summarize(carData, mean(mpg))
Source: local data frame [1 x 1]

  mean(mpg)
1  20.09062
```

We can summarize using any function we like, including custom-written functions. The only restrictions are that the function we use must expect a vector as the input and that it must return a single value. We cannot therefore use a function such as range because this returns a vector of length 2. However, we can make as many summaries as we like in a single call to summarize.

```
> summarize(carData, min(mpg), median(mpg), max(mpg))
Source: local data frame [1 x 3]

  min(mpg) median(mpg) max(mpg)
1     10.4        19.2     33.9
```

When creating multiple summaries in this way, it can be helpful to be able to manually control the labels of the resulting data. In order to do so we simply specify the name of the resulting output column when creating the summary, as follows:

```
> mpgSummary <- summarize(carData, Min=min(mpg), Median=median(mpg), Max=max(mpg))
> mpgSummary
Source: local data frame [1 x 3]

   Min Median  Max
1 10.4   19.2 33.9
```

Sometimes we may find that we need to pass additional arguments to our summary functions. For example, we may need to specify `na.rm = TRUE` when summarizing a variable with missing values. In order to pass extra arguments to our summary functions, we pass the arguments as if we were calling the function directly. Here's an example:

```
summarize(airquality, mean(Ozone, na.rm = TRUE)).
```

Grouped Data

If all we needed to do was summarize columns of data using standard numeric summary functions, then **dplyr** doesn't really offer anything new. If anything, it makes the process more tedious. However, the real advantage of using the `summarize` function is that it facilitates easy "by" operations. In order to summarize our data by variable(s), we use the `group_by` function to define a grouping within our data. We can actually group our data at any time, and the grouping will be retained by any other operations we perform. We can group by as many variables as we like.

To demonstrate the concept of grouped data, let's group `carData` by the `cyl` variable and observe what happens when we filter the data by `carb`. The code for the operation is shown in Listing 12.3.

LISTING 12.3 The Effect of `group_by`

```
1: > cylGrouping <- group_by(carData, cyl)
2: > head(cylGrouping)
3: Source: local data frame [6 x 11]
4: Groups: cyl
5:
6:    mpg cyl disp  hp drat    wt  qsec vs am gear carb
```

```
 7: 1 21.0    6   160 110 3.90 2.620 16.46   0   1    4    4
 8: 2 21.0    6   160 110 3.90 2.875 17.02   0   1    4    4
 9: 3 22.8    4   108  93 3.85 2.320 18.61   1   1    4    1
10: 4 21.4    6   258 110 3.08 3.215 19.44   1   0    3    1
11: 5 18.7    8   360 175 3.15 3.440 17.02   0   0    3    2
12: 6 18.1    6   225 105 2.76 3.460 20.22   1   0    3    1
13: >
14: > filter(cylGrouping, carb == 4)
15: Source: local data frame [10 x 11]
16: Groups: cyl
17:
18:       mpg cyl  disp  hp drat    wt  qsec vs am gear carb
19: 1   21.0    6 160.0 110 3.90 2.620 16.46  0  1    4    4
20: 2   21.0    6 160.0 110 3.90 2.875 17.02  0  1    4    4
21: 3   14.3    8 360.0 245 3.21 3.570 15.84  0  0    3    4
22: 4   19.2    6 167.6 123 3.92 3.440 18.30  1  0    4    4
23: 5   17.8    6 167.6 123 3.92 3.440 18.90  1  0    4    4
24: 6   10.4    8 472.0 205 2.93 5.250 17.98  0  0    3    4
25: 7   10.4    8 460.0 215 3.00 5.424 17.82  0  0    3    4
26: 8   14.7    8 440.0 230 3.23 5.345 17.42  0  0    3    4
27: 9   13.3    8 350.0 245 3.73 3.840 15.41  0  0    3    4
28: 10 15.8    8 351.0 264 4.22 3.170 14.50  0  1    5    4
```

Notice first of all that grouping by the `cyl` variable has the effect of adding a line to the output (see line 4). As can be seen in line 16, the `cyl` grouping was retained when we filtered the data. In both cases the sort order remains unaffected by the grouping. The effect of grouping our data is only felt when we summarize it. In the following example, we summarize the `mpg` column in our grouped data, `cylGrouping`:

```
> mpgSummaryByCyl <- summarize(cylGrouping, min(mpg), median(mpg), max(mpg))
> mpgSummaryByCyl
Source: local data frame [3 x 4]

  cyl min(mpg) median(mpg) max(mpg)
1   4     21.4        26.0     33.9
2   6     17.8        19.7     21.4
3   8     10.4        15.2     19.2
```

The result of performing a summary operation on grouped data is that the output is summarized by each level of the grouping variable(s). In keeping with the concept of tidy data, the output is a data frame (in fact, a `tbl_df`). The operation returns a separate column for each variable that we grouped by, with additional columns for each summary we specified.

Other Uses of `group_by`

You have already seen that when we filter our data, the grouping variables are retained. However, we can also use the grouping to our advantage within the filter itself. In the following example, we use a grouping on the `cyl` variable to extract the maximum `mpg` value for each value of `cyl`. The comparison `mpg == max(mpg)` is performed within each group (that is, each value of `cyl`).

```
> cylGrouping <- group_by(carData, cyl)
> # Extract maximum mpg by for each cyl category
> filter(cylGrouping, mpg == max(mpg))
Source: local data frame [3 x 11]
Groups: cyl

   mpg cyl  disp  hp drat    wt  qsec vs am gear carb
1 21.4   6 258.0 110 3.08 3.215 19.44  1  0    3    1
2 33.9   4  71.1  65 4.22 1.835 19.90  1  1    4    1
3 19.2   8 400.0 175 3.08 3.845 17.05  0  0    3    2
```

Grouping our data also facilitates the generation of new aggregation variables. For example, we could create a new variable, `meanMPGbyCyl`, that is the mean of the `mpg` column for each value of `cyl`, as shown here:

```
> mutate(cylGrouping, meanMPGbyCyl = mean(mpg))
Source: local data frame [32 x 12]
Groups: cyl

    mpg cyl  disp  hp drat    wt  qsec vs am gear carb meanMPGbyCyl
1  21.0   6 160.0 110 3.90 2.620 16.46  0  1    4    4     19.74286
2  21.0   6 160.0 110 3.90 2.875 17.02  0  1    4    4     19.74286
3  22.8   4 108.0  93 3.85 2.320 18.61  1  1    4    1     26.66364
4  21.4   6 258.0 110 3.08 3.215 19.44  1  0    3    1     19.74286
5  18.7   8 360.0 175 3.15 3.440 17.02  0  0    3    2     15.10000
6  18.1   6 225.0 105 2.76 3.460 20.22  1  0    3    1     19.74286
7  14.3   8 360.0 245 3.21 3.570 15.84  0  0    3    4     15.10000
8  24.4   4 146.7  62 3.69 3.190 20.00  1  0    4    2     26.66364
9  22.8   4 140.8  95 3.92 3.150 22.90  1  0    4    2     26.66364
10 19.2   6 167.6 123 3.92 3.440 18.30  1  0    4    4     19.74286
.. ...  ...   ... ...  ...   ...   ... .. ..  ...  ...          ...
```

NOTE

Remove a Grouping

We can remove any groupings in our data using the `ungroup` function.

The Pipe Operator

Functions in **dplyr** have been written in order to take advantage of what is commonly referred to as the "pipe" operator. The pipe operator, `%>%`, originates in the **magrittr** package and is by no means restricted to usage within **dplyr**. The pipe operator allows us to chain functions together such that the output from one function becomes the input to the first argument (by default) of the next. This has led to it being called the "then" operator in some quarters (do this, *then* this, *then* this, and so on). It is particularly useful if we have many steps to perform on a single type of object such as a data frame. The advantage of this approach is that it avoids intermediary objects (that is, those that we create simply to break up nested function calls).

NOTE

Piping to Other Arguments

When you use the pipe operator, the output from a function does not have to be used as the input to the *first* argument of the next function. It can in fact become the input to any argument within the following function. However, the code is generally a lot more readable if we feed the output into the first argument of the following function.

The **dplyr** package has been written with the pipe operator very much in mind. In a typical analysis workflow we might `arrange`, `filter`, `select`, `mutate`, `group_by`, and `summarize` several times over. Each of these functions takes a data frame as its first input and returns another data frame as the output. This is ideal for piping together function calls. Consider the example in Listing 12.4 using `mtcars`. In the first instance we use the traditional approach to data processing. To avoid nesting, we end up creating three intermediate datasets on the way to obtaining our summary. We then perform the same operations using the pipe operator. In the second case, no intermediate datasets are required.

LISTING 12.4   Workflow Examples With and Without the Pipe Operator

```
 1: > # A standard workflow, mean mpg by cyl for manual cars
 2: > # The traditional way:
 3: > carsByCyl <- arrange(mtcars, cyl)
 4: > groupByCyl <- group_by(carsByCyl, cyl)
 5: > manualCars <- filter(groupByCyl, am == 1)
 6: > summarize(manualCars, Mean.MPG=mean(mpg))
 7: Source: local data frame [3 x 2]
 8:
 9:   cyl Mean.MPG
10: 1   4 28.07500
11: 2   6 20.56667
12: 3   8 15.40000
13: >
14: > # Using pipes
15: > mtcars %>%
16: +    arrange(cyl) %>%
17: +    group_by(cyl) %>%
18: +    filter(am == 1) %>%
```

```
19: +    summarize(Mean.MPG=mean(mpg))
20: Source: local data frame [3 x 2]
21:
22:    cyl Mean.MPG
23: 1    4 28.07500
24: 2    6 20.56667
25: 3    8 15.40000
```

The pipe operator is not to everyone's taste, and it can be harder to debug than well-written code using a traditional syntax. However, it is becoming an increasingly popular means of working with data—and before long it may not be possible to avoid it!

Efficient Data Handling with data.table

The **data.table** package predates **dplyr** by several years, having been first released to CRAN in April 2006. However, it is still actively maintained by its primary author and maintainer Matt Dowle, and despite the growing popularity of the **dplyr** package, **data.table** remains one of the most popular and well-documented packages on CRAN. In addition to the standard help and a quick-start guide, Matt Dowle has written an extensive FAQ document for the package tackling some of the less-obvious aspects of the package.

The focus of the package is very much on reading, processing, and aggregating large data efficiently. The data.table object is essentially an enhancement to the data.frame class. It allows us to index, merge, and group data much faster than we can with standard data frames.

Creating a data.table

Like any analysis workflow the data.table workflow begins with importing data. In Hour 10 we looked briefly at the performance of the fread function contained within **data.table**. The fread function is similar to read.table in terms of usage, though it's much faster for large datasets. Conveniently, the output of the function is a data.table object.

```
> dji <- fread("djiData.csv")
> dji
            Date DJI.Open DJI.High  DJI.Low DJI.Close DJI.Volume DJI.Adj.Close
  1: 12/31/2014 17987.66 18043.22 17820.88  17823.07   82840000      17823.07
  2: 12/30/2014 18035.02 18035.02 17959.70  17983.07   47490000      17983.07
  3: 12/29/2014 18046.58 18073.04 18021.57  18038.23   53870000      18038.23
  4: 12/26/2014 18038.30 18103.45 18038.30  18053.71   52570000      18053.71
  5: 12/24/2014 18035.73 18086.24 18027.78  18030.21   42870000      18030.21
 ---
248: 01/08/2014 16527.66 16528.88 16416.69  16462.74  103260000      16462.74
249: 01/07/2014 16429.02 16562.32 16429.02  16530.94   81270000      16530.94
```

```
250: 01/06/2014 16474.04 16532.99 16405.52  16425.10   89380000    16425.10
251: 01/03/2014 16456.89 16518.74 16439.30  16469.99   72770000    16469.99
252: 01/02/2014 16572.17 16573.07 16416.49  16441.35   80960000    16441.35
```

The appearance of a data table is similar to that of a standard data frame. When we choose to print a small dataset (one containing 100 rows or less), the entire dataset is returned, but with the header row repeated at the base of the table. For larger datasets, only the first and last five rows are returned. We can turn existing data frames into `data.table` objects by directly calling a `data.table` function—for example, `air <- data.table(airquality)`. We can also create a `data.table` from scratch in the same way we would using the `data.frame` function.

TIP

Keeping Track of Tables

If we create many data table objects, the `tables` function can be used to find out what tables we have, what they contain, and how much memory they have been allocated.

Setting a Key

One of the primary focuses of the **data.table** package is performance. To achieve this performance, we define a key. In some ways this is similar to a primary key that would be used in a relational database. However, in **data.table** the key can be made up of several columns and does not have to be unique. In fact, it is often more useful if the key is not unique. The key is used for sorting, indexing, and summarizing. It is defined using a function called `setkey`. In Listing 12.5 we define a simple `data.table` using the demoData data in the **mangoTraining** package and then set the key based on the variables `Sex` and `Smokes`.

LISTING 12.5 Defining a Key

```
 1: > # Create a data.table and define the key
 2: > demoDT <- data.table(demoData)
 3: > setkey(demoDT, Sex, Smokes)
 4: > head(demoDT)
 5:    Subject Sex Age Weight Height  BMI Smokes
 6: 1:       3   F  23     72    170 25.1     No
 7: 2:       6   F  29     67    169 23.5     No
 8: 3:      12   F  32     77    182 23.1     No
 9: 4:      15   F  27     73    172 24.8     No
10: 5:      23   F  26     82    175 26.8     No
11: 6:      26   F  25     58    175 18.9     No
```

The obvious effect of defining a key is that when printing, the data is sorted by the key variables from left to right as we defined them. In Listing 12.5 they are sorted by `Sex` and then by `Smokes`.

The purpose of defining the sort key is not just for printing purposes, however. It enables faster indexing when subscripting.

Notice that we wrote `setkey(demog, Sex, Smokes)` as opposed to `demog <- setkey(demog, Sex, Smokes)`. Functions in **data.table** update the data table directly, so we do not need to use `<-` to copy/replace the original data. Updating by reference in this way reduces the memory required to perform manipulation tasks and improves speed.

TIP

Querying the Key

We can find out if a data table has a key using the function `haskey`, which returns `TRUE` if the data table has a key and `FALSE` otherwise.

The `key` function tells us what the key is.

Subscripting

In the **data.table** syntax, we can reference columns directly as if they were objects in their own right. In other words, we can drop the "`dataName$`" syntax. This saves some typing, though the real benefit is the speed gain we get from using **data.table** in the first place.

```
> demoDT[Sex == "F",]
     Subject Sex Age Weight Height  BMI Smokes
 1:        3   F  23     72    170 25.1     No
 2:        6   F  29     67    169 23.5     No
 3:       12   F  32     77    182 23.1     No
 4:       15   F  27     73    172 24.8     No
 5:       23   F  26     82    175 26.8     No
 6:       26   F  25     58    175 18.9     No
 7:       28   F  28     69    172 23.4     No
 8:       30   F  33     61    175 19.9     No
 9:       17   F  41     62    172 20.9    Yes
10:       27   F  36     82    190 22.6    Yes
```

If our data table has a key and we want to subset by that key, we can go one step further and drop the reference to the variable we want to subset altogether (for example, `demoDT["F",]`). In fact, we don't even need the comma to specify rows as we would with a data frame, though it can be sometimes be confusing to leave it out.

If we have defined a key using multiple variables, we can provide the subset values by separating with a comma. We enclose the values using `J()`, where `J` stands for "join." In the following example, we subset the demography data to return female smokers:

```
> key(demoDT)
[1] "Sex"    "Smokes"
> demoDT[J("F", "Yes"),]
   Subject Sex Age Weight Height  BMI Smokes
1:      17   F  41     62    172 20.9    Yes
2:      27   F  36     82    190 22.6    Yes
```

NOTE

Alternatives to J

The J function is the **data.table** specification of a "join" of two keys. The practice of joining based on keys has its roots in SQL, but in practice it is just a means of separating variables. As an alternative, the function list (**base**) or . (**plyr**) could be used in exactly the same way.

Occasionally we may want to return a subset in which the variables of interest match multiple criteria. To achieve this we can specify a vector of values. If we have defined a key from multiple variables, any vector we specify must be contained within a call to the J function. An example of this is shown here:

```
> setkey(demoDT, Sex, Weight)
> demoDT[J("M", c(76, 77)),]
   Subject Sex Age Weight Height  BMI Smokes
1:       4   M  25     76    188 21.4     No
2:      31   M  25     76    174 25.1     No
3:      13   M  21     77    180 23.6     No
4:      20   M  22     77    183 23.1     No
```

CAUTION

Numeric Keys

The **data.table** package allows us to define a key using numeric variables. However, in order to subset using these keys we must use the . function. This is because, like data frames, data tables also allow us to subset by specifying the row numbers. If we wanted to return all the rows in demoDT for which Weight is equal to 72, we would write the following:

```
> setkey(demoDT, Weight)
> demoDT[.(72),]
   Subject Sex Age Weight Height  BMI Smokes
1:       3   F  23     72    170 25.1     No
```

Adding New Columns and Rows

The **data.table** package makes adding variables to an existing data table much easier and quicker than when working with standard data frames. Whenever we add a column to a standard data frame, we make a copy of the data. When we work with data tables, the new column is instead appended by reference; in other words, R points to the existing table and tells it to add a new column. This makes it much faster and more efficient.

Adding and Renaming Columns

We create new variables in our data, by reference, using the := operator. To create variables by reference we use square, subscript brackets with the existing data table. We avoid any standard R assignment. If we are generating the new variable from existing variables, we refer to them directly as in the following example:

```
> demoDT[, HeightInM.sq := (Height^2)/10000]
> head(demoDT)
   Subject Sex Age Weight Height  BMI Smokes HeightInM.sq
1:       1   M  43     57    166 20.7     No       2.7556
2:       2   M  22     71    179 22.2     No       3.2041
3:       3   F  23     72    170 25.1     No       2.8900
4:       4   M  25     76    188 21.4     No       3.5344
5:       5   M  29     82    175 26.8     No       3.0625
6:       6   F  29     67    169 23.5     No       2.8561
```

CAUTION

Updating the Values in the Key

If we update the values in any of the columns that make up our key, we need to redefine the key.

To create multiple new columns, we must provide the names of the new columns as a character vector and the transformations as a list. The vector of names and list of transformations should be separated by the := operator, as shown in Listing 12.6. We can also remove columns by setting them to NULL using the := operator.

LISTING 12.6   Creating New Columns

```
1: > demoDT[, c("SexNum", "SmokesNum") := list(as.numeric(Sex),
➥as.numeric(Smokes))]
2: > head(demoDT)
3:    Subject Sex Age Weight Height  BMI Smokes HeightInM.sq SexNum SmokesNum
4: 1:       1   M  43     57    166 20.7     No       2.7556      2         1
5: 2:      26   F  25     58    175 18.9     No       3.0625      1         1
6: 3:      30   F  33     61    175 19.9     No       3.0625      1         1
7: 4:      22   M  27     61    170 21.0     No       2.8900      2         1
8: 5:      17   F  41     62    172 20.9    Yes       2.9584      1         2
9: 6:      14   M  26     64    170 22.0     No       2.8900      2         1
```

We can rename columns using the `setnames` function. Once again the renaming is performed by reference to avoid copying the entire dataset. The `setnames` function expects a data table as its first argument, with further arguments `old` and `new`, which respectively expect a vector of column names to change from and to.

NOTE

Multiple Ways to Create New Variables

There are normally several ways of doing the same thing with **data.table**, and everyone tends to have their preference. In order to create new variables in Listing 12.6, we could also have used the following syntax:

```
demoDT[, `:=` (SexNum = as.numeric(Sex), SmokesNum = as.numeric(Smokes))]
```

We could also have used the `set` function to achieve the same result.

Adding Rows

Although the `rbind` function in **base** can be used to append rows to a data table, the function `rbindlist` is optimized for speed and memory efficiency. The `rbindlist` function can be used to join data tables and/or regular data frames that are stored as a list. We can join together as many datasets as we wish, but we must first store them together in a list. Unlike the standard `rbind` that we looked at in Hour 11, `rbindlist` will permit us to bind together datasets for which the column names do not match by setting `fill` = `TRUE`. An example of this is shown in Listing 12.7. First we generate a list by splitting the `airquality` data by the `Month` variable and combine this back together in line 5. Then we use `rbindlist` again in line 24 to add on new rows of data.

LISTING 12.7   Adding New Rows

```
 1: > # Create a list containing airquality data for each available month
 2: > airSplit <- split(airquality, airquality$Month)
 3: >
 4: > # Bind these together into a single data table
 5: > airDT <- rbindlist(airSplit)
 6: > airDT
 7:       Ozone Solar.R Wind Temp Month Day
 8:   1:     41     190  7.4   67     5   1
 9:   2:     36     118  8.0   72     5   2
10:   3:     12     149 12.6   74     5   3
11:   4:     18     313 11.5   62     5   4
12:   5:     NA      NA 14.3   56     5   5
13:   ---
14: 149:     30     193  6.9   70     9  26
15: 150:     NA     145 13.2   77     9  27
```

```
16: 151:      14       191 14.3    75     9  28
17: 152:      18       131  8.0    76     9  29
18: 153:      20       223 11.5    68     9  30
19: >
20: > # Now assume two new records arrive but with missing columns
21: > month10 <- data.table(Ozone = c(24, 28), Month = 10, Day = 1:2)
22: >
23: > # Bind this to our original data
24: > newAirDT <- rbindlist(list(airDT, month10), fill = TRUE)
25: > tail(newAirDT)
26:      Ozone Solar.R Wind Temp Month Day
27: 1:      NA     145 13.2   77     9  27
28: 2:      14     191 14.3   75     9  28
29: 3:      18     131  8.0   76     9  29
30: 4:      20     223 11.5   68     9  30
31: 5:      24      NA   NA   NA    10   1
32: 6:      28      NA   NA   NA    10   2
```

Merging

Merging data tables works in the much same way as a typical merge on a data frame using the merge function. However, the default behavior of merge for data tables is to use the respective keys for the two data tables. We must therefore either define keys for the two data tables or specify the "by" variables manually. In Listing 12.8 we create two data tables from the demoData and pkData data frames contained within the **mangoTraining** package and set the keys accordingly. In line 8 we perform a merge, similar to that used in Hour 11.

LISTING 12.8 Merging Two Data Tables

```
 1: > # Create data tables and define the keys accordingly
 2: > demoDT <- data.table(demoData)
 3: > setkey(demoDT, Subject)
 4: > pkDT <- data.table(pkData)
 5: > setkey(pkDT, Subject)
 6: >
 7: > # Merge the two data tables together
 8: > allPKDT <- merge(demoDT, pkDT)
 9: > allPKDT
10:      Subject Sex Age Weight Height  BMI Smokes Dose Time   Conc
11:   1:       1   M  43     57    166 20.7     No   25    0   0.00
12:   2:       1   M  43     57    166 20.7     No   25    1 660.13
13:   3:       1   M  43     57    166 20.7     No   25    6 178.92
14:   4:       1   M  43     57    166 20.7     No   25   12  88.99
15:   5:       1   M  43     57    166 20.7     No   25   24  42.71
16:   ---
17: 161:      33   M  30     80    180 24.8     No   25    0   0.00
```

```
18: 162:      33  M  30      80     180 24.8     No   25    1 453.13
19: 163:      33  M  30      80     180 24.8     No   25    6 205.30
20: 164:      33  M  30      80     180 24.8     No   25   12 146.69
21: 165:      33  M  30      80     180 24.8     No   25   24  46.84
```

For large datasets you will notice that using `merge` with data tables is significantly faster than the with data frames. For those that need that little bit of extra performance, however, the package offers an alternative that is even faster. To perform the data table merge, we return to using square brackets. For a standard merge (a.k.a. an inner join), we put one data table inside the brackets and one outside. An example of an inner join or standard merge is shown here:

```
> demoDT[pkDT]
      Subject Sex Age Weight Height  BMI Smokes Dose Time    Conc
  1:        1   M  43     57    166 20.7     No   25    0    0.00
  2:        1   M  43     57    166 20.7     No   25    1  660.13
  3:        1   M  43     57    166 20.7     No   25    6  178.92
  4:        1   M  43     57    166 20.7     No   25   12   88.99
  5:        1   M  43     57    166 20.7     No   25   24   42.71
 ---
161:       33   M  30     80    180 24.8     No   25    0    0.00
162:       33   M  30     80    180 24.8     No   25    1  453.13
163:       33   M  30     80    180 24.8     No   25    6  205.30
164:       33   M  30     80    180 24.8     No   25   12  146.69
165:       33   M  30     80    180 24.8     No   25   24   46.84
```

Aggregation

In addition to transforming and manipulating our data, we can also use **data.table** to summarize our data. As usual, we start by specifying the name of the data and use square brackets to create a summary. We can perform simple summary operations on columns using standard statistical summary functions such as `mean`.

```
> # Calculate the mean height
> demoDT <- data.table(demoData)
> demoDT[ , mean(Height)]
[1] 176.1515
```

So far we have seen nothing special. However, **data.table** permits the use of a "by" argument, which allows aggregation. The return object is also a data table. Here, we calculate the mean height again by sex:

```
> demoDT[ , mean(Height), by = Sex]
    Sex       V1
1:    M  176.5652
2:    F  175.2000
```

TIP

Counting Records

In **data.table** we can use `.N` to count records within by-groups. For example, to count the number of males and females in the `demoDT` data table, we would write `demoDT[, .N, by = Sex]`.

We can summarize by multiple variables by providing them as a list using `.` or `list`. The result is another data table with a column for each "by" variable and an additional column for the summary.

```
> demoDT[ , mean(Height), by = list(Sex, Smokes)]
   Sex Smokes       V1
1:   M     No 177.3158
2:   F     No 173.7500
3:   M    Yes 173.0000
4:   F    Yes 181.0000
```

We can provide multiple summaries and name them using a list. Again, the result is a data table.

```
> demoDT[ , list(Mean.Height = mean(Height), Mean.Weight = mean(Weight)),
+ by = list(Sex, Smokes)]
   Sex Smokes Mean.Height Mean.Weight
1:   M     No    177.3158    74.10526
2:   F     No    173.7500    69.87500
3:   M    Yes    173.0000    74.25000
4:   F    Yes    181.0000    72.00000
```

CAUTION

Summary Functions That Return Multiple Values

It is possible to summarize using functions that return multiple values, such as `range` and `quantile`. However, the effect is that a new row is created for each element of the return vector—for example, one for the minimum and one for the maximum if using `range`. Other than the sort order, there is no way to tell which row corresponds to which value in the output vector.

The aggregation that we have seen thus far creates a new data table that we can use for publishing, plotting, or modeling. The original table is unaffected by the operation. However, if we want to merge the results of the aggregation back on to the original data, we can easily do so using the `:=` operator.

```
> demoDT[, MeanWeightBySex := mean(Weight), by = Sex]
> head(demoDT, 5)
   Subject Sex Age Weight Height  BMI Smokes MeanWeightBySex
1:       1   M  43     57    166 20.7     No        74.13043
```

```
2:        2   M   22      71     179 22.2      No            74.13043
3:        3   F   23      72     170 25.1      No            70.30000
4:        4   M   25      76     188 21.4      No            74.13043
5:        5   M   29      82     175 26.8      No            74.13043
```

In order to generate multiple summaries, we may use any of the methods associated with := for creating new variables.

More with data.table

There are always many ways of achieving the same goal using **data.table**, and we have presented just a small selection of options in most cases. There are also many more features, such as rolling means, that we simply do not have the time to cover in any detail. If you are interested in digging into **data.table** further, Matt Dowle has crammed the package help files full of examples. The package FAQ offers further guidance.

Too Large for data.table

For the vast majority of readers, **dplyr** and **data.table** will be more than sufficient for your data needs. In particular, **data.table** has been shown to be extremely performant. On a standard desktop, it can comfortably handle basic summary operations on datasets with a billion rows, containing several thousand groups, within a matter of minutes. However, for some that might still not be enough!

Without parallelizing your code and/or turning to high-performance computing solutions, you might find two further packages to be of assistance. The first of these is **bigmemory**. The **bigmemory** package is designed to work with matrices that can be held in your computer's memory but cannot be processed by standard R functions for data structures. The package takes advantage of C++ and allows objects to be shared across multiple sessions on the same machine.

An alternative approach to handling very large datasets is to use the **ff** package. Instead of storing large datasets in memory, the **ff** package stores data on disc. Only a tiny portion of the data is ever mapped to memory. Though the data is stored on disk, it behaves in very much the same way as standard R objects held in memory. On the back end, C++ is used to perform the requested operations.

Still further options are available beyond the two packages covered in this hour, though typically they involve parallelizing your operation and are beyond the scope of this tutorial.

Summary

In this hour, we have looked at the two most popular packages for efficient data handling in R: **dplyr** and **data.table**. We have looked at the basic syntax of the packages as well as common data-handling tasks such as sorting, subscripting, merging, and aggregation. If you are still unsure as to which is right for you, you can now have a go at using them both during the workshop.

Having seen how R can be used to import and manipulate data, we will spend the next three hours looking at how we can visualize our data using the **graphics** package and the popular alternatives **lattice** and **ggplot2**.

Q&A

Q. Which is better, dplyr or data.table?

A. In short, it depends! In terms of speed, most benchmarking examples show the packages to be comparable to a point, but as the number of rows and/or groups increases, **data.table** comes out on top. If speed or memory usage matter to you and you have more than a million rows or 100,000 groups within your data, you should probably use **data.table**. If data size (and hence performance) is not that important to you, choose whichever you feel more comfortable with.

Q. We have now seen a `data.frame`, a `tbl_df`, and a `data.table`. Why do I need to learn about three different structures?

A. First of all, both a `tbl_df` and a `data.table` are just an extension to a `data.frame`. Generally, there is therefore very little difference, though functions such as `print` behave in a slightly different manner for `tbl_df` and `data.table` objects than they do with a `data.frame`. This is due to R's S3 class system, which we will look at more closely in Hour 16, "Introduction to R Models and Object Orientation," and then again in Hour 21, "Writing R Classes."

Workshop

The workshop contains quiz questions and exercises to help you solidify your understanding of the material covered. Try to answer all questions before looking at the "Answers" section that follows.

Quiz

1. True or false? When using `select`, you must provide a character vector of columns names.

2. Which of the following is a **dplyr** function that allows you to create new columns?

    A. `transform`

    B. `subset`

    C. `mutate`

3. Assuming you have created a `data.table` object called `demoDT` from the `demoData` data frame and set the key to be the `Smokes` column, which of the following would return a subset containing all records for subjects that smoke?

   A. `demoDT[demoDT$Smokes == "Yes", ]`

   B. `demoDT[Smokes == "Yes", ]`

   C. `demoDT["Yes", ]`

   D. `demoDT["Yes"]`

4. What is "wrong" with the following syntax when working with a **data.table** called `demoDT`?

   `demoDT$Height.Sq <- demoDT$Height^2`

Answers

1. False. You specify each column name as a separate argument. In fact, if you do try to use a character vector, the function will return an error.

2. C. The `transform` and `subset` functions are contained in the **base** R package. The `transform` function is actually quite similar to `mutate`, though it does not allow you to base new variables on other variables that you are creating within the call to transform. The `subset` function offers similar functionality to the **dplyr** functions `filter` and `select`.

3. **A**, **B**, **C** and **D**. The **data.table** syntax is extremely flexible, and all four methods achieve the same end result.

4. Nothing is technically "wrong" with the statement, though **data.table** is optimized for efficiency, and the command shown is a standard, less efficient way of creating a new column, `Height.Sq`. The more efficient method in **data.table** would be

   `demoDT[, Height.Sq := Height^2]`

Activities

1. Using the **dplyr** package, perform the following actions:

   ▶ Create a `tbl_df` object named `air` from the `airquality` data frame.

   ▶ Sort the data by the `Wind` column.

   ▶ Remove any rows for which the `Ozone` column has a missing value.

   ▶ Remove the `Solar.R` column and create a new column containing the ratio of `Ozone` to `Wind`.

   ▶ Create a subset of the original `airquality` data containing just three columns: `Month`, `Day`, and `Solar.R`. The data should only contain data for June and July. Name the output `solar`.

▶ Merge the `air` and `solar` datasets together, retaining all records from the `air` dataset (that is, a left join).

▶ Calculate the median `Ozone` value by `Month` for the merged data.

2. Now using the **data.table** package, perform the same following actions:

▶ Create a `data.frame` object named `air` from the `airquality` data frame.

▶ Sort the data by the `Wind` column.

▶ Remove any rows for which the `Ozone` column has a missing value.

▶ Remove the `Solar.R` column and create a new column containing the ratio of `Ozone` to `Wind`.

▶ Create a subset of the original `airquality` data containing just three columns: `Month`, `Day`, and `Solar.R`. The data should only contain data for June and July. Name the output `solar`.

▶ Merge the `air` and `solar` datasets together, retaining all records from the `air` dataset (that is, a left join).

▶ Calculate the median `Ozone` value by `Month` for the merged data.

HOUR 13
Graphics

What You'll Learn in This Hour:

- ▶ How to use graphics devices
- ▶ High-level graphics functions
- ▶ Low-level graphics functions
- ▶ Graphical parameters
- ▶ How to control the device layout

After all the manipulations to our data, we want to be able to start to do something with it. In this hour, we look at how to create graphics using the base graphics functionality. You may be aware that there are other packages for creating graphics, including **ggplot2** and **lattice**, which we will look at in the next two hours. Here, however, we look at some of the basics, including how to send graphics to devices such as a PDF and the standard graphics functions. Finally, we look at how to control the layout of graphics on the page.

Graphics Devices and Colors

Before we start to create graphics, we need to think about where we will create them and how we will color them. In this section, you learn how to control the device that is used to create the graphic, whether this is the default plot device or a specific file type. You will also see the options for defining color in R graphics.

Devices

Whenever we create a graphic in R, it is returned to a device. This may be the RStudio Plot tab or it may be a physical file, such as a PDF, that we want to return to. A number of graphics devices are available, including PDF, PNG, JPEG, and bitmap. If we do not specify the device, the default device will be opened, and in RStudio this is the Plot tab.

If we want to create a graphic in a specific device, we do so by first creating that device. We create devices with a series of functions that take the name of the file type (for instance, pdf or png). This opens a connection between R and the device, and any graphics we now create will be written to that file. A vital step is to then close the device using the function dev.off. As an example, let's create a graphic in a PDF file that we will name myFirstGraphic.pdf:

```
> pdf("myFirstGraphic.pdf")
> hist(rnorm(100))
> dev.off()  # remember to close the device!
```

In our current working directory we will now have the PDF file myFirstGraphic. We can, of course, give the full file path to an alternative location to save our device. Attributes of the device, such as width, height, and resolution, can all be set in the specific device functions.

TIP

Closing Graphics Devices

When you start to create graphics in devices in this way, you may find that you have unintentionally opened a number of devices and you are not certain where the graphic is being written to anymore. If this happens, try using the function graphics.off, with no arguments. This will close all active devices and allow you to start again with creating your graphic.

Colors

When it comes to specifying colors in R, we have a few options. The easiest is to simply name the color. To know what colors we can name in this way, we can use a function in R called colors (or colours) that will return a vector of all the colors that R recognizes by name. Here's an example:

```
> sample(colors(), 10)
 [1] "wheat3"     "lightblue1" "wheat"      "olivedrab1" "lightblue4" "grey11"
 [7] "peru"       "grey39"     "firebrick2" "peachpuff4"
```

Alternatively, we can provide the exact hexadecimal value for the color we want to use. For instance, #FF0000 is the hexadecimal value for red. If you are not certain of the hexadecimal value but do know the red, green, and blue color values, you can use the rgb function to help you out. For example, here's how to find the hexadecimal value for green:

```
> rgb(0, 255, 0, maxColorValue = 255)
[1] "#00FF00"
```

High-Level Graphics Functions

Graphics functions in the base graphics package are split into two types. High-level functions are those that allow us to create the graphic. Low-level functions allow us to add content, such as points and lines to an existing graphic. In this section, we look at the high-level functions available to us. These have been split into univariate graphics and the `plot` function. We also look at how to control aesthetics and the type of plot we create.

Univariate Graphics

In this section, we look at graphics that we may create with a single variable. This includes histograms, boxplots, and bar charts, as well as QQ plots. Throughout this section we use simple vectors of simulated values to plot.

To start with, let's look at histograms and QQ plots. Both are very simply created by passing a vector of data to the appropriate function, `hist` or `qqnorm`. In the case of the QQ plot, if we want to add a QQ line, we need to additionally use the function `qqline`.

```
> x <- rnorm(100)
> hist(x, col = "lightblue")
> qqnorm(x)
> qqline(x)
```

In all these functions there is an argument, `col`, that allows us to set the color, as can be seen in the preceding `hist` example. The graphics that these calls generate can be seen in Figure 13.1.

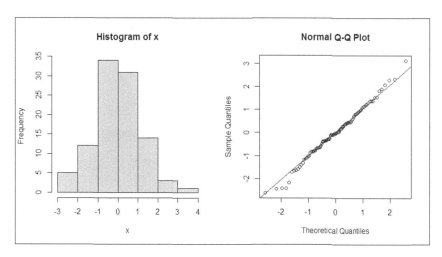

FIGURE 13.1
Examples of the default histogram and QQ plot, with corresponding QQ line

For boxplots, again we can simply provide a vector of the data we want to plot. Here's how:

```
> boxplot(x)
```

If, however, we want to plot the data split by another variable, we would need to provide a formula for that representation. As an example, we will create a new vector that is simply a random sampling of values from "F" and "M" to assign a gender to each value in the vector x. We then want to plot the data x split by the corresponding gender we have sampled.

```
> gender <- sample(c("F", "M"), size = 100, replace = TRUE)
> boxplot(x ~ gender)
```

The two graphics generated here can be seen in Figure 13.2. In the case where we have the data stored in a data frame, we can simply provide the variable names and then specify the dataset with the data argument. Here's an example:

```
> genderData <- data.frame(gender = gender, value = x)
> boxplot(value~gender, data = genderData)
```

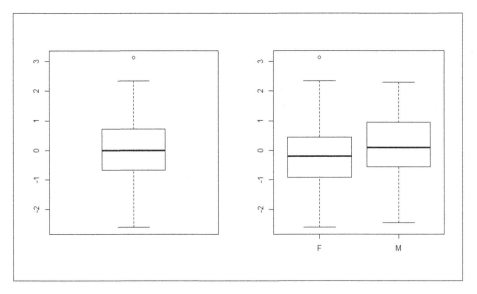

FIGURE 13.2
A simple univariate boxplot and boxplot split by a second variable, in this case gender

The final example to consider is the `barplot` function. This allows us to create a bar chart where the heights of the bars are based on the values given by the vector input. Consider this simple example of a vector of just three elements:

```
> barplot(c(3, 9, 5))
```

This bar chart is shown in Figure 13.3. There are additional options for giving names to each of the bars, for instance, and for coloring the bars, as you have seen for other plots. This function also works well with the `table` function you saw in Hour 6, "Common R Utility Functions." Consider the gender vector that we created. Suppose we want to count the number of cases of each gender and generate a bar chart showing these counts:

```
> genderCount <- table(gender)
> barplot(genderCount)
```

This is also shown in Figure 13.3. You will notice that in this case the bars are already named. This is because the output from the `table` function is a named vector, so the names of the categories in the data are passed through to the `barplot` function to label the bars.

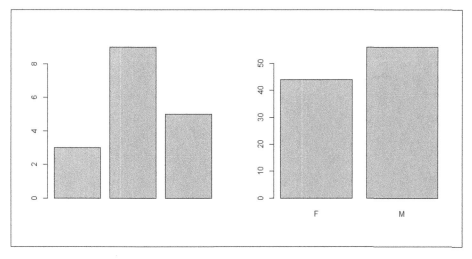

FIGURE 13.3
Bar charts created from a single vector and a named vector, the output of the `table` function

The `plot` Function

The main function you will use for generating graphics is the `plot` function. As you will see, this is a very versatile function and can be used to easily generate diagnostic plots for models. In this hour we use it only to plot vectors of data.

Let's start with just a single vector of data. In this case, just as with the preceding univariate graphics, we can simply pass the vector to the `plot` function:

```
> plot(x[1:10])
```

This plot is shown in Figure 13.4, where you can see that in this instance the values of the vector are plotted against the Y axis. On the X axis we have the index of the position of the element in the vector.

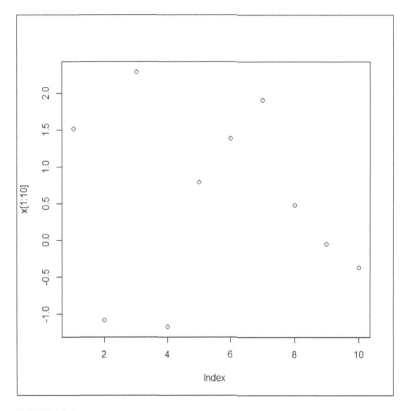

FIGURE 13.4
Using `plot` for a single vector. Here, the values in the vector are plotted against their index, or position in the vector

When it comes to plotting two variables, we need to give the X and Y axis variables in that order. So the first argument to `plot` is the vector of values on the X axis, and the second is the vector of values on the Y axis. Therefore, let's create a plot using the `airquality` data. In this instance, we are going to plot `Ozone` against `Wind`, so we want the `Wind` vector on the X axis and `Ozone` on the Y axis:

```
> plot(airquality$Wind, airquality$Ozone, pch = 4)
```

In this example, the result of which can be seen in Figure 13.5, we have also changed the plotting symbol, which you will see in more detail in the next section. You will notice that this has, by default, added axis labels that are simply the names of the objects we passed and that there is no title. All of these things, which contribute to the appearance of the plot, we will look at in the next section.

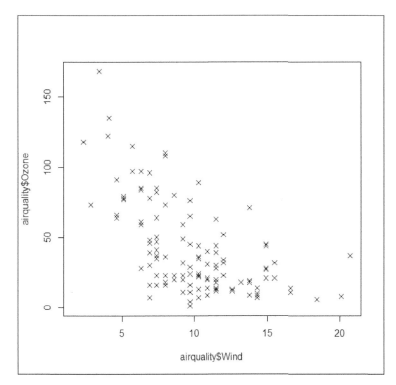

FIGURE 13.5
Using `plot` to create a bivariate scatterplot. Here, we have also changed the plotting symbol

Aesthetics

For all of the plotting functions that we have looked at in this hour, there are a number of arguments we can use to change the way that the plot looks. This could be adding a title, changing the point styles, or adding the correct axis labels. In this section, we discuss how to do all these things.

Titles and Axis Labels

We need three arguments to change the main title of the plot along with the X and Y axis labels:

- ► `main`, for controlling the plot title
- ► `xlab`, for setting the X axis label
- ► `ylab`, for setting the Y axis label

We can use these arguments in all the plotting functions from this hour:

```
> hist(x, main = "Histogram of Random Normal Data", xlab = "Simulated Normal Data")
> require(mangoTraining)
> plot(pkData$Time, pkData$Conc,
+      main = "Concentration against Time", xlab = "Time",
+      ylab = "Concentration")
```

The plots for these examples are shown in Figure 13.6, where you can see we now have more appropriate titles and axis labels.

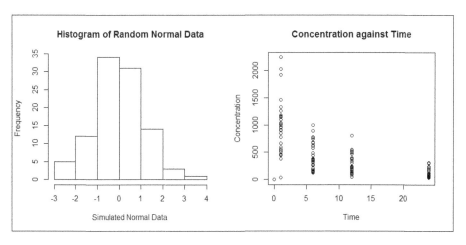

FIGURE 13.6
Changing titles and axis labels in both histograms and scatterplots

---

TIP

Including Special Characters

If you want to include special characters, such as Greek letters, in your titles and axis labels, you will need to use the `expression` function. As an example, the axis label may become this:

```
ylab = expression("Concentration ("*mu*"g/ml)")
```

Here, we are using the asterisk (*) to combine strings with the Greek character mu.

Axis Limits

The default behavior of the `plot` function is to set the range of the plot limits to cover the range of the data. In some instances this is sufficient; however, often this will not be suitable for the data in question—for instance, if the axis limits need to extend to zero. In this case, we need to make use of the arguments xlim and ylim.

Both of these arguments are provided in the same way. We need to give a single vector of length two. The first element of this vector is the minimum value for the axis and the second value is the maximum value for the axis. As an example, suppose we want to extend the maximum value of both axes in the Concentration against Time plot:

```
> plot(pkData$Time, pkData$Conc, xlim = c(0, 50), ylim = c(0, 3000))
```

The plot that is created by this code is shown in Figure 13.7. This functionality is particularly useful if we want to plot a subset of the data across the range of the full dataset. For instance, suppose we want to plot the Dose 25 data from the pkData dataset but with the axes based on the complete data:

```
> plot(pkData$Time[pkData$Dose == 25], pkData$Conc[pkData$Dose == 25],
+          ylim = range(pkData$Conc))
```

This plot can also be seen in Figure 13.7, and you can see how we have used the range function from Hour 6 to determine the minimum and maximum values of the Y axis of the plot.

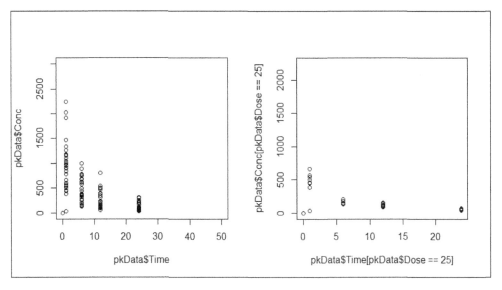

FIGURE 13.7
Changing axis limits

Plotting Symbols

In the graphics that we have created so far, we have mostly left the plotting symbol as the default, black, unfilled circle, although Figure 13.5 showed that we can change the symbol itself using the argument pch, and Figure 13.1 showed we can change color using the col argument.

You can change the plotting symbol by providing a numeric value to indicate the symbol you want to use. Figure 13.8 shows symbols 0 to 20. Additionally, a series of other symbols takes values in the region 21 to 25 (see Figure 13.9). The difference with these symbols is that, in addition to being able to set the color, we can also set the fill. The fill of the shapes is actually set with the argument bg, but just like with the argument col, we can give any color value.

FIGURE 13.8
Plotting symbols and their values

FIGURE 13.9
Plotting symbols 21 to 25 with just the col argument set (bottom) and with col and bg set (top)

As well as setting the color and shape of the symbols, we can also set the size. We do this with the argument cex. This argument is simply a numeric value indicating how many times bigger (or smaller) than the usual size we want our points. The default is 1.

The following example shows how we can create a graphic where all these arguments are set. Notice that we are using the plotting symbol 24, which allows us to use the bg argument:

```
> plot(pkData$Time, pkData$Conc,
+       main = "Concentration against Time", xlab = "Time",
+       ylab = "Concentration", pch = 24, col = "navyblue",
+       bg = "yellow", cex = 2)
```

You can see the graphic that is created from this code in Figure 13.10.

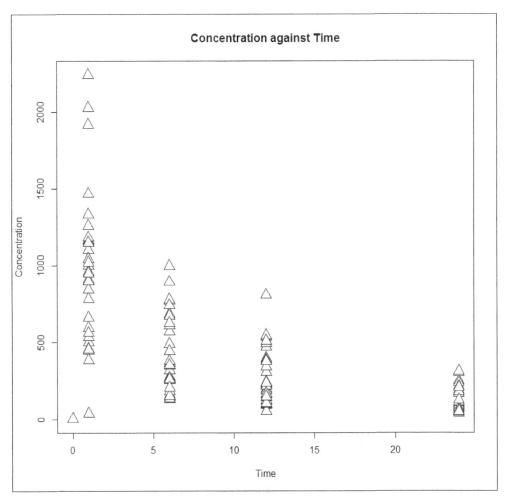

FIGURE 13.10
Updating the plotting symbol and its attributes

Plot Types

Clearly it is very simple to create scatterplots of our data, but what about alternative plot types? You haven't yet seen a line plot or step plot. How about lines and points? We can switch our plot to any of these graphics by using the `type` argument. We pass to the `type` argument one of a series of letters. The default is p, to indicate points, but we can also have l, o, and s, to name a few. The complete set of options is given in Table 13.1, and a series of graphics showing different types when plotting the same random 10 points is shown in Figure 13.11. Generating graphics of this type would look something like this:

```
> x   <- rnorm(100)
> plot(x, type = "l", main = 'type = "l"')
```

TABLE 13.1 Available Plot Types

Type	Description
p	Points (default)
l	Lines
b	Both points and lines
c	Just the lines component of a type b plot
o	Overlaid lines and points
h	Histogram like vertical bars
s	Step plot (horizontal first)
S	Step plot (vertical first)
n	No plotting

It is probably worth noting that just as we can style the points, as you saw in the previous section, we can also style lines. The argument `lty` lets us set the line type and again takes integer values. The argument `lwd` allows us to set the line width in the same way that we set the point size using `cex`. We will look at examples of setting line types in the next section.

Low-Level Graphics Functions

So far you have seen only the high-level graphics functions available in the base graphics package. This package has allowed us to create an entire plot. Often we will want to add a component to the graphic—such as lines showing the mean and confidence intervals, or text to identify an outlier. For this we need the low-level graphics functions. All the functions you will see in this section add a component to the existing graphics device rather than creating a new plot device. This is where the `type = "n"` option you saw in the previous section is particularly useful.

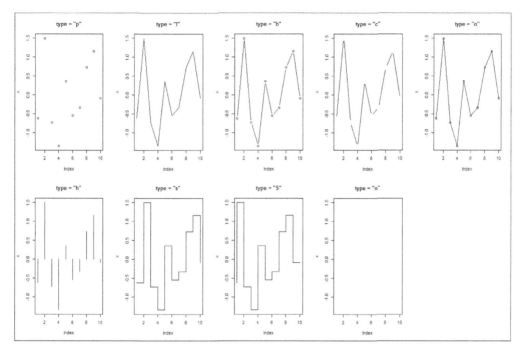

FIGURE 13.11
Setting the plot type

Points and Lines

We will start by adding simple points and lines to our graphics. For this we will use the functions
points and lines. Just as with the plot function, these functions add points at the X and Y
locations specified, or join the locations together in the case of lines. Just as with the plot function, therefore, the first two arguments are the vector of x values and the vector of y values. As
an example, let's take the first and second subjects from the pkData. On a single plot we will
add the points to show subject 1 and a line to show subject 2:

```
> subject1 <- pkData[pkData$Subject == 1, ]
> subject2 <- pkData[pkData$Subject == 2, ]
> plot(pkData$Time, pkData$Conc, type = "n")
> points(subject1$Time, subject1$Conc, pch = 16)
> lines(subject2$Time, subject2$Conc)
```

The resulting plot is shown in Figure 13.12. The lines function shown here has simply connected together supplied X and Y points. What if we wanted to add a straight line that shows
the median concentration value, or the time when the maximum occurs, or even some form of
trend? In this case, we would use the function abline. The default behavior of this function is to
add a line based on an intercept and slope. However, we can also use the arguments h and v to

add horizontal and vertical lines. So, here's how to add the median concentration and the time of the maximum concentration:

```
> abline(h = median(pkData$Conc), lty = 2)
> abline(v = pkData$Time[pkData$Conc == max(pkData$Conc)], lty = 3)
```

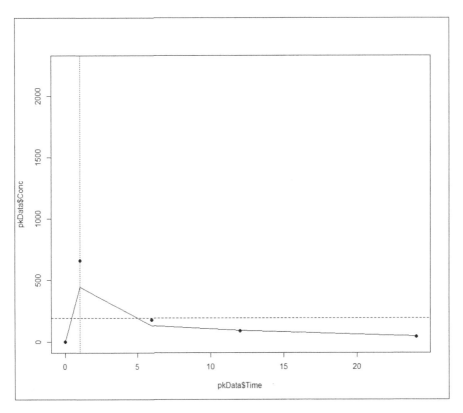

FIGURE 13.12
Adding points and lines to a plot

Text

The ability to add text to a graphic is incredibly useful. It may be that you actually want to use text as the plotting symbol itself but more often than not it will simply be that you want to label a particular point, typically an outlier. We would perform all of these tasks with the text function. Another low level function, this will allow us to add information to an existing plot and it doesn't matter if this was created using only a high level function or a combination of high and low level functions as we saw in the last section.

To start with, we will use the text function to add all of the content of our plot, using text as the plotting symbol. Just as other plot functions, the first two arguments are the vectors of the X and Y location for the points. The third argument to this function is then the text that we want at each location. This is typically a vector of the values for each X, Y pair. So if we were to plot the Concentration against Time plot of the pkData, using the Dose as the text to plot, it might look something like this:

```
> plot(pkData$Time, pkData$Conc, type = "n")
> text(pkData$Time, pkData$Conc, pkData$Dose)
```

This graphic is shown in Figure 13.13, and as you can see the doses appear as text on the plot. A more effective use of this function is to label specific points. We can use the text function in a very similar way with the X and Y location along with the text, but as you will notice, this centers the text on the location. If you also have a point here, this is a problem because the text will be obscured. You can, of course, manually adjust the X or Y location to handle this, though the text function includes a number of arguments for controlling the positioning. One argument, adj, lets us specify an X and Y adjustment for the text. We can also use the arguments pos and offset. The pos argument lets us control which side of the point to position the text and takes a value from 1 to 4, with 1 being the bottom, 2 to the left, 3 above, and 4 to the right. The offset argument is used in conjunction to determine how far away from the point to center the text.

As an example of using text in this way, we can consider labeling the maximum value at each time point, except 0, with the Subject number. Here, we are using the **dplyr** package to retain only the rows of data that correspond to the maximum concentration, and then we are using the text function to plot the Subject label to the right of the corresponding points. This graphic can be seen in Figure 13.13.

```
> library(dplyr)
> maxData <- filter(group_by(pkData, Time), Conc == max(Conc), Time != 0)
> plot(pkData$Time, pkData$Conc, pch = 16)
> text(maxData$Time, maxData$Conc, maxData$Subject, pos = 4, offset = 0.5)
```

Legends

Adding a legend to a graphic created with any of the base graphics functions requires us to use the low-level legend function. It can initially seem like a confusing function to work with, but in reality it is not too confusing if you remember to always give the groups in the same order as the text on the legend itself.

The first argument to this function is either an X and Y location for the position of the top-left corner of the legend or a single string of the form "topright" or "bottomleft", among others. A full list is available in the help file for the legend function.

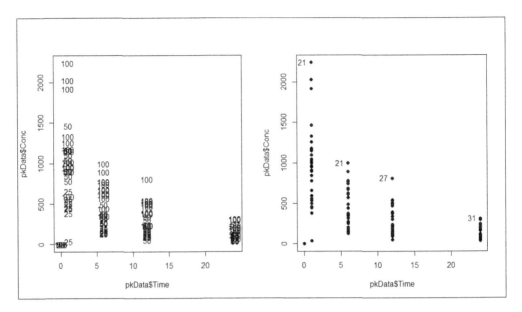

FIGURE 13.13
Using the text function to plot text or add text labels

We then need to specify the legend text. To the argument legend we pass a vector of character strings that will appear as the labels on the legend—for instance, legend = c("Subject 1", "Subject 2"). We can give the text in any order we want the groups to appear. The only thing we need to remember is that when we specify colors, points, and so on, we need to maintain this ordering.

In addition to the location and the legend text, we can then provide vectors of the values for any parameters we want to change. For instance, if we have set the color for each group, we may want to pass a vector of colors to the col argument. If we have changed the plotting symbol for each group, we may want to pass a vector of the plotting symbols—again, remembering for each to maintain the ordering we gave in the text.

As an example, suppose we want to add a legend to the pkData plot, where subject 1 is plotted with blue filled circles and subject 2 is plotted with red, unfilled squares:

```
> subj1 <- pkData[pkData$Subject == 1, ]
> subj2 <- pkData[pkData$Subject == 2, ]
> plot(subj1$Time, subj1$Conc, pch = 16, col = "blue")
> points(subj2$Time, subj2$Conc, pch = 0, col = "red")
> legend("topright", legend = c("Subject 1", "Subject 2"),
+       pch = c(16, 0), col = c("blue", "red"))
```

This graphic is shown in Figure 13.14, and you can see that in this case the legend has been pushed into the very top-right corner and sized appropriately based on the legend text provided.

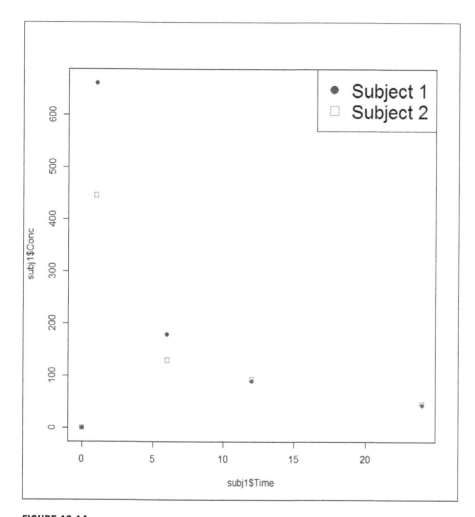

FIGURE 13.14
Adding a legend to a graphic

NOTE

Arguments to the `legend` **Function**

You will have noticed in the example that the arguments used were the same as those in the `plot` and `points` functions. For many of the graphics parameters, this will be the same. However, take care because some, such as `cex`, will actually change the legend itself. You can still change the size of the points in the legend, but you will need the argument `pt.cex` instead. Much more information is available in the help file.

Other Low-Level Functions

In addition to the low-level functions you have seen in this section, a few others are available. We will not go through them all here, but Table 13.2 lists many of the functions you may be interested in. This includes functions for controlling the title, text in the margins, and the axes.

TABLE 13.2 Low-Level Graphics Functions

Function	Purpose	Main Arguments
`title`	Add a main title	A character string
`text`	Add text to the plot area	X, Y positions + vector of text
`points`	Add points to the plot area	X, Y positions
`lines`	Add lines to the plot area	X, Y positions
`abline`	Add straight reference lines	Coefficients or reference values
`mtext`	Add text to the plot margin	An axis number and text
`axis`	Add an axis	An axis number and positions
`legend`	Add a legend	X, Y position + legend info
`polygon`	Add a polygon	X, Y positions

Graphical Parameters

In the graphics we created in this hour, we have set any parameters related to the graphics in the plotting functions. We can also set these inside a function called `par`. The `par` function actually returns a list that contains the settings for graphics parameters. This not only includes arguments such as `col` and `pch`, but also `mar` for setting the margins and `xpd`, which allows us to add graphics content outside of the figure region.

When it comes to setting margins for our graphic, it is useful to know how a graphics device in R is split. Figure 13.15 shows the sub-regions of a device, including the outer margins and the figure region. You will notice that the par function includes arguments for the outer margin. You may want to alter this when you have multiple graphics in one device, as you will see in the next section, because they all share an outer margin.

For all the options that can be set in the par function, their usage, and their default values, the help documentation is an invaluable resource.

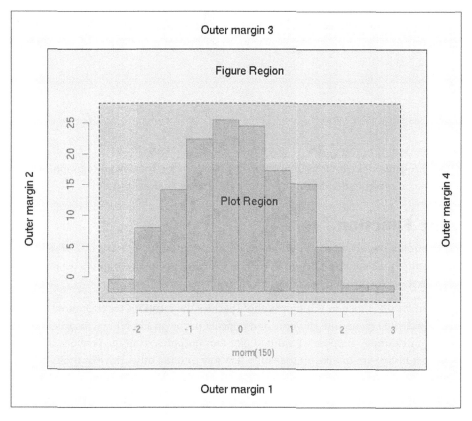

FIGURE 13.15
Regions in a graphics device

Controlling the Layout

Once we are able to create all the graphics we are interested in, we typically want to think about how we present that information. When we looked at creating a graphics device, we said that a PDF file would allow us to create a single, multipage document of all our individual plots. In this section, we look at options for creating a single page containing multiple graphics.

Grid Layouts

The simplest layout of our graphics is in a grid-like structure, where we have a specified number of rows and/or columns of graphics. We can set up a graphics device to have the format by using the `mfrow` option to the `par` function. This argument takes a vector of the number of rows and columns into which our device should be split. When we then create graphics, they will be entered into the device across the rows, starting in the top left of the grid.

As an example, suppose that we have some random data that we want to plot as a histogram, boxplot, QQ plot, and against its index. We may want to set this up as a 2×2 plot area, like so:

```
> par(mfrow = c(2, 2))
> x <- rnorm(100)
> hist(x)
> boxplot(x)
> qqnorm(x)
> plot(x)
```

The graphic that this generates can be seen in Figure 13.16. Once set, this layout of graphics will be maintained. We can revert to the default by setting the `mfrow` argument to `c(1, 1)`.

The `layout` Function

For much finer control of the layout of our graphics we can use the `layout` function. As well as being able to control the width and height of each of the columns in our graphics device, we have much finer control of which regions a graphic appears in.

The main argument for this function is a matrix that specifies the locations for each graphic. Each graphic is represented by an integer value and appears in the grid in all regions where that value appears. As an example, suppose we want to plot four graphics, as in the previous section, but we want the first histogram to take up the entire first row and the other three graphics to appear underneath in one row. In that case, we would create the following matrix:

```
> mat <- rbind(1, 2:4)
> mat
     [,1] [,2] [,3]
[1,]    1    1    1
[2,]    2    3    4
```

Thus, the first graphic would fill all cells containing the value 1—in this case, the entire first row. The second graphic would appear in the position of the 2, and so on. To set this as our layout, we pass it to the `layout` function, followed by the graphics in order:

```
> layout(mat)
> x <- rnorm(100)
> hist(x)
```

```
> boxplot(x)
> qqnorm(x)
> plot(x)
```

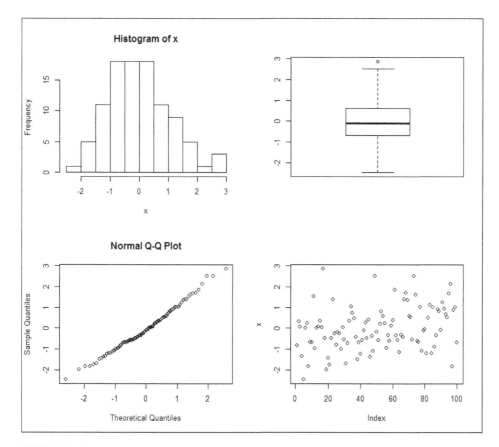

FIGURE 13.16
Splitting up the plot region using mfrow

The result is shown in Figure 13.17. Clearly this gives us a large amount of flexibility over which graphics appear where and their size. If you don't want a region to include a graphic, you can set the value in the matrix to 0. To see the layout you have specified, use the layout.show function. This will generate a graphic showing the specified layout.

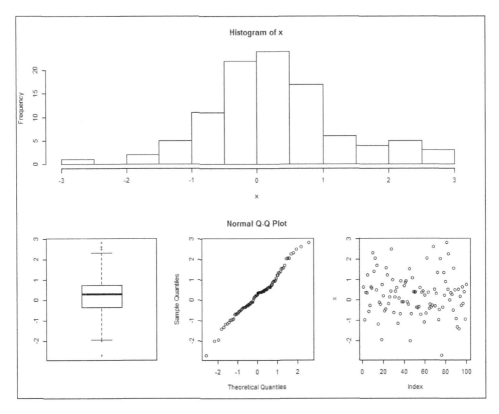

FIGURE 13.17
Splitting up the plot region using `layout`

TIP

Finer Control of the Layout

We can control the appearance of the layout further by using the `widths` and `heights` arguments to the `layout` function. We simply need to provide a vector the same length as the number of columns (for widths) or rows (for heights) specifying the sizes.

Summary

In this hour, you saw how to create graphics using the base R functionality. Functions for graphics are split into two: The high-level functions create a whole plot, and the low-level functions allow us to add components to an existing graphic. The base **graphics** package is not the only option for graphics, and in the next two hours you will see how to create graphics using the **ggplot2** and **lattice** packages.

Q&A

Q. Why isn't my plot appearing in the Plot tab?

A. This is usually because you have an open connection to a graphics device other than the default Plot tab in RStudio. In that case, your graphics are being written to an alternative graphics device. You can use the function `dev.off` to close the current connection, but if you are not sure how many graphics devices you have open, try `graphics.off`. This will close all active devices, and you can start again.

Q. The argument `bg` isn't changing anything in my graphic. What am I doing wrong?

A. What plotting symbol are you using? The argument `bg` is only compatible with plotting symbols in the range 21 to 25. If you are using any other symbol, this argument won't change anything about your graphic.

Q. How can I remove lines or points after I have added them with the low-level functions?

A. The approach taken by R in drawing graphics with the base graphics functions is similar to a pen-and-paper approach. If you want to remove a component, you will need to run the code again, excluding the component you don't want anymore.

Q. I changed the layout of my device and now I just want to see one plot. How can I change it back?

A. You can change the layout back to the default (one row, one column) by setting the argument `mfrow` of the `par` function to `c(1, 1)`.

Q. Can I put the legend outside of the plot region?

A. Yes, you can. You will need to extend the margins and set the argument `xpd` (in the `par` function) to `NA` to allow you to draw in the margins.

Workshop

The workshop contains quiz questions and exercises to help you solidify your understanding of the material covered. Try to answer all questions before looking at the "Answers" section that follows.

Quiz

1. What is a device and why do you need to set one?

2. Which functions allow you to create the following graphics?

    A. A QQ plot with corresponding line

    B. A bar chart of counts

    C. A plot of a variable against another

    D. A histogram

3. What effect would setting `pch` = 6 have on a scatterplot?

4. Which low-level graphics function can you use to add text to the margins?

5. When would you use the `mfrow` argument of the `par` function and when would you use the `layout` function?

Answers

1. A device is what your graphic is created in. This could be the default RStudio device or a specific file type, such as PDF or PNG. If you want to use a device that is not the default device, you need to set it. You use a function such as `pdf` or `png` to set the device and `dev.off` to close the connection.

2. You would need the following functions:

    A. `qqnorm` and `qqline`

    B. `barplot`

    C. `plot`

    D. `hist`

3. It would change the plotting symbol to an upside-down triangle.

4. To add text in the margins, you would need to use the `mtext` function.

5. You would use both to change the layout of a device to include multiple graphics in a single device. The `mfrow` argument is sufficient if you want the graphics to be in a grid layout with a specified number of rows and columns. The `layout` function gives you much more control over exactly where graphics should appear and the widths and heights of rows and columns.

Activities

1. Sample 100 values from a Normal distribution. Create a histogram of this data.

2. For each month in the `airquality` data, create a plot of `Ozone` against `Wind`. Ensure that all the plots are on the same axis and include a suitable title that indicates the month—for example, "`Ozone` against `Wind` for `Month` X."

3. Create a five-page PDF document from the graphics in the previous exercise.

4. Create a single-page PNG file that includes all five graphics created in Activity 2. Choose a suitable layout to show the data.

5. Create a single graphic of `Wind` against `Day`, where each month is a single line, each in a different color. Add a legend to the graphic.

The ggplot2 Package for Graphics

What You'll Learn in This Hour:

▶ Creating simple plots
▶ Changing plot types
▶ Control of aesthetics
▶ Groups and panels
▶ Themes and legend control

In Hour 13, "Graphics," you saw how the **graphics** package can be used to create highly customized graphics. However, as you have seen, the **graphics** package can be hard work when used as an exploratory tool. To compare levels of a variable, we typically need to use "for" loops or a clever application of factors. Items such as the legend must be added manually.

The **lattice** and **ggplot2** packages offer alternatives to the graphics package that are much easier to use for data exploration. Each has been built using Paul Murrell's **grid** package, thus enabling plots to be created as objects that are then printed when required. In this hour we start by looking at the hugely popular **ggplot2** package, developed (once again) by Hadley Wickham.

The Philosophy of ggplot2

The **ggplot2** package was inspired by Leland Wilkinson's book *The Grammar of Graphics*. The grammar of graphics philosophy breaks a graphic into a series of layers. Different layers describe the mapping of the data to plot features, the plot type, the coordinate system, and the associated scaling of plot features. To follow the grammar of graphic using **ggplot2**, we need just one plot function, ggplot, to which we add the required layers. Different plot types can be achieved through geometric layers, or "geoms."

In addition to the relatively pure implementation of the grammar of graphics via the ggplot function, **ggplot2** offers an additional graphical function, qplot, designed to speed up the creation of graphics by making assumptions about the layers we want to use. The existence of qplot in **ggplot2** is divisive: Several vocal supporters of the grammar of graphics concept advocate scrapping qplot. However, as passionate **ggplot2** supporters that use and teach the package on a daily basis, the authors of this book cannot relate to this opinion. Our clients want to be able to create powerful visualizations as quickly and easily as possible. Why would anyone want to remove a function that makes it quicker and easier to create high quality graphics?! By the end of the hour, you can decide for yourself whether you prefer the quick-and-easy approach, the true grammar of graphics, or a combination of the two. For now let's take a look at some **ggplot2** basics using the qplot function.

Quick Plots and Basic Control

The "q" in qplot stands for "quick." The speed mainly relates to typing; the function requires a lot less typing than its ggplot counterpart. It achieves this by making assumptions; however, the function is also far more flexible than most people realize and can be used in conjunction with a layered grammar of graphics approach.

Using qplot

We have stated that qplot is quick because it makes assumptions. Thankfully there are very few assumptions, and they are all very sensible! Indeed, most of the assumptions are no different from the assumptions made by **graphics** functions such as plot and hist. In addition to assumptions about the coordinate system, axes, plotting character, and so on, qplot also makes an assumption about the plot type. For example, if we provide a single variable to qplot, it is assumed that we want to draw a histogram. If we provide two variables, it is assumed that we want to draw a scatter plot.

Later, you'll see how to easily vary the plot type using qplot, but for now we start with a simple scatter plot using the mtcars data. We specify mtcars as the data frame that we are using and refer to the wt and mpg variables directly. The output is displayed in Figure 14.1.

```
> # Load package and create a simple plot
> require(ggplot2)
> theme_set(theme_bw(base_size= 14))    # Set the theme to a white background (more
                                        later)
> qplot(x = wt, y = mpg, data = mtcars)
```

TIP

Changing the Default Theme

In the code block that creates Figure 14.1, we include a line to set the "theme". This line of code changes the default background color from grey with white gridlines to white with grey gridlines. At the same time we increase the default font size. This is a global setting that changes the appearance of each of the subsequent graphics produced in this hour. We look at themes in more detail later in the hour.

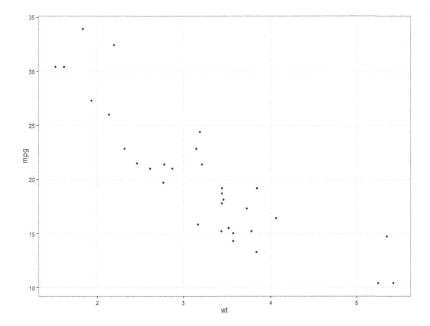

FIGURE 14.1
Creating a scatter plot using the `qplot` function

NOTE

Working with Vectors

The `qplot` function allows us to directly pass individual vectors—for example, `qplot(1:10, rnorm(10))`. However, it is generally more common to have the data that you wish to plot stored within a data frame. In this case, it is much easier to specify the name of the data frame using the `data` argument so that we can refer to variables directly.

Titles and Axes

As with the plotting functions contained within the base **graphics** package, we can add a main title to our plot using qplot via the `main` argument. The arguments `xlab` and `ylab` control the axis labels for the X and Y axes, respectively. Similarly, arguments `xlim` and `ylim` allow users to control the X and Y axis limits. These arguments must be provided with a vector of length 2. We can also add these features using "layers."

Working with Layers

To follow the grammar of graphics, we build a plot in layers. We don't have to do this with qplot, but each of the title/axis elements that we have looked at could instead have been added using a layer. A main title as well as X and Y axis labels can also be added as layers using the ggtitle function and the xlab and ylab functions, respectively. For the X and Y axis limits, we can use xlim and ylim functions. Listing 14.1 contains two sections of code for re-creating the graphic in Figure 14.1 with an appropriate title and axis labels. The two code sections produce an identical graphic; the first, starting on line 2, uses a single call to qplot, and the second, starting on line 10, uses a layered approach.

LISTING 14.1   Optional Layering

```
 1: > # Version 1: Using a single call to qplot
 2: > qplot(x = wt, y = mpg, data = mtcars,
 3: +       main = "Miles per Gallon vs Weight\nAutomobiles (1973-74 models)",
 4: +       xlab = "Weight (lb/1000)",
 5: +       ylab = "Miles per US Gallon",
 6: +       xlim = c(1, 6),
 7: +       ylim = c(0, 40))
 8: >
 9: > # Version 2: qplot with additional layers
10: > qplot(x = wt, y = mpg, data = mtcars) +
11: +       ggtitle("Miles per Gallon vs Weight\nAutomobiles (1973-74 models)") +
12: +       xlab("Weight (lb/1000)") +
13: +       ylab("Miles per US Gallon") +
14: +       xlim(c(1, 6)) +
15: +       ylim(c(0, 40))
```

To add plots as layers, we use the "+" symbol. By placing a + at the end of the line, we tell R to expect more layers to our plot, much like adding numbers. When we add **ggplot2** functions in this way, we say we are adding "layers."

TIP

Fixing One End of an Axis

Sometimes we're only interested in fixing one end of an axis scale. For example, we may wish to fix the lower end at zero. In this case, NA can be used to specify that we are happy to let **ggplot2** choose a bound for us.

Plots as Objects

Both **lattice** and **ggplot2** are built using Paul Murrell's **grid** package. This allows us to save plots as objects. The qplot function creates a ggplot object. A ggplot object is essentially a set of instructions that explain how to create the graphic. Only when we ask R to print the object are the instructions followed and the graph created. The instructions can be saved and used at any time—for example, after we have altered some theme settings and we are ready to export our graphics.

```
> # Create a basic plot and save it as an object
> basicCarPlot <- qplot(wt, mpg, data = mtcars)
> # Modify the plot to include a title
> basicCarPlot <- basicCarPlot +
+   ggtitle("Miles per Gallon vs Weight\nAutomobiles (1973-74 models)")
> # Now print the plot
> basicCarPlot
```

We can use layers to modify a ggplot object, adding new instructions as to what to draw. This is extremely powerful for data exploration because it allows us to create a base graphic and use a variety of different additional layers to explore covariates.

TIP

Exporting ggplot2 Graphics

In Hour 13 you saw how to write a plot to file by opening the device, drawing the plot, and then closing the device with dev.off. The **ggplot2** package provides an alternative workflow via ggsave. To export using ggsave, we first save our plot as an object. When we are ready to write the plot to file, we pass ggsave the filename and ggplot the object name, for example:

```
> carPlot <- qplot(x = wt, y = mpg, data = mtcars)    # Create ggplot object
> ggsave(file = "carPlot.png", carPlot)               # Save object as a png
Saving 10.6 x 7.57 in image
```

The function handles the opening and closing of devices for us, selecting the device based on the file extension that we provide.

Changing Plot Types

Using the grammar of graphics terminology, plot types are considered to be geometric shapes that describe how the data are displayed. We vary the plot type using the geom (short for "geometric") argument to qplot, negating the need for separate plotting functions. A sample call is shown here with the resulting graphic shown in Figure 14.2:

```
> # Ensure cyl variable is of the right type by fixing in the data
> mtcars$cyl <- factor(mtcars$cyl)
> qplot(cyl, mpg, data = mtcars, geom = "boxplot")
```

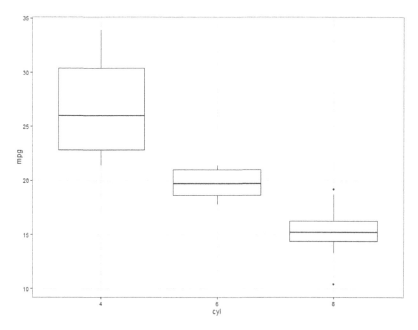

FIGURE 14.2
Generating boxplots

Know Your Factors!

When you're working within the **ggplot2** framework, it is really important to know your data types. You need to pay particular attention to categorical data that might be stored as numeric (for example, the `cyl` variable in `mtcars`). Such variables must be converted to factors to ensure appropriate representation on the end graphic. Generally, it is better to make any necessary conversions within the data as opposed to within the call to `qplot` or subsequent layers.

Plot Types

When we specify the `geom` argument within `qplot`, we are in fact calling out to one of many geometric functions that tell R how to display the graphic. Each function has a `geom_` prefix. We can therefore use a regular expression to find all geometric functions within the **ggplot2** package.

```
> grep("^geom", objects("package:ggplot2"), value = TRUE)
 [1] "geom_abline"    "geom_area"      "geom_bar"       "geom_bin2d"
 [5] "geom_blank"     "geom_boxplot"   "geom_contour"   "geom_crossbar"
```

```
 [9] "geom_density"     "geom_density2d"  "geom_dotplot"   "geom_errorbar"
[13] "geom_errorbarh"   "geom_freqpoly"   "geom_hex"       "geom_histogram"
[17] "geom_hline"       "geom_jitter"     "geom_line"      "geom_linerange"
[21] "geom_map"         "geom_path"       "geom_point"     "geom_pointrange"
[25] "geom_polygon"     "geom_quantile"   "geom_raster"    "geom_rect"
[29] "geom_ribbon"      "geom_rug"        "geom_segment"   "geom_smooth"
[33] "geom_step"        "geom_text"       "geom_tile"      "geom_violin"
[37] "geom_vline"
```

CAUTION

Line Graphs!

There are two geoms for creating a standard line graph in **ggplot2**: geom_line and geom_path. The geom_path function is analogous to using the low-level lines function in the **graphics** package. The geom_line function is best used with time series data because it ensures that the x-values are plotted from low to high by reordering the coordinates before plotting.

When working with qplot, we simply remove the "geom_" from the function name and pass the rest, in quotes, to the geom argument. As with the title, axis labels, and axis limit options, we can call the geometric functions directly as separate layers. However, one of the features that makes qplot "quick" is that it assumes a geometric shape or plot type to draw. If we don't specify a plot type, qplot chooses one for us. The following code therefore fails to exactly re-create Figure 14.2. Instead, the boxplots are drawn over the top of a scatter plot as shown in Figure 14.3.

```
> qplot(cyl, mpg, data = mtcars) + geom_boxplot()
```

The previous example might imply that it is difficult to use qplot to create complex graphics. However, with a good understanding of the working of qplot and the **ggplot2** layers, almost anything is possible!

Combining Plot Types

Although the previous example (overlaying points and a boxplot) may in itself be undesirable, it highlights the possibility of using two or more geometric layers in conjunction with one another. One example is using multiple layers to create the **ggplot2** equivalent to a type = "o" plot that we saw in the previous hour by overlaying points and lines. However, there are many more possible combinations. The following example adds a linear smoothing line to a plot of mpg against wt using mtcars:

```
> qplot(wt, mpg, data = mtcars) + geom_smooth(method = "lm")
```

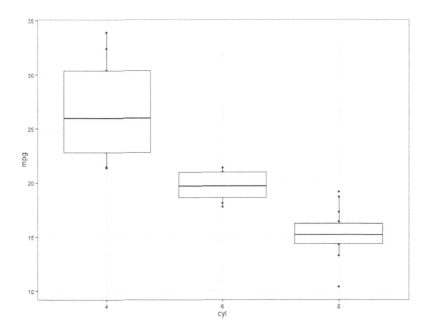

FIGURE 14.3
The effect of adding a geom_boxplot layer to a standard qplot call

We do not necessarily need to add geometric layers to create the desired plot. It is possible to create the exact same plot as the preceding line using a single call to qplot. We do so by providing the geom argument with a character vector of geometric names. In this case, we specify a vector containing both "point" and "smooth". Note that any additional arguments to the geometric functions, such as method = "lm" in this case, can also be passed to qplot. An example of this with the output displayed follows in Figure 14.4.

```
> qplot(wt, mpg, data = mtcars, geom = c("point", "smooth"), method = "lm")
```

When combining two or more plot types together, it can often be clearer to use the ggplot function instead of qplot. We will look more closely at ggplot later in the hour.

Aesthetics

In **ggplot2** terminology, the word "aesthetic" has a special meaning and can refer to any graph element that is affected by columns within our data. This could include what we traditionally think of as aesthetics, such as the color, shape, or size of plotting characters, but also arguments such as x and y. We will look more closely at the idea of x and y as being aesthetics toward the end of the hour, but for now let's focus on the traditional meaning.

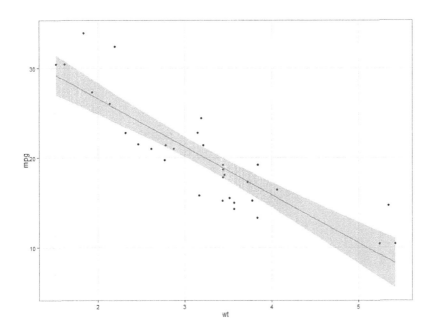

FIGURE 14.4
Passing additional arguments to geoms when using qplot

A big advantage of **ggplot2** over the **graphics** package is the ease with which we can visually explore our data using aesthetic elements. Using qplot, we can link an attribute such as color directly to a variable. Doing so creates a legend automatically. In order to use aesthetics, we can either specify the same arguments to the par function (col, pch, cex) that we saw in Hour 13 or we can use more memorable, user-friendly terms: color, shape and size. We can also use alpha to vary the transparency, fill to control shaded areas, and linetype to vary the line type. As can be seen in the following code block and Figure 14.5, we can create extremely attractive graphics using very little code. In this example, we create a plot of earthquake locations in a region of Fiji, where the size of the plot character represents the magnitude of the earthquake, and the color represents the depth at which it occurred.

```
> qplot(x = long, y = lat, data = quakes, size = mag, col = -depth) +
+    ggtitle("Locations of Earthquakes off Fiji") +
+    xlab("Longitude") + ylab("Latitude")
```

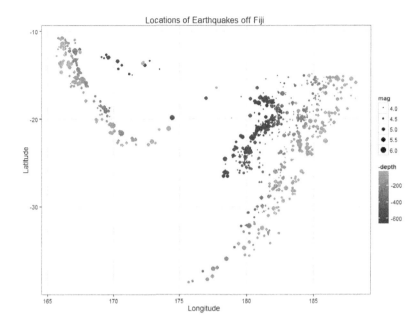

FIGURE 14.5
Varying the aesthetics of a plot

CAUTION

Make Everything Blue!

The qplot function has been written to make it as easy as possible to link aesthetic elements with variables in our data. As a consequence, it's not quite so easy to just color every point blue! To do so, we have to use a function called I. Here's an example:

```
> qplot(wt, mpg, data = mtcars, colour = I("blue"))
```

Neglecting to use the I function in this example would result in the text "blue" being treated as a variable in our data. This does not cause an error but does yield some interesting results!

Control of Aesthetics

One of the great things about using **ggplot2** for data exploration is that the package handles the aesthetics for us. However, when it comes to presenting or publishing our results, there are usually one or two styling elements we would like to tweak. In **ggplot2** the appearance of the aesthetics is controlled by scaling layers. The scale layer functions follow a very consistent naming convention that depends on the element we want to control and the type of data we are controlling. The general format is

```
scale_[aestheticElement]_[scaleType]
```

Using this convention, we replace `aestheticElement` with the aesthetic used (for example, color). We replace `scaleType` by an appropriate scale for our data type (for example, continuous). In addition to the more obvious `discrete` and `continuous` scales, a number of other useful aesthetic scales are available in **ggplot2**. For example, `scale_color_gradientn` creates a continuous color through n colors, e.g., `scale_color_gradientn(colours = rainbow(6))`.

Consider a plot of `mpg` against `wt` using `mtcars` for which we decide to vary the shape by the `cyl` variable. To change the shapes used for the three levels of the `cyl` variable, we use the scale layer function `scale_shape_manual`. The example is shown here with the corresponding output displayed in Figure 14.6:

```
> # Create a basic plot
> carPlot <- qplot(x = wt, y = mpg, data = mtcars, shape = cyl, # cyl is a factor
+        main = "Miles per Gallon vs Weight\nAutomobiles (1973-74 models)",
+        xlab = "Weight (lb/1000)",
+        ylab = "Miles per US Gallon",
+        xlim = c(1, 6),
+        ylim = c(0, 40))
>
> # Edit plotting symbols and print
carPlot + scale_shape_manual("Number of\nCylinders", values = c(3,5,2))
```

The scale function chosen must match the data type. In the previous example, we used the `manual` suffix, which allows us to be specific about which shapes we want to use. This `manual` suffix only works with discrete data. We provided the function with a list of three shapes because the factor version of the `cyl` variable is discrete and has three levels.

NOTE

Universal Spelling

Hadley Wickham is a New Zealander who has spent much of his adult life living in the USA. The **ggplot2** package is a universally friendly package that accounts for variants in the English language, such as the two ways of spelling color/colour, by duplicating functionality. This has resulted in several identical functions such as `scale_color_manual` and `scale_colour_manual`.

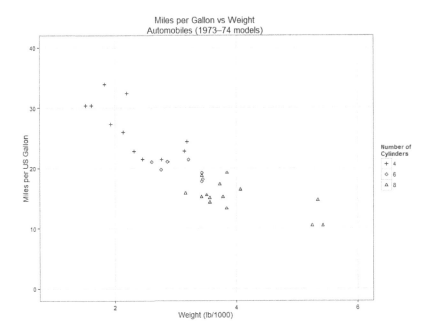

FIGURE 14.6
Manual control of the aesthetics

Scales and the Legend

In **ggplot2** there is a direct link between the aesthetic elements and the legend. It is this link that causes a legend item to be generated whenever we vary an aesthetic such as color by a variable in our data. This link extends to the aesthetic scaling functions, which, in addition to controlling the aesthetics themselves, can be used to control the way in which the aesthetics are portrayed within the legend. As you may have noted from the code block that creates Figure 14.6, the first argument to each of the aesthetic scaling functions controls the name that appears with that element within the legend. An example of updating the legend titles is shown here with the output displayed in Figure 14.7:

```
> # Create a basic plot
> carPlot <- qplot(x = wt, y = mpg, data = mtcars,
+                  shape = cyl, size = disp,
+                  main = "Miles per Gallon vs Weight\nAutomobiles (1973-74
➡models)",
+                  xlab = "Weight (lb/1000)",
+                  ylab = "Miles per US Gallon",
```

```
+                    xlim = c(1, 6),
+                    ylim = c(0, 40))
>
> # Change legend titles via scale layers
> carPlot +
+    scale_shape_discrete("Number of Cylinders") +
+    scale_size_continuous("Displacement (cu.in.)")
```

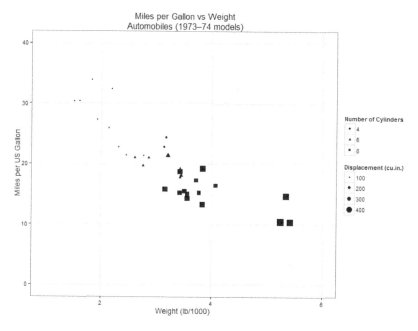

FIGURE 14.7
Updating the legend titles

In the previous example we chose to vary the size of the plotting character by each car's displacement value. The physical size of the points representing low displacement and high displacement is chosen for us. However, we can use the scale layers to control these physical properties. For a continuous scale we use the range argument to control the minimum and maximum values that a scale can take. Here's an example with the effect displayed in Figure 14.8:

```
> carPlot + scale_size_continuous("Displacement (cu.in.)", range = c(4,8))
```

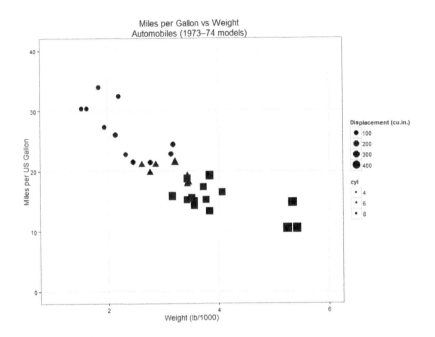

FIGURE 14.8
Using the `range` argument to control the symbol scaling

We can also control the appearance of each aesthetic in the legend. We do so using the `breaks` argument. We use `limits` to ensure that the values we provide to `breaks` are within the scale limits. Figure 14.9 shows a complete example using `scale_size_continuous` to control the size of points on the graph as well as the legend title and breaks. The corresponding code is shown here:

```
> carPlot +
+    scale_shape_discrete("Number of cylinders") +
+    scale_size_continuous("Displacement (cu.in.)",
+                          range = c(4,8),
+                          breaks = seq(100, 500, by = 100),
+                          limits = c(0, 500))
```

For a full list of available scales, type the following line into the console:

```
> grep("^scale", objects("package:ggplot2"), value = TRUE)
```

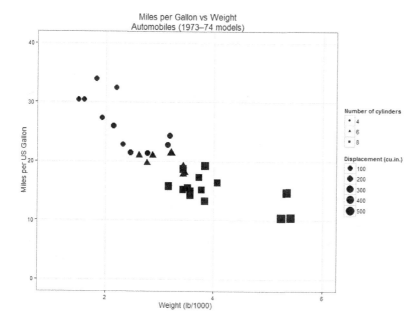

FIGURE 14.9
Control of aesthetics

NOTE

Axis Scales

In addition to scales for `color`, `shape`, `size`, `fill`, `alpha`, and `linetype`, there are further scales to control the X and Y axes. The axis scales work in much the same way as the other scales. We can use these scales to control axis titles, limits, breakpoints, and so on.

Working with Grouped Data

Occasionally our data may be inherently grouped, but we are not interested in visually exploring the differences between these groups with aesthetics. A good example of this is repeated measures or longitudinal data. Consider the following `pkData` dataset. The dataset contains repeated measures data for 33 subjects. For each subject, five drug concentration values were collected at times 0, 1, 6, 12, and 24. We can think of the concentration records as grouped by subject.

```
> library(mangoTraining)
> head(pkData)
  Subject Dose Time   Conc
1       1   25    0   0.00
2       1   25    1 660.13
```

3	1	25	6	178.92
4	1	25	12	88.99
5	1	25	24	42.71
6	2	25	0	0.00

To see how this grouping affects a plot, consider a line plot of Conc against Time. Using qplot, we could specify either geom = "path" or geom = "line". Here's an example:

```
qplot(data = pkData, x = Time, y = Conc, geom = "line")    # Not the desired
                                                             result!
qplot(data = pkData, x = Time, y = Conc, geom = "path")    # Not the desired
                                                             result!
```

If you draw these plots for yourself, you can see that there is something wrong with each one. To understand what is happening, imagine drawing the plot by hand but not taking the pen off the page. Specifying geom = "line" causes the data to be sorted by Time before plotting. Because there are multiple values at each time point, we end up with a slightly odd-looking plot with vertical lines at each time point where every Conc value has been joined before moving to the next time point. By specifying geom = "path", we create what, at a glance, looks like the desired plot; however, because we don't take the pen off the page, we end up with lots of unwanted lines linking the 24-hour value for one subject back to the zero-hour value for the next.

At this point we could use an aesthetic such as color or linetype to separate the lines. However, this would result in each subject being plotted in a different color or using a different line type. Because we are not interested in investigating subjects individually, this does not help us. We need a group option. By specifying group = Subject, we metaphorically take the pen off the page to draw each new subject. The grouping is not linked to any other physical property of the plot and so each line remains consistent in appearance. The result is shown in Figure 14.10, and the corresponding code is shown here:

```
> qplot(data = pkData, x = Time, y = Conc, geom = "path", group = Subject,
+        ylab = "Concentration")
```

The concept of groups is also useful when plotting geographical data using maps because groups can be used to ensure state boundaries are separated correctly but remain a consistent color.

Paneling (a.k.a Faceting)

There can come a point when a plot is simply too busy to effectively compare groups using aesthetics. As an alternative, we can split the information into separate subplots, commonly known as panels, and instead compare the information contained within each panel. In **ggplot2** terminology, the concept of paneling is known as "faceting." To panel/facet by a variable, we must invoke one of two facet_* functions: facet_grid or facet_wrap.

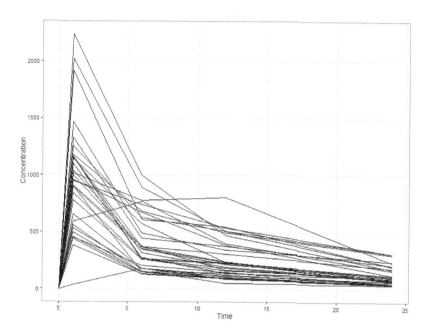

FIGURE 14.10
Using groups to separate lines

Using `facet_grid`

To see the difference between the two functions, let's suppose that we want to explore the relationship between mpg and wt for each gear in the mtcars data. We create a graphic with a separate panel for each level of gear and plot, say, side by side. We start with our basic carPlot that we looked at earlier.

Next, we add a facet_grid layer. The aim of the facet_grid function is to allow us to compare plots either vertically or horizontally across the levels of a factor. The facet_grid function expects a formula object. In R, a formula is a class of object that is commonly used for statistical modeling; therefore, we will look at formula objects in greater detail in Hour 16, "Introduction to R Models and Object Orientation." A formula object is based around a tilde (~). The facet_grid function expects a formula of the form *rows ~ cols* for which we replace rows and cols with variables in our data. Any variables specified on the left side of the formula are split across the rows. In other words, the resulting panels are stacked on top of each other. Any variables specified on the right side are split across columns (that is, side by side). In order to compare the various gears side by side, we must put the gear variable on the right side of the formula. For now, we are not interested in comparing anything else, so we do not provide a variable in the left side of the formula. In order for facet_grid to work, we must provide a period (.) as an alternative to any variables. This results in the graphic shown in Figure 14.11, which features a separate panel for each of the three gears. Note that the varying of aesthetics defined in `carPlot` are still present despite the faceting performed.

```
> carPlot + facet_grid(. ~ gear)
```

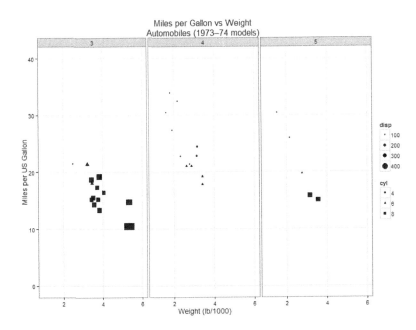

FIGURE 14.11
Faceting with `facet_grid`

Had we decided to stack the same three panels vertically, we could have written the following instead:

```
> carPlot + facet_grid(gear ~ .)
```

Now let's take this concept further and look at paneling by a second variable, `cyl`. Given that we decided to compare `gear` side by side, we compare `cyl` vertically. We replace the period on the left side of the formula with the `cyl` variable. This creates a 3×3 plot, with each row representing a different value of `cyl` and each column representing a different value of `gear`. It is worth noting that within the `mtcars` dataset there are no records of cars that have four gears and eight cylinders. The panel that represents the four-gear, eight-cylinder combination is displayed but is empty.

Alternatively, we may prefer to visualize each combination of `cyl` and `gear` side by side as shown in Figure 14.12. In this case, we literally add `cyl` as a variable to the right side of our formula using a + sign, leaving the left side untouched.

```
> carPlot + facet_grid(. ~ gear + cyl)
```

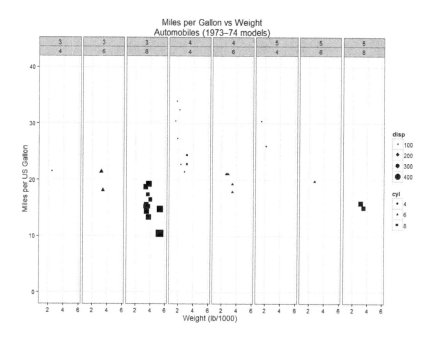

FIGURE 14.12
Multiple variables on the right-hand side of the `facet_grid` formula

The result is a 1×8 plot with eight panels representing the eight combinations of `gear` and `cyl` for which we have data to plot. The levels of the `gear` and `cyl` variables appear in the panel headers, commonly known as "strip headers." The strip header is split into two rows of text. In the first are the levels of `gear`, and in the second are the levels of `cyl`.

Using `facet_wrap`

In most cases it is much easier to compare plots if they are presented side by side or vertically stacked on top of each other. However, if the faceting variable has many levels, then this may not be practically possible. The `facet_wrap` function offers an alternative to `facet_grid` that "wraps" the plots around to best fill the available page and avoid long and thin or short and squat panels, which may result from comparing too many levels with `facet_grid`.

To illustrate this, consider the same basic `carPlot` from before, but let's now look to the panel by the `carb` variable, representing the number of carburetors for each car in the data. Plotting panels for each of the six possible values for the `carb` variable side by side using `facet_grid` creates some very tall, thin panels. Using `facet_wrap`, we get back the same six plots but laid out in a 2×3 grid, starting in the top left and moving left to right, then down the page through each of the possible `carb` values. A `facet_wrap` function call differs from a `facet_grid` call in that we leave the left side of the faceting formula blank. The following line generates the graphic shown in Figure 14.13:

```
> carPlot + facet_wrap( ~ carb)
```

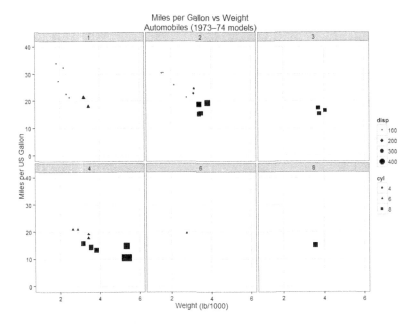

FIGURE 14.13
Faceting with `facet_wrap`

If we want to facet by multiple variables, these must be listed on the right side, each one separated by a +.

NOTE

Axis Scales

Neither `facet_grid` nor `facet_wrap` requires a factor in order to create the separate panels.

Faceting from `qplot`

It is possible to create faceted plots directly using `qplot` without having to add a `facet_grid` or `facet_wrap` layer. We can do so via the `facets` argument to `qplot`, providing it with an appropriate formula to determine which of `facet_grid` or `facet_wrap` is invoked. The key to determining which of the two functions is invoked by `qplot` is the left side of the faceting formula. To invoke `facet_grid`, we supply either a variable or period as we would when calling `facet_grid` directly. To invoke `facet_wrap`, we leave the left side blank.

Custom Plots

Each of the examples we have seen thus far has either been created directly using `qplot` or with `qplot` and additional layers. In the vast majority of cases this is absolutely fine; however, as the examples become more complex, the code may become difficult to follow. In such cases, the `ggplot` function may offer a more readable alternative.

Working with `ggplot`

Unlike `qplot`, `ggplot` makes no assumptions about the plot type or even the coordinate system. It simply creates a template `ggplot` object from which to build. On its own the object is useless, and we get an error message if we try to print it. It is the equivalent of an empty recipe. We must build our recipe piece by piece (layer by layer) telling R precisely how to build the plot.

Let's start by re-creating Figure 14.1, this time by fully embracing the grammar of graphics with the `ggplot` function. For comparison, remind yourself of the two `qplot` approaches in Listing 14.1 that can be used to create the plot. To achieve the desired scatter plot of mpg against wt, we start by adding a `geom_point` layer to a base `ggplot` object. We need to ensure that `geom_point` knows what the x and y variables are. Unfortunately, however, it is not as simple as specifying x = wt and y = mpg. As you may note from the following code, we must use a new function, `aes`:

```
> ggplot() + geom_point(data = mtcars, aes(x = wt, y = mpg))
```

If we want to add elements such as the title, axis limits, and labels, we must do so using additional layers. This layered approach is, in essence, the grammar of graphics.

The `aes` Function

For the **ggplot2** newcomer, the `aes` function can be one of the more confusing aspects of the package. I've taught training courses to people who have been using the package for several years but tell me that they still don't fully understand how or when to use it! In fact, there's only one rule you need to know, and it's quite straightforward once you know it. First, let's briefly look at what `aes` means and where it comes from.

In the grammar of graphics, the term "aesthetics" refers not only to the appearance of points on a graph but the points themselves. In fact, it need not necessarily refer to points at all. It could be lines, boxes, or bars because the plot type is defined by the geometric shape or "geom." The aesthetics are essentially just information about how variables in the data are to be represented (or "mapped," to use the grammar of graphics). They depend on the plot type, coordinate system, faceting, scaling, and so on.

In short, the aesthetics describe how columns of data are to be mapped to elements of the plot. This leads to the following rule for **ggplot2** layers:

▶ Any reference to a variable must be wrapped within a call to the aes function.

Perhaps what confuses people is that the rule does not apply to facet_grid and facet_wrap, which use a formula. As we have seen, it also does not apply to qplot. However, it does apply to subsequent layers that are added to an object generated by qplot. Let's return to our carPlot example and suppose we now wish to plot each point using a different plotting character depending on the value of the factor cyl.

```
> ggplot() + geom_point(data = mtcars, aes(x = wt, y = mpg, shape = cyl))
```

In this example, we mapped the three variables wt, mpg, and cyl to the aesthetics x, y, and shape, respectively. We placed each mapping within a call to aes. The data frame itself is never placed within a call to aes.

Working with ggplot

Switching between qplot and ggplot with layers can be confusing at first. When working outside of qplot, we don't need to use the I function to refer to plot elements that are not based on variables within our data. For example, to create a scatter plot of mpg against wt using large triangles as the plotting character, we write the following:

```
> ggplot() + geom_point(data = mtcars, aes(x = wt, y = mpg), shape = 17, size = 3)
```

We place the shape and size arguments outside the call to aes because they do not refer to variables in the data. The resulting plot is shown in Figure 14.14.

Where to Specify Aesthetics

So far we have looked at building a graphic using an empty ggplot object. However, if you look for **ggplot2** help online, you can find plenty of examples that do not start with an empty object. If we're working with a single data frame, we can save ourselves some typing by defining the data, and any aesthetics that we wish to pass to subsequent geometric layers, within the ggplot call.

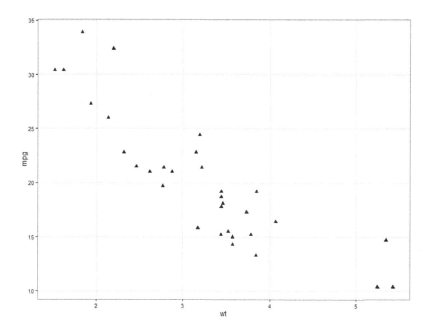

FIGURE 14.14
When to use the aes function

Suppose we want to add a linear line of best fit through our mpg against wt plot. We use two geometric layers: geom_point and geom_smooth. Rather than pass the data and aesthetics to each layer separately, we define them up front:

```
> ggplot(data = mtcars, aes(x = wt, y = mpg)) +
+    geom_point(shape = 17, size = 3) +
+    geom_smooth(method = "lm", se = FALSE, col = "red")
```

An advantage of writing the code in this way is to save typing. Providing data and aesthetic arguments within the ggplot function call does not prevent us from changing or adding new aesthetics in subsequent layers. For example, as shown in Figure 14.15, we can modify the previous code block to vary the geom_point plotting symbol by the cyl variable:

```
> ggplot(data = mtcars, aes(x = wt, y = mpg)) +
+    geom_point(aes(shape = cyl), size = 3) +
+    geom_smooth(method = "lm", se = FALSE, col = "red")
```

There is nothing to stop us creating this plot by starting with qplot and adding the geom_smooth layer. However, in order to ensure that we keep a single best-fit line, we do need to "undo" the definition of cyl as the shape variable by setting shape = NULL in the call to geom_smooth:

```
> qplot(data = mtcars, x = wt, y = mpg, shape = cyl, size = I(3)) +
+    geom_smooth(method = "lm", se = FALSE, col = "red", aes(shape = NULL))
```

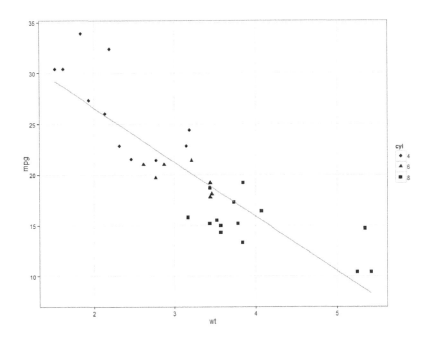

FIGURE 14.15
Use of aes in layers

Note that these examples draw a single smoothing line through the data. If we want a separate smoothing line for each level of cyl, we either need to specify this in the geom_smooth layer using aes(linetype = cyl) or we could move aes(shape = cyl) in geom_point into the original ggplot call.

Working with Multiple Data Frames

The qplot function cannot directly handle multiple data frames. However, it is possible to use qplot so long as you have a good understanding of layers and know when and where to use the aes function. We therefore do not technically *need* to use ggplot to work with multiple data frames, but it is generally much easier and can improve readability.

In the following example we use **ggplot2** to create a "shadow" plot. We panel by the cyl variable in mtcars but plot a copy of the full data in the background using light grey to create the shadow effect. The resulting plot can be seen in Figure 14.16. In order to achieve the shadow effect, we create a second data frame that does not contain the `cyl` variable in order to avoid the paneling.

```
> # Create a copy of the mtcars data to be used as a "shadow"
> require(dplyr)     # To use select function
> carCopy <- mtcars %>% select(-cyl)
>
> # Use layers to control the color of points
> ggplot() +
+   geom_point(data = carCopy, aes(x = wt, y = mpg), color = "lightgrey") +
+   geom_point(data = mtcars, aes(x = wt, y = mpg)) +
+   facet_grid( ~ cyl) +  # Note that cyl only exists in mtcars not carCopy
+   ggtitle("MPG vs Weight Automobiles (1973-74 models)\nBy Number of Cylinders") +
+   xlab("Weight (lb/1000)") +
+   ylab("Miles per US Gallon")
```

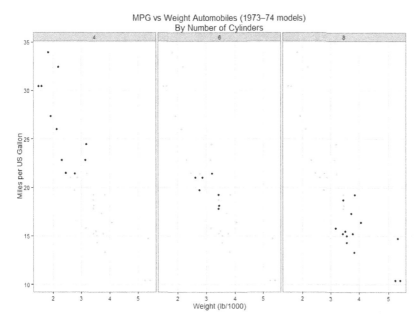

FIGURE 14.16
A "shadow" plot using the `mtcars` data

The previous example uses what might be considered a trick to create the shadow affect. However, a similar approach can be used plot any information contained within two or more separate data frames. The only restriction is that the axes remain on the same scale. It is not possible to use **ggplot2** to obtain a plot with two completely different y variables.

TIP

Quick Data Summaries

The `stat_summary` function enables us to summarize our y variable at each unique x value. This is particularly useful when plotting confidence intervals for repeated measures data.

Coordinate Systems

The layered grammar of graphics approach that **ggplot2** uses enables us to change the coordinate system completely via a single coordinate layer. Examples include transposing the axes (`coord_flip`), switching from a Cartesian to a polar coordinate system (`coord_polar`), and allowing for the Earth's curvature when plotting maps (`coord_map`). Borrowing functionality from the `mapproj` package, we can plot geographical data using a number of known map projections such as the default `"mercator"` projection as well as `"cylindrical"`, `"mollweide"`, and many, many more. The following code block generates the graphic in Figure 14.17.

```
> nz <- map_data("nz")          # Extract map coordinates for New Zealand
> nzmap <- ggplot(nz, aes(x=long, y=lat, group=group)) +
+   geom_polygon(fill="white", colour="black")
>
> # Now let's add a projection
> nzmap + coord_map("cylindrical")
```

A similar principle can be used to create a pie chart. If you look through the various "geom" layers available in **ggplot2**, you will notice the lack of a `geom_pie`. In the grammar of graphics, a pie chart is actually just another representation of a bar chart. To create a pie chart we must therefore start by creating a stacked bar chart. We then add to this a `coord_polar` layer. The `coord_polar` layer converts the coordinate system from a Cartesian system to a polar coordinate system, and with a little extra work to modify the axes and other features we end up with a reasonably decent-looking pie chart.

Themes and Layout

One of the reasons that the **ggplot2** package is so popular is that the "out-of-the-box" graphics are so visually appealing. However, if we're sharing our graphic either in a document, a slide show, or via a web application, we typically need to make some tweaks to the general appearance. Thankfully the concept of themes in **ggplot2** makes it very straightforward to control both the global styling options and the styling for individual plots.

At first the **ggplot2** theme settings can appear a little daunting, but once you understand the basic format that is required, modifying the elements is a very straightforward, logical process. Let's look first at how we can make minor theme alterations to an individual plot using a "theme" layer.

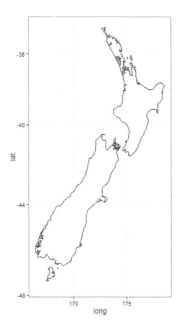

FIGURE 14.17
Adding map projections

Tweaking Individual Plots

Theme layers can be used to control styling elements for a plot such as axis ticks and labels, panel headers, and the legend. We can add a theme layer to a plot using the `theme` function. The `theme` function accepts a number of arguments relating to specific plot items. Plot items are classified as either text, such as the plot title; an area, such as the panel background; or a line, such as the X or Y axis. Depending on the classification, we choose one of four `element_*` functions, corresponding to the classifications described, or `element_blank` if we do not want the item to appear on our plot.

The modification of theme elements for a plot is best illustrated with an example. Suppose we are looking to publish a graphic and need to match some predefined criteria for graphics that prevent the use of gridlines and require that strip header backgrounds be blank. We re-use the basic `carPlot` example from earlier in the hour and panel by the `cyl` column. To make the necessary modifications, we add theme layers to `carPlot` as follows:

```
> carPlot +
+   facet_grid(~ cyl) +
+   theme(
+     strip.background = element_rect(colour = "grey50", fill = NA),
```

```
+       panel.grid.minor = element_blank(),
+       panel.grid.major = element_blank()
+     )
```

In this example, we modified the strip background, `strip.background`, and the major and minor grid lines, `panel.grid.major` and `panel.grid.minor`, respectively. Each was specified using a single theme layer called using the `theme` function. To modify the strip background, we used the `element_rect` function, which defines settings for an area. The gridlines are lines and would typically be modified using the `element_line` function. However, in this example we needed to remove them and so we chose `element_blank`. If we had needed to control the appearance of the strip text, we would have used `element_text`.

Global Themes

Rather than modify plots on an individual basis, it is usually much more desirable when creating several graphics to modify plot styles at a global level. We can define and modify a global theme using the `theme_set` and `theme_update` functions, respectively. The `theme_set` function allows us to define a new global theme based on predefined global themes. We pass the `theme_set` function one of a number of predefined global themes, which include the default gray theme and a black-and-white theme that could be used to create the figures in this hour.

Themes are actually functions in their own right, with arguments that control the size and font family used for plotting. Each follows the convention `theme_[themeName]`, where *[themeName]* would be `gray` or `bw` in the examples just described. For example, the default theme could be defined by calling `theme_set(theme_gray())`. At the beginning of this hour we set the global theme for graphics with the line `theme_set(theme_bw(base_size = 14))`. The `base_size` argument controls the base font size used for titles and axis labels. Similarly the `base_family` argument controls the font family.

The global theme settings are independent from the `ggplot` objects that we create during an R session. When we ask R to print a `ggplot` object, the list of instructions that make up the object are combined with the global theme settings to create the plot. In other words, once we have created the `ggplot` object we can easily draw and redraw using any theme we like.

Having selected a base global theme, we can use the `theme_update` function to make minor modifications. The `theme_update` function allows us to make or adjust specific plot elements in the same way as the `theme` function. However, with `theme_update` the changes are made globally.

TIP

More Themes

The **ggthemes** package provides a more extensive array of available themes, including `theme_economist` and `theme_wsj` for the popular newspapers as well as color scales such as `scale_color_excel`!

Legend Layout

You saw earlier how scaling layers can be used to control the legend appearance, including both the title and the display of legend information. We have also now seen how themes can be used to control the styling of plot elements, including the legend. For example, if we want to move the legend from the right side to the base of the plot, we could add a theme layer specifying the option `legend.position = "bottom"`.

Additional legend control is provided via the `guides` function. We usually end up using a combination of `guides` and the `guide_legend` function to control the layout of categorical variables for plot aesthetics such as `color`, `shape`, and `size`, particularly where there are multiple categories. For example, suppose we have created a `ggplot` object, `mapOfUSA`; this is a map of the USA where each state is represented in a different color. To ensure that all 50 states appear in the legend, we would likely need to specify exactly how the fill color is represented. Instead of listing all 50 states in a single column, we could use the `ncol` argument to `guide_legend` to specify, say, 10 columns, as in the following example:

```
> mapOfUSA + guides(fill = guide_legend(title = "State",
+                                nrow =10, title.position = "top"))
```

The code required to create the `mapOfUSA` object is provided on the book's website, http://www.mango-solutions.com/wp/teach-yourself-r-in-24-hours-book/. Note that the call to `guide_legend` is linked directly to the `fill` aesthetic. This link means that we can also call `guide_legend` from within the aesthetic scale layers.

TIP

Removing the Legend

We can use the `guides` function to remove the legend by setting the aesthetic to `"none"` or `FALSE`—for example, `guides(color = FALSE)`. Alternatively, we can use the aesthetic scale layers, setting the `guide` argument to `FALSE` instead—for example, `scale_color_discrete(guide = FALSE)`.

The ggvis Evolution

As you have seen, the **ggplot2** package is a fantastic package for creating high-quality static images. In recent years, however, many industries have seen a shift away from static graphics toward interactive web visualizations. Today there are several R packages such as **rCharts** that provide an interface to JavaScript graphical libraries. The **ggvis** package is built on top of **vega** and enables interactivity using a **ggplot2**-like syntax.

The **ggvis** package is still under development and does not fully replicate **ggplot2**. However, it is already a useful package. Listing 14.2 creates a very simple **ggvis** (non-interactive) version of the mpg against wt plot we explored during this hour. Note how we use the `fill` argument to vary the color (as opposed to `color` in **ggplot2**) by the wt variable. Note also the use of the piping operator from **magrittr**, which you were introduced to in Hour 12, "Efficient Data Handling in R."

LISTING 14.2 A Simple Example Using ggvis

```
1: > # Load the package
2: > require(ggvis)
3: >
4: > # Vary the colour by the factor variable: cyl
5: > ggvis(mtcars, x = ~wt, y = ~mpg, fill = ~cyl) %>%
6: +   layer_points()
```

The example in Listing 14.2 produces a static graphic, one much less appealing than its **ggplot2** counterpart. However, this example doesn't do **ggvis** justice. The **ggvis** package is at its best when graphics are interactive and accessed from a web browser. In Hour 24, "Building Web Applications with Shiny," you will see how interactive graphics can be embedded within a simple web application that we build entirely with R code.

Summary

In this hour, you have discovered the immensely popular graphical package **ggplot2**. Along the way you have been introduced to the concept of the grammar of graphics and the concept of layered graphics. You saw how to quickly create stylish plots using `qplot` and take a layered approach to graphics with `ggplot`. In the "Activities" section, you have a chance to try out many of the techniques you just read about.

In Hour 15, "Lattice Graphics," we look at the **lattice** approach to graphics, and see how it can be used to create highly customized panel plots.

Q&A

Q. I'm still confused as to whether I should use `qplot` or `ggplot`. What does everyone else use?

A. The `ggplot` function follows the grammar of graphics. The `qplot` function does not. As such, you will find that the principled `ggplot` fans tend to be more vocal on social media and in help forums. However, most of Hadley Wickham's own examples were written with `qplot`. Besides, there are enough **ggplot2** users these days for it not to matter which you choose.

Q. Is it worth taking the time to learn more about ggplot2 if ggvis is going to supersede it?

A. It has taken some time for **ggvis** to get to where it is today, and yet it still feels very much like a package under development when compared with **ggplot2**. The decision boils down to whether you ever need to produce static graphics. If you do, and most people do, then **ggplot2** is worth the investment. There are also initiatives underway that allow us to convert **ggplot2** graph outputs to interactive formats, such as the `ggplotly` function from the **plotly** package.

Workshop

The workshop contains quiz questions and exercises to help you solidify your understanding of the material covered. Try to answer all questions before looking at the "Answers" section that follows.

Quiz

1. Which of the following is not a **ggplot2** function for adding layers to a plot?

    A. `main`

    B. `xlab`

    C. `ylim`

    D. `scale_x_log10`

2. Which of the following lines creates an orange histogram?

    A. `qplot(Wind, data = airquality, binwidth = 5, fill = "orange")`

    B. `qplot(Wind, data = airquality, binwidth = 5, fill = I("orange"))`

    C. `qplot(Wind, data = airquality, binwidth = 5, aes(fill = "orange"))`

3. True or false? In order to create a paneled plot with `qplot`, you must explicitly add either a `facet_grid` or `facet_wrap` layer to your plot.

Answers

1. **A.** To add a main title as a layer, we use the `ggtitle` function. We haven't seen the `scale_x_log10` function in this hour, but it can be used to create an X axis in base 10 log.

2. **B.** When using `qplot`, you must use the `I` function whenever you are not using variables to control an aesthetic. The `aes` function is used when referencing variables in a layered approach and is never used within `qplot`.

3. **False.** If using `qplot`, you can use the `facets` argument to create a paneled plot.

Activities

1. Create a histogram of the `Wind` column from `airquality`. Use the `binwidth` argument to adjust the width of the bins.

2. Create a boxplot of the `Wind` values for each `Month` using `airquality`.

3. Create a plot of `Ozone` against `Wind` from `airquality`. Ensure that the plot has appropriate titles and axis labels:

   ▶ Ensure that the `Wind` axis begins at zero.

   ▶ Add a linear smoothing line to the plot, removing the error bars.

4. Create a scatter plot of `Height` against `Weight` using `demoData`. Use a different color to distinguish between males and females and a different plotting symbol dependent on whether the subject smokes or not.

5. Re-create the basic plot of `Height` against `Weight` using `demoData`. This time, panel/facet the plot to create a 2×2 grid such that the first column contains data for nonsmokers and the first row contains data for females.

6. Using the **maps** and **mapproj** packages, import the state data using `map_data("state")` and create a plot of the USA, where each state is represented by a different color.

   ▶ Ensure that there is sufficient space for the legend by moving it to the bottom of the plot. Spread the states across 10 columns.

   ▶ Transform the plot in order to view the country with a Mercator projection.

Lattice Graphics

What You'll Learn in This Hour:

▶ How to create simple lattice graphics

▶ How to show structure in data using groups and panels

▶ How to create custom graphics

▶ How to control styles and legends

In the previous two hours, you saw how to create graphics using either the base graphic system or the **ggplot2** package. In this hour, we will look at a third way of creating graphics: using the **lattice** package. This graphic system is well suited to plotting highly grouped data, with the code designed to closely resemble the modeling capabilities of R that we'll need later in Hour 16, "Introduction to R Models and Object Orientation."

In this hour, we'll look at how to create simple lattice graphics, building up to more fine control of styling and the creation of highly customized plots.

The History of Trellis Graphics

As mentioned in Hour 1, "The R Community," the R language can be considered an implementation of the S language, originally developed at AT&T Bell Labs. A good analytic software needs strong graphical capabilities, so the base graph system was created (the evolution of which was described in Hour 13, "Graphics").

During the 1990s, researchers at AT&T designed a new graphic system, whose evolution is detailed in books such as the landmark 1993 book *Visualizing Data* by William Cleveland. Following the release of the book, William Cleveland and Rick Becker evolved the system, eventually implementing the ideas in the S language. They named the graphic system "trellis" because the display style (panels arranged in regular grids) reminded the authors of garden trelliswork.

The Lattice Package

The **lattice** package in R, which can be thought of as a port of the S Trellis graphic system, was created by Deepayan Sarkar of the University of Wisconsin. Like **ggplot2**, it is based on Paul Murrell's **grid** package and therefore requires the **grid** add-on package. One of the design aims of **lattice** was to be, as far as possible, backward compatible with code created in trellis, although a number of significant changes were made.

Like trellis, the lattice system is designed primarily for the visualization of multivariable datasets. The prominent design feature is the arrangement of graphics in a series of "panels," set out in a regular grid, with each "panel" graphing a subset of the data. This provides strong capabilities, in particular, for understanding how a response depends on a range of explanatory variables.

Creating a Simple Lattice Graph

Because **lattice** is a recommended package, the first thing we need to do is to load the package, providing access to its capabilities. We can do this using either the `library` or `require` function:

```
> # Load the lattice package
> require(lattice)
Loading required package: lattice
```

To create a lattice graphic, we need three things:

- ▶ A lattice plotting function
- ▶ A formula specifying the relationship between variables to create
- ▶ The data to plot, typically contained in a data frame

For our lattice plotting function, let's start with `xyplot`, which allows us to create a scatter plot. To define the relationship between variables to graph, we use the ~ symbol in the form (Y axis ~ X axis). As with the previous hour, let's start by creating a scatter plot of `mpg` vs. `wt` using the `mtcars` data frame.

```
> xyplot( mpg ~ wt, data = mtcars )
```

The resulting plot can be seen in Figure 15.1.

Here, we specified the data frame containing our data using the `data` argument, and we specified `mpg ~ wt` as the relationship to visualize.

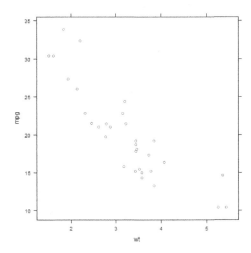

FIGURE 15.1
A simple scatter plot of mpg vs. wt

NOTE

Working with Vectors

Like ggplot2 functions, we can specify vector data inputs to our lattice function, so the preceding command could be replaced by xyplot(mtcars$mpg ~ mtcars$wt). However, it is more common to specify the name of the data frame using the data argument so that we can refer to variables directly.

Lattice Graph Types

Unlike qplot from the **ggplot2** package, which selects the most appropriate graph type to create, with the **lattice** package we specify the graph type we want based on the function we select. In the preceding example we used the xyplot function to create a scatter plot, but there are many others to choose from. A complete list of lattice graph functions can be seen in Table 15.1.

TABLE 15.1   Lattice Graph Functions

Function	Type	Description
histogram	Univariate	Univariate histogram
densityplot	Univariate	Univariate density line plot
qq	Bivariate	Normal QQ plot

Function	Type	Description
barchart	Bivariate	Bar chart
xyplot	Bivariate	Scatter plot
bwplot	Bivariate	Box and whisker plot
dotplot	Bivariate	Label dot plot
stripplot	Bivariate	Categorical scatter plot
cloud	3D	3D scatter plot
wireframe	3D	3D surface plot
splom	Data	Scatter matrix plot
parallelplot	Data	Multivariate parallel plot

Note that there are four types of lattice graph functions: univariate, bivariate, 3D, and data. When we choose a lattice graph function, the type of function we use determines the structure of the formula we must use to specify the plotting variables.

Univariate Lattice Graphics

The **lattice** package contains two univariate graphic functions that allow us to plot a single variable. We specify the variable we want to plot using a formula that only has a variable on the right, such as ~ mpg. Let's see a simple example using the histogram function. The created histogram can be seen in Figure 15.2.

```
> histogram( ~ mpg, data = mtcars )
```

TIP

Controlling Binning

As with other implementations (such as hist or geom_histogram), a default binning mechanism is used. With the histogram function we can specify the number of bins to use with the nint argument.

The densityplot function allows us to produce a density plot of a single variable. Let's see a densityplot of the wt variable. The resulting density plot can be seen in Figure 15.3.

```
> densityplot( ~ wt, data = mtcars )
```

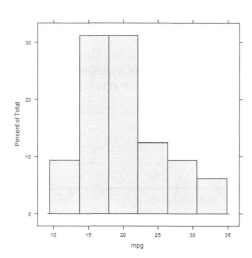

FIGURE 15.2
A histogram of mpg

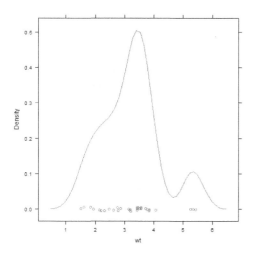

FIGURE 15.3
A density plot of wt

TIP

Controlling the Points

The default behavior with `densityplot` is to add "jittered" points along the X axis indicating the positions of the observations. Although this is highly useful, we can control (or suppress) these points using the `plot.points` argument to `densityplot`, which accepts four possible inputs, as listed in Table 15.2.

TABLE 15.2 Inputs to the `plot.points` Argument

Input	Behavior
`"jitter"`	Adds "jittered" points along the X axis (default)
`"rug"`	Adds a "rug" plot (vertical lines) along the X axis
TRUE	Adds a row of points along the X axis (with no jitter)
FALSE	Suppresses the printing of any points along the X axis

Bivariate Lattice Graphics

The **lattice** package contains five bivariate graph functions: `qq`, `barchart`, `xyplot`, `bwplot`, `dotplot`, and `stripplot`. As seen with the earlier `xyplot` example, we specify the relationship with a two-sided formula with the structure Y ~ X. When you are using these functions, it is important to understand which variables are (by default) placed on the Y axis (specified by the left side of the formula) and which variables are placed on the X axis (specified by the right side of the formula). These variables are listed in Table 15.3.

TABLE 15.3 Bivariate Graph Axes Definitions

Function	Left Hand Side of Formula	Right Hand Side of Formula
`xyplot`	Numeric, factor, or date variable	Numeric, factor, or date variable
`bwplot`	Factor variable	Numeric variable
`dotplot`	Factor variable	Numeric variable
`stripplot`	Factor variable	Numeric variable
`barchart`	Factor variable	Numeric variable
`qq`	Numeric variable	A factor variable with two levels

From Table 15.3 we can see that for the functions `bwplot`, `dotplot`, `stripplot`, and `barchart`, the factor variable is by default on the Y axis. Let's see an example using `dotplot` with our mtcars data, this time looking at how the miles per gallon (mpg) varies based on the number of carburetors (carb). The output can be seen in Figure 15.4.

```
> dotplot( carb ~ mpg, data = mtcars )
```

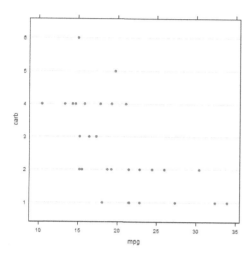

FIGURE 15.4
A dot plot of carb vs mpg

NOTE

The Use of Factor Axes

In the preceding example, we specified carb as the (factor) variable on the Y axis. In fact, carb is a numeric variable. Where a factor is expected, the provided variable will be converted to a factor.

Transposing the Axes

We previously noted that the functions bwplot, dotplot, stripplot, and barchart specify the categorical variable on the Y axis and the numeric variable on the X axis. This is based on the design in the book *Visualizing Data* by William Cleveland, but this behavior may be unexpected. For example, boxplots are more commonly produced with the numeric variable on the Y axis and the categorical variable on the X axis. Each of these functions has the argument horizontal, which, by default, is set to TRUE (producing "horizontal" charts). We can instead set the value of horizontal to FALSE to create vertical charts, but we also need to change the order of the variables in the formula (with the categorical variable on the X axis). Let's see an example using the bwplot function. The resulting plot can be seen in Figure 15.5.

```
> bwplot( mpg ~ carb, data = mtcars, horizontal = FALSE )
```

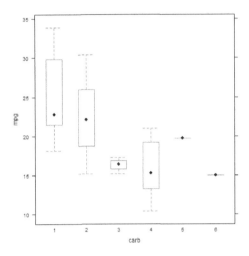

FIGURE 15.5
A vertical box and whisker plot of mpg vs. carb

3D Lattice Graphics

The lattice graph functions cloud and wireframe can be used to plot 3D scatter plots and surfaces, respectively. When you're specifying the variables to graph, your formula should be of the format z ~ x * y, with the z variable used as the "height" of the plot. Let's use the cloud function to create a 3D scatter plot of some variables from our mtcars data, which can be seen in Figure 15.6.

```
> cloud( mpg ~ wt * hp, data = mtcars)
```

An alternative way to provide data for a 3D lattice graph function is in the form of a matrix. When a matrix is provided, the lattice graph functions will use the rows and columns of the matrix as the X and Y axes, and use the value in each cell as the height of the plot. Let's see an example using the internal volcano matrix, which contains topological information for Maungawhau, one of 50 active volcanoes in the Auckland volcanic field. This time we'll use the wireframe function to create a 3D surface plot. The resulting 3D plot can be seen in Figure 15.7.

```
> dim(volcano)   # Dimensions of the volcano matrix
[1] 87 61
> wireframe( volcano, shade = TRUE )
```

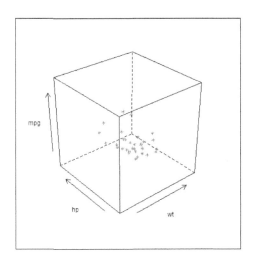

FIGURE 15.6
A 3D scatter plot of mpg vs. wt and hp

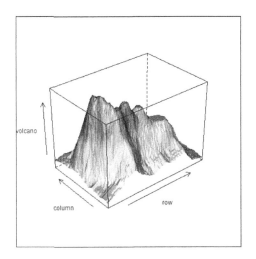

FIGURE 15.7
A 3D surface plot of the volcano matrix

TIP

Controlling the Color Shading

Note the use of the `shade` argument in this example, which specifies that color shading should be used on our 3D surface using an illumination model with a single light source. We can additionally control the colors used with the `shade.colors.palette` argument, and the light source itself using the `light.source` function. For more information, see the help file for the `panel.3dwire` function (`?panel.3dwire`).

When creating 3D graphics in this way, you'll often want to control the perspective of the graph—in other words, the view point from which you are looking at the graph. For example, in the previous graph we cannot really see the crater of the volcano, but we could rotate the graph so we're looking at the other side of the volcano. We can achieve this using the `screen` argument, which accepts a list with elements x, y, and z specifying the rotation to apply. Let's use the `screen` argument to view the volcano from a different perspective so we can see the crater. This can be seen in Figure 15.8.

```
> wireframe( volcano, shade = TRUE,
+            screen = list(x = -60, y = -40, z = -20))
```

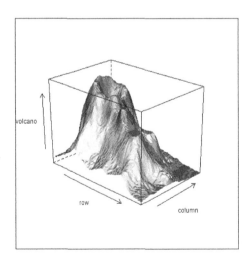

FIGURE 15.8
A 3D surface plot of the `volcano` matrix with the volcano's crater visible

"Data" Lattice Graphics

Two lattice graph functions can be used to graph the structure of a data frame: `splom` and `parallelplot`. To use these functions, we specify the data frame in a one-sided formula

(~Data). Let's first look at the `splom` function, which creates a scatter-plot matrix (analogous to the `pairs` function seen in previous hours). Instead of using the whole dataset, we'll select four columns from the `mtcars` data to plot. In Figure 15.9, we can see that each of our four variables are plotted against each other in a matrix of scatter plots:

```
> splom( ~ mtcars[,c("mpg", "wt", "cyl", "hp")])
```

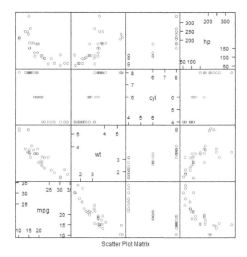

Scatter Plot Matrix

FIGURE 15.9
A scatter-plot matrix of the mpg, wt, cyl, and hp variables from `mtcars`

TIP
_____

The `pairs` Function

The `pairs` function is the base graphics equivalent of the `splom` function, and can also produce a scatter-plot matrix of our data.
_____

Plotting Subsets of Data

All lattice graph functions contain a `subset` argument that allows you to filter the data as you're plotting. This is useful for plotting sections of the data without having to create a filtered dataset before plotting. Let's see an example of this, where we'll create a scatter plot of mpg vs. wt using only manual cars (where am == 1). The resulting plot can be seen in Figure 15.10.

```
> xyplot( mpg ~ wt, data = mtcars, subset = am == 1 )
```

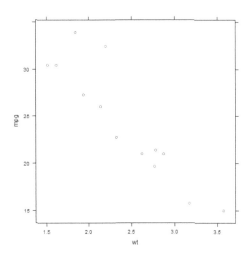

FIGURE 15.10
Using the subset argument to graph a section of the data

Graph Options

As with base and **ggplot2** graphics, each of the **lattice** graphics listed in Table 15.1 accepts common graph options that control aspects of the graph. The option names generally follow the conventions used in the **graphics** package.

Titles and Axes

First, let's use arguments such as main, xlab, and xlim to control our plot titles and axes, as seen in Figure 15.11. For now, we'll use the xyplot function, but this works for all lattice graph functions.

```
> xyplot(mpg ~ wt, data = mtcars, main = "Miles per Gallon vs Weight",
+        xlab = "Weight (lb/1000)", ylab = "Miles/(US) Gallon",
+        xlim = c(1, 6), ylim = c(10, 40))
```

Plot Types and Formatting

As with the **graphics** system, we can use the type argument to control the type of (scatter) plot created and use arguments such as col and lwd to control the style of the elements graphed, as seen in Figure 15.12. For this example, let's use a different dataset—we'll use the **cranlogs** package to extract data on package downloads. First, let's install the **cranlogs** package from CRAN:

```
> install.packages ("cranlogs")
```

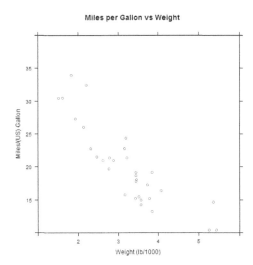

FIGURE 15.11
Adding titles and axis controls for a scatter plot

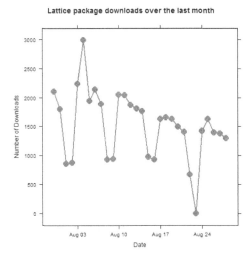

FIGURE 15.12
Scatter plot of downloads over time

Next, let's load the library and download some data using the `cran_downloads` function. For this exercise, we'll download the CRAN logs for **lattice** and **ggplot2** over the last month:

```
> library(cranlogs)
> cranData <- cran_downloads(packages = c("lattice", "ggplot2"), when =
➡ "last-month")
> head(cranData)
        date count package
1 2015-07-30 2100 lattice
2 2015-07-31 1804 lattice
3 2015-08-01  858 lattice
4 2015-08-02  874 lattice
5 2015-08-03 2234 lattice
6 2015-08-04 2991 lattice
```

Now we'll create a scatter plot of the number of downloads (count) vs. date for the **lattice** package.

```
> xyplot(count ~ date, data = cranData, subset = package == "lattice",
+       main = "Lattice package downloads over the last month",
+       ylab = "Number of Downloads", xlab = "Date",
+       type = "b", col = "red", lwd = 2, cex = 2, pch = 16)
```

CAUTION

Background Colors of Plot Characters

Using the base graphic system, we can use plot characters with filled backgrounds using pch values 21 to 25. When we use these plot characters, we use the bg argument to control the background color of each plot symbol. In lattice, we can also use pch values 21 to 25, but the argument for controlling the background color is fill instead of bg.

Multiple Variables

When we use the lattice graph functions, we can choose to plot multiple variables. We achieve this by specifying multiple variables in the formula of the format Y1 + Y2 ~ X1 + X2. By default, this will superimpose the variables onto the same plot using different colors for each variable, as see in Figure 15.13. In this example, we are plotting Miles per Gallon (mpg) on the Y axis vs. two X axes: Displacement (disp) and Gross Horsepower (hp).

```
> xyplot(mpg ~ disp + hp, data = mtcars, auto.key = TRUE, pch = 16, cex = 2)
```

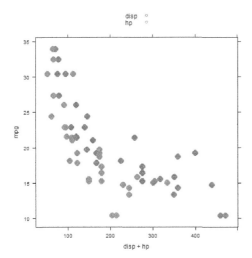

FIGURE 15.13
Scatter plot with multiple X axes plotted on the same graph

CAUTION

Mismatched legend

In this example, we used the `pch` and `cex` arguments to make the plot clearer. We also use the `auto.legend` argument to automatically create a legend for the plot that indicates that the `disp` variable is represented with blue points and the `hp` variable is represented with pink points. Although this allows us to identify each variable, notice that the legend doesn't completely match the plot (the legend shows empty circles). Later in this hour, you'll see how to fix this issue.

As you can see in Figure 15.13, the two variables on the X axis (`disp` and `hp`) appear superimposed on the same graph, and the color of the plotting symbols allows us to distinguish between the two variables. We can use the `outer` argument to control whether the multiple variables should be represented as groups on the same plot (the default behavior) or should be split into separate plots. We can specify that separate plots should be created by specifying `outer = TRUE`, as shown in Figure 15.14.

```
> xyplot(mpg ~ disp + hp, data = mtcars, pch = 16, cex = 2, outer = TRUE)
```

As you can see, the two graphs are produced in separate "panels," each with the same X and Y axis scales. This is very similar to the "facets" you saw in Hour 14, "The ggplot2 Package for Graphics." You'll see more on panels later in this hour.

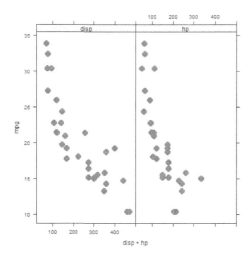

FIGURE 15.14
Scatter plot with multiple X axes plotted in different "panels"

Groups of Data

If we have groups in our data, we can represent them by varying plot aspects using the groups argument. Let's start with a simple example using our mtcars data. Here, we will plot mpg vs. wt, but vary the color of the plot based on the number of cylinders (cyl) using the groups argument. This can be seen in Figure 15.15.

```
> xyplot(mpg ~ wt, data = mtcars, groups = cyl,
+    pch = 16, cex = 2, auto.key = TRUE)
```

If we use a grouping variable together with multiple variables, the outer argument is set to TRUE, such that the multiple variables are split into panels. This can be seen in Figure 15.16, where we group by cyl but also use multiple X axis variables:

```
> xyplot(mpg ~ disp  + hp, data = mtcars, groups = cyl,
+        pch = 16, cex = 2, auto.key = TRUE)
```

NOTE

Plot Layout

When we create graphs in multiple panels, such as in this example, the layout of the plots is determined based on the size of the plot device available. For example, in RStudio, we may see different panel layouts by resizing the plot window. We can control the layout of panels explicitly using the layout argument. This argument also allows us to create multiple pages of plots when our partitioning variable has a high number of levels.

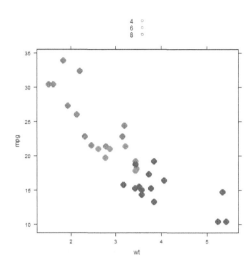

FIGURE 15.15
Scatter plot with levels of `cyl` grouped

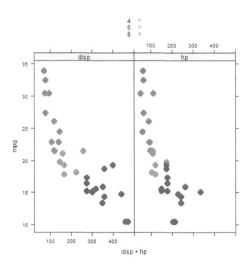

FIGURE 15.16
Scatter plot with multiple X axes plotted in different "panels" and the plot grouped by `cyl`

TIP

More Control of the Legend

The `auto.key` argument can, instead, accept a list of settings. This can be used to further control the format and placement of the legend. For example, we can place the legend on the right side of the plot with `auto.key = list(space = "right")`.

Using Panels

As you've seen already in this hour, the **lattice** package is able to create graphics in separate "panels." We can specify a variable to be used to partition our data into panels directly in the formula. To achieve this, we simply append a | symbol to our formula and specify the variable by which to partition the graph. Let's first revisit the data we downloaded that compared recent downloads of the **lattice** and **ggplot2** packages. A simple plot of count versus date can be seen in Figure 15.17.

```
> xyplot(count ~ date | package, data = cranData, type = "o")
```

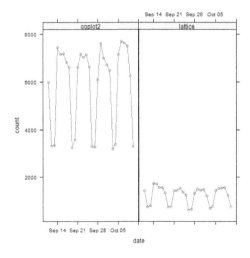

FIGURE 15.17
Scatter plot of downloads partitioned by package (*lattice* vs. *ggplot2*)

As you can see, the plot is now partitioned into two separate panels based on the `package` variable. The axis scales are the same for each panel, with the levels of the package variable ("ggplot2" and "lattice") displayed at the top of each plot.

Alternating Axis Ticks

The default behavior of lattice is to alternate the tick marks between panels, which explains why the X axis ticks appear at the top of the graph for the "lattice" panel. We can control this behavior with the `alternating` attribute of the `scales` argument, which is described further in the help file for the `xyplot` function.

Controlling the Strip Headers

Let's see another simple example, where we'll attempt to create a plot of Miles per Gallon (mpg) vs. Weight (wt) partitioned on levels of cylinder (cyl). This can be seen in Figure 15.18.

```
> xyplot( mpg ~ wt | cyl, data = mtcars,
+         main = "Miles per Gallon vs Weight by Number of Cylinders")
```

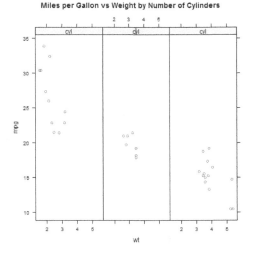

FIGURE 15.18
Scatter plot of miles per gallon vs. weight partitioned by number of cylinders

In Figure 15.18 we created a graph containing three panels, corresponding to the three levels of the cyl variable. However, the labels at the tops of each panel (the "strip headers") are not correctly formed. Instead, the text "cyl" is repeated for each strip header, along with some darker orange segments. The strip header labeling worked in the previous example (Figure 15.17) but not this example because of the class of the partitioning variable. In Figure 15.17, the partitioning variable (package) was a factor variable. In this more recent example (Figure 15.18), the partitioning variable (cyl) is a numeric variable. To ensure the strip headers are correct for our data, we need to ensure our partitioning (or "by") variables are factors. We can use the `factor` function directly to fix this, as seen in Figure 15.19.

```
> xyplot( mpg ~ wt | factor(cyl), data = mtcars,
+           main = "Miles per Gallon vs Weight by Number of Cylinders")
```

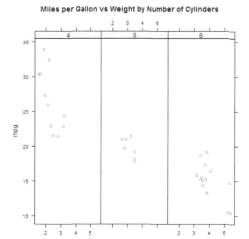

FIGURE 15.19
Scatter plot of miles per gallon vs. weight partitioned by number of cylinders (fixing headers)

TIP
More Control of the Strip Header
We can further control the strip headers in one of two ways:

▶ Using the `factor` function to further define labels and the order of levels

▶ Using the `strip` argument to the lattice functions

More information on the `factor` function can be found in the `factor` help file (`?factor`). More information on the use of the `strip` argument can be found in the help file for the `strip.default` function (`?strip.default`).

Multiple "By" Variables

In the preceding examples, we used a single "by" variable to create a partitioned plot. If we want to use more than one variable, we list them separated by the asterisk (*) symbol. Therefore, if we want to create a plot of Miles per Gallon (mpg) vs. Weight (wt) partitioned on levels of cylinder (cyl) and Automatic/Manual indicator (am), we include both cyl and am in the formula. This can be seen in Figure 15.20. Here, instead of providing am directly as a factor, the ifelse function is used to create a variable containing the values "Automatic" and "Manual."

```
> xyplot( mpg ~ wt | factor(cyl) * ifelse(am == 0, "Automatic", "Manual"),
+    data = mtcars, cex = 1.5, pch = 21, fill = "lightblue",
+    main = "Miles per Gallon vs Weight \nby Number of Cylinders and Transmission
➡Type")
```

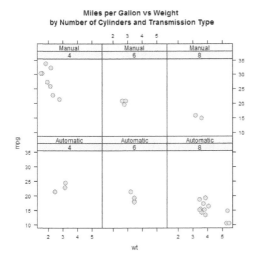

FIGURE 15.20
Scatter plot of miles per gallon vs. weight partitioned by number of cylinders and transmission type

Panel Functions

Each lattice graph function operates in a similar fashion. First, the data is partitioned based on the formula specified, and the panels are created based on the number of partitions to be plotted. Then, the data for each panel is passed to a "panel function" that draws each subset of data. The panel function is specified with the panel argument to each lattice function. The default panel function for each lattice graph function follows a specific naming convention: panel.functionName. Therefore, the default panel function for xyplot is panel.xyplot. The panel.xyplot help file lists the arguments to panel.xyplot as follows:

```
panel.xyplot(x, y, type = "p", groups = NULL, pch, col, col.line, col.symbol,
font, fontfamily, fontface, lty, cex, fill, lwd, horizontal = FALSE, ...,
grid = FALSE, abline = NULL, jitter.x = FALSE, jitter.y = FALSE, factor = 0.5,
amount = NULL, identifier = "xyplot")
```

Note that the first two arguments are x and y, corresponding to the X and Y data to plot for each panel. Let's further explore the workings of the panel functions using a simple example. Here, we will re-create our plot of mpg vs. wt by cyl, but will replace the default panel function (panel.xyplot) with a simple function of our own. The resulting graph is shown in Figure 15.21.

```
> myPanel <- function(x, y, ...) {
+    cat("Panel Function Called!\n")
+ }
> xyplot( mpg ~ wt | factor(cyl), data = mtcars, panel = myPanel)
Panel Function Called!
Panel Function Called!
Panel Function Called!
```

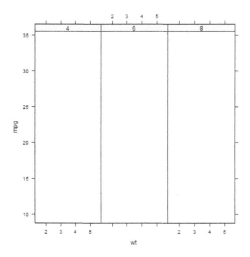

FIGURE 15.21
Empty (!) scatter plot of miles per gallon vs. weight partitioned by number of cylinders

In this example, we have replaced the default panel function with myPanel, which prints a short message but does nothing else. In particular, note that myPanel does nothing with x and y (that is, no graph elements are produced). The result is that our call prints our simple message three times, one for each panel of data drawn. Because myPanel performs no graphing, each panel is left empty.

Let's change the myPanel function now so that it performs some graphical routines. We can achieve this be reinserting the panel.xyplot function call within myPanel. The resulting graph can be seen in Figure 15.22.

```
> myPanel <- function(x, y, ...) {
+   panel.xyplot(x, y, ...)
+ }
> xyplot( mpg ~ wt | factor(cyl), data = mtcars, panel = myPanel)
```

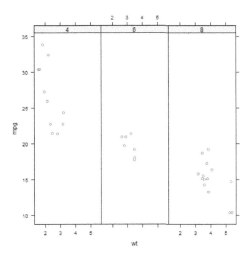

FIGURE 15.22
Scatter plot of miles per gallon vs. weight partitioned by number of cylinders

Now the plot is again created, but this time xyplot is using our myPanel function to pass the inputs on to panel.xyplot.

Using Other Panel Functions

Now that we have xyplot using our panel function, we may choose to alter the graph created in each panel. A simple way to do that is to include other "panel" functions. Let's use the apropos function to list all the available panel.* functions:

```
> apropos("^panel")
 [1] "panel.3dscatter"     "panel.3dwire"            "panel.abline"
 [4] "panel.arrows"        "panel.average"           "panel.axis"
 [7] "panel.barchart"      "panel.brush.splom"       "panel.bwplot"
[10] "panel.cloud"         "panel.contourplot"       "panel.curve"
[13] "panel.densityplot"   "panel.dotplot"           "panel.error"
[16] "panel.fill"          "panel.grid"              "panel.histogram"
[19] "panel.identify"      "panel.identify.cloud"    "panel.identify.qqmath"
[22] "panel.levelplot"     "panel.levelplot.raster"  "panel.linejoin"
[25] "panel.lines"         "panel.link.splom"        "panel.lmline"
[28] "panel.loess"         "panel.mathdensity"       "panel.number"
```

```
[31]  "panel.pairs"            "panel.parallel"      "panel.points"
[34]  "panel.polygon"          "panel.qq"            "panel.qqmath"
[37]  "panel.qqmathline"       "panel.rect"          "panel.refline"
[40]  "panel.rug"              "panel.segments"      "panel.smooth"
[43]  "panel.smoothScatter"    "panel.spline"        "panel.splom"
[46]  "panel.stripplot"        "panel.superpose"     "panel.superpose.2"
[49]  "panel.superpose.plain"  "panel.text"          "panel.tmd.default"
[52]  "panel.tmd.qqmath"       "panel.violin"        "panel.wireframe"
[55]  "panel.xyplot"
```

The set of panel functions available includes the default panel functions for each of the lattice graph functions listed in Table 15.1 (such as `panel.histogram` and `panel.bwplot`). However, there are many other panel functions listed that we can use to perform alternative behaviors within each panel. As a simple example, let's use the `panel.abline` function to add vertical and horizontal reference lines as the median x and y points in each panel. We can achieve this by specifying the h and v inputs to `panel.abline`, as seen next. The output can be seen in Figure 15.23.

```
> myPanel <- function(x, y, ...) {
+   medX <- median(x, na.rm = TRUE)                    # Median of X values
+   medY <- median(y, na.rm = TRUE)                    # Median of Y values
+   panel.abline(v = medX, h = medY, lwd = 2, col = "red")   # Add reference lines
+   panel.xyplot(x, y, ...)                            # Draw the points
+ }
> xyplot( mpg ~ wt | factor(cyl), data = mtcars, panel = myPanel, pch = 16)
```

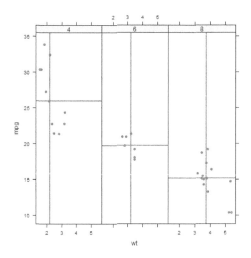

FIGURE 15.23
Scatter plot of miles per gallon vs. weight by number of cylinders with reference lines at the medians

There are many other `panel.*` functions we could use in a similar manner. A selection of these are listed in Table 15.4.

TABLE 15.4 Sample of Useful Panel Functions

Function	Description
panel.abline	Adds straight reference lines to the panel
panel.lmline	Adds a linear regression line to the panel
panel.loess	Adds a loess smooth line to the panel
panel.average	Adds lines at the mean (or other function) Y points for each unique X
panel.grid	Adds grid lines to the panel
panel.fill	Adds a background color to the panel
panel.rug	Adds a rug plot to either, or both, axes
panel.polygon	Adds a polygon to the panel
panel.text	Adds text at X/Y coordinates to the panel
panel.points	Adds points at X/Y coordinates to the panel
panel.lines	Adds lines at X/Y coordinates to the panel

Using Other Panel Functions

In the previous section you saw a range of "panel" functions we can use to customize our graphics. Let's have a closer look at a few of the panel functions mentioned:

```
> panel.points
function (...)
lpoints(...)
<bytecode: 0x0efed2c8>
<environment: namespace:lattice>
> panel.text
function (...)
ltext(...)
<bytecode: 0x0f80702c>
<environment: namespace:lattice>
> panel.lines
function (...)
llines(...)
<bytecode: 0x2f2a1acc>
<environment: namespace:lattice>
```

Many of the `panel.*` functions use low-level graph calls to add elements to the graph. These are "lattice" equivalents of the low-level graph functions you saw in Hour 13. Table 15.5 lists a few of these low-level graph functions.

TABLE 15.5   Low-Level Lattice Graph Functions

Function	Description
lpoints	Adds points to the plot
llines	Adds lines to the plot
ltext	Adds text to the plot
lpolygon	Adds polygons to the plot
lrect	Adds rectangles to the plot

Let's see an example using the ltext function to add some text in each panel. Here, we'll use the lm function to fit a linear regression line in each panel and use ltext to report the intercept and slope. The resulting graph can be seen in Figure 15.24.

```
> myPanel <- function(x, y, ...) {
+    myLm <- lm(y ~ x)                          # Fit a linear regression line
+    panel.abline(myLm, col = "red")            # Add the regression line
+    panel.xyplot(x, y, ...)                     # Draw the points
+    params <- paste(c("Intercept:", "Slope:"), # Parameters
+      signif(coef(myLm), 3), collapse="\n")
+    ltext(max(x), max(y), params, adj = 1, cex = .8) # Add text to plot
+ }
> xyplot( mpg ~ wt | factor(cyl), data = mtcars, panel = myPanel, pch = 16)
```

This example correctly calculates and prints the parameters of the regression line. In this example, we used the maximum X and Y positions to place the text, which doesn't produce a good output. We could "hard-code" the positions of the text, but then we'll not be able to reuse our code if the data changes. We can resolve this issue by passing another variable to the panel function directly, as discussed next.

Passing Additional Arguments

In the previous example, we saw that positioning the text is difficult. Let's resolve this by passing the positions as additional arguments to the lattice call. If we list these also as inputs to the panel function, the arguments will be available to us. Here we'll specify inputs xPos and yPos to the panel function and pass them directly into our high level xyplot call. The result can be seen in Figure 15.25.

```
> myPanel <- function(x, y, xPos, yPos, ...) {
+    myLm <- lm(y ~ x)                          # Fit a linear regression line
+    panel.abline(myLm, col = "red")            # Add the regression line
+    panel.xyplot(x, y, ...)                     # Draw the points
+    params <- paste(c("Intercept:", "Slope:"), # Parameters
+                  signif(coef(myLm), 3), collapse="\n")
```

```
+    ltext(xPos, yPos, params, adj = 1, cex = .8) # Add text to plot
+ }
> xyplot( mpg ~ wt | factor(cyl), data = mtcars, panel = myPanel, pch = 16,
+    xPos = max(mtcars$wt), yPos = max(mtcars$mpg))
```

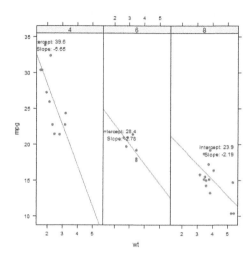

FIGURE 15.24
Scatter plot of miles per gallon vs. weight by number of cylinders with linear regression line

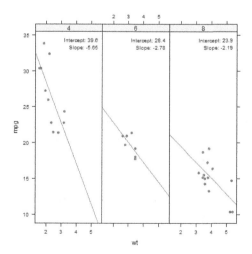

FIGURE 15.25
Scatter plot of miles per gallon vs. weight by number of cylinders with linear regression line (and label justified on the plot)

Controlling Styles

Earlier, in Figure 15.13, you saw the use of the `auto.key` argument to automatically add a legend to our graphics. However, you also saw that the style of the legend didn't directly reflect the styling used in the plot. Let's see another simple example of this by adding a grouping variable to our plot. Figure 15.26 shows the resulting plot, where the plot character is varied based on the transmission type.

```
> xyplot( mpg ~ wt | factor(cyl), data = mtcars,
+    pch = c(15, 16), col = c("navy", "orange"),
+    groups = ifelse(am == 0, "Auto", "Manual"), auto.key = TRUE)
```

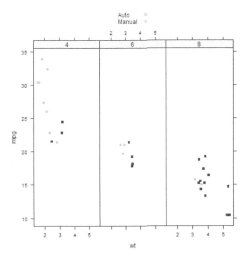

FIGURE 15.26
Scatter plot of miles per gallon vs. weight by number of cylinders grouped by transmission type

In this graph, we specify that the two groups levels should be represented by specific colors (navy and orange) and plot characters (filled squares and filled circles). The plot seems to be created correctly, but the styles in the legend produced do not match.

This situation occurs because the styling of lattice graphics is controlled by underlying stylesheets (or "themes"). When the `auto.key` option is set, the legend is constructed based on these underlying styles and not by the style parameters used in the lattice call.

Previewing the Styles

We can see the styles currently in use for lattice graphics using the `show.settings` function. This function produces a set of graphics to visualize the range of styles in use, as seen in Figure 15.27.

```
> show.settings()
```

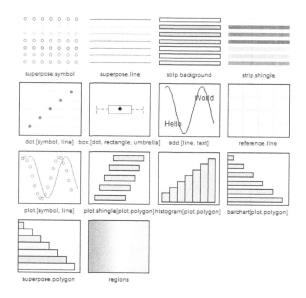

FIGURE 15.27
Visualization of the current lattice styles in use

From this visualization, we can see a number of the characters shown in the preceding figures. Here are some examples:

▶ The `histogram[plot.polygon]` style matches the style of the histogram we created in Figure 15.2.

▶ The `dot.[symbol, line]` style matches the style of the dot plot we created in Figure 15.4.

▶ The `strip.background` style controls the color of the strip header on each plot. The default color is the light orange color on the bottom of this visualization, but the second level (the pale green) was seen when we used multiple by variables in Figure 15.20.

▶ The `superpose.symbol` style shows the default plot symbols and colors, which are also the ones used to create the legend (blue open circle, pink open circle).

Creating a Theme

The styles themselves are stored as nested lists of vectors. To create a theme, it is easiest to create a copy of the existing styles and then alter specific aspects of them. We can create a copy of the current styles using the `trellis.par.get` function, as shown here:

```
> myTheme <- trellis.par.get()  # Get the list of styles
```

```
> names(myTheme)                   # Look at the element names
 [1] "grid.pars"        "fontsize"          "background"        "panel.background"
 [5] "clip"             "add.line"          "add.text"          "plot.polygon"
 [9] "box.dot"          "box.rectangle"     "box.umbrella"      "dot.line"
[13] "dot.symbol"       "plot.line"         "plot.symbol"       "reference.line"
[17] "strip.background" "strip.shingle"     "strip.border"      "superpose.line"
[21] "superpose.symbol" "superpose.polygon" "regions"           "shade.colors"
[25] "axis.line"        "axis.text"         "axis.components"   "layout.heights"
[29] "layout.widths"    "box.3d"            "par.xlab.text"     "par.ylab.text"
[33] "par.zlab.text"    "par.main.text"     "par.sub.text"
```

```
> myTheme$superpose.symbol      # Look at the superpose.symbol element
$alpha
[1] 1 1 1 1 1 1 1

$cex
[1] 0.8 0.8 0.8 0.8 0.8 0.8 0.8

$col
[1] "#0080ff"   "#ff00ff"   "darkgreen" "#ff0000"   "orange"    "#00ff00"   "brown"

$fill
[1] "#CCFFFF" "#FFCCFF" "#CCFFCC" "#FFE5CC" "#CCE6FF" "#FFFFCC" "#FFCCCC"

$font
[1] 1 1 1 1 1 1 1

$pch
[1] 1 1 1 1 1 1 1
```

Once we have our styles, we can update the elements we need. For example, let's change the default styles for the points. Let's also change the default color of the strip header:

```
> ss <- myTheme$superpose.symbol  # Extract the superpose.symbol element
> names(ss)                        # Names of the superpose.symbol element
[1] "alpha" "cex"   "col"   "fill"  "font"  "pch"
> ss$col                           # Current colors
[1] "#0080ff"   "#ff00ff"   "darkgreen" "#ff0000"   "orange"    "#00ff00"   "brown"
```

```
> ss$col <- c("orange", "navy", "green", "red", "grey") # Update plot colors
> ss$pch <- c(16, 15, 17, 18, 19) # Updated plot symbols
> myTheme$superpose.symbol <- ss   # Update the styles
> myTheme$strip.background$col      # Current strip header color
[1] "#ffe5cc" "#ccffcc" "#ccffff" "#cce6ff" "#ffccff" "#ffcccc" "#ffffcc"
> myTheme$strip.background$col <- c("lightgrey", "lightblue", "lightgreen")
```

We can use the show.settings function to check the changes we've made to our stylesheet. The changes above can be seen in Figure 15.28.

```
> show.settings(myTheme)
```

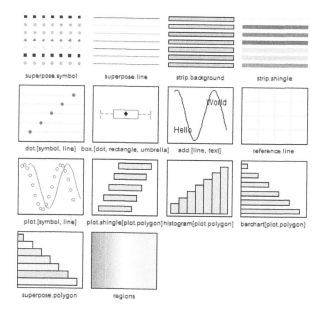

FIGURE 15.28
Visualization of our updated stylesheet

Using a Theme

Now we can use our theme to create with our plot using the par.settings argument. This way, the styles in the plot and legend will match. To see this, let's use our previous example, but this time using our new theme. The resulting plot can be seen in Figure 15.29.

```
> xyplot( mpg ~ wt | factor(cyl), data = mtcars, par.settings = myTheme,
+          groups = ifelse(am == 0, "Auto", "Manual"), auto.key = TRUE)
```

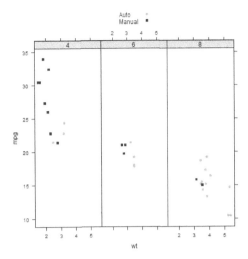

FIGURE 15.29
Scatter plot of miles per gallon vs. weight by number of cylinders grouped by transmission type (using custom stylesheet)

TIP

Overwriting Default Settings

In the last section we created a new theme and used it in our graph with the `par.settings` argument. If instead we wanted to overwrite the default theme globally, we can use the `trellis.par.set` function as follows: `trellis.par.set(theme = myTheme)`. Unlike **ggplot2** this change only applies to current active devices, so care must be taken when exporting to multiple devices.

Summary

The **lattice** package provides a rich set of graphic functions that are particularly useful for visualizing relationships in grouped data. In this hour, you saw how to create simple lattice graphics and control the appearance of the graph using standard options. You also saw how the grouping and, in particular, panel capabilities of lattice can help you to better explore levels of information in your data. With base graphics, **ggplot2**, and **lattice**, R has an incredible array of graphical capabilities to suit the needs of the R user community.

Q&A

Q. We've seen the base, ggplot2 and lattice systems. Which graph system should I use?

A. This is a difficult question to answer. A familiarization with the base graphic system is strongly recommended, because it is still (perhaps) a preferred system to create highly bespoke graphics. There are also elements of base graphics that are reflected throughout **ggplot2** and **lattice**. Beyond that, it is good advice to learn at least one of **ggplot2** or **lattice**. In terms of capability, the **ggplot2** and **lattice** packages have almost 100% overlap, so when choosing between them it's a question of style and future direction. **Lattice** is an older system, and those users familiar with the S-PLUS Trellis capabilities may find it a more natural fit. However, **ggplot2** is the more modern implementation, with more support and documentation and more ongoing development.

Q. Can I stop each panel having the same X and Y axis limits?

A. Yes. The `scales` argument to each lattice graph allows you to control a number of aspects of the axes, including the relationship between them. The `scales` argument itself takes a list of controls, which can include an element called `relation` that controls the relationship between axes. In particular, `relation = "same"` is the default, whereas `relation = "free"` specifies that each panel can be drawn on a different scale.

Q. What does the latticeExtra package do?

A. The **latticeExtra** package extends the **lattice** package, adding many new features. Notable features include the addition of new plot types, new panel functions (including one with a transparent smoother), and more styles.

Q. How do I control the ordering of panels?

A. There are two ways to control the panel order. First, the order of panels will reflect the order of levels in the "by" variables. By default, the order of the levels will be alphabetical, so a variable may have levels ordered "High > Low > Medium." The `factor` function can help you order the levels correctly. The other thing to note is that, by default, panels are positioned on the device from the bottom left to the top right. If you wish to change this, you can use the `as.table` input to the lattice functions. Setting `as.table = TRUE` will result in panels positioned from the top left to the bottom right.

Q. Can I place more than one graph on the same page?

A. Yes. Each lattice graph can be saved as an object and then placed on a page using the `print.trellis` function. For more information, see the `print.trellis` help file.

Workshop

The workshop contains quiz questions and exercises to help you solidify your understanding of the material covered. Try to answer all questions before looking at the "Answers" section that follows.

Quiz

1. How do you specify the variables to plot with a univariate lattice graph function?

2. Which lattice function creates a scatter-plot matrix of a data frame?

3. How do you specify multiple "by" variables for a lattice graph?

4. What argument can be used to automatically add a legend?

5. How can you customize the content in each graph panel?

Answers

1. You use a one-sided formula, such as `histogram( ~ Y)`.

2. The `splom` function can be used to create a scatter-plot matrix of a data frame.

3. You specify multiple "by" variables with the * symbol. For example, to partition a plot of Y vs. X by variables BY1 and BY2, you would specify the formula as Y ~ X | BY1 * BY2.

4. You can use the `auto.key` argument to add a legend, although care must be taken to ensure the styles match that of the plot.

5. You can create a "panel" function and then provide it as the `panel` input to a lattice graph function.

Activities

1. Using the `airquality` data frame, create a histogram of the Wind variable.

2. Create a scatter plot of Ozone vs. Wind using the `xyplot` function. Add titles and change the style of the plotting symbol.

3. Extend this example by varying the color of the plotting symbol by Month. Add a legend to your plot.

4. Change this graph so that, instead, each Month of data is produced in a separate panel.

5. Use a panel function to add a linear regression line to each panel.

Introduction to R Models and Object Orientation

What You'll Learn in This Hour:

▶ How to fit a simple statistical model

▶ How to assess the model's appropriateness

▶ The basic concepts of object orientation

The R Language (and, before that, S) was created by statisticians to enable them to perform statistical analyses. As such, R is primarily a statistical software and provides the richest set of analytic methods available in any technology. In this hour, you see how to fit a simple linear model and assess its performance using a range of textual and graphical methods. Beyond this, you'll be introduced to "object orientation" and see how the R statistical modeling framework is built on this concept. In Hour 17, "Common R Models," we'll extend this by looking at other modeling approaches, such as nonlinear, survival, and time series models. For each model type we will explain some of the basic principles behind the model and any associated terminology. However, the focus of both this hour and Hour 17 is on the practical implementation of the models as opposed to the mathematics behind the models.

Statistical Models in R

Statistical modeling is a vital technique that allows us to understand and confirm whether, and how, responses are influenced by other data. R provides the richest set of statistical modeling capabilities and was designed from the outset with modeling in mind, making it the perfect environment in which to fit and assess models. In fact, at the time of writing, approximately 2,500 packages are available on CRAN that supply model-fitting functions (based on an analysis of package descriptions). The majority of statistical model-fitting routines are designed in a similar fashion, allowing us to change our model-fitting approach without having to relearn a completely new syntax. In many ways, this consistent design and approach to model fitting is every bit as valuable as the range of models available. Let's focus first on simple linear models and then move on to more complex model-fitting approaches.

Simple Linear Models

A linear model allows us to relate a response, or "dependent," variable to one or more explanatory, or "independent," variables using a linear function of parameters. For a linear model, the dependent must be continuous; however, the independent variables may be either continuous or discrete.

The lm function in R allows us to fit a range of linear models. However, we'll start with a simple linear regression of one continuous dependent variable and one continuous independent variable. In this case, our model is of the form $Y = \alpha + \beta * X + \varepsilon$, where the Y term represents our dependent variable, and X represents our independent variable(s). The α and β are parameters to be estimated and ε is our error term. For this hour, let's use the mtcars data to fit simple models, starting with a linear regression of mpg versus wt, which can be visualized in Figure 16.1.

```
> plot(mtcars$wt, mtcars$mpg, main = "Miles per Gallon vs Weight",
+       xlab = "Weight (lb/1000)", ylab = "Miles per Gallon", pch = 16)
```

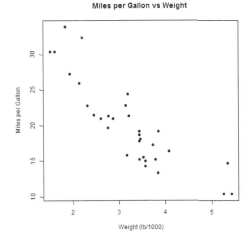

FIGURE 16.1
A scatter plot of mpg versus wt

NOTE

Base Graphics

For this section, we will use the base graphics system to produce plots, because that is the system in which most model-fitting "diagnostic" plots are implemented.

This example creates a scatter plot of mpg versus wt. From the plot, it is clear that a relationship exists between mpg and wt that looks approximately linear, with miles per gallon reducing based on increased vehicle weights.

Fitting the Model

To create the plot in Figure 16.1, we stated our x and y variables explicitly using the $ syntax. However, we can also create the same basic plot using formula and data arguments, plot(mpg ~ wt, data = mtcars). The lm function works in much the same way. The first argument to lm (and, in fact, most model-fitting functions) is a "formula" defining the specific relationship to model. As with lattice graphics, we use the ~ symbol to establish a relationship as part of a formula. To specify a linear relationship between two variables, we use Y ~ X, which corresponds to a model of Y = α + β * X + ε. It should be noted, in particular, that specifying Y ~ X denotes a relationship that includes an intercept term (α). Let's go ahead and fit our linear model of mpg versus wt using the lm function. We will save the output from the model fit as an object and print the value of the object.

```
> model1 <- lm(mpg ~ wt, data = mtcars)  # Fit the model
> model1

Call:
lm(formula = mpg ~ wt, data = mtcars)

Coefficients:
(Intercept)            wt
     37.285        -5.344
```

NOTE

The data Argument

Note that lm, like the majority of model-fitting functions in R, accepts a data argument that specifies the data frame from which the model variables are taken. If preferred, we can omit this argument and fit the model by specifying vector inputs, such as lm(Y ~ X) or, in our example, lm(mtcars$mpg ~ mtcars$wt).

TIP

Removing the Intercept

As mentioned, the default behavior when specifying a model of Y ~ X is to include an intercept term. If appropriate, we can remove the intercept term by instead defining the formula as Y ~ X - 1.

Assessing a Model in R

In the previous section, we fitted a simple linear regression of mpg versus wt. Printing the resulting object from the lm function, we see a concise text output containing two elements:

▶ The "call" that was made to the function. (A model always knows how it was created.)

▶ The estimated coefficients of the model (α = 37.285 and β = -5.344).

The next step is to assess whether our model is a "good" model and look for areas of improvement. To assess a model's appropriateness, we can investigate the following:

▶ The overall measures of fit, such as the Residual Standard Error

▶ Plots of "predicted" (or "fitted") values and model "residuals" (where the residuals values are calculated by subtracting the fitted values from the observed responses)

▶ Metrics on the influence of each independent variable

Clearly, the printed output from our model object provides very little insight into the model fit itself. For that, we need to use further functions that allow us to explore other aspects of our model.

Model Summaries

As seen in the previous section, the printed output from a model is rather concise, reporting only the function call and the estimated parameters. We can generate a more detailed textual output from our model using the summary function, which accepts a model object as the input. The output from this is shown in Listing 16.1.

LISTING 16.1 Output from Summary of Model

```
 1: > summary(model1)  # Summary of the lm model
 2:
 3: Call:
 4: lm(formula = mpg ~ wt, data = mtcars)
 5:
 6: Residuals:
 7:     Min      1Q  Median      3Q     Max
 8: -4.5432 -2.3647 -0.1252  1.4096  6.8727
 9:
10: Coefficients:
11:             Estimate Std. Error t value Pr(>|t|)
12: (Intercept)  37.2851     1.8776  19.858  < 2e-16 ***
13: wt           -5.3445     0.5591  -9.559 1.29e-10 ***
14: ---
```

```
15: Signif. codes:  0 '***' 0.001 '**' 0.01 '*' 0.05 '.' 0.1 ' ' 1
16:
17: Residual standard error: 3.046 on 30 degrees of freedom
18: Multiple R-squared:  0.7528,  Adjusted R-squared:  0.7446
19: F-statistic: 91.38 on 1 and 30 DF, p-value: 1.294e-10
```

As you can see, the summary function results in considerably more metrics. The information returned is shown in Table 16.1, which describes the output shown in Listing 16.1.

TABLE 16.1 Metrics from Summary of Model

Lines	Information
4	The function call, describing how the model was created.
7–8	Distribution of residuals of the model in the form.
11–13	Table of model coefficients, including each parameter estimate, standard error, T-statistic, and corresponding (two-sided) p-value. Each p-value is suffixed with a "significance star" display, reporting the significance level of the p-value.
15	Key for significance based on the two-sided p-value for each coefficient.
17	The Residual Standard Error (RSE) calculated as the square root of the estimated variance of the error, together with the degrees of freedom (number of observations minus number of parameters) on which the RSE was based.
18	The Multiple R-squared and Adjusted R-squared values, designed to describe the fraction of variance explained by the model.
19	The F-statistic for the whole model, along with the corresponding p-value.

There are a small number of additional arguments we can provide to the summary function, including the correlation input, which allows us to additionally include the correlation matrix of estimated parameters, as shown in the following example. For more information, see the help file for ?summary.lm.

Model Diagnostic Plots

In Hour 13, "Graphics," we introduced the plot function, which allows us to produce scatter plots of our data. In fact, we used the plot function earlier in this hour to create the scatter plot in Figure 16.1. We can also use the plot function to create diagnostic plots for model objects, such as our model1 object. By default, four diagnostic plots will be created, so we will first use the mfrow layout parameter to create a 2x2 plot surface that is displayed in Figure 16.2:

```
> par(mfrow = c(2, 2))    # Set up a 2x2 Graph Page
> plot(model1)            # Create diagnostic plots for model1
```

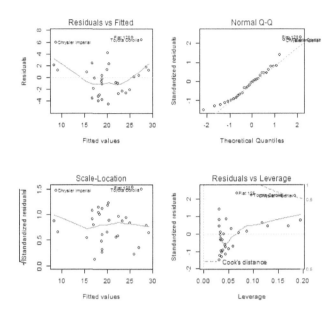

FIGURE 16.2
Diagnostic plots for linear regression

The four plots created by the call to the plot function are described in Table 16.2.

TABLE 16.2   Diagnostic Plots Created

Position	Description
Top left	A scatter plot of model residuals versus fitted values. A horizontal reference line is added at 0. By default, a loess smooth line is added and the more "extreme" (highest absolute residual) points are identified with the row names from the input data.
Top right	A Normal Quantile-Quantile (QQ) plot of the (standardized) model residuals allows us to assess whether the residuals are normally distributed.
Bottom left	A Scale-Location (or "S-L") plot of the square root of absolute (standardized) residuals versus fitted values.
Bottom right	A plot of (standardized) residuals versus each observation's "leverage" (the "hat" values calculated with the lm.influence function) with Cook's distance overlaid as contour lines.

Additional Arguments to `plot`

We can provide a number of additional arguments to `plot`. Most of these are concerned with the formatting of each plot (such as the `id.n` input, which controls the number of "extreme" values to be identified on each plot). Perhaps the most interesting is the `which` argument, which controls which plots are to be produced by `plot`. By default, `which` is set to `c(1:3, 5)`, indicating the index of the four plots to be created. If, instead, we specify `which = 1:6`, the `plot` function will create six plots (the four described previously plus two that visualize Cook's distance measures). For more information, see the help file for `?plot.lm`.

Extracting Model Elements

R provides three functions that will return key elements of a linear model object (and, in fact, the majority of model types). The three functions are described in Table 16.3.

TABLE 16.3 Model Extractor Functions

Function	Description
resid	Extracts the residuals from the model
fitted	Extracts the fitted values from the model
coef	Extracts the coefficients from the model

The use of these functions can be seen here:

```
> coef(model1)          # Model coefficients
(Intercept)          wt
  37.285126    -5.344472
> head(resid(model1))   # Fitted Values
        Mazda RX4      Mazda RX4 Wag        Datsun 710
       -2.2826106         -0.9197704        -2.0859521
  Hornet 4 Drive Hornet Sportabout           Valiant
        1.2973499         -0.2001440        -0.6932545
> head(fitted(model1))  # Residuals (observed - fitted)
        Mazda RX4      Mazda RX4 Wag        Datsun 710
         23.28261           21.91977          24.88595
  Hornet 4 Drive Hornet Sportabout           Valiant
         20.10265           18.90014          18.79325
```

Let's use the `resid` function to create scatter plots of our residuals versus the other nine variables from `mtcars` (seen in Figure 16.3):

```
> whichVars <- setdiff(names(mtcars), c("wt", "mpg"))   # Names of other variables
                                                           in mtcars
> par(mfrow = c(3, 3))                                   # Set plot layout
> for (V in whichVars) {                                 # Loop through create
                                                           scatter plots
+    plot(mtcars[[V]], resid(model1), main = V, xlab ="", pch = 16)
+    lines(loess.smooth(mtcars[[V]], resid(model1)), col = "red")
+ }
```

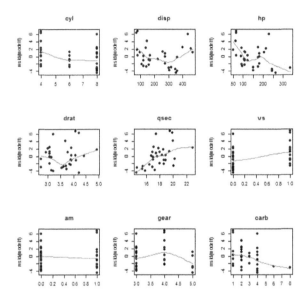

FIGURE 16.3
Plots of model residuals versus other variables in mtcars

From these plots, it seems that there are other variables we should include in our model—we'll do that later in this hour.

Models as List Objects

In the previous sections, you saw a number of ways of accessing information from a model:

▶ Printing the contents of the model object

▶ Using the summary function to create a more detailed textual output

▶ Using the plot function to create a range of diagnostic plots

▶ Using functions resid, coef, and fitted to extract key model elements

These approaches all use the information stored in the model object (returned from the call to lm). From the "Value" section of the lm help file (?lm), we can see that the function returns "an object of class lm," which is a "list" containing a number of components. Because our object is, fundamentally, a list, we can show the names of its elements using the names function (as seen in Hour 4, "Multi-Mode Data Structures"). Let's check the class of our model1 object and see the elements it contains:

```
> class(model1)    # The class of model1
[1] "lm"
> is.list(model1) # Is model1 a list?
[1] TRUE
> names(model1)    # The element names of model1
 [1] "coefficients"  "residuals"     "effects"      "rank"
 [5] "fitted.values" "assign"        "qr"           "df.residual"
 [9] "xlevels"       "call"          "terms"        "model"
```

The "Value" section of the lm help file also describes these elements; this information can be seen in Table 16.4.

TABLE 16.4 Model Elements

Name	Description
coefficients	A named vector of coefficients
residuals	The residuals (that is, response minus fitted values)
fitted.values	The fitted mean values
rank	The numeric rank of the fitted linear model
weights	The specified weights (only for weighted fits)
df.residual	The residual degrees of freedom
call	The matched call
terms	The terms object used
contrasts	The contrasts used (only where relevant)
xlevels	A record of the levels of the factors used in fitting (only where relevant)
offset	The offset used (missing if none were used)
y	If requested, the response used
x	If requested, the model matrix used
model	If requested (the default), the model frame used
na.action	Information returned by model.frame on the special handling of NAs (where relevant)
call	The function call that was made to create the model
terms	Independent variables of the model

Given that our object is a list and we know the element names, we can directly extract elements using the $ symbol, as shown here:

```
> model1$coefficients            # Model Coefficients
(Intercept)        wt
  37.285126    -5.344472
> quantile(model1$residuals,     # Specific quantiles of residuals
+        probs = c(0.05, 0.5, 0.95))
       5%        50%        95%
-3.8071897 -0.1251956  6.1794815
```

Model Summaries as List Objects

You have seen that the summary function allows us to produce a detailed textual summary of our model fit. In fact, the summary function (when applied to an lm object) also returns a list object that can be queried. This is shown in the following example:

```
> sModel1 <- summary(model1)    # Summary of model1
> class(sModel1)                # Class of summary object
[1] "summary.lm"
> is.list(sModel1)              # Is it a list?
[1] TRUE
> names(sModel1)                # Element names
 [1] "call"          "terms"        "residuals"     "coefficients"
 [5] "aliased"       "sigma"        "df"            "r.squared"
 [9] "adj.r.squared" "fstatistic"   "cov.unscaled"
> sModel1$adj.r.squared         # Adjusted R Squared
[1] 0.7445939
> sModel1$sigma^2               # Estimate variance
[1] 9.277398
```

The elements of this object are described in Table 16.5 (taken from the summary.lm help file).

TABLE 16.5 Summary Model Elements

Name	Description
residuals	The weighted residuals, the usual residuals rescaled by the square root of the weights specified in the call to lm.
coefficients	A p x 4 matrix with columns for the estimated coefficient, its standard error, T-statistic, and corresponding (two-sided) p-value. Aliased coefficients are omitted.
aliased	Named logical vector showing if the original coefficients are aliased.
sigma	The square root of the estimated variance of the random error $\sigma^2 = 1/(n\text{-}p)\ \text{Sum}(w[i]\ R[i]^2)$, where $R[i]$ is the i-th residual, residuals[i].

Name	Description
df	Degrees of freedom, a three-vector (p, n-p, p*), the first being the number of non-aliased coefficients, the last being the total number of coefficients.
fstatistic	For models including non-intercept terms, a three-vector with the value of the F-statistic with its numerator and denominator degrees of freedom.
r.squared	R^2, the "fraction of variance" explained by the model $R^2 = 1 - Sum(R[i]^2) / Sum((y[i] - y^*)^2)$, where y^* is the mean of y[i] if there is an intercept, and zero otherwise.
adj.r.squared	The preceding R^2 statistic "adjusted," penalizing for higher p.
cov.unscaled	A p x p matrix of (unscaled) covariances of the coef[j], j=1, ..., p.
correlation	The correlation matrix corresponding to the preceding cov.unscaled, if correlation = TRUE is specified.
symbolic.cor	Only if correlation is true, the value of the argument symbolic.cor.
na.action	Information returned by model.frame on the special handling of NAs (where relevant). Identical to the na.action value returned from the model object.
call	The function call that was made to create the model.
terms	Independent variables of the model.

Adding Model Lines to Plots

At the start of this hour, we created a scatter plot of mpg vs. wt (refer to Figure 16.1). We can add a linear regression line to this plot based on our model fit using the abline function (which you also saw earlier in Hour 13). The following code adds a solid line representing our model fit; the resulting plot can be seen in Figure 16.4.

```
> plot(mtcars$wt, mtcars$mpg, main = "Miles per Gallon vs Weight",
+        xlab = "Weight (lb/1000)", ylab = "Miles per Gallon", pch = 16)
> abline(model1)
```

CAUTION

Additional Arguments to plot

When our models are more complex, involving multiple variables or nonlinear relations, a simple abline call will not work and other approaches must be taken. However, for simple models such as the one in this example, it works well.

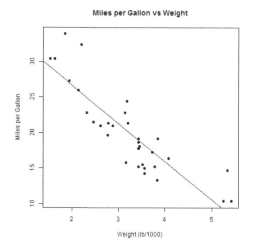

FIGURE 16.4
Scatter plot of mpg versus wt with overlaid regression line

Making Model Predictions

Once we have a model, we can make predictions using the predict function. If we supply only the model object to predict, then fitted values are returned:

```
> head(predict(model1))   # Model Predictions using model1
        Mazda RX4       Mazda RX4 Wag          Datsun 710
         23.28261            21.91977            24.88595
   Hornet 4 Drive Hornet Sportabout             Valiant
         20.10265            18.90014            18.79325
> head(fitted(model1))    # Fitted Values of model1
        Mazda RX4       Mazda RX4 Wag          Datsun 710
         23.28261            21.91977            24.88595
   Hornet 4 Drive Hornet Sportabout             Valiant
         20.10265            18.90014            18.79325
```

We can, instead, provide a data frame containing the set(s) of independent variables for which out-of-sample predictions are to be made. This data frame is supplied as the newdata input to predict, as shown here:

```
> wtDf <- data.frame(wt = 1:6)               # Independent Variables
> predVals <- predict(model1, newdata = wtDf)  # Make predictions using
                                               model1
> data.frame(wt = wtDf$wt, Pred = round(predVals, 1))  # Form as data frame
  wt Pred
1  1 31.9
2  2 26.6
3  3 21.3
```

```
4   4 15.9
5   5 10.6
6   6  5.2
```

Other arguments to the `predict` function allow us to customize our predictions in a number of ways. For example, we can use the `se.fit` and `interval` arguments to provide standard errors and confidence intervals related to our predictions, as shown here:

```
> predict(model1, newdata = wtDf, se.fit = TRUE, interval = "confidence")
$fit
        fit      lwr       upr
1 31.940655 29.18042 34.700892
2 26.596183 24.82389 28.368481
3 21.251711 20.12444 22.378987
4 15.907240 14.49018 17.324295
5 10.562768  8.24913 12.876406
6  5.218297  1.85595  8.580644

$se.fit
          1         2         3         4         5         6
1.3515519 0.8678067 0.5519713 0.6938618 1.1328743 1.6463754

$df
[1] 30

$residual.scale
[1] 3.045882
```

Multiple Linear Regression

Figure 16.3 showed a plot of the residuals from our model versus other variables in the `mtcars` data frame. We can include more than one independent variable in a model by separating variables by a + symbol on the right side of the formula. Therefore, we can specify a formula as Y ~ X1 + X2, which corresponds to a model of $Y = \alpha + \beta1 * X1 + \beta2 * X2 + \varepsilon$. Here, α, $\beta1$ and $\beta2$ are parameters to be estimated and ε is our error term. Let's define a new model including both wt and the hp variable:

```
> model2 <- lm(mpg ~ wt + hp, data = mtcars)   # Fit new model
> summary(model2)

Call:
lm(formula = mpg ~ wt + hp, data = mtcars)

Residuals:
   Min     1Q Median     3Q    Max
-3.941 -1.600 -0.182  1.050  5.854
```

```
Coefficients:
            Estimate Std. Error t value Pr(>|t|)
(Intercept) 37.22727    1.59879  23.285  < 2e-16 ***
wt          -3.87783    0.63273  -6.129 1.12e-06 ***
hp          -0.03177    0.00903  -3.519  0.00145 **
---
Signif. codes:  0 '***' 0.001 '**' 0.01 '*' 0.05 '.' 0.1 ' ' 1

Residual standard error: 2.593 on 29 degrees of freedom
Multiple R-squared:  0.8268,  Adjusted R-squared:  0.8148
F-statistic: 69.21 on 2 and 29 DF,  p-value: 9.109e-12
```

You can see from this output that the coefficient of the hp variable is significant at the 1% level, so including it would initially seem to be a good idea.

Updating Models

In the last example, we created a new model (model2) including two independent variables (wt and hp). It is common, when model fitting, to create a new model by varying the aspects of a previous model. That could include the following:

▶ Adding or removing a model term

▶ Removing outlying observations

▶ Changing a model-fitting option

Instead of creating new models directly, we can create new models by updating existing models with the update function. To achieve this, we supply an existing model and identify what to change. As an example, let's re-create model2, this time using the update function:

```
> model2 <- update(model1, mpg ~ wt + hp)      # Create model2 based on model1
> model2

Call:
lm(formula = mpg ~ wt + hp, data = mtcars)

Coefficients:
(Intercept)           wt           hp
   37.22727     -3.87783     -0.03177
```

Although this example is very simple, when we have more complex models, this approach can be very efficient.

TIP

Updating Formula

When updating the model in this example, we specified the new formula as `mpg ~ wt + hp`. However, we can reduce the amount of typing using the period character to denote all formula elements of the previous model. Therefore, we could rewrite the previous example as follows:

```
> model2 <- update(model1, . ~ . + hp)      # Create model2 based on model1
```

Again, when we have large models, this can be a far more efficient way of developing models.

Comparing Nested Models

In the previous section, we created a new model, `model2`, with an added term (`hp`). An initial look at the summary from `model2` suggests that `hp` should be included in our model. Note that the independent variables in `model1` are a subset of those in `model2`. The models are otherwise identical. In cases such as this, we say that `model1` is nested within `model2`. Instead of looking at the models in isolation, we can compare two (or more) nested models using the following approaches:

- ▶ Creating comparative diagnostic plots
- ▶ Computing analysis of variance tables

Comparative Diagnostic Plots

Because we can access the information in each model, either directly or using functions such as `resid` and `fitted`, we can create plots that overlay data from two or more models. Let's start by creating a plot of residuals vs. fitted values for each of our two models. The output can be seen in Figure 16.5.

```
> # Extract elements
> res1 <- resid(model1)
> fit1 <- fitted(model1)
> res2 <- resid(model2)
> fit2 <- fitted(model2)

> # Calculate axis range
> resRange <- c(-1, 1) * max(abs(res1), abs(res2))
> fitRange <- range(fit1, fit2)

> # Create plot for model1 > add points for model2
> plot(fit1, res1, xlim = fitRange, ylim = resRange,
+    col = "red", pch = 16, main = "Residuals vs Fitted Values",
+    xlab = "Fitted Values", ylab = "Residuals")
> points(fit2, res2, col = "blue", pch = 16)
```

```
> # Add reference and smooth lines
> abline(h = 0, lty = 2)
> lines(loess.smooth(fit1, res1), col = "red")
> lines(loess.smooth(fit2, res2), col = "blue")
> legend("bottomleft", c("mpg ~ wt", "mpg ~ wt + hp"), fill = c("red", "blue"))
```

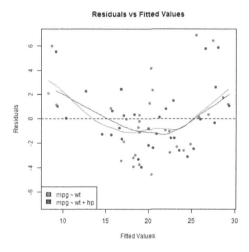

FIGURE 16.5
Scatter plot of residuals vs. fitted values for two linear models

We can use a similar approach to see how different models deal with variables in our data. For example, let's see how the addition of the hp variable in model2 has helped to deal with the relationship between the model1 residuals and hp shown in Figure 16.3. The resulting plot can be seen in Figure 16.6.

```
> # Create plot for model1 > add points for model2
> plot(mtcars$hp, res1, ylim = resRange,
+      col = "red", pch = 16, main = "Residuals vs Fitted Values",
+      xlab = "Fitted Values", ylab = "Residuals")
> points(mtcars$hp, res2, col = "blue", pch = 16)

> # Add reference and smooth lines
> abline(h = 0, lty = 2)
> lines(loess.smooth(mtcars$hp, res1, span = .8), col = "red")
> lines(loess.smooth(mtcars$hp, res2, span = .8), col = "blue")
> legend("bottomleft", c("mpg ~ wt", "mpg ~ wt + hp"), fill = c("red", "blue"))
```

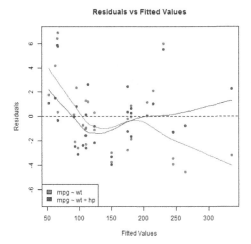

FIGURE 16.6
Scatter plot of residuals vs hp for two linear models

Analysis of Variance

We can create an analysis of variable table for one or more linear models using the anova functions. For this to make statistical sense, the models provided should be nested. For each model, the residual degrees of freedom and sum of squares is reported. In addition, an F test is performed for each step, with the p-value report. Let's create an analysis of variance table to compare model1 and model2:

```
> anova(model1, model2)
Analysis of Variance Table

Model 1: mpg ~ wt
Model 2: mpg ~ wt + hp
  Res.Df    RSS Df Sum of Sq      F   Pr(>F)
1     30 278.32
2     29 195.05  1    83.274 12.381 0.001451 **
---
Signif. codes:  0 '***' 0.001 '**' 0.01 '*' 0.05 '.' 0.1 ' ' 1
```

You can see from the p-value (the value below Pr(>F)) that the inclusion of the hp variable significantly improved the model fit (assuming a p-value of 0.05).

Interaction Terms

We may wish to test whether there is a significant interaction term in the model. For example, we may hypothesize that wt has a different effect on mpg depending on differing values of hp. To test an interaction term, we specify it using the : symbol. Therefore, we can specify a formula as Y ~ X1 + X2 + X1:X2, which corresponds to a model of Y = α + $\beta 1$ * X1 + $\beta 2$ * X2 + $\beta 2$ * X1 * X2 + ε. Here, α, $\beta 1$, $\beta 2$, and $\beta 3$ are parameters to be estimated and ε is our error term. Let's update model2 to include this interaction term.

```
> model3 <- update(model2, . ~ . + wt:hp)
> summary(model3)

Call:
lm(formula = mpg ~ wt + hp + wt:hp, data = mtcars)

Residuals:
    Min      1Q  Median      3Q     Max
-3.0632 -1.6491 -0.7362  1.4211  4.5513

Coefficients:
             Estimate Std. Error t value Pr(>|t|)
(Intercept) 49.80842    3.60516  13.816 5.01e-14 ***
wt          -8.21662    1.26971  -6.471 5.20e-07 ***
hp          -0.12010    0.02470  -4.863 4.04e-05 ***
wt:hp        0.02785    0.00742   3.753 0.000811 ***
---
Signif. codes:  0 '***' 0.001 '**' 0.01 '*' 0.05 '.' 0.1 ' ' 1

Residual standard error: 2.153 on 28 degrees of freedom
Multiple R-squared:  0.8848,  Adjusted R-squared:  0.8724
F-statistic: 71.66 on 3 and 28 DF,  p-value: 2.981e-13
```

Assess Addition of Interaction Term

From the preceding summary output, the interaction terms certainly seem highly significant, as are the other parameters when assessed in the presence of the interaction. Let's compare our models with a quick graphic, seen in Figure 16.7. This time, we'll add horizontal reference lines at the 5% and 95% residual quantiles.

```
> # Extract elements for model 3
> res3 <- resid(model3)
> fit3 <- fitted(model3)

> # Calculate axis range
> resRange <- c(-1, 1) * max(resRange, abs(res3))
> fitRange <- range(fitRange, fit3)
```

```
> # Create plot for model1 > add points for model2
> plot(fit1, res1, xlim = fitRange, ylim = resRange,
+       col = "red", pch = 16, main = "Residuals vs Fitted Values",
+       xlab = "Fitted Values", ylab = "Residuals")
> points(fit2, res2, col = "blue", pch = 16)
> points(fit3, res3, col = "black", pch = 16)

> # Add reference and smooth lines
> abline(h = 0, lty = 2)
> lines(loess.smooth(fit1, res1), col = "red")
> lines(loess.smooth(fit2, res2), col = "blue")
> lines(loess.smooth(fit3, res3), col = "black")

> # Add 5% and 95% reference lines for each model
> refFun <- function(res, col) abline(h = quantile(res, c(.05, .95)), col = col,
➥lty = 3)
> refFun(res1, "red")
> refFun(res2, "blue")
> refFun(res3, "black")

> legend("bottomleft", c("mpg ~ wt", "mpg ~ wt + hp", "mpg ~ wt + hp + wt:hp"),
+      fill = c("red", "blue", "black"))
```

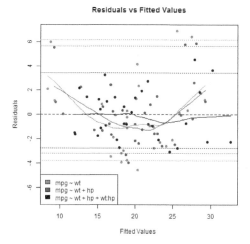

FIGURE 16.7
Scatter plot of residuals vs fitted values for three linear models

The addition of the interaction term certainly seems to have improved our model. As a last check, let's create an analysis of the variance table for our three models:

```
> anova(model1, model2, model3)
Analysis of Variance Table

Model 1: mpg ~ wt
Model 2: mpg ~ wt + hp
Model 3: mpg ~ wt + hp + wt:hp
  Res.Df    RSS Df Sum of Sq      F    Pr(>F)
1     30 278.32
2     29 195.05  1    83.274 17.969 0.0002207 ***
3     28 129.76  1    65.286 14.088 0.0008108 ***
---
Signif. codes:  0 '***' 0.001 '**' 0.01 '*' 0.05 '.' 0.1 ' ' 1
```

In this case, the F test and corresponding p-values are derived by testing each model against the largest model provided (in this case `model3`). The significance of the two comparisons supports our claim that `model3` is an improvement over each of the previous models.

TIP

Linear Combinations Including Interactions

In the previous section, you saw that we can create models with linear combinations of variables and interaction terms using a formula such as `Y ~ X1 + X2 + X1:X2`. Another way of writing this is as `Y ~ X1*X2`, which expands to `Y ~ X1 + X2 + X1:X2`. This works for any number of variables; for example, we could use `Y ~ X1*X2*X3` to create a model of `Y ~ X1 + X2 + X3 + X1:X2 + X1:X3 + X2:X3 + X1:X2:X3`!

Factor Independent Variables

So far in this hour, we have used only continuous independent variables. In fact, the `lm` function allows us to include factor variables as independent variables. In the `mtcars` dataset, there are a number of variables we could treat as factor variables, each of which may be influential in our model. Let's first look at the residuals from our current model (`model3`) versus some of these factor variables, seen in Figure 16.8. Let's focus on three variables that we'll treat as categorical:

▶ The `vs` variable, an indicator for whether the engine is a "straight" (0) or "V" engine (1)

▶ The `am` variable, an indicator of the transmission type: 0 for automatic, 1 for manual.

▶ The `cyl` variable, which contains the number of cylinders (4, 6, or 8).

These variables are actually stored as numeric, so we will need to convert them to factors first:

```
> par(mfrow = c(1, 3))
> plot(factor(mtcars$vs), resid(model3),  col = "red",
```

```
+    xlab = "0 = Straight Engine \ 1 = 'V Engine'", ylab = "Residuals",
+    main = "Residuals versus\n'V Engine' Flag")
> plot(factor(mtcars$am), resid(model3), col = "red",
+    xlab = "0 = Automatic \ 1 = Manual", ylab = "Residuals",
+    main = "Residuals versus\nTransmission Type")
> plot(factor(mtcars$cyl), resid(model3), col = "red",
+    xlab = "Number of Cylinders", ylab = "Residuals",
+    main = "Residuals versus\nNumber of Cylinders")
```

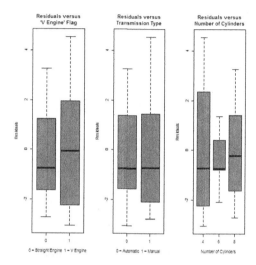

FIGURE 16.8
Model residuals versus `vs`, `am`, and `cyl`

Including Factors

Let's add `cyl` to our model and see what impact it has. To achieve this, we will specify `cyl` as a factor variable; otherwise, it would be handled as a continuous independent variable.

```
> model4 <- update(model3, . ~ . + factor(cyl))
> summary(model4)

Call:
lm(formula = mpg ~ wt + hp + factor(cyl) + wt:hp, data = mtcars)

Residuals:
    Min      1Q  Median      3Q     Max
-3.5309 -1.6451 -0.4154  1.3838  4.4788
```

```
Coefficients:
              Estimate Std. Error t value Pr(>|t|)
(Intercept)  47.337329   4.679790  10.115 1.67e-10 ***
wt           -7.306337   1.675258  -4.361 0.000181 ***
hp           -0.103331   0.031907  -3.238 0.003274 **
factor(cyl)6 -1.259073   1.489594  -0.845 0.405685
factor(cyl)8 -1.454339   2.063696  -0.705 0.487246
wt:hp         0.023951   0.008966   2.671 0.012865 *
---
Signif. codes:  0 '***' 0.001 '**' 0.01 '*' 0.05 '.' 0.1 ' ' 1

Residual standard error: 2.203 on 26 degrees of freedom
Multiple R-squared:  0.888,  Adjusted R-squared:  0.8664
F-statistic: 41.21 on 5 and 26 DF,  p-value: 1.503e-11
```

The coefficients are reported for cyl = 6 and cyl = 8, with the first level (cyl = 4) taken as the baseline. This is because "treatment" contrasts are the default contrast method for unordered factors. The treatment "contrast" method contrasts each level with a baseline level, taken (by default) as the first level of the variable.

TIP
_____

Control of Contrasts

There are five contrast methods available in R: contr.treatment (the default), contr.sum, contr.poly, contr.helmert, and contr.SAS. Each of the contrast options is represented by a function that is used to create a contrast matrix of the appropriate size. The following is an example for a factor with three levels:

```
> contr.treatment(3)     # Matrix of dummy variables to use for a 3-level factor
                           (like cyl)

  2 3
1 0 0
2 1 0
3 0 1
```

We view and set the default contrast using options("contrasts").
_____

From the model output, it is clear that the cyl variable is not significant in the model. This is further supported by an analysis of variance, which shows that very little additional variance is explained with the addition of the cyl variable between model3 and model4:

```
> anova(model1, model2, model3, model4)
Analysis of Variance Table

Model 1: mpg ~ wt
Model 2: mpg ~ wt + hp
```

```
Model 3: mpg ~ wt + hp + wt:hp
Model 4: mpg ~ wt + hp + factor(cyl) + wt:hp
  Res.Df    RSS Df Sum of Sq      F    Pr(>F)
1      30 278.32
2      29 195.05  1    83.274 17.1624 0.0003219 ***
3      28 129.76  1    65.286 13.4552 0.0011040 **
4      26 126.16  2     3.606  0.3716 0.6932114
---
Signif. codes:   0 '***' 0.001 '**' 0.01 '*' 0.05 '.' 0.1 ' ' 1
```

One interesting thing from the summary output, however, is that the significance of the hp variable (and the interaction term) were slightly lessened with the inclusion of cyl. The reason for this is that hp and cyl are highly correlated (as seen in Figure 16.9), so the "information" provided by hp is very similar to that supplied by cyl.

```
> plot(factor(mtcars$cyl), mtcars$hp, col = "red",
+       xlab = "Number of Cylinders", ylab = "Gross Horsepower",
+       main = "Gross Horsepower vs Number of Cylinders")
```

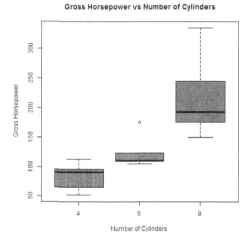

FIGURE 16.9
Gross horsepower vs. number of cylinders (cyl versus hp)

We could, as a next step, replace hp with cyl in the model and also look at interaction terms between wt and cyl.

Variable Transformations

If we look back at Figure 16.1, which plotted mpg versus wt, there is a suggestion of curvature. Let's see this plot again, this time alongside of plot of log(mpg) versus wt. This can be seen in Figure 16.10.

```
> par(mfrow = c(1, 2))
> plot(mtcars$wt, mtcars$mpg, pch = 16, xlab = "Weight (lb/1000)",
+       ylab = "Miles per Gallon", main = "MPG Gallon versus Weight")
> lines(loess.smooth(mtcars$wt, mtcars$mpg), col = "red")
> plot(mtcars$wt, log(mtcars$mpg), pch = 16, xlab = "Weight (lb/1000)",
+       ylab = "log(Miles per Gallon)", main = "Logged MPG versus Weight")
> lines(loess.smooth(mtcars$wt, log(mtcars$mpg)), col = "red")
```

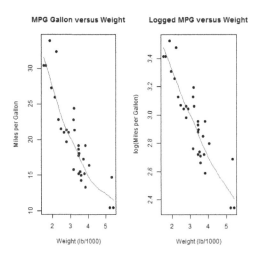

FIGURE 16.10
Scatter plots of miles per gallon and logged miles per gallon versus weight

Based on this visualization, we may decide to try to model logged miles per gallon. If we want to transform any of our dependent or independent variables, we can apply a transformation function directly in the formula. Let's create a simple model of logged miles per gallon versus weight horsepower. We'll look at the detailed summary output and also create some diagnostic plots (seen in Figure 16.11).

```
> lmodel1 <- lm(log(mpg) ~ wt, data = mtcars)
> summary(lmodel1)

Call:
lm(formula = log(mpg) ~ wt, data = mtcars)
```

```
Residuals:
      Min        1Q    Median        3Q       Max
-0.210346 -0.085932 -0.006136  0.061335  0.308623

Coefficients:
            Estimate Std. Error t value Pr(>|t|)
(Intercept)  3.83191    0.08396   45.64  < 2e-16 ***
wt          -0.27178    0.02500  -10.87 6.31e-12 ***
---
Signif. codes:  0 '***' 0.001 '**' 0.01 '*' 0.05 '.' 0.1 ' ' 1

Residual standard error: 0.1362 on 30 degrees of freedom
Multiple R-squared:  0.7976, Adjusted R-squared:  0.7908
F-statistic: 118.2 on 1 and 30 DF,  p-value: 6.31e-12

> par(mfrow = c(2, 2)) # Set plot layout
> plot(lmodel1)        # Create diagnostics plots
```

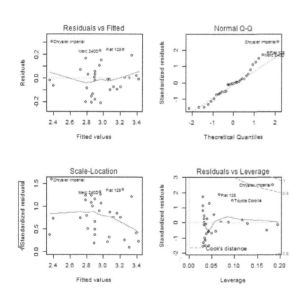

FIGURE 16.11
Diagnostic plots for log model fit

If we want to overlay this model onto our original data, it is better to exponentiate some predicted results and use the lines function to add the line to the plot. Let's compare the original model of mpg vs. wt with the new model of log(mpg) vs. wt. The output can be seen in Figure 16.12.

```
> plot(mtcars$wt, mtcars$mpg, pch = 16, xlab = "Weight (lb/1000)",
+       ylab = "Miles per Gallon", main = "MPG Gallon versus Weight")
> abline(model1, col = "red")   # Add (straight) model line (based on earlier
                                  model1 object)

> wtVals <- seq(min(mtcars$wt), max(mtcars$wt), length = 50)     # Weights to
                                                                  predict at
> predVals <- predict(lmodel1, newdata = data.frame(wt = wtVals)) # Make
                                                                  predictions
> lines( wtVals, exp(predVals), col = "blue")                   # Add (log) model
                                                                  line
> legend("topright", c("mpg ~ wt", "log(mpg) ~ wt"), fill = c("red", "blue"))
```

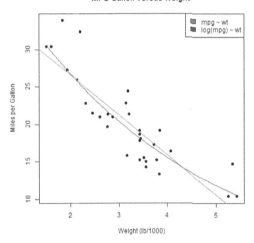

FIGURE 16.12
Scatter plot of miles per gallon versus weight, overlaid with two models

CAUTION

Inhibiting Interpretation

If we want to transform dependent or independent variables, it is worth noting that some model formula syntax has special meaning. For example, if we wanted to model a response Y against a continuous variable X, we'd use Y ~ X. However, if we instead wanted to model Y against "X - 1" (the values of X with 1 subtracted), we might try Y ~ X - 1. However, this syntax denotes a model of Y against X without an intercept term. If we literally want to model Y against "X - 1", we need to include the I function, which inhibits the interpretation of the formula. Therefore, our formula would become Y ~ I(X - 1). For more information on the formula syntax, including the I function, see the ?formula help file.

R and Object Orientation

In the preceding sections, we used functions such as `summary` and `plot` to understand our models. However, we have seen these functions used in earlier hours to summarize and graph other objects. In addition to the outputs from summary related to the preceding models, consider the following uses of the `summary` function:

```
> summary(mtcars$mpg)             # Summary of a numeric vector
   Min. 1st Qu.  Median    Mean 3rd Qu.    Max.
  10.40   15.42   19.20   20.09   22.80   33.90
> summary(factor(mtcars$cyl))     # Summary of a factor vector
  4  6  8
 11  7 14
> summary(mtcars[,1:4])           # Summary of a data frame
      mpg              cyl             disp              hp
 Min.   :10.40   Min.   :4.000   Min.   : 71.1   Min.   : 52.0
 1st Qu.:15.43   1st Qu.:4.000   1st Qu.:120.8   1st Qu.: 96.5
 Median :19.20   Median :6.000   Median :196.3   Median :123.0
 Mean   :20.09   Mean   :6.188   Mean   :230.7   Mean   :146.7
 3rd Qu.:22.80   3rd Qu.:8.000   3rd Qu.:326.0   3rd Qu.:180.0
 Max.   :33.90   Max.   :8.000   Max.   :472.0   Max.   :335.0
```

In these examples, the `summary` function produces different output depending on the type of object it is provided. The `summary` help file describes it as a "generic" function, which provides "methods" for many "classes" of objects. But what does this mean?

Object Orientation

Many features of the R language are based on the object-oriented programming paradigm. To describe object orientation, let's consider the following:

▶ If someone asks us to **open a door**, we would **turn the handle.**

▶ If someone asks us to **open a bottle**, we would **twist the top.**

▶ If someone asks us to **open a box**, we would **lift the lid.**

For each of these statements, the "command" is the same: "open." However, we behave differently based on the type of object we are to "open." The idea behind object-oriented programming is similar. Here, the "command" is called a "method," and the "type" of object is called the "class" of the object. We have seen a number of examples of this behavior in this hour, such as the previous `summary` function uses, which are described in Table 16.6.

TABLE 16.6 Summary Methods

Object "Class"	Action
Numeric vector	Numeric summaries (quantiles plus the mean)
Factor vector	Frequency count of levels
Data Frame	Summary of each column
Output from Linear Model	Detailed summary of the model fit

R contains a number of systems for object-oriented programming. The majority of the statistical modeling functionality available in R is based on the "S3" system, which implements generic functions and uses a simple naming convention. When a method is called, the class of the object is appended to the name of the method, separated by a period character, and the process is redirected to this function. So when we perform a `summary` of an object of class "factor," we instead call function `summary.factor`, as shown in the following example:

```
> cylFactor <- factor(mtcars$cyl)
> class(cylFactor)
[1] "factor"
> summary(cylFactor)
 4  6  8
11  7 14
> summary.factor(cylFactor)
 4  6  8
11  7 14
```

NOTE

Using R Classes

In Hour 21, "Writing R Classes," and Hour 22, "Formal Class Systems," we will look more closely at S3 and other object-oriented programming systems provided by R.

Linear Model Methods

For most of this hour, we've been using functions such as `summary` and `plot` to evaluate linear models, which we fitted with the `lm` function. The "class" of these objects can be seen with the `class` function:

```
> class(model1)
[1] "lm"
> class(model2)
[1] "lm"
> class(model3)
```

```
[1] "lm"
> class(model4)
[1] "lm"
```

Using this fact, we now know the names of the functions we have been calling throughout the previous sections of this hour, many of which are summarized in Table 16.7.

TABLE 16.7   Methods for "lm" Objects

Method	Function Called	Action
print	print.lm	Concise summary of model. (print is executed invisibly when we run the name of the object.)
summary	summary.lm	Detailed summary of the model fit.
plot	plot.lm	Diagnostic plots illustrating the model fit.
anova	anova.lm	Analysis of variance for the model, or many nested models.
update	update.lm	Used to change some aspect of the model to create a new model.
predict	predict.lm	Used to make predictions based on the model.

Perhaps the most important reason to understand this mechanism is to know which is the relevant help file to read to understand the options available to us. For example, if we're using the summary function for an lm object, we know that summary.lm is the help file we need to refer to.

Summary

In this hour, you saw how to fit a series of simple linear models in R. This includes the way in which we define our linear model via the use of a "formula" as well as a number of ways to assess the appropriateness of our model using textual and graphical means. We also introduced the concept of object-oriented programming by looking at the behavior of generic functions such as print, summary, and plot when given linear model outputs. Although we focused on linear models in this hour, the concepts and approach we used is similar across a wide range of statistical models provided by R. In the next hour, we'll look at some of these models and see how similar the approach is to the fitting of linear models covered in this hour.

Q&A

Q. Can we return different types of residuals from our model fits?

A. Yes. Other types of residuals (such as Pearson and partial residuals) can be also be returned from the `resid` function. See the `?residuals.lm` help file for more information.

Q. What other high-level metrics relating to model fit are available?

A. A number of additional metrics are available, such as Akaike's Information Criteria (`?AIC`), Bayesian Information Criteria (`?BIC`), and Log-Likelihood (`?logLik`). This is not an exhaustive list, and we recommend searching the www.r-project.org site for specific methods if they have not been covered here.

Q. How do I extract the variance-covariance matrix of model parameters?

A. The `vcov` function allows you to extract the variance-covariance matrix of parameters given a model.

Q. How does `lm` deal with missing values?

A. The handling of missing values in `lm` is controlled by the `na.action` argument. By default, the `na.action` argument is set to `na.omit`, which removes rows including at least one missing based on the variables involved in the model.

Q. Can I perform polynomial regression using `lm`?

A. Yes. You can include independent variables in a polynomial manner. However, care must be taken because the `^` symbol in a formula has a particular meaning (it represents parameter crossing, as described in the `?formula` help page). Therefore, to include variables in a polynomial manner you need the `I` function (for example, `mpg ~ wt + I(wt^2)`). An alternative approach is to use the `poly` function, which allows you to specify this as `mpg ~ poly(wt, 2, raw = T)`.

Q. Is there functionality for stepwise regression in R?

A. Yes. The `step` function can be used to perform stepwise regression, which uses AIC as the basis for deciding which steps to take.

Workshop

The workshop contains quiz questions and exercises to help you solidify your understanding of the material covered. Try to answer all questions before looking at the "Answers" section that follows.

Quiz

1. How can we fit a model of Y against X without an intercept term?

2. What would a formula of Y ~ X1*X2 denote?

3. Which function can you use to extract the residuals from a model fit?

4. What help file would you refer to if you wanted to control the behavior of the `plot` function when producing diagnostic plots of a linear model?

5. What are the default contrast methods in R?

Answers

1. You would use Y ~ X - 1.

2. This denotes a model of Y against X1, X2 and the interaction of X1 and X2. Therefore, Y ~ X1*X2 is equivalent to Y ~ X1 + X2 + X1:X2.

3. You can use the `resid` function to extract residuals from a linear model.

4. If you are using the `plot` function with an object of class "lm" (which contains a linear model output), then the `plot.lm` help file would be the one to refer to.

5. The default contrast methods for an (unordered) factor variable in R are "treatment" contrasts, where the first level of the factor is taken as the baseline (as described in the `?contr.treatment` help file).

Activities

1. Using the `airquality` data frame, fit a linear model of Ozone versus Wind.

2. Create detailed textual summaries and diagnostic plots to assess your model fit.

3. Use the `update` function to add Temp as an independent variable. Evaluate your new model *and create an analysis of variance of these nested models*.

4. Assess the inclusion of an interaction term (Wind:Temp) in your model.

5. Add Month as a categorical independent variable in your model.

HOUR 17
Common R Models

What You'll Learn in This Hour:

▶ How to fit GLM Models

▶ How to fit Nonlinear Models

▶ How to fit Survival Models

▶ How to fit Time Series Models

In Hour 16, "Introduction to R Models and Object Orientation," we explored the ways in which we can fit and assess statistical models in R. To achieve this, we used a simple linear modeling approach using the `lm` function. However, as mentioned, R has the most rich analytic feature set in any technology today. In this hour, we'll extend the ideas of the previous hour to other modeling approaches. Specifically, we'll look at Generalized Linear Models, Nonlinear Models, Time Series Models, and Survival Models. We'll finish this hour by looking at other modeling approaches provided by R, and see where to access further information on these model types.

NOTE

Theory versus Code

In this hour, we provide a high-level overview of the theory for each modeling approach and then show how the models can be implemented in R. Consequently, we will not spend too much time on the detailed theory, or on the assessment of model performance, beyond that which helps you understand how methods can be applied to model objects.

Generalized Linear Models

In Hour 16, we used the `lm` function to fit Linear Models to our data. The "linear" aspect, here, refers to the fitting of a dependent variable against a linear function of independent variables. Here's an example:

$$Y = \theta_0 + \theta_1 X_1 + \theta_2 X_2 + \dots + \theta_N X_N + \varepsilon$$

Here, our Dependent Variable (Y) is modeled against N Independent Variables (X_1 to X_N), with parameters (θ_0 to θ_N) to be estimated by the model-fitting process. With the Linear Model, such as that fit by the `lm` function, we make a number of assumptions. In particular, we assume that the Dependent Variable (Y) is continuous and Normally distributed. Furthermore, we assume the errors (ε) are independent and identically distributed such that $E(\varepsilon) = 0$ and $var(\varepsilon) = \sigma^2$. We also assume that the errors (ε) are Normally distributed with mean 0 and variance σ^2 for the purposes of tests.

GLM Definition

The Linear Model, described here, can be considered a special case of the Generalized Linear Model (GLM) framework. The GLM approach allows us to fit models where

▶ The Dependent Variable may not be continuous and Normally distributed.

▶ The variance of the Dependent Variable may depend on the mean.

The GLM framework uses four elements to fit a model:

▶ A probability distribution from the exponential family

▶ A "linear predictor" to be modeled

▶ A "link function" defining how the linear predictor is related to the Dependent Variable

▶ A "variance function" explaining how the variance depends on the mean

In the GLM framework, the Dependent Variable (Y) is assumed to be generated from a specific distribution from the exponential family, a large range of distributions. A number of common distributions are listed in Table 17.1.

TABLE 17.1 Selection of Distributions from the Exponential Family

Distribution	Description
Normal	Continuous probability distribution, defined by a mean and variance
Binomial	Discrete probability distribution of a number of successes in a sequence of n independent yes/no experiments, which yields success with probability p
Poisson	Discrete probability distribution for the number of (independent) events occurring in a specified interval

The linear predictor is of the following form:

$$\gamma = \theta_0 + \theta_1 X_1 + \theta_2 X_2 + \dots + \theta_N X_N$$

Here, the linear predictor (γ) is linearly related to N Independent Variables (X_1 to X_N), with parameters (θ_0 to θ_N) to be estimated by the model-fitting process.

The link function (g) is of the format $g(\mu) = \gamma$ and specifies how the linear predictor (γ) is related to the mean of the Dependent Variable, $E(Y) = \mu$.

The variance function (V) explains how the variance of the Dependent Variable $var\ (Y)$, depends on its mean (μ), specified as $var\ (Y) = \phi V(\mu)$. The variance function is typically dictated by the selected probability distribution.

Fitting a GLM

We can use the `glm` function to fit a Generalized Linear Model (GLM) in R. The key inputs to the `glm` function are listed in Table 17.2.

TABLE 17.2   Key Inputs to `glm`

Method	Description
formula	Formula specifying the model (that is, relationship) to be fitted.
data	(Optional) Data frame containing the data (if variables are referenced directly).
family	A description of the error distribution and link function to be used in the model.
na.action	A function that controls the behavior when missing values are encountered. By default, observations involved in the model that include at least one missing value are excluded using the `na.omit` function.

The `formula`, `data`, and `na.action` inputs are similar to the arguments seen with the `lm` function. Here, the formula describes the linear predictor we wish to model. The `family` input describes the link and variance function to be applied by the GLM framework. The `family` argument is typically specified as a character string or function. Some common examples are seen in Table 17.3, with further detail found in the `?family` help file.

TABLE 17.3   GLM Family Inputs

Family	Link Function	Variance Function
gaussian	Identity: $g(\mu) = \mu$	$V(\mu) = 1$
binomial	logit: $g(\mu) = logit(\mu) = \log\left(\dfrac{\mu}{1-\mu}\right)$	$V(\mu) = \mu(1 - \mu)$
poisson	log: $g(\mu) = log(\mu)$	$V(\mu) = \mu$

Fitting Gaussian Models

In Hour 16, we used the lm function to fit Linear Models to our data. This is, perhaps, the simplest case of the GLM framework, where

▶ The probability distribution is Gaussian.

▶ The link function is the identity function (because the linear predictor describes the Dependent Variance directly, without transformation).

Thus, we can re-create a model from the previous chapter by instead using the glm function, as shown here:

```
> lmModel <- lm(mpg ~ wt * hp + factor(cyl), data = mtcars)    # Model fit with lm
> lmModel

Call:
lm(formula = mpg ~ wt * hp + factor(cyl), data = mtcars)

Coefficients:
 (Intercept)             wt              hp   factor(cyl)6   factor(cyl)8           wt:hp
    47.33733       -7.30634        -0.10333       -1.25907       -1.45434         0.02395

> glmModel <- glm(mpg ~ wt * hp + factor(cyl), data = mtcars) # Model fit with glm
> glmModel

Call:  glm(formula = mpg ~ wt * hp + factor(cyl), data = mtcars)

Coefficients:
 (Intercept)             wt              hp   factor(cyl)6   factor(cyl)8           wt:hp
    47.33733       -7.30634        -0.10333       -1.25907       -1.45434         0.02395

Degrees of Freedom: 31 Total (i.e. Null);  26 Residual
Null Deviance:      1126
Residual Deviance: 126.2     AIC: 148.7
```

We can see that the coefficients of both models match, as do the residuals produces from the models:

```
> all(signif(resid(lmModel), 10) == signif(resid(glmModel), 10))
[1] TRUE
```

NOTE

Default Family

Note here that "gaussian" is the default value of the family input, so we do not need to specify it here.

The `glm` **Object**

As with our earlier `lm` examples, the `glm` function returns an object that can be interrogated using a series of standard methods. A number of these standard methods can be seen in Table 17.4.

TABLE 17.4 Common GLM Methods

Method	Action
print	Concise summary of model. (`print` is called invisibly when we run the name of the object.)
summary	Detailed summary of the model fit.
plot	Diagnostic plots illustrating the model fit.
anova	Analysis of Variance for the model, or many nested models.
update	Change some aspect of the model to create a new model.
predict	Make predictions based on the model.
resid	Extract residuals from the model.
fitted	Extract fitted values of the model.
coef	Extract model coefficients.
deviance	Return the deviance of the model.

Detailed Summary

We can see a detailed model summary using the `summary` function, as shown here:

```
> summary(glmModel)

Call:
glm(formula = mpg ~ wt * hp + factor(cyl), data = mtcars)

Deviance Residuals:
    Min       1Q   Median       3Q      Max
-3.5309  -1.6451  -0.4154   1.3838   4.4788

Coefficients:
              Estimate Std. Error t value Pr(>|t|)
(Intercept)  47.337329   4.679790  10.115 1.67e-10 ***
wt           -7.306337   1.675258  -4.361 0.000181 ***
hp           -0.103331   0.031907  -3.238 0.003274 **
factor(cyl)6 -1.259073   1.489594  -0.845 0.405685
factor(cyl)8 -1.454339   2.063696  -0.705 0.487246
```

```
wt:hp          0.023951   0.008966   2.671 0.012865 *
---
Signif. codes:  0 '***' 0.001 '**' 0.01 '*' 0.05 '.' 0.1 ' ' 1

(Dispersion parameter for gaussian family taken to be 4.852119)

    Null deviance: 1126.05  on 31  degrees of freedom
Residual deviance:  126.16  on 26  degrees of freedom
AIC: 148.71

Number of Fisher Scoring iterations: 2
```

Diagnostic Plots

We can use the `plot` function to generate diagnostic plots of our model fit, as seen in Figure 17.1.

```
> par(mfrow = c(2, 2))
> plot(glmModel)
```

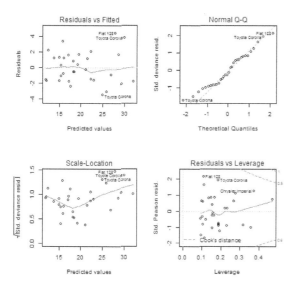

FIGURE 17.1
Diagnostic plots for GLM

Functions such as `coef`, `resid`, and `fitted` can be used to extract model aspects, as seen in the following example. This includes the creation of a plot of residuals versus fitted values, as seen in Figure 17.2.

```
> coef(glmModel)    # Model Coefficients
 (Intercept)           wt           hp factor(cyl)6 factor(cyl)8       wt:hp
 47.33732893  -7.30633653  -0.10333117  -1.25907265  -1.45433929   0.02395121
>
> res1 <- resid(glmModel)                     # Extract residuals
> fit1 <- fitted(glmModel)                    # Extract fitted values
> yRange <- c(-1, 1) * max(abs(res1))         # Calculate Y axis Range
> xRange <- range(fit1)                       # Calculate X axis Range
> xRange <- xRange + c(-1, 1) * diff(xRange)/5  # Extend X axis Range
>
> plot(fit1, res1, type = "n",                # Empty plot with axes specified
+    ylim = yRange, xlim = xRange,
+    xlab = "Fitted Values", ylab = "Residuals",
+    main = "Residuals vs Fitted Values")
> text(fit1, res1, row.names(mtcars), cex=1.2)  # Add text based on car names
> abline(h = 0, lty = 2)                      # Add horizontal reference line at 0
```

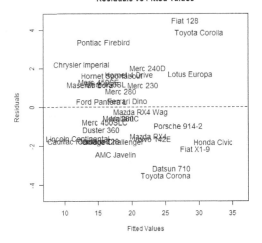

FIGURE 17.2
Plot of residuals versus fitted values for GLM

Logistic Regression

Logistic regression, or Logit Regression, is part of the GLM framework and can be implemented with the glm function. We use logistic regression to model the probability of some event occurring, based on a "dichotomous" Dependent Variable (that is, a variable with two levels specifying whether an event occurred). To achieve this, we model the log odds, so our link function (*g*) relates the Dependent Variable (Y) to the linear predictor (γ) via the logit function. Thus, $g(\mu) = \text{logit}(\mu)$ = $\log\left(\dfrac{\mu}{1 - \mu}\right)$. The Variance Function (V) is $V(\mu) = \mu(1 - \mu)$.

Fitting a Logistic Regression

We fit a Logistic Regression using the `glm` function by specifying the `binomial` family. Our response variable must contain values 0 and 1 (or `FALSE` and `TRUE`). As a simple example, let's model the am variable from the `mtcars` data based on `wt`. Here, we model the log-odds of the car having a manual transmission (am == 1) rather than an automatic transmission (am == 0), given the `wt` variable. The odds of interest can be calculated as the ratio of the probability of a manual transmission over that of an automatic one. Thus, log-odds are obtained through log transformation from the odds:

```
> lrModel <- glm(am ~ wt - 1, data = mtcars, family = binomial)
> summary(lrModel)

Call:
glm(formula = am ~ wt - 1, family = binomial, data = mtcars)

Deviance Residuals:
    Min       1Q   Median       3Q      Max
-0.9397  -0.8525  -0.7549   1.4023   1.5541

Coefficients:
   Estimate Std. Error z value Pr(>|z|)
wt  -0.2388     0.1166  -2.049   0.0405 *
---
Signif. codes:  0 '***' 0.001 '**' 0.01 '*' 0.05 '.' 0.1 ' ' 1

(Dispersion parameter for binomial family taken to be 1)

    Null deviance: 44.361  on 32  degrees of freedom
Residual deviance: 39.717  on 31  degrees of freedom
AIC: 41.717

Number of Fisher Scoring iterations: 4
```

NOTE

Removing the Intercept

We've removed the intercept in this example to better understand the resulting model coefficients.

CAUTION

Modeling Factor Levels

If the Dependent Variable specified is a two-level factor variable, R will model the probability of the second level occurring (so the first level is set as 0, and the second level as 1). If our Dependent Variable is a factor with levels "0" and "1," this works as expected; however, care should be taken if you are using an unordered factor where the levels are defined alphabetically. For example, in the following, we would be modeling the probability of Y being "Low" instead of "High" because of the default alphabetic ordering of the factor levels:

```
> lrDf <- data.frame(Y = sample(c("Low", "High"), 10, T), X = rpois(10, 3))
> lrObj <- glm(Y ~ X, data = lrDf, family = binomial)     # Logistic Model
> levels(lrDf$Y)                                           # Ordering of levels
[1] "High" "Low"
```

Predictions from a Logistic Regression

When we use the `predict` function, we are (by default) predicting on the scale of the linear predictors (that is, we're not directly predicting the responses). As such, the prediction function for our logistic example will return the log-odds of a car having a manual transmission. If we wish to see the predictions on the scale of the response, we set the `type` input to `"response"`, which instead returns the probabilities.

```
> newDf <- data.frame(wt = 1:5)
> round(predict(lrModel, newDf), 4) # Log Odds
      1       2       3       4       5
-0.2388 -0.4776 -0.7164 -0.9552 -1.1940
> round(predict(lrModel, newDf, type = "response"), 4)   # Probability
      1       2       3       4       5
0.4406  0.3828  0.3282  0.2778  0.2325
```

Coefficients from a Logistic Regression

As with predictions, the coefficients from a Logistic Regression are reported on the scale of the linear predictor. If we want to interpret the estimated effects as relative odds ratios, we simply exponentiate our coefficients as follows:

```
> round(coef(lrModel), 3)          # Log-Odds
    wt
-0.239
> round(exp(coef(lrModel)), 3)     # Odds
    wt
0.788
```

So, for every single unit increase in Weight, the odds of the car being manual (am = 1) are exected to decrease by a factor of 21% (e.g. Weight = 1, Odds = 0.79; Weight = 2, Odds = $0.79^2 = 0.62$).

Confidence Intervals for Coefficients

The `confint` function will provide confidence intervals for coefficients in a `glm` (and `lm`) model. For example, we could provide estimates and confidence intervals for model coefficients on the log-odds scale using the following:

```
> cbind(coef(lrModel), confint(lrModel))
Waiting for profiling to be done...
              [,1]          [,2]
2.5 %   -0.2388045 -0.48456168
97.5 %  -0.2388045 -0.02093423
```

Poisson Regression

We can use Poisson regression, another example from the GLM framework, to model count data. This way, we can model the number of independent "events" to occur within a fixed "interval." For a Poission regression, the link function (g) relates the Dependent Variable (Y) to the linear predictor (γ) via the log function, so $g(\mu) = log\ \mu$. The Variance Function (V) is $V(\mu) = \mu$.

Let's fit a simple Poisson regression using `glm`. For this example, we'll use the `InsectSprays` data frame, which has the counts of the number of insects based on the use of a variety of insecticides (see the `?InsectSprays` help file for more information). Before we fit the model, let's have a look at the data (seen here and in Figure 17.3):

```
> head(InsectSprays)
  count spray
1    10     A
2     7     A
3    20     A
4    14     A
5    14     A
6    12     A
> plot(factor(InsectSprays$spray), InsectSprays$count,
+      xlab = "Insecticide", ylab = "Insect Count",
+      main = "Insect Count by Insecticide")
```

Let's fit a simple Poisson model of count versus spray with no intercept term. We achieve this with `glm` by specifying `poisson` as the family input:

```
> prModel <- glm(count ~ factor(spray) - 1, data = InsectSprays, family = poisson)
> summary(prModel)

Call:
glm(formula = count ~ factor(spray) - 1, family = poisson, data = InsectSprays)
```

```
Deviance Residuals:
    Min       1Q    Median      3Q      Max
-2.3852   -0.8876   -0.1482   0.6063   2.6922


Coefficients:
               Estimate Std. Error z value Pr(>|z|)
factor(spray)A  2.67415    0.07581  35.274  < 2e-16 ***
factor(spray)B  2.73003    0.07372  37.032  < 2e-16 ***
factor(spray)C  0.73397    0.20000   3.670 0.000243 ***
factor(spray)D  1.59263    0.13019  12.233  < 2e-16 ***
factor(spray)E  1.25276    0.15430   8.119 4.71e-16 ***
factor(spray)F  2.81341    0.07071  39.788  < 2e-16 ***
---
Signif. codes:  0 '***' 0.001 '**' 0.01 '*' 0.05 '.' 0.1 ' ' 1


(Dispersion parameter for poisson family taken to be 1)

    Null deviance: 2264.808  on 72  degrees of freedom
Residual deviance:   98.329  on 66  degrees of freedom
AIC: 376.59

Number of Fisher Scoring iterations: 5
```

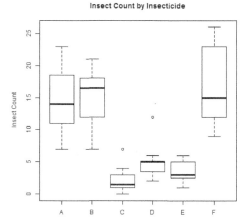

FIGURE 17.3
Plot of InsectSprays data

NOTE

Including the Intercept

Note that, by suppressing the intercept, all levels of the factor variable are estimated (as opposed to the standard use of contrasts, where the first level would be set as the baseline). If, instead, we included an intercept term, then spray "A" would be set as the baseline and other coefficients would be interpreted in relation to this level:

```
> summary(glm(count ~ factor(spray), data = InsectSprays, family = poisson))$coef
                  Estimate Std. Error   z value      Pr(>|z|)
(Intercept)      2.67414865  0.0758098 35.2744434 1.448048e-272
factor(spray)B   0.05588046  0.1057445  0.5284477 5.971887e-01
factor(spray)C  -1.94017947  0.2138857 -9.0711059 1.178151e-19
factor(spray)D  -1.08151786  0.1506528 -7.1788745 7.028761e-13
factor(spray)E  -1.42138568  0.1719205 -8.2676928 1.365763e-16
factor(spray)F   0.13926207  0.1036683  1.3433422 1.791612e-01
```

We can exponentiate the coefficients to see them on the scale of the response (that is, counts). Let's see the exponentiated coefficients next to the confidence intervals:

```
> lc <- cbind(Est = coef(prModel), confint(prModel))
Waiting for profiling to be done...
> round(exp(lc), 2)
                 Est 2.5 % 97.5 %
factor(spray)A 14.50 12.45  16.76
factor(spray)B 15.33 13.22  17.66
factor(spray)C  2.08  1.37   3.01
factor(spray)D  4.92  3.77   6.28
factor(spray)E  3.50  2.55   4.67
factor(spray)F 16.67 14.46  19.08
```

GLM Extensions

So far we have looked at some Generalized Linear Model examples. Specifically, we have seen an example of a General Linear Model, a Logistic Regression, and a Poisson Regression. There are many related approaches and extensions that may be useful, including the following:

▶ We have bypassed the fitting of Analysis of Variance models, which can be achieved with the aov function (see the ?aov help file for details).

▶ There are many other distributions supported by glm, which can be seen in the ?family help file.

▶ There are many extensions to the glm function itself, such as the glm.nb function from the **MASS** package, which includes the estimation of the additional parameter "theta."

▶ Extensions such as Generalized Estimating Equations (GEEs) allow for correlations between observations and are implemented in packages such as **gee** and **geepack**.

▶ Mixed models allow for random effects in the linear predictor and can be fit using packages such as **lme4**, **nlme**, and **glmm**.

▶ Generalized Additive Models (GAMs) allow the linear predictor to use smoothing functions applied to the Independent Variables. They are implemented in the **gam** package.

Nonlinear Models

The Generalized Linear Modeling approach allows us to fit a range of models where a Dependent Variable is related to a set of Independent Variables in a linear manner. However, R provides a range of functionality for fitting models where the function is a Nonlinear combination of parameters and depends on one or more Independent Variables.

Nonlinear Regression

The simplest form of Nonlinear model is a Nonlinear regression, which we can fit in R via least-squares estimation using the `nls` function. For Nonlinear regression,

$$Y = f(\theta_{0, ..., M}, X_{1,...,N}) + \varepsilon$$

Here, our Dependent Variable (Y) is modeled against N Independent Variables (X_1 to X_N) and M parameters (θ_0 to θ_M) to be estimated by the model-fitting process. We assume the errors (ε) are independent and identically distributed such that $E(\varepsilon) = 0$ and $var(\varepsilon) = \sigma^2$. We also assume that the errors (ε) are Normally distributed with mean 0 and variance σ^2 for the purposes of the tests.

Fitting a Nonlinear Regression

We can fit a Nonlinear model using least squares estimation with the `nls` function. The primary arguments accepted by `nls` can be seen in Table 17.5.

TABLE 17.5   Key Inputs to the `nls` Function

Argument	Description
formula	Formula specifying the relationship to be modeled
data	Data frame containing the columns used in the model
start	Named list or vector of starting values for the model
na.action	Function that controls the behavior in the presence of missing values

When we fit a Nonlinear model, it is common to define the relationship in terms of a function that accepts independent variables and parameters and returns a response.

As a very simple example, just to illustrate the use of nls, let's fit our earlier linear model (of mpg vs wt). First, we'll define a function we can use in our model fit and illustrate the use of the function with a two possible sets of input parameters (seen in Figure 17.4):

```
> linFun <- function(wt, a, b) a + b * wt
> plot(mtcars$wt, mtcars$mpg,
+       main = "Miles per Gallon versus Weight",
+       xlab = "Weight", ylab = "Miles per Gallon")
> lines(1:6, linFun(1:6, a = 40, b = -6), col = "red")
> lines(1:6, linFun(1:6, a = 35, b = -4.5), col = "blue")
> legend("topright", paste("Model", 1:2), fill = c("red", "blue"))
```

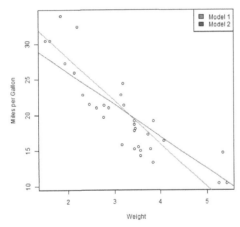

FIGURE 17.4
Plot of miles per gallon versus weight with two candidate models

If we want to fit this as a Nonlinear(!) model, we use the nls function as follows:

```
> nlsMpg <- nls(mpg ~ linFun(wt, a, b), data = mtcars)
Warning message:
In nls(mpg ~ linFun(wt, a, b), data = mtcars) :
  No starting values specified for some parameters.
Initializing 'a', 'b' to '1.'.
Consider specifying 'start' or using a selfStart model
```

Unfortunately, our model process fails because we have not provided starting values for the parameters (a and b). We can provide these as a named list or named vector of inputs. Based on the previous graph, let's choose a = 40 and b = -5 as suitable starting parameters for our model:

```
> nlsMpg <- nls(mpg ~ linFun(wt, a, b), data = mtcars,
+              start = c(a = 40, b = -5))
> nlsMpg
Nonlinear regression model
  model: mpg ~ linFun(wt, a, b)
   data: mtcars
      a      b
37.285 -5.344
 residual sum-of-squares: 278.3

Number of iterations to convergence: 1
Achieved convergence tolerance: 1.765e-09
```

As you can see, we have successfully fit our model and retrieved the parameters we would have achieved using a linear model (with the lm function):

```
> coef(nlsMpg)                     # Coefficients from the nls fit
        a         b
37.285126 -5.344472
> coef(lm(mpg ~ wt, data = mtcars))     # Coefficients from the lm fit
(Intercept)          wt
  37.285126    -5.344472
```

Let's switch to using a more appropriate example.

Nonlinear Regression of the Puromycin Data

The Puromycin data frame in R contains data on the reaction velocity versus substrate concentration in an enzymatic reaction with Puromycin (an antibiotic). The data contains measurements involving untreated and treated cells. Let's look at the data before we perform any model fitting, including a plot of the data in Figure 17.5:

```
> head(Puromycin)        # A look at the data
  conc rate    state
1 0.02   76 treated
2 0.02   47 treated
3 0.06   97 treated
4 0.06  107 treated
5 0.11  123 treated
6 0.11  139 treated
> plot(Puromycin$conc, Puromycin$rate, pch = 21, cex = 1.5,    # Plot the data
+    xlab = "Instantaneous reaction rates (counts/min/min)",
+    ylab = "Substrate Concentrations (ppm)",
+    main = "Instantaneous reaction rates vs Substrate Concentrations",
+    bg = ifelse(Puromycin$state == "treated", "red", "blue"))
> legend("bottomright", c("Treated", "Untreated"), fill = c("red", "blue"))
```

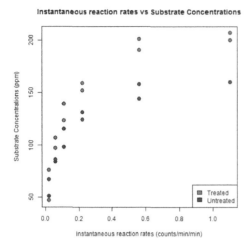

Instantaneous reaction rates vs Substrate Concentrations

FIGURE 17.5
Plot of reaction rates versus concentration from the Puromycin data

Let's attempt to fit a Michaelis-Menten model to this data, which is one of the best-known models of enzyme kinetics. Given the preceding plot, we'll fit separate models for "Treated" and "Untreated." First, we'll define the function and look at some possible starting values, overlaid on the previous plot. The output can be seen as Figure 17.6.

```
> micmen <- function(conc, Vm, K) Vm * conc / (K + conc)   # Define function
> X <- seq(0, 1.1, length = 25)                            # Set of Concentrations
>
> lines(X, micmen(xConcs, 200, 0.1), col = "pink")         # Treated: Vm = 200, K = 0.1
> lines(X, micmen(xConcs, 210, 0.03), col = "pink")        # Treated: Vm = 210, K = 0.03
> lines(X, micmen(xConcs, 210, 0.05), col = "red")         # Treated: Vm = 210, K = 0.05
>
> lines(X, micmen(xConcs, 150, 0.05), col = "lightblue")   # Untreated: Vm = 150, K = 0.05
> lines(X, micmen(xConcs, 170, 0.1), col = "lightblue")    # Untreated: Vm = 170, K = 0.1
> lines(X, micmen(xConcs, 165, 0.05), col = "blue")        # Untreated: Vm = 165, V = 0.05
```

Based on this, let's fit Nonlinear models to both the "Treated" and "Untreated" data:

```
> mmTreat <- nls(rate ~ micmen(conc, Vm, K), data = Puromycin,
+    start = c(Vm = 210, K = 0.05), subset = state == "treated")
> mmUntreat <- nls(rate ~ micmen(conc, Vm, K), data = Puromycin,
+    start = c(Vm = 165, K = 0.05), subset = state == "untreated")
> round(coef(mmTreat), 3)    # Coefficients for Treated data
     Vm       K
212.684    0.064
> round(coef(mmUntreat), 3)  # Coefficients for Untreated data
     Vm       K
160.280    0.048
```

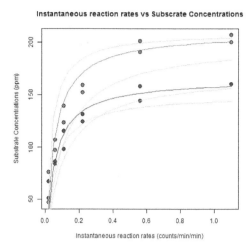

Instantaneous reaction rates vs Subscrate Concentrations

FIGURE 17.6
Plot of reaction rates versus concentration with candidate starting parameters

TIP

Self-Starting Functions

In these examples, we need to specify starting values for our model fit. However, there are a number of "self-starting" functions in R that deduce starting values as part of the modeling process. These functions start with "SS" and can be listed using the following syntax:

```
> apropos("^SS")
 [1] "SSasymp"     "SSasympOff"   "SSasympOrig"  "SSbiexp"
 [5] "SSD"         "SSfol"        "SSfpl"        "SSgompertz"
 [9] "SSlogis"     "SSmicmen"     "SSweibull"
```

Notice the SSmicmen function, which is a "self-starting" function that implements the Michaelis-Menten model. As such, we could simplify the preceding call as follows:

```
> nls(rate ~ SSmicmen(conc, Vm, K), data = Puromycin, subset = state == "treated")
Nonlinear regression model
  model: rate ~ SSmicmen(conc, Vm, K)
   data: Puromycin
       Vm          K
212.68371    0.06412
 residual sum-of-squares: 1195

Number of iterations to convergence: 0
Achieved convergence tolerance: 1.93e-06
```

Making Predictions

We can use the `predict` function to make predictions from a Nonlinear model and then use the `lines` function to add the model lines to our plot. The result of this can be seen in Figure 17.7.

```
> plot(Puromycin$conc, Puromycin$rate, pch = 21, cex = 1.5,
+       xlab = "Instantaneous reaction rates (counts/min/min)",
+       ylab = "Substrate Concentrations (ppm)",
+       main = "Instantaneous reaction rates vs Substrate Concentrations",
+       bg = ifelse(Puromycin$state == "treated", "red", "blue"))
>
> predDf <- data.frame(conc = seq(0, 1.1, length = 25))       # Set of
                                                              Concentrations
> lines(predDf$conc, predict(mmTreat, predDf), col = "red")   # Model for Treated
                                                              data
> lines(predDf$conc, predict(mmUntreat, predDf), col = "blue") # Model for
                                                              Untreated data
> legend("bottomright", c("Treated", "Untreated"), fill = c("red", "blue"))
```

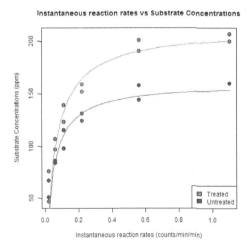

FIGURE 17.7
Plot of reaction rates versus concentration with Nonlinear model fits

Extended Model

We could extend our example to fit a single model that includes both the treated and untreated data. At the same time, we could add a new parameter to explain the difference in Vm between the two states. The outcome can be seen in Figure 17.8.

```
> # Add new parameter to out function (vTrt)
> micmen <- function(conc, state, Vm, K, vTrt) {
+    newVm <- Vm + vTrt * (state == "treated")
```

```
+    newVm * conc / (K + conc)  # Define function
+ }
> mmPuro <- nls(rate ~ micmen(conc, state, Vm, K, vTrt), data = Puromycin,
+     start = c(Vm = 160, K = 0.05, vTrt = 50))
> summary(mmPuro)

Formula: rate ~ micmen(conc, state, Vm, K, vTrt)

Parameters:
       Estimate Std. Error t value Pr(>|t|)
Vm    166.60396    5.80742  28.688  < 2e-16 ***
K       0.05797    0.00591   9.809 4.37e-09 ***
vTrt   42.02591    6.27214   6.700 1.61e-06 ***
---
Signif. codes:  0 '***' 0.001 '**' 0.01 '*' 0.05 '.' 0.1 ' ' 1

Residual standard error: 10.59 on 20 degrees of freedom

Number of iterations to convergence: 5
Achieved convergence tolerance: 9.239e-06


>
> plot(Puromycin$conc, Puromycin$rate, pch = 21, cex = 1.5,
+     xlab = "Instantaneous reaction rates (counts/min/min)",
+     ylab = "Substrate Concentrations (ppm)",
+     main = "Instantaneous reaction rates vs Substrate Concentrations",
+     bg = ifelse(Puromycin$state == "treated", "red", "blue"))
> xConc = seq(0, 1.1, length = 25)           # Set of Concentrations
> trtPred <- data.frame(conc = xConc, state = "treated")
> untrtPred <- data.frame(conc = xConc, state = "untreated")
>
> lines(predDf$conc, predict(mmPuro, trtPred), col = "red")      # Model for Treated
                                                                          data
> lines(predDf$conc, predict(mmPuro, untrtPred), col = "blue")  # Model for
                                                                    Untreated data
> legend("bottomright", c("Treated", "Untreated"), fill = c("red", "blue"))
```

If we extract the coefficients from our model, we can see the highly significant vTrt variable:

```
> round(cbind(Est = coef(mmPuro), confint(mmPuro)), 3)
Waiting for profiling to be done...
        Est    2.5%   97.5%
Vm  166.604 154.617 179.252
K     0.058   0.046   0.072
vTrt 42.026  28.957  55.199
```

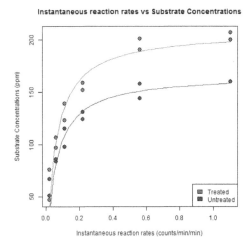

FIGURE 17.8
Plot of reaction rates versus concentration with Nonlinear model fit

Nonlinear Model Extensions

The previous section contained a very simple introduction to the Nonlinear model-fitting features of R. There are a number of extensions, including the following:

▶ The `gnls` function, which additionally allows for the correlated errors. For more information, see the `?gnls` help file.

▶ The **gnm** package, which fits Generalized Nonlinear models (analogous to the `glm` function for Nonlinear fits).

▶ The **nlme** package, which provides functionality for fitting Nonlinear Mixed Effects models.

Survival Analysis

Earlier in this hour, you saw how logistic regression can be used to model the probably of an event occurring. Survival analysis, instead, allows us to model the time until an event happens. For example, Survival analysis is used heavily in the field of medicine to understand the time until an event occurs, such as failure of an organ following transplant or time until death for someone with a terminal disease. We are interested in how a set of covariates may influence the time to event.

The `ovarian` **Data Frame**

Throughout this section we'll use a data frame called `ovarian`, which contains data from a randomized trial comparing two treatments for ovarian cancer. This data frame can be found in the **survival** package:

```
> library(survival)
> head(ovarian)
  futime fustat      age resid.ds rx ecog.ps
1     59      1 72.3315        2  1       1
2    115      1 74.4932        2  1       1
3    156      1 66.4658        2  1       2
4    421      0 53.3644        2  2       1
5    431      1 50.3397        2  1       1
6    448      0 56.4301        1  1       2
```

The columns from the `ovarian` data frame are described in Table 17.6.

TABLE 17.6   Columns of the `ovarian` Data Frame

Variable	Description
`futime`	Survival time
`fustat`	Censoring status
`age`	Age (years)
`resid.ds`	Residual disease present (1 = no, 2 = yes)
`rx`	Treatment group
`ecog.ps`	ECOG performance status

Censoring

When we are analyzing the time until an event occurs, a particular challenge is that the data may be "censored." In this case, the event has not yet occurred, so we record the last times at which we know the events had not yet occurred and flag these observations. Consider if we wanted to understand the time an organ survives following a transplant. There are three possible outcomes:

▶ The organ is still functioning, so the failure of this organ has not yet occurred.

▶ The patient died as a result of something other than the organ failing.

▶ The organ failed, so the "event" has occurred.

In the first two situations, the time is "censored" as we know the time until the "event" had not occurred, but cannot observe the time until the "event" itself.

In the case of our `ovarian` data frame, the time and "censor" flag are recorded in the `futime` and `fustat` variables.

```
> aggregate(ovarian$futime, list(State = ovarian$fustat),
+   function(x) c(Min = min(x), Median = median(x), Max = max(x)))
  State x.Min x.Median  x.Max
1     0 377.0    786.5 1227.0
2     1  59.0    359.0  638.0
```

Here, the censored times are those with State 0. We can create an object that combines these variables into a single object with the `Surv` function, as follows:

```
> ovSurv <- Surv(ovarian$futime, event = ovarian$fustat)
> ovSurv
 [1]   59   115   156   421+  431   448+  464   475   477+  563   638   744+  769+
➥770+
[15]  803+  855+ 1040+ 1106+ 1129+ 1206+ 1227+  268   329   353   365   377+
```

Note the + suffix for censored values (that is, observations where the event has not yet occurred).

Estimating the Survival Function

Much of Survival analysis is concerned with modeling and estimating the "Survival Function" (S), which provides the probability that an individual will survive a certain time (t). Formally,

$S(t) = P(T > t)$ for times $T \geq 0$

Consider the graphical representation of an example of a Survival Function shown in Figure 17.9.

Note that the probability of surviving past time t = 40 in Figure 17.9 is 39%. There are other characteristics of a Survival Function as t ranges from 0 to ∞, such as the following:

▶ The Survival Function is decreasing (or at least is non-increasing).

▶ Typically, the probability of surviving past time 0 is 1, so S(0) = 1.

▶ The probability of surviving at time ∞ is 0, so S(∞) = 0.

We can estimate the Survival Function using either non-parametric or parametric approaches.

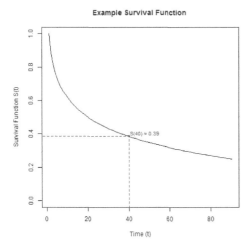

FIGURE 17.9
Example of a Survival Function

Kaplan-Meier Estimate

The "Kaplan-Meier" estimator (or "product limit" estimator) is the most popular non-parametric method statistic used to estimate the Survival Function. We can produce a Kaplan-Meier estimate in R using the `survfit` function. The first argument to the `survfit` function should be a formula with a survival object (such as the one we produced earlier) on its left hands side. To estimate a single Survival Function, we specify "1" on the right side, as follows:

```
> kmOv   <- survfit(ovSurv ~ 1)
> kmOv
Call: survfit(formula = ovSurv ~ 1)


records   n.max n.start  events  median 0.95LCL 0.95UCL
     26      26      26      12     638     464      NA
```

The `survfit` function returns an object of class "survfit," which has a few methods available. The `summary` method returns the estimated Survival Function along with confidence intervals:

```
> summary(kmOv)
Call: survfit(formula = ovSurv ~ 1)

 time n.risk n.event survival std.err lower 95% CI upper 95% CI
   59     26       1    0.962  0.0377        0.890        1.000
  115     25       1    0.923  0.0523        0.826        1.000
  156     24       1    0.885  0.0627        0.770        1.000
```

268	23	1	0.846	0.0708	0.718	0.997
329	22	1	0.808	0.0773	0.670	0.974
353	21	1	0.769	0.0826	0.623	0.949
365	20	1	0.731	0.0870	0.579	0.923
431	17	1	0.688	0.0919	0.529	0.894
464	15	1	0.642	0.0965	0.478	0.862
475	14	1	0.596	0.0999	0.429	0.828
563	12	1	0.546	0.1032	0.377	0.791
638	11	1	0.497	0.1051	0.328	0.752

The `plot` method allows us to produce a graph of the Kaplan-Meier estimate, seen in Figure 17.10.

```
> plot(kmOv, col = "blue",
+    main = "Kaplan-Meier Plot of Ovarian Data",
+    xlab = "Time (t)", ylab = "Survival Function S(t)")
```

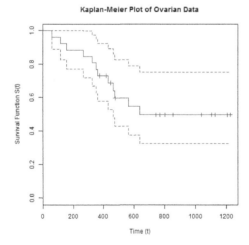

FIGURE 17.10
Kaplan-Meier plot of ovarian data

Parametric Methods

We can estimate the Survival Function using parametric methods with probability distributions such as Weibull, Exponential, and Log-Normal. In this case, we use maximum likelihood estimation to estimate the (unknown) parameters of the selected distribution. Let's use the Weibull distribution to model the Survival, such that $S(t) = \exp(-\alpha * t^\gamma)$. We can fit a parametric survival model using the `survreg` function, which has a `dist` input for specifying the distribution:

```
> wbOv <- survreg(ovSurv ~ 1, dist = "weibull")
> summary(wbOv)

Call:
survreg(formula = ovSurv ~ 1, dist = "weibull")
            Value Std. Error      z        p
(Intercept)  7.111      0.293 24.292 2.36e-130
Log(scale)  -0.103      0.254 -0.405  6.86e-01

Scale= 0.902

Weibull distribution
Loglik(model)= -98   Loglik(intercept only)= -98
Number of Newton-Raphson Iterations: 5
n= 26
```

If we want to plot the line, there are two possible options:

▶ Manually transform the parameters into a Weibull curve

▶ Use the `predict` function

Let's use the `predict` function, which allows us to produce a number of predictions from a "survfit" object. We can specify "quantile" predictions using `type = "quantile"`, using the p argument to specify the quantiles for which to provide predictions. Because we have no covariates, we need to provide a "dummy" dataset for the `newdata` argument as follows:

```
> pct <- seq(.0,.99,by=.01)                 # Quantiles at which to predict
> dummyDf <- data.frame(1)                   # Dummy dataset
> predOv <- predict(wbOv, newdata = dummyDf, # Make Quantile predictions
+   type = "quantile", p = pct)
> head(predOv)
[1]  0.00000 19.28838 36.22041 52.46544 68.33554 83.97347
```

This returns a set of predicted time points for the specified quantiles. We can overlay these predictions onto our Kaplan-Meier plot, the output of which can be seen in Figure 17.11.

```
> plot(kmOv, col = "blue",
+      main = "Kaplan-Meier Plot of Ovarian Data",
+      xlab = "Time (t)", ylab = "Survival Function S(t)")
> lines(predOv, 1 - pct, col = "red")
> legend("bottomleft", c("Kaplan-Meier", "Weibull"), fill = c("blue", "red"))
```

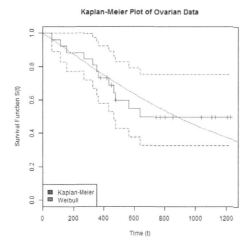

FIGURE 17.11
Survival plot of ovarian data with Kaplan-Meier and Weibull

Adding Covariates

We can easily add independent variables in the parametric model fit by specifying them on the right side of our formula. Let's model survival against age using our `ovarian` data:

```
> wbOv2 <- survreg(ovSurv ~ age, dist = "weibull", data = ovarian)
> summary(wbOv2)

Call:
survreg(formula = ovSurv ~ age, data = ovarian, dist = "weibull")
             Value Std. Error     z        p
(Intercept) 12.3970     1.4821  8.36  6.05e-17
age         -0.0962     0.0237 -4.06  4.88e-05
Log(scale)  -0.4919     0.2304 -2.14  3.27e-02

Scale= 0.611

Weibull distribution
Loglik(model)= -90   Loglik(intercept only)= -98
    Chisq= 15.91 on 1 degrees of freedom, p= 6.7e-05
Number of Newton-Raphson Iterations: 5
n= 26
```

Let's again use the `predict` function to create estimated Survival curves from different age groups. The output can be seen in Figure 17.12.

```
> ageDf <- data.frame(age = 10*4:6)          # Set of ages for predictions
> theCols <- c("red", "blue", "green")       # Colors to use
> predOv <- predict(wbOv2, newdata = ageDf,  # Make Quantile predictions
+   type = "quantile", p = pct)
> matplot(t(predOv), 1-pct, xlim = c(0, 1200),  # Matrix plot of predicted survival
+   type = "l", lty = 1, col = theCols,
+   main = "Parametric Estimation of Survival Curve by Age",
+   xlab = "Time (t)", ylab = "Survival Function S(t)")
> legend("bottomleft", paste("Age =", ageDf$age), fill = theCols)
```

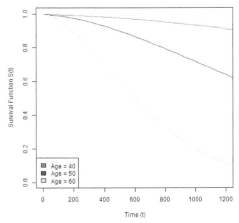

FIGURE 17.12
Estimated survival by age

Proportional Hazards

Proportional Hazards regression (or "Cox" regression) provides an excellent framework for modeling time to event data when we want to test many independent variables. In particular, Proportional Hazards regression provides a framework for understanding how differing levels of covariates increase the "risk" on a subject.

Proportional Hazards regression focuses on models of the "Hazard" Function (h), which can be considered as the probability of an event during an infinitesimally small period of time, and thus represents the "risk" of an event occurring at a specific point in time given that it hasn't happened up to that point.

When we introduce Independent Variables into a Proportional Hazards regression, we can consider the Survival Model to have two components:

▶ An underlying baseline Hazard Function describing the "risk" over time at baseline levels of covariates

▶ The effect parameters describing how the Hazard varies due to other (non-baseline) levels of covariates

For a Proportional Hazards model to be suitable, the "Proportional Hazards condition" must hold, which states that covariates are related to the hazard in a multiplicative sense. We'll check this assumption later.

To fit a Proportional Hazards model in R, we use the coxph function, and again we define the model to fit as a formula with a survival object on the left side:

```
> coxModel <- coxph(ovSurv ~ age + factor(rx), data = ovarian)
> summary(coxModel)
Call:
coxph(formula = ovSurv ~ age + factor(rx), data = ovarian)

  n= 26, number of events= 12

                coef exp(coef)  se(coef)       z Pr(>|z|)
age          0.14733   1.15873   0.04615   3.193  0.00141 **
factor(rx)2 -0.80397   0.44755   0.63205  -1.272  0.20337
---
Signif. codes:  0 '***' 0.001 '**' 0.01 '*' 0.05 '.' 0.1 ' ' 1

            exp(coef) exp(-coef) lower .95 upper .95
age            1.1587      0.863    1.0585     1.268
factor(rx)2    0.4475      2.234    0.1297     1.545

Concordance= 0.798  (se = 0.091 )
Rsquare= 0.457   (max possible= 0.932 )
Likelihood ratio test= 15.89  on 2 df,   p=0.0003551
Wald test          = 13.47  on 2 df,   p=0.00119
Score (logrank) test = 18.56  on 2 df,   p=9.341e-05
```

The age variable is significant in our model, but not the rx variable. Because the model is based on the hazard, the coefficients of the model can be interpreted in relation to the baseline level for each covariate. In fact, the coefficients returned are the log-hazards relative to the baseline, so the exponentiated coefficients (also reported) are the relative risk of change.

▶ For factor variables, the exp(coef) values are the risks relative to the baseline level. So, in our example, the risk in treatment group 2 is approximately 45% of that of group 1.

▶ For continuous variables, the `exp(coef)` values are the risks relative to a unit change in the covariate. So, in our example, the increased risk for a subject 5 years older than another is `exp(5 * 0.147) = 2.085`.

TIP

Testing the Proportional Hazards Assumption

We can use the `cox.zph` function to test the assumption of Proportional Hazards. We look for small p-values as an indication that the proportionality assumption is not met.

```
> cox.zph(coxModel)
             rho chisq     p
age      -0.0918 0.113 0.736
factor(rx)2 0.2072 0.518 0.472
GLOBAL        NA 0.729 0.695
```

So, it looks like the assumption holds for our model.

Plotting a Proportional Hazards Model

The `plot` and `survfit` functions can be used together to produce survival plots on the basis of a Proportional Hazards model. First of all, we call `survfit` with our model object. Note that we are including only the significant age variable in this model:

```
> coxModel <- coxph(ovSurv ~ age, data = ovarian)
> coxSurv <- survfit(coxModel)
> summary(coxSurv)
Call: survfit(formula = coxModel)
```

time	n.risk	n.event	survival	std.err	lower 95% CI	upper 95% CI
59	26	1	0.988	0.0142	0.961	1.000
115	25	1	0.974	0.0244	0.927	1.000
156	24	1	0.955	0.0364	0.886	1.000
268	23	1	0.933	0.0482	0.844	1.000
329	22	1	0.897	0.0621	0.783	1.000
353	21	1	0.862	0.0724	0.732	1.000
365	20	1	0.824	0.0819	0.678	1.000
431	17	1	0.775	0.0934	0.612	0.982
464	15	1	0.724	0.1032	0.548	0.958
475	14	1	0.673	0.1112	0.487	0.931
563	12	1	0.596	0.1226	0.398	0.892
638	11	1	0.520	0.1287	0.321	0.845

Now we can use the plot function to produce our survival curves, as seen in Figure 17.13.

```
> plot(coxSurv, col = "blue", xlab = "Time (t)",
+      ylab = "Survival Function S(t)",
+      main = "Proportional Hazards Model")
```

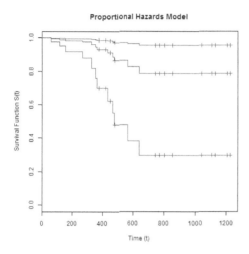

FIGURE 17.13
Estimated survival using Proportional Hazards model

We can provide a new data frame to the survfit function if we want to produce Survival curves for different sets of covariates. For example, let's produce different Survival curves for the different age values as we did for the parametric model fits. We'll overlay the original parametric model fits for these age values using dashed lines for comparison. The output can be seen in Figure 17.14.

```
> coxSurv <- survfit(coxModel, newdata = ageDf)     # Survival curves for age
                                                       values
> plot(coxSurv, col = theCols, xlab = "Time (t)",   # Plot the survival curves
+      ylab = "Survival Function S(t)",
+      main = "Proportional Hazards Model")
> matlines(t(predOv), 1-pct,                         # Add parametric curves
+    type = "l", lty = 2, col = theCols)
> legend("bottomleft", paste("Age =", ageDf$age), fill = theCols)
```

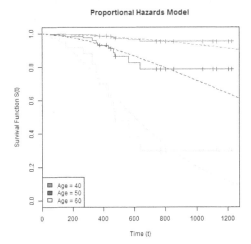

FIGURE 17.14
Estimated survival for different ages using Proportional Hazards model

Survival Model Extensions

R provides a rich set of capabilities for the analysis of time to event data. The best source of information is the Survival Analysis Task View (https://cran.r-project.org/web/views/Survival. html), which lists over 200 packages that are related the study of survival data.

Time Series Analysis

R is used heavily in areas such as quantitative finance and econometrics; unsurprisingly, it provides a wide range of time series analysis functionality. Although a number of packages provide time series analysis capabilities, we will focus here on the functions loaded in the basic **stats** package that is loaded when we start R. In this section, we will see

- ▶ How to create and manage time series objects
- ▶ How to perform simple decomposition and smoothing
- ▶ How to fit an ARIMA model

Time Series Objects

We can create a time series object in R with the `ts` function. Once created, these objects can be used in a range of analytic and graphical routines. The `ts` function accepts a vector or matrix containing the data.

As an example, the website boxofficemojo.com reports daily gross income for film releases. One of the highest grossing films of 2015 was *Avengers: Age of Ultron*, which grossed over $425m in its first month (May 2015). The daily takings during that first month are as follows:

```
> ultron <- c(84.4, 56.5, 50.3, 13.2, 13.1, 9.4, 8.6, 21.2, 33.8, 22.7,
+    5.4, 6, 4.3, 4, 10, 17.2, 11.6, 3.4, 3, 2.3, 2.4, 5.4, 8.3, 8, 6.5,
+    1.9, 1.4, 1.4, 2.9, 4.9, 3.6)
```

If we wanted to create a time series of this data, we could use the `ts` function. We often specify time series elements such as the "start" date/time of the series, but for this example we'll simply specify the data and the frequency as 7 (that is, weekly data).

```
> tsUltron <- ts(ultron, frequency = 7)
> tsUltron
Time Series:
Start = c(1, 1)
End = c(5, 3)
Frequency = 7
 [1] 84.4 56.5 50.3 13.2 13.1  9.4  8.6 21.2 33.8 22.7  5.4  6.0  4.3
[14]  4.0 10.0 17.2 11.6  3.4  3.0  2.3  2.4  5.4  8.3  8.0  6.5  1.9
[27]  1.4  1.4  2.9  4.9  3.6
```

Once we have a time series object created, we can use the `plot` function to create a simple time series plot, as shown in Figure 17.15.

```
> plot(tsUltron, main = "Daily Box Office Daily for Avengers: Age of Ultron",
+       xlab = "Week during May 2015", ylab = "Daily Gross ($m)")
> points(tsUltron, pch = 21, bg = "red")
```

If, as in this example, the data is not linear, we may want to apply a transformation. For example, let's apply a log transformation to our example, which can be seen in Figure 17.16.

```
> plot(log(tsUltron), main = "Daily Box Office Daily for Avengers: Age of Ultron",
+       xlab = "Week during May 2015", ylab = "Log Daily Gross ($m)")
> points(log(tsUltron), pch = 21, bg = "red")
```

TIP

Selecting a Subset of the Time Series

If we want to subset a time series, we can use the `window` function. To specify the subset, we need to provide a start and/or end relative to the frequency. So, to select only data for the first week, we request the series up to the seventh element of the first week, as follows:

```
> window(tsUltron, end = c(1, 7))
Time Series:
Start = c(1, 1)
End = c(1, 7)
Frequency = 7
[1] 84.4 56.5 50.3 13.2 13.1  9.4  8.6
```

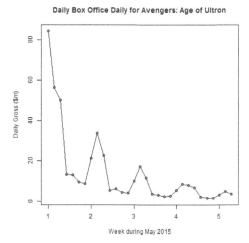

FIGURE 17.15
Time series plot of daily grossing of *Avengers: Age of Ultron*

FIGURE 17.16
Time series plot of (logged) daily grossing of *Avengers: Age of Ultron*

Decomposing Time Series

A common task in the field of time series analysis is decomposition, where we attempt to separate a time series into components. This could include

▶ A seasonal element (for example, weekly, monthly, or annually)

▶ An overall trend

▶ Remaining data not fully explained by the first two elements

We can perform a simple seasonal decomposition in R using the `stl` function, which uses loess smoothers to decompose a time series into seasonal, trend, and irregular components. Let's use the `stl` function to perform a simple decomposition of our *Age of Ultron* data, which we can graph directly using the `plot` function. The resulting graphic can be seen in Figure 17.17.

```
> stlUltron <- stl(log(tsUltron), s.window = "periodic")
> plot(stlUltron, main = "Decomposition of the Ultron Time Series")
```

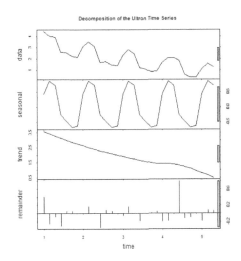

FIGURE 17.17
Decomposition of (logged) daily grossing of *Avengers: Age of Ultron*

The output from the `stl` function is an object of class "stl." It includes a `time.series` element we can query or plot directly:

```
> window(stlUltron$time.series, end = c(1, 7))
Time Series:
Start = c(1, 1)
End = c(1, 7)
Frequency = 7
          seasonal     trend    remainder
1.000000  0.4330473  3.598952   0.403568367
1.142857  0.8490648  3.441404  -0.256228394
```

```
1.285714   0.7104135 3.283857 -0.076264998
1.428571  -0.2510144 3.131462 -0.300230859
1.571429  -0.4588637 2.979068  0.052408283
1.714286  -0.6741455 2.868556  0.046299129
1.857143  -0.6085021 2.758045  0.002219731
```

We can also use this to remove components from our time series. For example, we could remove the seasonal element from our time series and then plot the remaining data, as seen in Figure 17.18.

```
> seUltron <- log(tsUltron) - stlUltron$time.series[,"seasonal"]
> plot(seUltron,
+    main = "Logged Daily Box Office Gross\n(Weekly seasonality removed)",
+    xlab = "Weeks in May 2015", ylab = "Logged Daily Box Office Gross ($m)")
```

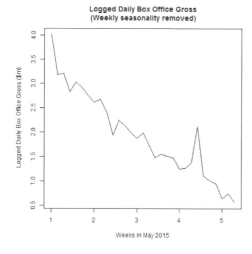

FIGURE 17.18
Logged daily grossing of *Avengers: Age of Ultron* with seasonality removed

NOTE

Outlying Value

The large spike in this time series was May 25, 2015, which was Memorial Day, so figures were higher than expected for a Monday.

Smoothing

We may want to perform some smoothing on our time series to provide short-term forecasts. Exponential smoothing techniques apply exponentially, decreasing weights to less recent observations, and therefore can be a more appropriate approach than using moving averages. However, simple exponential smoothing can only be used for data without systematic trend or seasonality.

The Holt-Winters method can be applied to time series, which contain both trend and seasonality. This approach can be performed using the `HoltWinters` function in R. The primary inputs to the `HoltWinters` function are described in Table 17.7.

TABLE 17.7   Key Inputs to the `HoltWinters` Function

Input	Description
x	The time series object (of class `ts`).
alpha	The alpha parameter of the Holt-Winters filter.
beta	The beta parameter of the Holt-Winters filter. If it's set to `FALSE`, the function will perform exponential smoothing.
gamma	The gamma parameter of the Holt-Winters filter. If it's set to `FALSE`, a non-seasonal model is fitted.
seasonal	Version of the method to apply: "additive" (default) or "multiplicative."

Let's use the Holt-Winters method with our *Age of Ultron* data. The results are visualized in Figure 17.19.

```
> hwUltron <- HoltWinters(log(tsUltron))
> plot(hwUltron)
```

Once we have used the Holt-Winters method, we can make predictions using the `predict` function, which accepts the argument `n.ahead` to specify the number of predictions to make. We can also specify the argument `prediction.interval` to request for (95% by default) prediction intervals. Because we have the actual values, we have overlaid these too, as shown in Figure 17.20.

```
> predUltron <- predict(hwUltron, n.ahead = 7,          # Predict 7 days with
                                                         #   H-W method
+   prediction.interval = TRUE)
> plot(hwUltron, predUltron, col = "red",               # Plot data and
                                                         #   predictions
+   col.predicted = "blue", col.intervals = "blue",
+   lty.intervals = 2)
> actuals <- c(1.08, 1.26, .97, .95, 1.84, 2.66, 1.84)  # Actual values
```

```
> tsActuals <- ts(actuals, frequency = 7, start = c(5, 4))   # Create time series
> lines(log(tsActuals), col = "darkgreen")                    # Add line
> points(log(tsActuals), pch = 4, col = "darkgreen")          # Add points
> legend("bottomleft", c("Original Data", "Holt-Winters Filter", "Actual Data"),
+     fill = c("red", "blue", "grey"))
```

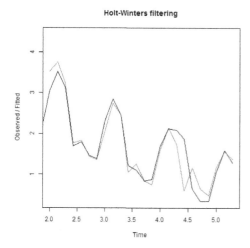

FIGURE 17.19
Holt-Winters filtering of the logged daily box office takings for *Avengers: Age of Ultron*

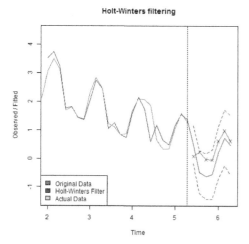

FIGURE 17.20
Holt-Winters predictions versus actual logged daily box office takings for *Avengers: Age of Ultron*

Autocorrelations

Although smoothing approaches can provides us with a mechanism for generating short-term forecasts, to understand the mechanisms for a time series we must first investigate its autocorrelation. That is, the cross-correlation of a time series with lagged values of the same series. We can create a plot of the Autocorrelation Function (a "correlogram") using the acf function in R. We can also create Partial Autocorrelation plots using the pacf function. Both of these plots can be seen in Figure 17.21.

```
> par(mfrow = c(1, 2))
> acf(log(tsUltron), main = "Autocorrelation")
> pacf(log(tsUltron), main = "Partial Autocorrelation")
```

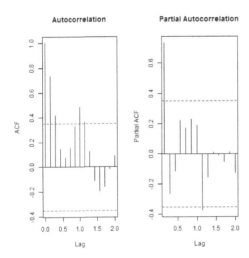

FIGURE 17.21
Correlograms of logged daily box office takings for *Avengers: Age of Ultron*

TIP

The forecast Package

The **forecast** package provides excellent resources for time series analysis. Among other things, it provides enhanced versions of acf and pacf called Acf and Pacf.

Fitting ARIMA Models

An Autoregressive Integrated Moving Average (or "ARIMA") Model can be fit to understand and predict time series data. The ARIMA Model consists of three components:

▶ **AR**: Autoregressive

▶ **I**: Integrated (differencing that can be applied)

▶ **MA**: Moving Average

We can fit an ARIMA Model in R using the `arima` function, which accepts a time series object. We specify the order of the time series using a vector of length three (p, d, q), which specifies

▶ **p**, the AR order

▶ **d**, the degree of differencing

▶ **q**, the MA order

Based on these autocorrelations, let's fit an ARIMA (1, 0, 1) Model to our time series:

```
> arimaUltron <- arima(log(tsUltron), order = c(1, 0, 1))
> arimaUltron

Call:
arima(x = log(tsUltron), order = c(1, 0, 1))

Coefficients:
          ar1     ma1    intercept
       0.7627  0.3782       2.1785
s.e.   0.1428  0.1883       0.5470

sigma^2 estimated as 0.3278:  log likelihood = -27.46,  aic = 62.93
```

We can see a visual representation of the time series fit using the `tsdiag` function, which produces diagnostic plots for time series fits. Specifically, it will plot standardized residuals, an autocorrelation of the residuals, and p-values from a Portmanteau test. This output is shown in Figure 17.22.

```
> tsdiag(arimaUltron)
```

The residuals still exhibit signs of seasonality, which is understandable since we are fitting an ARIMA Model to a time series with seasonality. At this point, we could de-trend the time series and remove the seasonal trend (for example, using the `stl` function) and then refit the model. Alternatively, we could fit a seasonal ARIMA Model using the `seasonal` argument to `arima`, which also accepts a vector of length 3 (specifying the autoregressive, differencing, and moving average components of the seasonal element to the time series). Let's fit a seasonal ARIMA model to our data, as seen in Figure 17.23.

```
> sarimaUltron <- arima(log(tsUltron), order = c(1, 0, 1),
+    seasonal = list(order = c(1, 0, 1)))
> tsdiag(sarimaUltron)
```

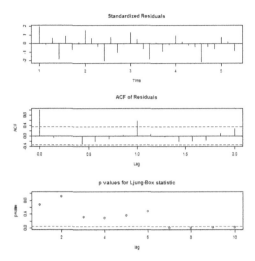

FIGURE 17.22
Diagnostic plots from ARIMA (1, 0, 1) fit

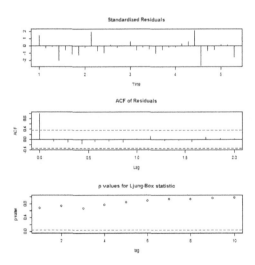

FIGURE 17.23
Diagnostic plots from seasonal ARIMA (1, 0, 1) fit

Predicting from ARIMA Models

We can predict values from an ARIMA Model using the `predict` function, which accepts an `n.ahead` input. Let's see our model predictions plotted against the real observations. The output can be seen in Figure 17.24.

```
> predUltron <- predict(sarimaUltron, n.ahead = 7,    # Predict next 7 days with
                                                          ARIMA model
+       prediction.interval = TRUE)
> plot(log(tsUltron), type = "n",
+       main = "Predictions from ARIMA(1,0,1) Model",
+       ylab = "Logged Daily Box Office Takings",
+       xlab = "Day", xlim = c(1, 6.3), ylim = c(-1, 5))
> lines(log(tsUltron), col = "red")                      # Add original data
> lines(predUltron$pred, col = "blue")                   # Add predictions
> lines(predUltron$pred - 2 * predUltron$se, col = "blue", lty = 2)  # Add errors
> lines(predUltron$pred + 2 * predUltron$se, col = "blue", lty = 2)  # Add errors
> lines(log(tsActuals), col = "darkgreen")               # Add line
> points(log(tsActuals), pch = 4, col = "darkgreen")     # Add line
>
> legend("bottomleft",
+   c("Original Data", "ARIMA Predictions", "Actual Data"),
+   fill = c("red", "blue", "grey"))
```

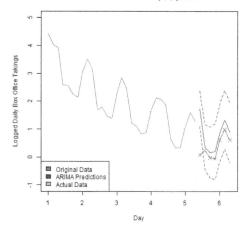

FIGURE 17.24
Time series predictions from ARIMA Model

TIP

Covariates

We can add covariates to an ARIMA Model using the `xreg` input to the `arima` function.

NOTE

Time Series Analysis Extensions

The Time Series Task View, found at https://cran.r-project.org/web/views/TimeSeries.html, lists a wider range of packages that allow the user to perform a range of time series tasks and analyses.

Summary

This hour covered a range of modeling approaches that can be used to study different data types. Specifically, we saw how the `glm` function allows us to fit Generalized Linear Models, looked at the `nls` function for Nonlinear Model Nonlinearfits, used the **survival** package to model time-to-event data, and covered a few of the time series analysis capabilities of R. The capabilities seen in this and the previous hour demonstrate only a small portion of the analytic functionality provided by R.

Q&A

Q. Is there a way of fitting Generalized Linear Models on very large data sizes?

A. Although limitations exist, the **biglm** package provides the function `bigglm`, which allows out-of-memory Generalized Linear Model fitting.

Q. Can I create my own "self-starting" functions?

A. Yes, the `selfStart` function can be used to define a self-starting function that can then be used in a function such as `nls`.

Q. How do I define left or interval censored data?

A. The `Surv` function allows you to specify left, right, or interval censored data using the `time`, `time2`, and `type` arguments.

Q. Does R provide ARCH time series modeling capabilities?

A. Yes, there are a number of packages (such as **fGarch**) that implement (G)ARCH models.

Workshop

The workshop contains quiz questions and exercises to help you solidify your understanding of the material covered. Try to answer all questions before looking at the "Answers" section that follows.

Quiz

1. What argument in `glm` controls the probability distribution to use?

2. How would you fit a logistic regression?

3. Under what condition would you not have to specify starting values in an `nls` fit?

4. In which package would you find the `coxph` function?

5. How would you fit a "seasonal ARIMA" model?

Answers

1. The `family` argument.

2. You specify a dichotomous response variable and select "binomial" as the distribution.

3. When you are using a "self-starting" modeling function.

4. In the **survival** package.

5. Using the `arima` function, specifying the `order` and `seasonal` inputs.

Activities

1. Using the `mtcars` data frame, fit a logistic model of `vs` versus other variables in the data.

2. For a (Nonlinear) logistic function of `circumference` versus `age` from the `Orange` data frame, either specify the model function directly or use the `SSlogis` function.

3. Fit a Cox Proportional Hazards regression model to the `lung` data frame from the **survival** package.

4. Fit an ARIMA model of the `LakeHuron` time series.

Code Efficiency

What You'll Learn in This Hour:

▶ How to profile code to find the bottlenecks

▶ How to vectorize code

▶ What initialization is and how it makes code more efficient

▶ How to handle memory usage

▶ The basics of **Rcpp**

Up to this point we have thought a lot about the data analysis workflow in R—how we can read in data, analyze the data, and produce professional graphics—but we have not really thought about the impact of what we are doing and how long it will take to run the code in practice. Although we have already looked at packages such as **dplyr** and **data.table** that will help us to make working with data more efficient, we should do more to ensure our code is performant and robust. In this chapter, we are going to look at some of the techniques we can use to improve the efficiency and, importantly, the professionalism of our R code.

Determining Efficiency

Before we dive in and start spending large amounts of time making our code more efficient, it's worth thinking about where we should start on improving our code and how we know if a change has made a difference. We will start by looking at ways in which we can profile code to find out where the slow points are and then look at functions we can use to see how long it takes to run our code.

TIP

Making Accurate Changes

As well as making updates that ensure that our code runs faster, we also need to ensure that any changes do not impact the accuracy. Although it would be great to have a function that is 1,000 times faster, it is no use if this adversely changes what the function does. At a basic level, we can simply compare the output of different variants of the function. For more professional and robust code, we can use a unit test framework such as `testthat` to continuously check our changes. See Hour 20, "Advanced Package Building," for more information on unit testing.

Profiling Code

Profiling allows us to determine where the bottlenecks are in code, what is actually slowing us down. Profiling allows us to see which lines or functions we are spending the most time running. The benefit of this is that by knowing where our code is slowest, we can spend our time on increasing the efficiency of the right components of our code. After all, there is little point in increasing the efficiency of a line of code that is only a tiny percentage of the overall running time. You may as well put your time and effort into making changes in the right place.

A number of different packages are available for profiling R code, but here we will use the `Rprof` function available in base R. When we use this function, we run our code between start and close instances. This will then check at a specified interval what function is being run by our code. The output is returned to file, and we can then analyze it to determine where our code was spending most of its time. In more recent versions of R, it is possible to return this output at the line level so that we can see which lines of code we spent the most time on.

As an example, we will profile the function in Listing 18.1 shown in the next section. Because this function will run quite quickly, we will run the function a number of times using `replicate`.

```
> tmp <- tempfile()
> Rprof(filename = tmp, line.profiling = TRUE)
> replicate(100, f1(100))
> Rprof(NULL)
> summaryRprof(filename = tmp, lines = "show")
$by.line
    self.time self.pct total.time total.pct
#9       0.06      100       0.06       100
```

In this example, we have included line profiling, which makes it much easier to see which line the most time was spent on. In this particular case, the output returns only one line (line 9), which would indicate that the most time is spent performing the `ifelse` inside of the `for` loop (see Listing 18.1 in the next section). This suggests that this is the component we should focus on trying to improve. Note that the specific output you see in this case will depend on exactly how long the code takes to run, which will depend upon the machine used and the operating system, among other things.

Benchmarking

If we are going to start making changes to code, we want to know that it is making a difference and actually speeding up our functions. Benchmarking tools let us time the running of code, typically at the nanosecond level. Just as with profiling, there are a number of ways of doing this, but here we will use the **microbenchmark** package, which is widely used for code analysis. Using the `microbenchmark` function, we can pass any number of functions to be run. Each will be run a specified number of times, as defined by the `times` argument. We need to run a function more than once to determine the average time to run because there may be faster and slower occurrences, which would impact our results if we compared on a single run. The `microbenchmark` function helps us handle this and returns a series of statistics, such as the median and upper and lower quantiles of all the times.

As an example of benchmarking, we will start with the function defined in Listing 18.1. This is a simple function that samples 0 and 1 to give a vector of the length specified by the argument `len`. We will use this function as an example throughout this hour to show how we can improve our code. We can use this function in the `microbenchmark` function by simply passing the function call—for example, `f1(100)`. By default, this will be replicated 100 times.

```
> microbenchmark(f1(100))
Unit: microseconds
     expr     min      lq     mean  median      uq      max neval
 f1(100) 597.087 616.146 731.2236 624.21 662.5125 2026.94   100
```

As you can see, the output to this function is a series of summary statistics for the running time of each `replicate`. The main value of interest is the median, though in some instances the spread may also be of interest.

LISTING 18.1   Sampling Function

```
 1: f1 <- function(len){
 2:
 3:    x <- NULL
 4:
 5:    for(i in seq_len(len)){
 6:
 7:      s <- runif(1)
 8:
 9:      x[i] <- ifelse(s > 0.5, 1, 0)
10:
11:    }
12:
13:    x
14:
15: }
```

TIP

How Fast Is Fast Enough?

Before you start to make changes to your code, it is worth having an aim for how much you are looking to speed up your code by. How long will be sufficient to wait for your code to run? There are many small changes you can make to improve efficiency, but this will typically take more of your time than it is worth for the speed up you will achieve. Having an aim will allow you to focus on the changes that will help you achieve that rather than endlessly making changes for minimal gains.

Initialization

When you first start writing code, and particularly if you have a background in other languages such as C++, you are likely to write lots of loops. You have seen functions, such as the `apply` family of functions, that allow you to write some of these actions in an alternative way that would be recommended for production code.

However, sometimes you do just need to use a `for` loop. One of the common pitfalls when you do this is to create an object and then simply append to it each time you work around the loop. You can see an example of this in Listing 18.1. In this example, you can see that on line 3 an object called x is created, and then inside the `for` loop, on line 9, we append to this for each iteration of the loop. In R, this makes our code much slower because a copy is made of the vector at each iteration.

A very simple way to speed this up is to prevent R from making the copy each time. We can do this via initialization, or pre-allocation. This simply means that we create the object (in this case, a vector) before we start our loop as an object of the appropriate type and size (for instance, a numeric vector of length 10 or character vector of length 5). Now each time we work around our loop, we simply overwrite the values. This alternative implementation can be seen in Listing 18.2.

LISTING 18.2   Initialized Sampling Function

```
 1: f2 <- function(len){
 2:
 3:    x <- numeric(len)
 4:
 5:    for(i in seq_len(len)){
 6:
 7:      s <- runif(1)
 8:
 9:      x[i] <- ifelse(s > 0.5, 1, 0)
10:
11:    }
12:
```

```
13:    x
14:
15: }
```

Let's compare this to the original version of the function using `microbenchmark`.

```
> microbenchmark(f1(100), f2(100))
Unit: microseconds
      expr     min       lq      mean   median       uq       max neval
  f1(100) 582.059 616.6960  637.9074 631.3575  651.883   744.434   100
  f2(100) 532.576 567.5805  642.1922 583.8910  602.401  2666.544   100
```

You can see that this has made the function faster, though in this case there is still a significant amount more we can do to improve the efficiency.

TIP

Creating the Correct Type

In this example, we have used the function `numeric` to create a numeric vector of 0s. We can also create character and logical vectors with the functions `character` and `logical`, respectively. The advantage of this is that the vector is of the correct type before we start, and this will prevent R from having to convert the object to a different type. It can also help us out because we don't need to change the value unless we want to change it from 0 (for numeric), `""` (for character), or `FALSE` (for logical).

Vectorization

As stated in the previous section, one of the common pitfalls when starting to write R code, especially for those coming to R from other programming languages, is to use a `for` loop to perform an action over a vector of values. In R this is actually often unnecessary and makes our code run much slower. Instead, we can use R's vectorization to perform a series of actions at the same time. This will not only make the code much faster, but is a much more professional approach to take in coding in R.

What Is Vectorization?

Vectorization allows us to perform an action on an array of values, such as a vector, simultaneously. As an example, suppose we wanted to multiply the values 1 to 10 by 4. Rather than first multiply 1 by 4 and then 2 by 4 and so on, we can use vectorization to perform all 10 calculations at the same time. In R we would do the following:

```
> 4 * (1:10)
 [1]   4   8  12  16  20  24  28  32  36  40
```

As you can see, we were able to perform 10 calculations with just a single expression and no need for any loops. This will significantly speed up the code, as you will see when we look again at the example from Listing 18.1.

Note that in this particular example the brackets are not strictly necessary, but they help to make your code much clearer to read, particularly for someone picking up your code for the first time. Because we are looking at efficiency, it is worth mentioning that brackets will slow down your code very slightly, so where your preference is for very fast code, you may want to remove them. However, this will not generally be the primary cause of slow-running code, and in the latest versions of R the difference is barely measurable.

How Code Can Be Vectorized

Vectorization in R is very simple because most functions have been designed to accept a vector of values as input rather than a single, scalar value. As an example, think about the `paste` function introduced in Hour 6, "Common R Utility Functions." We actually made use of vectorization there to create a vector of values that were the strings of fruits with numeric values pasted together:

```
> fruits <- c("apples", "oranges", "pears")
> nfruits <- c(5, 9, 2)
> paste(fruits, nfruits, sep = " = ")
[1] "apples = 5"  "oranges = 9" "pears = 2"
```

So rather than having to loop round and paste the fruit to the number in turn, we do it all in one step. Some functions have even been written as a vectorized version of functions that you know. For instance, the function `ifelse` used in the examples in this hour is a vectorized version of the `if/else` structure introduced in Hour 7, "Writing Functions: Part I." Other examples include `pmin` and `pmax`, which we can use to find the minimum and maximum, respectively, for each value in a vector of values. Here's an example:

```
> pmin(0, -1:1)
[1] -1  0  0
> pmax(-1:1, 1:-1)
[1] 1 0 1
```

Let's now return to our sampling function that we have been improving. You saw how we could initialize this function in Listing 18.2, but we can actually remove the loop here altogether by vectorizing the code. There are multiple ways we can do this, and two are shown in Listing 18.3.

LISTING 18.3 Vectorized Sampling Function

```
1: f3 <- function(len){
2:
3:   s <- runif(len)
```

```
 4:
 5:   x <- ifelse(s > 0.5, 1, 0)
 6:
 7:   x
 8:
 9: }
10:
11:
12: f4 <- function(len){
13:
14:   x <- numeric(len)
15:
16:   s <- runif(len)
17:
18:   x[s > 0.5] <- 1
19:
20:   x
21:
22: }
```

In the first of these functions, f3, we have used the ifelse function. Rather than generate a single value from a uniform distribution, we have generated a complete vector of values that we will use in a single step (line 3). We can then use the vectorized ifelse (line 5) to test all values and return the appropriate 1 or 0 for each value in the vector. Before we look at the second way of doing this, let's compare f3 to our previous implementations:

```
> microbenchmark(f1(100), f2(100), f3(100))
Unit: microseconds
     expr     min       lq      mean   median       uq      max neval
  f1(100) 570.696 593.6045 999.40998 601.1185 616.8795 32061.20   100
  f2(100) 524.512 533.8590 598.32525 550.7200 562.4485  1758.27   100
  f3(100)  30.056  32.2560  47.34957  33.7220  36.8370  1211.40   100
```

Just looking at the median values here, you can see that this is a massive improvement over the original version, and even the initialized version. This approach gives us huge improvements in the running of our code, but in actual fact the second approach we can take to vectorizing this function will make even more gains.

Take a look at the function f4 that we defined in Listing 18.3 (starting on line 12). In this example, we are again initializing a vector that we will return. Just like in f3, we have generated our uniform samples in a single step, but rather than using ifelse, we have directly subscripted the vector x based on the values in the vector s. You might also notice that we have only done this to generate the values that need to be 1. This is because the initialization creates a vector of 0s, so we can cut out a step by only making a single change that we need. If we compare the two vectorized versions, we will see that this is faster yet.

```
> microbenchmark(f3(100), f4(100))
Unit: microseconds
    expr    min     lq     mean median     uq    max neval
 f3(100) 28.956 29.690 31.40153 30.057 30.973 59.012    100
 f4(100)  9.530 10.264 11.19091 10.630 11.363 50.583    100
```

Although there are vectorized functions that will speed up compared to the non-vectorized versions, it is sometimes better to work directly on the vector using basic subscripting methods.

TIP

Don't Remove Error Handling

Functions such as pmin and pmax are slower because they include a variety of arguments and
checks for the data types and such. As you can see, the direct version is much faster, but that
doesn't mean we should start to remove all error handling from our functions. If you are sharing your
code, it is much better practice—and key to production level code—to include the error handling and
make other parts of your code more efficient with the methods you have seen here.

Using Alternative Functions

Often we don't actually need to do much to our code other than use an alternative function
that has solved the problem for us or is more specific in its implementation. It is quite possible
that someone has already done what you are trying to do and solved the problem already, so
it is always worth searching available resources for an alternative function or package. As a
reminder of some of the ways in which you can search for functions and packages, take a look
at Hour 2, "The R Environment."

The example we have been using in this hour is a great illustration of such a case. The function
we wrote in Listing 18.1 is designed to randomly sample a series of 0s and 1s. In Hour 6, you
were introduced to the sample function. Clearly someone has already implemented the problem we are trying to solve, and it is likely that they have already put in the effort to make it as
efficient as possible. A final version of this function, f5, is given in Listing 18.4, where we have
simply changed the implementation to use the sample function. Let's compare this final implementation to all the other variants we have seen in this hour.

```
> microbenchmark( f1(100), f2(100), f3(100), f4(100), f5(100))
Unit: microseconds
    expr     min       lq      mean   median       uq      max neval
 f1(100) 574.727 582.4245 672.98853 596.7200 616.8795 1895.354   100
 f2(100) 524.146 545.4050 638.65877 554.0190 568.3130 1768.899   100
 f3(100)  30.423  32.6220  36.03099  33.7220  39.0365   78.806   100
 f4(100)  10.263  10.9970  23.79963  11.5465  12.0965 1211.766   100
 f5(100)   6.231   7.5145   9.31053   8.4310  10.4470   16.862   100
```

LISTING 18.4 Using the `sample` Function

```
1: f5 <- function(len){
2:
3:    sample(0:1, size = len, replace = TRUE)
4:
5: }
```

Obviously, if you don't know that the function exists, you can't use it. A great way to find functions that can help you solve a problem is to read other people's code and take a look online at the ways in which people solve similar problems to your own. Many resources are available that can help you out, and we have tried to introduce many useful functions to you in the appropriate places in this book.

Managing Memory Usage

When it comes to memory usage in R, there is actually very little we need to do to manage it ourselves. Although memory in R is taken up by temporary objects, it is automatically made available when it is needed. There is no need for us to manually free the memory on a regular basis. One of the main things we need to do is consider what objects we have created and how we will work with them.

Suppose we are working with big data sets. The packages you saw in Hour 12, "Efficient Data Handling in R," have been designed to use memory in an efficient manner, so they are strongly recommended in this case. If you do find that you are getting errors due to a lack of available memory, the first thing to do is to take a look at what objects you have created in your current R session, the size of those objects, and whether you can remove them.

In RStudio, this is made simple with the environment pane. This pane gives us summary information about all the objects in our environment, what each object is, and, importantly, its size.

TIP

Checking the Size of Objects

To see the size of an object in the environment pane, you will need to use the grid view. In the top-left corner of the pane, you will see a menu labeled either "Grid" or "List." If it says "List," you can use this to menu to switch your view. If you are not using RStudio, you will need to use the `object.size` function on each object. Remember that you can use a function such as `sapply` to do this for a number of objects at the same time.

We can remove objects from our session either using the interface in RStudio or programmatically using the function `rm`. For example, to remove object x, we would run

```
> rm(x)
```

If the object is large, we may want to force R to make the memory available again. We do this in R by using the function gc for garbage collection. This is usually done automatically when needed without the need for us to intervene.

TIP

Restart to Clear Completely

If you have been working on an analysis and creating objects to test out your method, you may want to restart R to completely clear the workspace of any unused objects, including classes and unused packages or functions. If you have been writing a script, it will be easy to re-run all of your code and get back to where you were in a completely clean environment.

Integrating with C++

We have been looking at some of the ways in which you can rewrite your code in R to make it more efficient, but in some instances it is simply not possible to improve the speed of your code using R. In those instances, you may want to turn to other tools that are more suitable for the task. In R, one of the simplest ways to extend code with much faster alternatives is by using C++, and more specifically the **Rcpp** package.

C++ is a statically typed language, which means we have to specify object types when they are created; it is also compiled, which tends to make it a much faster language than R. Although it has always been possible to integrate C and C++ code in R, the **Rcpp** package has made this much more accessible; you only need to take a look at the length of the list of reverse dependencies to see how popular it now is.

When to Think about C++ and Rcpp

Adding C++ code to your R packages obviously requires that you start to learn another programming language, so it may not always be the answer. The overhead in learning C++ in the first place may be larger than the gains it will give you. However, if you already know C++ or you find that there are a number of cases where your code could benefit from being written in C++, you may find that it is worth the effort.

There are two main cases when C++ will be beneficial to your code:

▶ When you have no choice but to use a for loop. For example, when there is a dependency on the previous value in the loop.

▶ When what you want to do has already been implemented efficiently in C++.

The advantage of using **Rcpp** for your C++ implementations is that it has solved many problems for you in terms of passing data between R and C++, handling the memory usage, and providing many commonly used R functions to C++. This means that rather than having to learn how to do all of these things yourself in C++, you can simply use existing, well-tested functionality.

A Basic Function

We won't go into lots of detail here on how to start writing C++ code, but we will introduce some of the basics with the aim of demonstrating how you can use the **Rcpp** package to integrate your C++ code with R in an easy way. To continue the theme of this hour, we will implement the sampling function. This actually uses a number of features specific to C++, so it's a helpful introduction. You can see an example of this implementation in Listing 18.5.

LISTING 18.5   Implementing with Rcpp

```
 1: #include <Rcpp.h>
 2: using namespace Rcpp;
 3:
 4: // [[Rcpp::export]]
 5: IntegerVector sampleInC(int len){
 6:
 7:    // Initialize x to create output
 8:    IntegerVector x(len);
 9:
10:    // Initialize and create s by using the Rcpp runif function
11:    NumericVector s = runif(len);
12:
13:    // Loop to do sampling, using if...else...
14:    for(int i = 0; i < len; ++i) {
15:
16:      if(s[i] > 0.5)
17:        x[i] = 1;
18:      else
19:        x[i] = 0;
20:    }
21:
22:    // Explicitly return x
23:    return x;
24: }
```

Differences Between R and C++

First of all, you should be aware of the key differences between R and C++ that you will come across when defining functions:

▶ You must declare the types of all objects, including the type of input and output objects and the type of any intermediate objects created.

▶ All expressions end with a semicolon.

▶ You define `for` loops in a different way, specifying the start value, the end condition, and the increment.

▶ Counting of indexes starts at zero in C++.

You saw all of these features in the code in Listing 18.5.

Writing a Function

We can write a C++ function directly in R using `cppFunction`; however, once our C++ function is more than a line or two long, this can be tricky, so it is much more sensible to write our function as a C++ script and then source this using `sourceCpp`. This is the approach we take here, so the code in Listing 18.5 should be saved in a file ending .cpp.

TIP

Rcpp and RStudio

Support for **Rcpp** is well integrated with RStudio. If you open a new script and instead of selecting R select "C++ File," you will get the template structure for **Rcpp**. You can then source this by using the Source button at the top of the script, which will run `sourceCpp` for you.

The first four lines of Listing 18.5 (1 to 4) need to be at the top of any C++ script, where you want to use **Rcpp**. These lines make the functionality of **Rcpp** available to C++. They also allow R to recognize this as a function you want to be available in R.

Data Types

Starting on line 5 of Listing 18.5 we have our function definition. You will notice that in C++ we do not use the `function` keyword, but we have stated `IntegerVector` before the function name (`sampleInC`). This is to indicate to C++ that the return value of the function will be an integer vector. It is very important in C++ to get this correct. You will also notice that we have specified that the argument `len` will be of type `int`, which means we will pass an integer to the function. All of this is done for us in R, so we need to remember to include it when we write C++. The definition of various data types for scalars, vectors, and matrices are shown in Table 18.1. Note that some of these types are specific to **Rcpp** and are not the standard type definitions for C++.

TABLE 18.1   Data Types in Rcpp

Data Type	Scalar	Vector	Matric
Integer	`Int`	`IntegerVector`	`IntegerMatrix`
Numeric	`double`	`NumericVector`	`NumericMatrix`
Character	`String`	`CharacterVector`	`CharacterMatrix`
Logical	`Bool`	`LogicalVector`	`LogicalMatrix`

When you look through the remainder of the code, you will notice that this is very similar to the original example in Listing 18.1. We have created our vector, x, and the samples, and we will return to them in the next section. Just like in the R version, we have used a `for` loop with an `if/else` structure, which is the same as the R equivalent of the `if/else` structure, although different from the `ifelse` function we have used in this hour. The main difference is the structure of the `for` loop.

Loops in C++

In C++ we define a `for` loop in a different manner. First of all, we create an object and give it a starting value. Notice that in the example in Listing 18.5, line 14, this is initialized to 0. This is because we are going to index a vector, and the counting starts at 0 in C++. This is very important to remember when working with C++. The next component of the `for` loop is the condition that will cause the loop to stop. In this case, we are looping while the object i is less than the length of the final vector. Note the "less than" here. Because we start counting at 0, the final element will be `len-1`. The final component is the increment for the loop. Note the syntax here of `++i`. In C++, this is special notation for adding one to the value of the object. So in this example, we are adding one to the value of i on each iteration.

Returning from Functions

To return from a function in R, we can optionally use the function `return`. In C++, this is not the case; we *must* use the keyword `return`. We must also ensure that what we return is of the same type that we stated the function would return. In this case we specified, on line 5 of Listing 18.5, that we would return an `IntegerVector`, so this is what we must return. Here, we are returning x, which we declared to be an `IntegerVector` on line 8.

Using R Functions in C++

You might have noticed that in the function in Listing 18.5 we used the function `runif`. This is because **Rcpp** provides many additional functions to C++ that you are familiar with in R, including distribution functions. In fact, thanks to the way the distribution functions are implemented, they make use of the same random number generation, meaning that you can still test your functions comparing to an R implementation.

Other than the distribution functions, we can implement in C++ vectorized versions of standard arithmetic operators (`+`, `-`, `*`, `/`, etc.) and many mathematical functions such as `sin`, `cos`, and so on, along with `round`, `abs`, `ceiling`, and `floor`.

In addition to the statistical distributions, there are also implementations of summary functions, such as `mean`, `sd`, `var`, `sum`, and `diff`. This is not an exhaustive list, and it is worth checking the vignette for Rcpp Sugar (`vignette("Rcpp-sugar")`) to see other functions that are available.

The advantage of this is that we can implement our R functions using **Rcpp** in a much faster way. Obviously to get the most from C++ you will need to learn more of the language itself, but as a means of quickly getting the benefits of speed gains, this is a great start.

TIP

Learning More

In this hour, we have only touched on the basics of C++, specifically for working with **Rcpp**. There are many available resources, but a good starting point is the user documentation provided with **Rcpp**. For a list of all the vignettes available in this package, you can use `vignette(package = "Rcpp")`.

Summary

In this hour, we looked at many of the methods you can use to not only make your code more efficient but also more professional. The more you use R, the more you will find that you implement many of these approaches—in particular, vectorization—without thinking about them as being a way to speed up your code. You will also find more and more functions that help you write more efficient code. We also briefly introduced the **Rcpp** package, which can be beneficial when other approaches we have suggested are not possible or simply make no difference. One of the key points to remember when you are adapting your code is to ensure that you test whether it is still performing in the same way. Although this can simply be an informal test, you will see in Hour 20 that you can, and should, make use of test frameworks to continuously verify that you are not adversely changing your code.

Q&A

Q. I don't mind waiting for my code to finish running. Do I need to do any of this?

A. If you are happy with the speed of your code, you don't need to make any changes; however, many of these points are what will make your code more professional and suitable for wider production usage. It is advisable that you take all of these points into consideration when writing R code (many you may be doing already), and eventually they will become a natural part of your R code.

Workshop

The workshop contains quiz questions and exercises to help you solidify your understanding of the material covered. Try to answer all questions before looking at the "Answers" section that follows.

Quiz

1. Before you jump into changing your code, what should you do and what function can you use to help you do it?

2. Why should you initialize when writing `for` loops?

3. Why are vectorized functions, such as `pmin`, slower than working directly with a vector?

4. Do you need to handle memory usage in R?

5. What are the main differences between R and C++?

Answers

1. Before making any changes, you should first profile your code to determine where the slowest components are. You can do this in R using the `Rprof` function, which will generate a series of summary statistics to show where your code spends most of its time.

2. Initializing objects when you are writing for loops means that R will not continuously make copies of the objects you are adding values to. This is more efficient because you are simply writing over a value.

3. Vectorized functions are typically slower because they contain several function arguments and a series of error checks on the arguments. This is to ensure that the function is run in the way intended, and if incorrect arguments are passed, a more informative error message is returned. For code that you will reuse regularly and particularly share with others, this error checking is vital and shouldn't be removed to make small speed gains.

4. No, this is done automatically when a temporary object is no longer being used. The main reason to manage memory would be to remove large objects that you no longer need but that you previously created.

5. There are four points that you should keep in mind:

   A. You must declare the type of all objects.

   B. All expressions end with a semicolon.

   C. Loops are defined in a different way.

   D. Indexes start counting from 0!

Activities

1. Write a function that takes a vector of input and, using a loop, iterates around all of the values, calculating the sum up to that value (that is, the cumulative sum) so that when you pass the vector of values 1 to 10, you get the following return value:

```
[1]   1   3   6 10 15 21 28 36 45 55
```

2. Use `microbenchmark` to determine the median time it takes to run your function.

3. Use any of the initialization and vectorization techniques to improve the speed of your function, using `microbenchmark` to check that you are making the code more efficient.

4. Can you find a function in R that will do this for you? Compare the speed of that function to your most efficient version.

5. Have a go at writing this function in C++ using **Rcpp**. If you are finding the cumulative sum a little tricky, start out with just taking the sum of all the values in the vector.

HOUR 19
Package Building

What You'll Learn in This Hour:

► Why you should build R packages

► What an R package contains

► What you need to include in all the directories and files

► Things to consider for maintaining good quality code

► How to easily create documentation with **roxygen2**

► How to build a package with **devtools**

In this hour, we will look at one of the key aspects for professionalizing your code: package building. When you put your code into a package, it helps you to ensure that your code is of a high standard and you are adhering to good practices such as documenting your code. In the next hour, we will look at some further components such as incorporating unit tests, but we will focus here on making sure our code is well written and documented. This is the starting point for high quality, professional code that is easy to share and reuse.

Why Build an R Package?

Most of us don't think about writing our own packages when we work with R despite the fact that we use other packages on a regular basis, as you have done in the previous hours in this book. We typically start out by writing code in one or more R scripts that contain lots of library/require calls or calls to source at the top of the script. This type of coding can cause us problems for many reasons.

Code written in this way is difficult to share. We have to determine all of the files that we need to run the code and all of the package dependencies. We also have to spend time explaining to our colleagues what the code does and how to use it if we do not document it. It can be difficult to know which version is the latest because we might have slightly different versions stored in different places. What's more, it can often be difficult to be certain that the code has not been affected by a change we have made.

However, as we know from using other R packages, we can solve many of these challenges. An R package allows us to keep all of our code and documentation in a single place and implement a more formal approach to testing. Building an R package allows us to do the following:

▶ Keep track of versions of our code and easily know whether we are using the same or different versions.

▶ Keep documentation with the code and save time in having to explain how to use functions and the workflow of the code.

▶ Easily provide demo code and examples.

▶ Easily use test frameworks to ensure that any changes to the code do not change the output of the function.

▶ Easily incorporate and call functions written in other languages such as C++.

Overall the advantages of converting our code to be structured as an R package are huge and well worth considering, and as you will see in this hour, it is very simple to do using tools such as **devtools** and **roxygen2**.

The Structure of an R Package

As you know, R packages contain various components and objects, including functions and documentation. You will see the basic structure and components in this hour, and in Hour 20, "Advanced Package Building," we will look at some of the additional components such as unit tests.

The basic structure of a package contains four components:

▶ A DESCRIPTION file

▶ A NAMESPACE file

▶ An R directory

▶ A man directory

We will look at all these components in turn, but before we do we will cover how to create the correct package structure—in particular, how to set up a package for working with RStudio.

Creating the Package Structure

Traditionally, we created the package structure by using a function called `package.skeleton`. Although we can still use this function, it is much better to use the `create` function in the package **devtools**. The **devtools** package has been created to simplify the package-building process by wrapping up functionality such as creating and building packages.

TIP
Creating a Package Project
In RStudio, you may also create an R package from the project menu in the top-right corner. By selecting New Project > New Directory > R Package, you will be given a menu that allows you to give the package name as well as the location for the package on your file system, and you can optionally select existing R files that will be included in the package.

The purpose of the create function is to set up the basic structure of an R package. As you will see later in this hour, it has been designed around a workflow whereby we add our own R code separately and document packages using **roxygen2**. As an example, as stated earlier, an R package requires a man directory. This will not be created when we run create but will instead be created when we generate our documentation.

To create the package structure, we simply give the name of the package by defining the file path to where the package directory should be created. Here's an example:

```
> create("../simTools", rstudio = TRUE)
Creating package simTools in .
No DESCRIPTION found. Creating with values:


Package: simTools
Title: What the package does (one line)
Version: 0.1
Authors@R: "First Last <first.last@example.com> [aut, cre]"
Description: What the package does (one paragraph)
Depends: R (>= 3.1.2)
License: What license is it under?
LazyData: true
Adding RStudio project file to simTools
```

You will see here that we have specified that the package structure should be created in a directory called simTools. Although it is not strictly necessary, it is good practice to give the directory the same name as your final package. You will also see in this code that a default DESCRIPTION file has been created that includes this package name. We will return to this shortly, but for now it is sufficient to note that a default set of values has been provided to this file.

You may also notice in the preceding code we have set an option called rstudio. If you are working in RStudio, you may find that this is a handy feature because it creates an RStudio package project. You can then open this from the projects menu by selecting Open Project and then navigating to and selecting the .Rproj file created. This is in fact the default behavior of this function. If you don't want to create an RStudio project you will need to set this option to FALSE.

Having run `create`, or using the project menu, you will now have a directory at the specified location that contains the directories and files listed (with the exception of the man directory). We will look at each of these in turn in the following sections.

TIP

Additional Package Files

Having used `create` or the project menu system, you may notice that some hidden files have been created. You will need to have your explorer window set up to show hidden files, which include .gitignore and .Rbuildignore. These files allow us to include files within our package locally but stop git and/or the R build process from using these files. By default, the .Rproj files will be listed in these files.

The DESCRIPTION File

The first file in an R package is the DESCRIPTION file. This file is used to list important package information, including the authors and the current maintainer of the package, the version number, and the license for the package. It is in this file that we also specify any package dependencies.

You will have noticed when we ran the `create` function that a DESCRIPTION file was being created with certain default values. We can actually specify options for **devtools** to automatically populate some of these fields for us, but for occasional packages it is simple enough to update the file. An example of a DESCRIPTION file for the **simTools** package for which we created the structure is given in Listing 19.1.

LISTING 19.1   Example of a DESCRIPTION File

```
Package: simTools
Title: Simulation Analysis Tools
Version: 1.0-0
Authors@R: c(
    person("Aimee", "Gott", email = "agott@mango-solutions.com", role = c("aut", "cre")),
    person("Andy", "Nicholls", email = "anicholls@mango-solutions.com", role = "aut"),
    person("Rich", "Pugh", email = rpugh@mango-solutions.com, role = "ctb")
    )
Description: A series of tools for simulation analysis used for learning about
    distributions.
Depends:
    R (>= 3.1.2)
Imports:
```

```
    ggplot2 (>= 1.0.0)
License: GPL-2
LazyData: true
```

TIP

Package License

Note that the default License is the relatively open GPL-2, the same license as R itself. There are several standard licenses for R packages that are listed on the R-Project website, https://www.r-project.org/Licenses/, although it is not necessary to apply one of these licenses. Licenses should be chosen carefully as they describe what others can do with your code.

The NAMESPACE File

The NAMESPACE file is now a compulsory file when you develop a package. It allows us to specify which functions in our package will be "exported" so that the end user can see them. This is useful if we want to have some utility functions that we want to use in our code but we don't want the end user to see them. It also allows us to import namespaces from other packages (that is, make the user-visible functions in another package available to our package). We will return to this topic later in this hour because it is possible to allow the "roxygen" headers we add to our functions to handle this for us.

The R Directory

The R directory is where all our R functions will be stored. When we have simply used the `create` function, this directory will be empty and we can start to add R script files (that is, files ending in ".R"). You could add all your functions in a single file, though it is good practice to include multiple R scripts for individual groups of functionality. It is worth noting, however, that you will often see a file called utils.R. This is typically where short utility functions (of just a couple lines) that are not intended to be used by the end user are stored.

For our sample package, we will create a function called `sampleFromData`. The code for this function can be seen in Listing 19.2. This code should be contained in an R script in the R directory.

LISTING 19.2 R Function for the simTools Package

```
sampleFromData <- function(data, size, replace = TRUE, ...){
  if (!is.numeric(size)) {
    stop("Size must be a numeric integer value")
  }
```

```
lengthData <- nrow(data)

if (!replace & size > lengthData){
  stop("Cannot sample greater than the data size without replacement")
}

# Sample a number of rows from the given dataset
samples <- sample(seq_len(lengthData), size = size, replace = replace, ...)
invisible(data[samples, ])

}
```

The man Directory

The man directory is where we store all the files that contain the user documentation for the functions in our package. We can, and should, create help files for all functions in a package. We must document any exported functions, i.e. functions that an end user will see.

Although you will be familiar with the HTML format of help files from running ?mean, for instance, this is not the way in which we write help files. They are written in a TeX-like format and saved in files ending with an .Rd extension. We need to generate one file for each of the functions and the package itself. Generating these files can be quite time consuming, and it is easy to forget to update the files if you make changes to the function itself. For these reasons we will instead generate the documentation using a package called **roxygen2**. We will return to this topic later in the hour.

Code Quality

When it comes to putting our code into a package, the quality of the code is of huge importance. Typically code in a package will be shared, will be returned to later, or is collecting together a large amount of functionality—or all these things. As such, it is vital that we think about the quality of our code.

Code quality doesn't just refer to whether the code works or not, but relates to the styling, documentation, and usability of the code. All these can be taken account by following some guidelines for writing code. At Mango, code quality is vital, and since there is typically more than one developer working on the code at a time, using a consistent style makes it much easier to work on the code in a collaborative manner. We have introduced many good coding practices throughout this book, and if you follow these practices you will be well on your way to high-quality, well-written code. Although we suggest some guidelines for styling in this section, you do not need to follow these guidelines specifically. However, we recommend that you decide on a consistent way to style your code and stick with it.

As mentioned, all of the R code for our packages is stored in the R directory in a series of files. These files should have descriptive names that help you to identify the contents when you return to the code. Also, they should all take the file extension ".R" (note the capitalization). The functions and objects referenced in these files should be named in a way that helps to inform the user of their purpose. A consistent means of naming the objects should be used. A popular convention, and one that is used at Mango, is `lowerCamelCase`, where each new word is capitalized.

In terms of the documentation, all functions should have a "roxygen" header, which will be discussed further in the next section. The code itself should be well commented to clarify its purpose, with comments for roughly every 10 lines of code.

When it comes to the layout of the code, it is considered a good practice to indent and space the code in a consistent manner. It is typical to include spaces after operators such as + or * as well as after a comma. It is convention to indent code inside a function call as well as inside `for` loops and `if`/`else` structures. We recommend two spaces for each indentation.

In addition to the styling of our code and the coding practices we have discussed, such as not appending in a `for` loop, we should also consider what our code does to the R session. It is considered bad practice to do anything inside a function that changes the environment in any way, including the assignment of objects and changing options or settings. If there is a need to make a change (for instance, if you need to change the working directory), your function should set it back to the original value before exiting.

Automated Documentation with roxygen2

To the end user, the most important part of your package is the documentation. A package that is well documented is much easier for someone to pick up and work with, and it's much easier to return to when you need to update or change the functionality in the future.

Package documentation can take many forms, though the most widely used, and the aspect we will focus on here, is the function help files. We can also write user guides, known as vignettes, which we will look at in Hour 20.

From reading help files for other functions, you will be familiar with the format of this documentation. Function help files list all the arguments and they detail the purpose and usage of each. We can also add information about the output of each function, additional details about the function, who wrote the function, and so on.

We are going to generate the documentation using roxygen headers. These headers go above the function to which they refer. This makes it much simpler to produce the documentation because we can do it alongside the function development. It is also easier to update if we make a change to the function because the header is there while we are working on the function.

TIP

Document as You Write

As you will see, it is very simple to create the roxygen headers for functions. As such, it is a good habit to write them even if you are not thinking of putting your functions into a package. This means that the code is well documented and easy for you or others to work with. It also means that if you do decide to turn the code into a package, it is already documented, so you don't have to go back and do so.

Function Headers

We include a roxygen header above the function definition. Each line of the roxygen header starts with the symbols #'. This allows R to treat the lines as comments, but they will be recognized by roxygen as function headers. Following this we use special tags to indicate a particular component of the help file. Some tags and their uses are shown in Table 19.1.

TABLE 19.1 roxygen2 Header Tags

Tag	Purpose
@param	Identifies each of the function arguments and the corresponding help text
@return	Details the output of the function
@author	Indicates who wrote the function
@seealso	Other functions for which the user should look at the help documentation
@examples	Code examples of running the function
@import/@importFrom	Indicate a package or function within a package to be imported
@export	Indicates that this function should be exported (that is, made visible to the end user)

Some components do not need their tags explicitly written out because the first three paragraphs without tags are treated in a special way. The first three paragraphs are as follows:

1. The title of the help page (short, one sentence)

2. The description for the help page (brief description of the function)

3. The details section, which can provide much more information about the function, what it implements, and so on

For including special formatting we can use LaTeX formatting components. If you are not familiar with LaTeX, this won't impact your ability to write documentation unless you need to include mathematical formulas. The main thing to point out is usage of %. In LaTeX the % symbol indicates a comment, so we actually need to use \% if we don't want everything after it to be treated as a comment.

Listing 19.3 shows how this might look for a sample function in the **simTools** package we created earlier. Notice that, although we have not included the complete function definition again, this header goes directly above the function definition, in this case the one given in Listing 19.2.

LISTING 19.3   Roxygen Header for the `sampleFromData` Function

```
 1: #' Sample from a dataset
 2: #'
 3: #' This function has been designed to sample from the rows of a two
 4: #' dimensional data set returning all columns of the sampled rows.
 5: #'
 6: #' @param data The matrix or data.frame from which rows are to be
 7: #' sampled.
 8: #' @param size The number of samples to take.
 9: #' @param replace Should values be replaced? By default takes the
10: #' value TRUE.
11: #' @param ... Any other parameters to be passed to the sample
12: #' function.
13: #'
14: #' @return Returns a dataset of the same type as the input data with
15: #' \code{size} rows.
16: #'
17: #' @author Aimee Gott <agott@@mango-solutions.com>
18: #'
19: #' @export
20: #' @examples
21: #' sampleFromData(airquality, 100)
22: #'
23: sampleFromData <- function(data, size, replace = TRUE, ...){
```

One of the key tags, which you can see here on line 19, is `@export`. This tag is what makes this function visible to the end user. When we generate the documentation, the NAMESPACE file will be automatically updated to indicate that it will be exported, meaning that we do not need to manually generate the NAMESPACE file. There are similar tags, `@import` and `@importFrom`, that allow us to specify functions or packages that we need to make available to run our functions.

Other tags to note include `@param`, which can be seen on lines 6, 8, 9, and 11. This tag is used to identify the arguments of the function. Notice that following the tag we give the name of the argument, and after a space the text that describes that particular argument. As you can see, the text can span multiple lines, and text is treated as belonging to the last tag until another, new tag is encountered.

You may also notice that in giving an email address in line 17 we have used @@. This is due to the fact that the @ symbol is used before a tag, so we need to indicate that we really want an @ symbol by duplication of the symbol.

Documenting the Package

In addition to documenting our functions using **roxygen2**, we can also document the package itself. Obviously in this case we do not have a function to put the header above. The typical approach to this documentation is to create a single file named with the package name. In the example we have used in this hour, that would be a file named simTools.R. The header itself is then contained above the statement NULL or NA.

An example of package documentation for the example we have used in this hour is given in Listing 19.4. Just like with the function documentation, the first line is the title of the help page, and the second is the description text. We can also include tags such as @author, @examples, and even @references, as we would in function headers.

LISTING 19.4   Roxygen Header for the simTools Package

```
1: #' A package for performing common simulation tasks
2: #'
3: #' This package provides a series of tools for common simulation tasks such as
4: #' sampling from a data frame and generating plots of simulation experiments.
5: #'
6: #' @author Aimee Gott \email{agott@@mango-solutions.com}
7: #' @docType package
8: #' @name simTools
9: NULL
```

The main difference is that we need to include the tags @docType and @name. For the first of these tags, we identify that the specific documentation is for a package. You can see this in line 7 of the example in Listing 19.4. As you will see in Hour 20, we will also use this tag when documenting other package components such as data. The tag @name is used to label the help document. This is what the user will call to see the help document for the package, and it takes the name of the package itself, as you can see in line 8 of Listing 19.4.

Creating and Updating the Help Pages

Once we have created the headers for all of the functions and for the package, we can generate the Rd files. The function roxygenize, in the **roxygen2** package, can be used to do this, but there is also a function available in **devtools** called `document`. Both functions work in the same way, but here we will demonstrate the use of `document`.

As you saw with the function `create` earlier in this hour, we need only point to the top level of the package directory to generate, or update where it already exists, the package documentation.

```
> document("../simTools")
Updating simTools documentation
Loading simTools
Writing NAMESPACE
Writing sampleFromData.Rd
Writing simTools.Rd
```

You can see from the output messages that this updates the NAMESPACE file along with the Rd files for the functions and the package itself. When we're working with RStudio, it is actually possible to open the Rd files and preview them. After opening an Rd file in RStudio, simply click the Preview button to see the HTML preview in the Help tab. Figure 19.1 shows the preview of the help file defined in Listing 19.3.

FIGURE 19.1
HTML preview of the `simFromData` help page

As part of the package building workflow, this stage should be completed before the build and check stages we will see in the next section. In practice, it is common to cycle around all of these stages multiple times in the process of creating and testing a package.

TIP

Documenting with Projects

As mentioned previously, if we are developing a package as a project in RStudio, we have quick access to a number of build features through the Build tab, which is made available in a package project. This includes the option to generate package documentation. This can be done by either selecting the Document option, typically in the More drop-down menu of the Build tab, or using the keyboard shortcut Ctrl+Shift+D.

Building a Package with devtools

Once we have put together all of the components of our package, whether that is simply R code and help files, as we have seen here, or additional components as we will see in Hour 20, we need to go through the process of preparing the package to be shared and then building it. Traditionally this was entirely done by using a series of command-line tools. We now have an easier way to handle this in the form of the package **devtools**. The package itself still uses the command-line tools but provides us with a simple, familiar interface to them.

CAUTION

Building a Package in Windows

In order to build packages in Windows, you will need to have installed RTools. This is an additional component available on CRAN that provides the command-line tools needed for R package development. It's important to make sure that the correct version of R is installed and that the system path has been set up correctly. For details of how to install RTools, see the Appendix, "Installation," of this book.

Checking

The first thing we should do before building our package to share is to run a series of checks. Before a package can be made available on CRAN, it must pass a series of checks relating to the structure of the package, aspects of the code, the documentation, and even whether the examples run without error. Even if we don't intend to make a package available on CRAN, it is good practice to run these checks and ensure that our own package passes all of them. We can run these checks in **devtools** with the function check.

You can see an example of running `check` and partial output in Listing 19.5. As you can see from the output in line 2, the first thing that `check` does is run the `document` function. This ensures that the documentation is up to date because there are a number of documentation-related checks. The package is then built into a source version. This is to ensure that there are no files included in the check that would not be present in the final version of the package. The checks themselves then start from line 20. In the lines shown in Listing 19.5, checks are being run against the DESCRIPTION and NAMESPACE files. In these cases, they pass the checks, which you can see from the OK line ending.

LISTING 19.5 Running the `check` Function

```
 1: > check("../simTools")
 2: Updating simTools documentation
 3: Loading simTools
 4: Writing NAMESPACE
 5: Writing sampleFromData.Rd
 6: Writing simTools.Rd
 7: "C:/PROGRA~1/R/R-31~1.2/bin/i386/R" --vanilla CMD build
 8: "C:\Users\agott\Documents\simTools" --no-manual --no-resave-data
 9:
10: * checking for file 'C:\Users\agott\Documents\simTools/DESCRIPTION' ... OK
11: * preparing 'simTools':
12: * checking DESCRIPTION meta-information ... OK
13: * checking for LF line-endings in source and make files
14: * checking for empty or unneeded directories
15: * building 'simTools_1.0-0.tar.gz'
16:
17: "C:/PROGRA~1/R/R-31~1.2/bin/i386/R" --vanilla CMD check  \
18:    "C:\Users\agott\AppData\Local\Temp\RtmpwNk65n/simTools_1.0-0.tar.gz"
➥--timings
19:
20: * using log directory 'C:/Users/agott/AppData/Local/Temp/RtmpwNk65n/
➥ simTools.Rcheck'
21: * using R version 3.1.2 (2014-10-31)
22: * using platform: i386-w64-mingw32 (32-bit)
23: * using session charset: ISO8859-1
24: * checking for file 'simTools/DESCRIPTION' ... OK
25: * this is package 'simTools' version '1.0-0'
26: * checking package namespace information ... OK
27: * checking package dependencies ... OK
28: ...
```

Where there are any issues, they will be raised with an ERROR, WARNING, or NOTE, depending on the severity. You should try to solve all issues that are raised; many can be solved easily, particularly those that relate to inaccurate documentation. However, although it is very important to resolve any ERRORs that are raised, it is less important for WARNINGs and NOTEs if you are not going to share your code, or at least not going to make it widely available or available on CRAN. For packages to be used in production code, we would recommend that you strive to resolve, or at least understand, all issues that are raised by the checks.

This `check` function can be repeatedly re-run until you are satisfied with the output and ready to build the package.

Building

We are now at a point where we can build the package. We do this using the `build` function in **devtools**. When building the package, we need to consider the type of package we want or need to create. We can either generate a source package or a binary package. A source package contains the source files for the code, whereas the binary versions have been compiled for either the Windows or OS X operating system. If you plan to share your code with other Windows (or OS X) users, you will typically want to create the binary package.

The only difference if we want to create the binary version of the package is that we set the value of the argument `binary` to be TRUE. An example of running the `build` function, along with the output generated, is shown in Listing 19.6.

LISTING 19.6   Building the Package

```
 1: > build("../simTools", binary = TRUE)
 2: "C:/PROGRA~1/R/R-31~1.2/bin/i386/R" --vanilla CMD INSTALL  \
 3:   "C:\Users\agott\Documents\simTools" --build
 4: * installing to library 'C:/Users/agott/AppData/Local/Temp/RtmpwNk65n/
➥file105078613584'
 5: * installing *source* package 'simTools' ...
 6: ** R
 7: ** preparing package for lazy loading
 8: ** help
 9: *** installing help indices
10: ** building package indices
11: ** testing if installed package can be loaded
12: *** arch - i386
13: *** arch - x64
14: * MD5 sums
15: packaged installation of 'simTools' as simTools_1.0-0.zip
16: * DONE (simTools)
17: [1] "C:/Users/agott/Documents/simTools_1.0-0.zip"
```

You can see from this example that when we generate the binary version of the package, it is first installed and then packaged up in the installed format. The package name and version number are taken from the DESCRIPTION file values that we set previously, so we do not need to separately inform the `build` function of these values. Because we have built a Windows binary package, you will notice on lines 15 and 17 that the package has the file extension .zip. If we had instead built a source package, it would have had the extension .tar.gz.

Installing

After we have built our package, whether that is in the form of a binary package or a source package, we are then ready to install it. The package that you have built is in the same format as any other package you would install, and as such can be installed, loaded, and used in the same way, as you can see below:

```
> install.packages("../simTools_1.0-0.zip", repos = NULL)
Installing package into 'C:/Users/agott/Documents/R/win-library/3.1'
(as 'lib' is unspecified)
package 'simTools' successfully unpacked and MD5 sums checked
> library(simTools)
> simDat <- sampleFromData(airquality, 2)
> simDat
   Ozone Solar.R Wind Temp Month Day
58    NA      47 10.3   73     6  27
36    NA     220  8.6   85     6   5
```

Summary

In this hour, we have looked at all the components required to create a simple R package with the basic components required. We have introduced some of the good practices for package development, including considerations around the code itself as well as how we can provide useful documentation components. We have looked at what is required to build a package and how to build one. In the next hour, we will discuss how to add further components to our packages to make them more production ready, including unit tests and user guides.

Q&A

Q. I use another package in my code. What do I need to do to make sure it is available for my package?

A. When it comes to dependencies of your code, you can list them in one of a number of ways. A package is typically listed under `Depends` or `Imports`, `Suggests` or `LinkingTo`. You use `LinkingTo` to specify that your function requires the C code of another package. A package listed as `Suggests` is one that is needed to run unit tests or examples, or for only very specific functionality as an option in maybe only one function in your package. Any package that contains functions required for the running of your package should be listed in either `Depends` or `Imports`. It is now best practice to use only the `Imports` field, although there are some occasions when `Depends` is still needed; hence, it is still available.

Q. Who should be listed as an author of a package?

A. This is entirely up to you. Typically an author has made substantial contributions to a package, whereas a contributor has made only a small contribution, such as a bug fix. The one role to consider with care is who is listed as the creator or maintainer (`cre`) or the package. This is the person who can be contacted by the R Core team or by users of the package. It is important that a single person is named in this role and that an email address is provided that can be used to contact the maintainer.

Q. I am just writing a couple of functions. Should I create a package from them?

A. When you are getting started with package building, you might find that it helps you to learn how to do so by creating a small package first. In general, although you may not actually build the package or want to share it further, by following the practices in this chapter and organizing code in this way, you make it much easier to work with, which means it's easy to create a package if you need to later.

Q. Can I use roxygen headers even if I am not creating a package?

A. Yes, and we would strongly recommend that you do. Documenting functions you write in this way makes them much easier to work with and return to, as well as to convert into a package at a later date.

Workshop

The workshop contains quiz questions and exercises to help you solidify your understanding of the material covered. Try to answer all questions before looking at the "Answers" section that follows.

Quiz

1. What are the minimum required components for an R package?

2. How can you generate help documentation for functions?

3. What extra tags do you need to document a package?

4. What is the difference between a source package and a binary package?

5. If you don't plan to make a package available on CRAN, do you need to ensure that all of the checks pass?

6. How do you install a package that you have developed?

Answers

1. At a minimum, you require the directories man and R and the files NAMESPACE and DESCRIPTION.

2. You can generate documentation for functions by including roxygen headers in the function R scripts. You use special tags that start with the @ symbol to document components of the function.

3. For the overall package documentation, you need to include the additional tags `@docType` and `@name`. The `name` tag should give the package name, which is what the user will call to access the help file. The `docType` tag simple needs to state the package.

4. A source package contains all the source code for the package but excludes the additional files that may be included in the package as you develop, such as RStudio project files. The binary package is the packaged-up version for a specific operating system such as Windows or OS X.

5. Although it is not a requirement to run the checks if you are not submitting to CRAN, it is good practice to do so. It is particularly recommended if you will be sharing your code with others or if it is intended to be used in production code. A package that passes the checks is generally considered to be of a higher quality than a package that does not.

6. You install a package that you have developed in the same way that you would install any other package you have been provided in source or binary format. Take a look back at Hour 2, "The R Environment," for a reminder on how to do this.

Activities

1. Use **devtools** to create a skeleton package for a package called **summaryTools**.

2. Add in the appropriate location of an R function called `numericSummary`. This function should take two arguments: a numeric vector and the argument `na.rm`. The function should call a helper function that generates numeric summaries, including the mean and standard deviation. It should also call a helper function that returns the number and proportion of missing values. The `numericSummary` function should return all this information in a suitable format.

3. Use **roxygen2** to create headers to document all three of the functions you have just written. Choose carefully which of these functions need to be visible to the end user.

4. Update the DESCRIPTION file and all other package documentation.

5. Build and check your package. Once you have resolved any issues raised by the check and have rebuilt the package, install it and then try calling your function.

Advanced Package Building

What You'll Learn in This Hour:

▶ What you can do to extend an R package

▶ Why testing is important and how to use **testthat**

▶ How to include datasets in a package

▶ How to include a user guide in a package

▶ What you need to do to use C++ code in a package

In the last hour, you saw how to put all of your code together in the form of a package to simplify the sharing and maintenance of code, as well as to aid in the development of high-quality, production-ready code. There are, however, a number of ways you can extend a package to make it more robust to changes and easier for users to get started with. You will see the most common of these extra components in this hour.

Extending R Packages

We have now managed to create a package that contains all the functions we need and even contains the help files for those functions—so why do we need to add more? Surely this is sufficient. In many respects, this is true. We can simply share our package as it is with no need to do anything more, but there are many advantages to the extensions you will see in this hour.

The first additional component we will cover is a test framework. As you have seen throughout this book, once we have code we may want to update it to make it more efficient or simply change the functionality as we find bugs or need new features. A test framework becomes a vital component here for ensuring that we do not introduce more errors into our code or revert back to issues we have already resolved.

There are many instances when we may need to share data with our end users. This may be simply for examples; it may be data relevant to the field that we want to share, or it may be reference data required by functions in the code. This last point is particularly common in the development of code for analytics. Whatever the reason for needing to share the data, we can incorporate it all in our package so there is no need to also send out data separately to the package we have developed.

The next component we'll implement is the user guide. Whether you are just sharing code with colleagues or you plan to share widely with the R community, the end users of your package are going to need to know how to use it. The individual function help files will help users with questions of "How do I use this function?" and "What are all the options for this function?" However, they will not typically help with the overall workflow of your package. A user guide is aimed at helping to get users started with a general workflow for your package. Just as with data, we have written this anyway and intended to simply email it to people who need it, but incorporating it in the package ensures that it is up to date and always available for the end users.

The final additional component we cover in this hour is C++ code, or more specifically, code we have written with **Rcpp**. This is not going to be a component that you will include in every package you write, but as you saw in Hour 18, "Code Efficiency," you may have chosen to incorporate such code into a function for efficiency, so you need to know how to include such code in an R package.

As you can probably see, inclusion of these two components, data and C++ code, will be dependent upon the package itself and its requirements and implementation. When it comes to the user guide and unit tests, they are again optional. However, it is considered to be a best practice to include these components, and we would recommend that you get into the habit of including them as standard in any package you write. As you will see in this hour, they are very simple to add, with **devtools** functionality available to help you with the package structure, and they don't take much additional effort once you are familiar with them.

Developing a Test Framework

Whenever we develop code, we test it in some way. As we start out this might just be with an ad-hoc running of a function to ensure it does what we expect. Usually this is with small amounts of data, and typically we test the main functionality we have implemented. As we write more code and begin to change it to handle any issues that arise, we might write a script that can be run regularly where there are known expected outputs we are looking for. This is the beginning of a test framework. For all development, but especially production development, it is recommended that these informal tests are formalized so that they can easily be re-run with specific cases at any point. We can then include these tests within a package so that they are always kept together, and even the end user can run them to ensure the package is still working as it should.

An Introduction to testthat

There are a number of options for providing a test framework in R, but the one introduced here, **testthat**, is both widely used and easy to get started with. Before we consider how to include tests in an R package, we will simply look at how to write what are known as "unit tests" using **testthat**.

As an example in this hour, we will implement tests for the function we included in the R package that we developed in the previous hour, `sampleFromData`. This function is defined in Listing 19.2 and simply randomly samples rows from a dataset we provide. You will also notice that this function includes some error handling by checking that sensible arguments have been provided.

While we write the tests, we will need to consider what we might test. We will return to this topic shortly, but for now we will simply write some tests to ensure that data is returned as expected. If we were to ask you to check that this function worked correctly, you would most likely pick a simple dataset and test the function with argument values that are easy to check the output of. For example, you might try the following:

```
> library(mangoTraining)
> set.seed(20)
> testData <- sampleFromData(demoData, 3)
> testData
   Subject Sex Age Weight Height  BMI Smokes
29      29   M  44     81    175 26.4    Yes
26      26   F  25     58    175 18.9     No
10      10   M  23     71    188 20.1     No
```

In this case, we have used the function `set.seed`, which allows us to set the value of the random seed to ensure that we can consistently reproduce the random sampling in this function. However many times we run all these lines of code, we will consistently reproduce these same sampled rows. This is a really useful function when it comes to testing. We use **testthat** to formalize this test and to check for us that the correct data is returned.

We create individual tests using functions named with the pattern `expect_`. The names are then appended with elements such as `equal`, `named`, `is`, and `error`, among others. All of the functions follow a similar pattern whereby we provide the object we want to test as the first argument, followed by the value we want to test against as the second argument. In the preceding example, we might ensure that the correct three rows are returned with tests such as these:

```
> expect_is(testData, "data.frame")
> expect_named(testData, c("Subject", "Sex", "Age", "Weight", "Height", "BMI",
➡"Smokes"))
> expect_equal(testData[,"Subject"], c(29, 26, 10))
```

So we have checked that the correct structure is returned, that it has the correct columns, and that the elements of the Subject column are correct. We could extensively test the whole returned structure, but in this case, because rows are unique based on the subject number, we can be confident that the same data has been returned if the subject values are the same each time. You will notice that if you run all of these statements, nothing is returned when the output is as expected. Only if the test fails will you see any output.

We can write such statements to test a range of functionality in the sampleFromData function. Typically we want to test that arguments work as expected and change the output in some way, and we want to ensure that errors and warnings are thrown when expected. It is also highly recommended that we write a test for what the correct behavior should be whenever a bug is identified. This will help us to resolve the bug and ensure that we don't do anything that puts the bug back into our code.

Rather than simply writing a script full of expect_ statements, we use a function called test_that to group expectations together. Therefore, we would typically group the statements we wrote previously as a test for expected default behavior, for instance, which would mean that our test script might look something like the example given in Listing 20.1.

LISTING 20.1 Example of a Test Script for **sampleFromData**

```
 1: context("sampleFromData must return data frames of the correct format")
 2:
 3: test_that("Default arguments return correctly", {
 4:
 5:   require(mangoTraining)
 6:
 7:   set.seed(20)
 8:
 9:   testData <- sampleFromData(demoData, 3)
10:
11:   expect_is(testData, "data.frame")
12:
13:   expect_named(testData,
14:             c("Subject", "Sex", "Age", "Weight", "Height", "BMI", "Smokes"))
15:
16:   expect_equal(testData[,"Subject"], c(29, 26, 10))
17:
18: })
19:
20: test_that("Throws an error correctly", {
21:
22:   expect_error(sampleFromData(airquality, "Subject"),
23:             "Size must be a numeric integer value")
24:
25: })
```

You can see that lines 5 to 16 are the same as we previously ran, but this time they are inside the test_that function. As you can see on line 3, the first argument is a character string to indicate what the purpose of this group of tests is, and the second is the group of code, contained inside curly brackets, that is to be run, including all of the expectations. In this example, we have included a second test_that function call that we are using to test that the function handles errors correctly. We can have as many `test_that` groups as we want in a single script. It is a best practice to collect `test_that` statements in a script for a single function or group of functionality so that tests are organized in an easy-to-find way. We will look in the next section at how to structure tests for a package.

You will also notice in this example that on line 1 we have called a function context and that it contains a character string. This is simply a way of grouping together a series of `test_that` statements. The context indicates that all of the following tests are related to a specific piece of functionality—in this case, the `sampleFromData` function.

When it comes to running these tests, we can make use of the functions `test_file` and `test_dir`. The function `test_file` will run all of the tests in a single file, whereas the function `test_dir` will run all of the scripts in a single directory. As an example, suppose that we had saved the code in Listing 20.1 as the file test-sampleFromData.R. We would run all of these tests with the following lines:

```
> test_file("test-sampleFromData.R")
sampleFromData must return data frames of the correct format : ....
```

Notice that the context has been used to label all the tests that have been run, and the `.` in the output indicates that a test has been run and has passed.

Incorporating Tests into a Package

Although we could simply write tests in a script that we can run as we did earlier, if we are writing a package it is much better to include the tests in the package. This way, we always know where to find tests for specific code, we can very easily re-run the tests for the whole package after we have made changes, and we can easily provide the tests to others who may want to re-run them. This final point is quite common in controlled environments where it is necessary to be certain that there have not been changes to the software or environment that impact the results of running specific code.

As you saw in the last hour, components of a package are structured in a specific way, and tests are no exception. Although the **devtools** functions we have seen so far have not created this for us, we can add a test structure to a package we have already created with the function `use_testthat`. Thus, to add the test structure to the package we started to develop in Hour 19, "Package Building," we can run the following line:

```
> use_testthat("../simTools")
```

This will create in the package structure a directory called "tests," which contains a file, testthat.R, that houses the required code to run the tests for the package and doesn't need to be changed, as well as a directory called "testthat." It is in this directory that we should store all our test scripts. We can include as many or as few scripts as we want, but all files need to start with "test-".

When you use **devtools** to set up the correct package structure for tests, you will also find that it updates the DESCRIPTION file to include **testthat** as a suggested package. The package is only included as a suggestion because it is not a requirement to have **testthat** to run your code; however, if someone wants to run your tests, they will need this package.

Once we have included tests inside our package, we no longer need to use the `test_file` and `test_dir` functions in **testthat** to run them. As with all the other components of package building, we can run the tests from RStudio using the Build tab options, or we can use the **devtools** function `test`. Running the tests in the **simTools** package would become

```
> test("../simTools")
Testing simTools
sampleFromData must return data frames of the correct format : ....
```

As you can see, the output is just the same as if we had run `test_file`. When we have structured the tests in this format, they will be run when we run the package checks from Hour 19. However, it is good practice to run your tests before this point if you have made changes to the code so that you don't get to building your package before you realize that you have introduced an error. Given the ease with which we can run tests inside a package, it won't take a lot of effort to run `test` on a regular basis.

TIP

Test-Driven Development

One means of code development that you might find useful is an idea known as test-driven development. In this approach to development, we start by writing tests for what we want our package to do that will initially fail, and then we develop the code. When the test passes, we have completed that component. This is a useful way to develop code if you have a large number of requirements or if you are adding requirements, because you can always see what you have done so far and what is left to do.

Including Data in Packages

As you will know from using other R packages, it is not only code that can be incorporated but also data. This is useful if you have a dataset that you want to be able to use for examples or that you want to make available to others for a specific purpose or even as a reference dataset for functionality in your package. Just as with all other components of a package, we can use **devtools** to simplify adding data to a package.

Where we add the data will depend on what its purpose is. Data that we want to be available to end users or available for examples or user guides should be stored in the "data" directory. If we haven't yet added data, this won't exist in our package structure but will be added when we run the use_data function. This function, in the **devtools** package, both sets up the correct structure and adds the data we want to include in an appropriately compressed format. The dual purpose of this function means that it is slightly different in usage from other **devtools** functions for which we simply provide the file path to the package. As an example, let's create a simple dataset that we will add to our package:

```
> exampleData <- data.frame(ID = 1:10, Value = rpois(10, lambda = 5))
> use_data(exampleData, pkg = "../simTools")
Saving exampleData to data/exampleData.rda
```

You will notice here that in the use_data function, we have first listed the data objects we want to have included. Because we can provide any number of data objects, we need to specify the package in which to include the data using the pkg argument. This will create the "data" directory for us as well as compress the data and add it to the package structure.

With the data in this format, we can now load the package and see the data, just as we use data in any other package, by giving the name of the data set. Note that it retains the name we gave the object when it was created (in this case, exampleData).

If you were to run the package checks now, you would find that this creates a warning in the check because any object that can be seen by the user must have a corresponding help file. So the next step we need to take is to provide the documentation. As you saw in Hour 19, we can use **roxygen2** to create package documentation, and this extends to help files for data sets. This is very similar to how we document a function, but we use an alternative tag, @format, to describe the structure of the dataset. In addition, rather than giving the function call after the header, we give the name of the dataset. As an example, consider Listing 20.2, where we have created simple documentation for the dataset we just added to the package. This header needs to be saved in an R script in the R directory. As discussed in the previous hour, the naming of these files is up to you but it is generally good practice to name so that it is easy to identify the file.

LISTING 20.2 Roxygen Header for a Dataset

```
1: #' Simple example of including data
2: #'
3: #' This is a simple example of how we can include data in a package
4: #' and provide the corresponding documentation.
5: #'
6: #'  @format A data.frame with 10 rows and two columns:
7: #'  \describe{
8: #'    \item{ID}{Unique identity variable}
9: #'    \item{Value}{Simulated value (g)}
```

```
10: #'  }
11: #'
12: #'  @source Simulated data
13: "exampleData"
```

You will see that we have documented each column of the data. It is a good idea here to state what the column of data contains as well as any units relevant to that column—for instance, "inches" or "pounds" if you were giving measurements of distance or weight. You might also notice in this example that we have used the tag @source, which is a handy way of detailing where the data came from—obviously, in this case, the data was simply simulated, but this may be details of the location of the original data.

TIP

Adding More Data

We can still use the use_data function to add datasets later in the package development, even if we have already set up the package structure. We use the function in the same way, but the function itself won't create (or overwrite) a data directory.

If we want to include reference data that is used by a function in our package but is not visible to the end user, we save the data in a file named sysdata.rda in the R directory. Again, we can use the use_data function to incorporate such data, but in this instance we add the argument internal = TRUE. Unlike the user-visible data in the data directory, we do not need to document this data. Including a dataset in this way would look like the following:

```
> hiddenData <- data.frame(ID = 1:5, Ref = rnorm(5))
> use_data(hiddenData, pkg = "../simTools", internal = TRUE)
Saving hiddenData to R/sysdata.rda
```

Including a User Guide

In R, a user guide is typically referred to as a vignette and is typically a means of extending the package help files to describe the typical workflow of your package or to give extended details of what you have implemented in your package. If you are sharing your package with others, you will typically need to provide some form of documentation to help them get started. By including this in the package itself, you can be sure that it is always available to the users, that you can easily keep it up to date, and that the code in the vignette actually runs without error because it is checked as part of the package checks.

You can see the vignettes available for a package by using the browseVignettes function. This will allow you to navigate vignettes for all packages or for a specific package. Here is an example:

```
> #browse all vignettes
> browseVignettes()
> # browse for a specific package
> browseVignettes("roxygen2")
```

A package can include multiple vignettes, which is useful if you want to include more detailed information about specific components of your package.

Including a Vignette in a Package

When it comes to writing a vignette, we now have multiple options for the tools we use. Traditionally we used Sweave, which requires knowledge of LaTeX, a markup language that allows us to combine text, R code, and mathematical expressions. Since R version 3.0.0, we can use any package to create a vignette that can produce HTML of PDF files. This means that we can now use the package **knitr**, which allows us to use R Markdown for our vignettes. In this section, we will look at how to incorporate a vignette in a package and get started with creating one.

As with all other aspects of our package, we are going to use **devtools** to help us get started. It is now a best practice to include package vignettes in a vignettes directory. We can of course create this directory directly; however, the use_vignette function will not only create that directory but it will add all the required components to the DESCRIPTION file, and it will create a template vignette file for us to start working with. To get started on a quick-start guide to using our **simTools** package, we would run the following line:

```
> use_vignette("QuickStart", pkg = "../simTools")
```

The first argument here gives the name of the vignette that we want to create so that the template file takes the correct filename. There will now be a vignette directory containing the file QuickStart.Rmd. You will also find that the package **knitr** has been added to the list of suggested packages in the DESCRIPTION file and that a new field, VignetteBuilder, will also have been added with **knitr** listed as the required package to build the vignette.

The vignette file incorporated in your package will be checked when you run the usual package checks, and it will be built into an HTML file when you build the package. During development of the vignette itself, the easiest way to preview the file you are creating is to simply use the Knit button in RStudio. First of all, open the file that was created for you. This is a ".Rmd," or RMarkdown, file. We will return to how to write this in the next section, but you will initially find that the file has been populated with some sample text. In RStudio, opening this file will have given you some alternative options across the top of the file viewer, one of which being "Knit." Selecting this option, you will build the file into the corresponding HTML file and a preview will be opened in the Viewer tab.

TIP

Building Vignettes Without RStudio

If you don't want to use the built-in options in RStudio, you can build your vignettes by running the function `build_vignettes` in the **devtools** package. This is used the same as other **devtools** functions, passing the package as the main argument. This will create the directory inst/docs, which will contain the .Rmd file, an R script, and the built HTML vignette.

Writing a Vignette

R Markdown is simple to read and write markup language that allows us to incorporate text, R code, and output in a single file. In this section, we introduce the basics of markdown. For more details on creating documentation and reports in R, see Hour 23, "Dynamic Reporting."

Because the step we took in the previous section created a sample file for us, we will start with this. All R Markdown documents use a header at the top of the file to give details such as the title, author, and date, as well as details on the type of file to generate. For a vignette we also have some extra components. Listing 20.3 shows what this template header looks like. As you can see, we have the title and author components that we can update as well as the date (which in this case updates dynamically). We can optionally remove these components, if we don't want the date to appear, for instance. The remainder of the header gives instructions relating to building the vignette and creating an index of vignettes, as we saw when we ran `browseVignettes`. The only thing that we need to change here is on line 7, where we need to update the `Vignette Title` text to match the title on line 2.

LISTING 20.3   Vignette Header

```
 1: ---
 2: title: "Vignette Title"
 3: author: "Vignette Author"
 4: date: "`r Sys.Date()`"
 5: output: rmarkdown::html_vignette
 6: vignette: >
 7:   %\VignetteIndexEntry{Vignette Title}
 8:   %\VignetteEngine{knitr::rmarkdown}
 9:   %\VignetteEncoding{UTF-8}
10: ---
```

The actual content of the guide is up to you to determine, but a useful guide to produce would walk the user through the main workflow. How do you get started using your package? What are the main functions in your package that a user should look at? There is no need to go into all of the details about all the function arguments, but this type of guide will point a user in the right direction, and they can then use your function help files for more details. As an example, we might produce a guide for our **simTools** package that guides the user to the `sampleFromData` function as a starting point for their simulation.

When it comes to starting to write the document, we need to know the basics of markdown. It is quite a limited markup language, but that shouldn't prevent you from being able to create a functional user guide to your package. Some examples of markdown syntax can be seen in Table 20.1.

TABLE 20.1 Basic Markdown Notation

Format	Code	Example
Level 1 Heading	`# heading text`	`# Introduction`
Level 2 Heading	`## heading text`	`## Loading the Package`
Level 3 Heading	`### heading text`	`### Main Functions`
Italic	`*italic*, _italic_`	
Bold	`**bold**, __bold__`	`The **devtools** package`
Superscript	`text^superscript^`	`Multiply by 4^2`
Strikethrough	`~~strikethrough~~`	`This ~~large~~ small` `document`
Bulleted List	`* Item 1` `* Item 2`	`* Load package` `* Run sampleFromData`
Numbered List	`1. Item 1` `2. Item 2`	`1. Load package` `2. Run sampleFromData`
Hyperlink	`[Text as link]` `(http://www.example.com)`	`[R](www.r-project.org)`
Quote	`> This is a block quote` `> That can span multiple lines`	`> All R Markdown documents` `> use a header.`

An example of how a user guide for the **simTools** package might look can be seen in Listing 20.4. You will notice that the file created for us by **devtools** contains text, which can be deleted, and that also includes examples of many of these features.

LISTING 20.4 Example of User Guide Content

```
1: This guide is intended as a means of quickly getting started with the package
2: **simTools**. It will introduce the main workflow of the package.
3:
4: ## Getting Started
5:
```

```
 6: The main function in the **simTools** package is `sampleFromData`. This
➥function will
 7: allow you to generate random samples from a given data set. It is useful for
 8: simulation experiments.
 9:
10: ### Loading the package
11:
12: Before starting you will need to load the package in the usual way using either
13: `library` or `require`.
14:
15: ### Running the main function
16:
17: Once the package is loaded we can run the function as follows:
```

One of the main components of interest to the reader of your vignette will be examples of code and how to run the functions in your package. We include code in vignettes in special code blocks. An example of a code block is shown in Listing 20.5. We use the triple back ticks to mark the start and end of the code block, as you can see on lines 1 and 5. You will also notice the {r} after the back ticks on line 1. This indicates that the code in this block should be executed as R code. We can also include options for the code block inside these curly brackets. We will return to this in Hour 23.

LISTING 20.5   Including a Code Block

```
1: ```{r}
2: library(mangoTraining)
3: example1 <- sampleFromData(demoData, size = 5)
4: example1
5: ```
```

Inside the code block we can include any executable code we want, including code that generates graphics. Note that the code will be checked during the standard package checks as well as the build, and any packages used to run examples in the vignette need to be included in the suggests field in your DESCRIPTION file as a minimum. When this code block is included in our vignette, it will include not only the code run but also the output generated. An example of how the code block in Listing 20.5 would be rendered is shown in Figure 20.1.

We can include as much text and as many code blocks as we want into a vignette, but it is worth remembering the reader. If you find your vignette is quite long, you may want to split it into multiple files so it does not seem as long and difficult to read. However, this is entirely up to you.

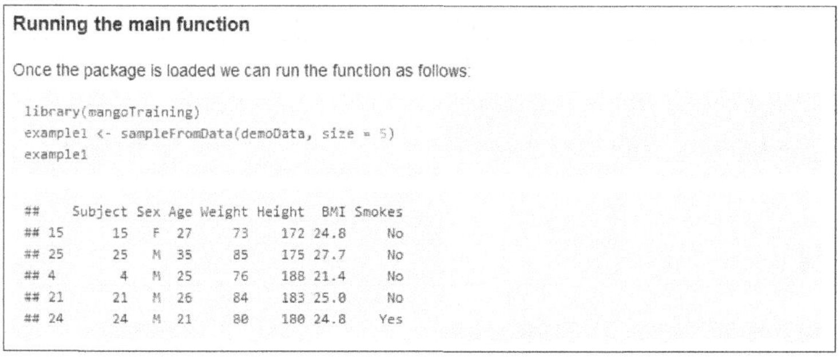

Running the main function

Once the package is loaded we can run the function as follows:

```
library(mangoTraining)
example1 <- sampleFromData(demoData, size = 5)
example1
```

```
##    Subject Sex Age Weight Height  BMI Smokes
## 15      15   F  27     73    172 24.8     No
## 25      25   M  35     85    175 27.7     No
## 4        4   M  25     76    188 21.4     No
## 21      21   M  26     84    183 25.0     No
## 24      24   M  21     80    180 24.8    Yes
```

FIGURE 20.1
Example of the HTML version of code blocks in vignettes

Code Using Rcpp

You saw in Hour 18 that we could easily incorporate code written in C++ using the package **Rcpp**. If we have done this and we then wanted to put that code into our packages, we would need to know how to include the code in our packages. As you have seen in the previous section, **devtools** has simplified all aspects of incorporating additional package components, and the function use_rcpp will help us at this point.

Any source code that is not R code is included in a directory called src. The use_rcpp function will create this directory for us, along with handling the updating of the DESCRIPTION file. As an example, in our **simTools** package we would run the following:

```
> use_rcpp("../simTools")
Adding Rcpp to LinkingTo and Imports
Creating src/ and src/.gitignore
Next, include the following roxygen tags somewhere in your package:
#' @useDynLib simTools
#' @importFrom Rcpp sourceCpp
```

You will notice that this also tells us to add some **roxygen** tags in the package. You can include this anywhere in the package, but the most sensible place would be in the overall package help file. These two tags will ensure that the C++ code is loaded when the package is loaded.

At this point, we can include the .cpp files, which we discussed in Hour 18, in the source directory. As an example, suppose that we included the sampleInC function that we wrote in Listing 18.5 of Hour 18 in our package. Including this in a .cpp file in the src directory with the same structure that we saw previously, we cause the check and build process for the R package to create the appropriate additional files in both the src and R directories for us. If we are simply using this function in other R functions and we do not intend the end user to see the function, this is all we need to do and we can start to use the function in our code. The function will not be exported but will be available to any code that requires it.

If we want to export this function to be visible to the end user, we will need to include an equivalent **roxygen** header in the .cpp file. This will be identical to the headers for R functions as we saw in Hour 19, but we use the C++ comment character to indicate the header rather than the R comment character. An example of what the file header would look like can be seen in Listing 20.6.

LISTING 20.6   Including a Code Block

```
1: #include <Rcpp.h>
2: using namespace Rcpp;
3:
4: //' Sample a series of 0s and 1s
5: //'
6: //' @param len A single integer giving the final length.
7: //' @export
8: // [[Rcpp::export]]
```

After you have updated the file, you will need to update the package documentation in the usual manner before building your package. You will then have the function `sampleInC` available to the end user and a corresponding help file for the user to reference. Of course, just like R functions, it is beneficial to include this header for all functions but simply omit the `@export` tag if you do not want the function to be available to the end user.

Summary

In this hour, you saw how to improve packages, making them more robust, user friendly, and easier to manage. Although these components are not a requirement of a package, they are considered to be best practices, and we would recommend that you get into the habit of structuring your packages in this way, in particular with tests and user guides. In the next hour, we will introduce classes and how to develop our own classes to make code more robust and user friendly.

Q&A

Q. Do I really need to include tests? Isn't it going to take a long time?

A. You do not need to include any of the package components mentioned in this hour; however, it is good practice to include tests and a vignette. Tests will help you to ensure the quality of your code and make it much easier to make changes to the code in the future knowing that they will not impact the code adversely. The first time you write tests it may take you longer as you get used to the structure, but this will quickly become second nature, and if you do it as you write the code rather than all at the end, it won't add much to the development time.

Q. Can I include data in a .csv file in my package?

A. Yes, you can include any raw data file that you like in your package, but this is done in a slightly different way. In this case, you should create a directory in the inst directory to contain the data (for instance, inst/extdata). You can then access this data using the `system.file` function and pointing to the rawdata directory of the package, like so:

```
system.file("extdata", "myFile.csv", package = "simTools")
```

Q. I know LaTeX. Can I use this for my vignette instead of markdown?

A. Yes, you can. You simply create your vignette in an .Rnw file rather than an .Rmd file. You will need to include lines 7–9 in Listing 20.3 in your document header.

Workshop

The workshop contains quiz questions and exercises to help you solidify your understanding of the material covered. Try to answer all questions before looking at the "Answers" section that follows.

Quiz

1. Why should you include tests in a package?

2. How would you include data in your package that is not intended to be seen by the end user?

3. What are user guides known as in R?

4. What is the simple markup language that you can use for vignettes?

5. In which directory do you put C++ code?

Answers

1. Tests help you to ensure that your code does what it is meant to do. If you make changes to the code, you can re-run the tests to ensure that the code still runs as expected. You can also write tests for any bugs you identify so that you can continually check that they don't end up back in your code due to changes that you make.

2. You can include data in your package using the `use_data` function. You can ensure that this is only available to the package by using the argument `internal = TRUE`, which will store the data in the R directory rather than the data directory.

3. Longer user guides in R are referred to as vignettes. You can see all of the package vignettes by using the `browseVignettes` function.

4. You use the markup language markdown. We can also use LaTeX for writing vignettes.

5. Any C++ code, or other compiled code, is included in the src directory.

Activities

1. In the activities for the last hour we developed a package called **summaryTools** and we wrote two functions for this package. Using the methods introduced in this hour, add a test framework and tests for each of the functions you created.

2. Update both functions to include some simple error checking of the arguments. Ensure that the tests you have written still pass, and add further tests to test the error handling.

3. Create a simple dataset, `summaryData`, that contains three columns: ID, which should be a numeric factor that is unique for each row; Group, which is a random sample of the values "A" and "B" to identify the group each value is in; and finally "Observed," which is a sample from a random normal distribution.

4. Include this data in your package and ensure that it is well documented.

5. Create a simple vignette for your package that explains how the user should run your functions.

6. Rebuild and check your package, ensure that all tests pass, and that you can access the data and vignette once your package is loaded.

HOUR 21
Writing R Classes

What You'll Learn in This Hour:

▶ What a class is

▶ How to create an S3 class

▶ Generic functions and methods

▶ Inheritance in S3

▶ Documenting in S3

▶ Limitations of S3

Now that you have seen how to build an R package, we will take a closer look at the class structures available in R and the benefits of implementing such structures in an R package. Classes and object orientation are concepts that will be more than familiar to anyone who has majored in computer science. Any readers familiar with these concepts will also be aware that despite many common themes between languages, there is no standard cross-language approach to object orientation.

It may come as no surprise to learn that R has several takes on what constitutes object-oriented programming. In this hour, we take a general look at some key features of object-oriented programming before focusing in on R's S3 implementation. In Hour 22, "Formal Class Systems," we will look more closely at some of the other options available to us in R.

What Is a Class?

In Hour 16, "Introduction to R Models and Object Orientation," and Hour 17, "Common R Models," you saw how to build and compare various types of models in R. In order to do so we took advantage of R's S3 class structure. Our model objects had classes such as lm and survreg. We used the print, plot, and summary functions to analyze the models. For each class of object, the print, plot, and summary functions behaved in different ways, producing output appropriate to the class of model. Functions that behave differently depending on the class of input are known as "methods."

The class and method concepts are fundamental to object-oriented programming. When we refer to a "class system" in R, we are talking about an object-oriented system, of which R has several.

Object Orientation in R

Back in Hour 1, "The R Community," we discussed the history of S and its impact on R today. Nowhere is this impact felt more greatly than on R's class system, particularly when it comes to modeling. Another claim we made in Hour 2, "The R Environment," was that R is "loosely" object-oriented. In R, everything is an object and has a name and a class. There is also a clear distinction between data objects and function objects. The distinction between objects and functions that act on objects is the basis of an object-oriented programming environment. However, the functions that we write do not have to be associated with a particular class of object. We must therefore choose to use the object-oriented features available in R. In R today, there are actually four common class implementations: S3, S4, reference classes (a.k.a R5), and R6. The "S" in S3 and S4 refers directly to S, whereas the numbers refer to the S versions within which the classes were unveiled. Those that use the term "R5" for reference classes or R6 are simply continuing the number sequence. The terms have absolutely nothing to do with R versions.

Despite the sequential release of new class structures in R, the vast majority of R packages on CRAN today either implement an S3 system or no system at all. The S3 system is particularly appealing for package developers with an analytical background due to its relative simplicity and less rigid rules. This makes it more accessible when sharing code with other analysts. As you will see in Hour 22, the more rigid structures of the other class systems lend themselves more toward application development in R. However, even these implementations could be considered relaxed when compared with traditional object-oriented development languages such as Java.

Why Bother with Object Orientation?

In order to write professional-level code, we need to ensure that we are following good programming practice. Everyone tends to have their own definition of precisely what this means, but the central concepts are based around

- Readability
- Maintainability
- Efficiency

In Hour 18, "Code Efficiency," we looked closely at code efficiency. In Hour 19, "Package Building," we then discussed code quality and talked about how adherence to a naming convention, regular commenting, and consistent layout and spacing can improve readability. In Hour 20, "Advanced Package Building," we looked at building a test framework to help improve the maintainability of our code. Object orientation builds upon the theme of maintainability.

It is much easier to develop, test, and hence maintain modular code. We write modular code by ensuring that functions remain small and, where possible, have a single purpose. The modular approach facilitates the development of unit tests. In many cases, just writing modular code is sufficient to ensure that our code base is maintainable. The concept of object-oriented programming extends the idea of modular code and introduces other useful concepts such as type checking and inheritance.

Fundamentally, a class structure lets us define a consistent behavior for objects of that class. Once we can be sure that an object is of a particular structure, we can construct methods (functions) that understand this structure and react accordingly.

Class Example

Let's imagine for a second that the `data.frame` class did not exist. Hopefully you would agree that with only vectors, matrices, arrays, and lists to store information, analyzing data would be pretty tough! We are used to thinking of data as a rectangular structure with a number of rows and columns. Each column contains a different type of information in which we are interested (dates, times, numeric values, character, and so on). Given that vectors, matrices, and arrays are all single-mode objects and can only store data of a single type, the only option available to us would be to store our data as a list. However, a list can store any object, whereas we only want to store columns of data. We therefore need to impose some rules on our list:

▶ Every element must be a vector (to ensure we have "columns" containing a single type of data)

▶ Each vector must have the same length (to ensure that we have a fixed dimension)

▶ Each "column" should have a name attribute (for easy referencing of columns)

These rules ensure that our list functionally behaves like a rectangular data structure, but we also need it to look like one. We therefore impose the further rule:

▶ The list *looks like* a rectangular data structure

To see what an object looks like, we usually just type its name and press Enter. In R, typing an object's name is a shortcut for calling the `print` function on the object. When we say, "the list *looks like* a rectangular data structure" what we really mean is, "when we call `print` on the object, it looks like a rectangular data structure." In summary, we have defined three rules that specify the structure of a data frame object and one rule that defines how the `print` function should behave when we pass it a data frame object. In other words, we have defined a "data frame" class and a print method for this class.

We don't just want to print data frames, however. Once we have defined the structure, we can also define what happens when we call `subset` on the structure. We can write additional methods such as head and tail, which return the first and last few rows of data, respectively. We can write nrow, ncol, and dim methods. We can also define what happens when we call plot or aggregate. What we get from defining classes is structure and control. So long as we create an object of the right structure, we know that our methods will function as expected.

Inheritance

In object-oriented programming, inheritance is extremely useful to us because it keeps our code modular and saves us from duplicating code. When programmers talk about the benefits of inheritance, they typically talk about defining animals. Let's imagine we want to define a cat object and a dog object. Cats and dogs have a lot in common. Among the many things they do, they eat and they sleep. However, a cat meows and a dog barks. Defining cats and dogs separately results in duplication; for each animal we must define what it means to eat and what it means to sleep. The idea of inheritance allows us to define an object hierarchy. First, we define what it means to be an "animal" object. An animal eats and an animal sleeps. We say that "cat" and "dog" objects inherit these properties from the "animal" object. We can then define the additional "meows" property for cats and "barks" property for dogs. Should we ever need to change what it means to eat or sleep, we need only make a single change to the "animal" object.

Each of the object-oriented systems in R benefits from inheritance. Consider the data.table class from the **data.table** package you saw in Hour 12, "Efficient Data Handling in R." We can think of a data.table object as a data frame that, among other things, prints nicely when there are many rows. There are actually only a handful of methods that respond specifically to data.table objects. The rest of the functionality is inherited primarily from the data.frame class. Where a method has not been defined for the data.table class, R defaults to the method for the data.frame class. Beyond that, R defaults to the default method for an S3 object (of which data.frame objects belong). For example, calling summary on a data.table object still returns a statistical summary of each column as it would for a data.frame object, even though no summary method has been specifically written for the data.table class. Inheritance is a powerful idea that enables us to easily build upon the work of others.

NOTE

Multi-Level Hierarchy

The tbl_df class actually inherits from a tbl class, which in turn inherits from a data.frame. This is an example of multi-level hierarchy. We can use this property to build hierarchical class structures.

Why Use S3?

We begin our tour of R classes by looking at R's most common class implementation, S3. Each of the basic data structures we have looked at throughout the book use an S3 structure. Standard linear models, generalized linear models, survival models, and mixed effects models all use an S3 class structure. We therefore know that we can print, plot, or summarize these objects in a consistent manner. By developing our own packages with S3, we can take advantage of this consistency by defining our own `print`, `plot`, and `summary` methods for a new class of object. We can also use S3 to create new methods specific to our new class of object.

The S3 class implementation is a form of generic function object-oriented programming. In generic function object-oriented programming, we call generic functions that then determine which function is appropriate to use with our object. For example, when we pass an object of class `lm` to the generic `plot` method, the method determines that the `plot.lm` function should be used. This type of implementation is rare among programming languages and is often frowned upon by experienced software developers. However, like R itself, the S3 class system is relatively straightforward to learn and is extremely popular among data scientists and statisticians alike. The implementation strikes a nice balance between the full flexibility of the R language and the more controlled rigor of other object-oriented programming languages.

Creating a New S3 Class

In most object-oriented programming environments, we begin by formally defining the structure of the class. We also place restrictions on each element of the class. However, S3 implements a lazy form of object-oriented programming that allows us to instantiate (create instances of) a new class without formally defining the class.

Instantiating S3 objects is incredibly straightforward. Remember that every object in R has a class. We can query the class of an object using the `class` function. Here's an example:

```
> x <- 5
> class(x)
[1] "numeric"
```

The same `class` function can be used to change the class of an object. In the following example, we change the class of our numeric x value to a new class called `superNumber`.

```
> class(x) <- "superNumber"
> x
[1] 5
attr(,"class")
[1] "superNumber"
```

In this ad-hoc manner, we can change the class of any object to anything we like, whether we have defined the new class or not. Note that the class of an object is returned as an attribute. Objects can have several attributes that are returned via the `attributes` function:

```
> attributes(x)
$class
[1] "superNumber"
```

TIP

Removing a Class

We can return an object without its class attribute using the `unclass` function. The `unclass` function removes the class attribute, leaving only the underlying object and any attributes, as shown here:

```
> aDF <- data.frame(X = 1:3, Y = rnorm(3))
> aDF
  X          Y
1 1  0.52409671
2 2 -2.26076788
3 3 -0.01967972
> unclass(aDF)
$X
[1] 1 2 3

$Y
[1]  0.52409671 -2.26076788 -0.01967972

attr(,"row.names") [1] 1 2 3
```

Note that `unclass` returns a new object and does not affect the original object.

A More Formal Approach to Creating Classes

As you have seen, it is very easy to change the class of an object. However, it is not considered good practice to do so, nor is it particularly useful, especially if our goal is writing packages. A more standard approach is to define the structure that our class should take and then write a function that creates objects of that class. This is known as a "constructor" function. Traditionally, functions that generate objects of a particular class are named after the class of object that they create. For example, the `ts` function creates time series (`ts`) objects.

Because we are introducing a formal method for creating a class, let's start with a more formal example and write a class for modular arithmetic. If you are not familiar with modular arithmetic, consider time as specified by a typical 12-hour clock. Imagine it is three o'clock (we ignore a.m. and p.m. for this example). In 10 hours' time, we will say it's one o'clock. We won't say it's 13 o'clock. A 12-hour clock is an example of "mod 12" arithmetic. We call the number 12 our "modulus." Numbers must always be between 0 and 11 (when we hit 12, we restart at zero). We now define this formally in R using an S3 class structure. In lines 1 to 11 in Listing 21.1, we create a new class called modInt. Our object consists of an integer value and a modulus attribute. Some examples are also provided to illustrate the behavior of the constructor function.

LISTING 21.1 Writing a Function to Generate a New Class

```
 1: > modInt <- function(x, modulus) {
 2: +   # Create the object from the starting number and modulus, "mod"
 3: +   # Divide by the modulus to get new number appropriate for that modulus
 4: +   object <- x %% modulus
 5: +   # Assign a class attribute to the object
 6: +   class(object) <- "modInt"
 7: +   # Store the modulus as an attribute
 8: +   attr(object, "modulus") <- modulus
 9: +   # Return the new object
10: +   object
11: + }
12: > # Examples
13: > modInt(3, 12)
14: [1] 3
15: attr(,"class")
16: [1] "modInt"
17: attr(,"modulus")
18: [1] 12
19: > modInt(13, 12)
20: [1] 1
21: attr(,"class")
22: [1] "modInt"
23: attr(,"modulus")
24: [1] 12
```

We have now created a constructor function that generates objects of our chosen modInt class. On its own this could perhaps be a useful function. However, to really see the benefit of the S3 class structure, we need to define some generic functions.

Generic Functions and Methods

Generic functions are functions that can behave differently depending on the class of object passed to them. The precise behavior is controlled by further functions known as methods. You saw the generic methods print, plot, and summary in Hour 16. If we inspect the source code of the `print` function, for example, we see that it calls the `UseMethod` function. It is the `UseMethod` function that determines which method function to call.

```
> print
function (x, ...)
UseMethod("print")
<bytecode: 0x00000000094cda60>
<environment: namespace:base>
```

As you saw in Hour 16, the S3 class structure provides a simple naming convention that we can use to create methods for a new class. The naming convention is as follows:

```
[genericFunction].[class]
```

A dot (.) is used to separate out the generic function from the class. The function `print.lm` defines what happens when we call the `print` function on an object with class `lm`. Let's return to our sample `modInt` class that we defined in Listing 21.1. The two examples from line 12 onward were functional but not particularly nice to look at. We start by defining a `print` method to control the appearance of `modInt` objects. In order to do so, we create a function called `print.modInt`, shown next, and let R's S3 class system do the rest:

```
> print.modInt <- function(aModIntObject){
+   # Extract the relevant components from the object
+   theValue <- as.numeric(aModIntObject)
+   theModulus <- attr(aModIntObject, "modulus")
+   # Print the object in the desired form
+   cat(theValue, " (mod ", theModulus, ")\n", sep = "")
+ }
> x <- modInt(3, 12)
> x
3 (mod 12)
```

NOTE

Naming Conventions

In the `print.modInt` function, we use the argument name `aModIntObject`. This is to illustrate that we should pass a `modInt` object to the function. However, it is much better practice to follow the naming convention of the generic function that will call the method (in this case, `print`). The `print` function takes `x` and an ellipsis (`...`), and in practice these are the arguments that a `print.modInt` function would take. The primary benefit of following this convention is that the help files are much easier to follow. A user unfamiliar with classes is far more likely to type `?print` than they are to type `?print.modInt`. Further, the names should be in the same order as the generic and adhere to any default values defined in the generic. Following these conventions will vastly improve the usability of your class.

NOTE

Updating Methods

As with any function, the impact of updating a method is immediate. For example, if we update the print method for a class, then the next time we print an object of that class, it will print differently.

We can see what methods have been defined for a class via the class argument to the methods function:

```
> methods(class = "modInt")
[1] print
see '?methods' for accessing help and source code
```

The same function can be used to query all methods for a particular generic:

```
> methods("plot")
 [1] plot.acf*           plot.data.frame*   plot.decomposed.ts*  plot.default
 [5] plot.dendrogram*    plot.density*      plot.ecdf            plot.factor*
 [9] plot.formula*       plot.function      plot.hclust*         plot.histogram*
[13] plot.HoltWinters*   plot.isoreg*       plot.lm*             plot.medpolish*
[17] plot.mlm*           plot.ppr*          plot.prcomp*         plot.princomp*
[21] plot.profile.nls*   plot.raster*       plot.spec*           plot.stepfun
[25] plot.stl*           plot.table*        plot.ts              plot.tskernel*
[29] plot.TukeyHSD*
see '?methods' for accessing help and source code
```

Defining Methods for Arithmetic Operators

Mathematical operators can also be used as generic functions. We define an operator in exactly the same way we do any generic function:

```
[operator].[class]
```

Returning to our modInt example, we can use the + operator to define what happens when we add two modInt objects together. The function and some examples are shown in Listing 21.2. Note than when defining methods that involve operators, we place back ticks around the function name to avoid errors.

CAUTION

Defining Each Operator Separately!

Defining a method for + does not automatically create a method for -, *, or /. These must be defined separately.

LISTING 21.2   Defining Operator Methods

```
 1: > # Define a new method 'add' method for the modInt class
 2: > `+.modInt` <- function (x, y){
 3: +   # We can only add objects that are of the same modulus
 4: +   if(attr(x, "mod") != attr(y, "mod")){
 5: +     stop("Cannot add numbers of differing modulus")
 6: +   }
 7: +   # Add the numbers together
 8: +   totalNumber <- as.numeric(x) + as.numeric(y)
 9: +   # Ensure a number in the correct modulus is returned
10: +   theResult <- modInt(totalNumber, attr(x, "mod"))
11: +   # Next step useful for inheritance (later)
12: +   class(theResult) <- class(x)
13: +   theResult
14: + }
15: >
16: > # Examples
17: > a <- modInt(7, 12)
18: > b <- modInt(9, 12)
19: > a + b
20: 4 (mod 12)
21: > c <- modInt(3, 4)
22: > a + c
23: Error in `+.modInt`(a, c) : Cannot add numbers of differing modulus
```

CAUTION

Operations on Different Classes of Objects

If we try to use an arithmetic operator such as + to combine objects of differing classes, R will attempt to use the method that is higher up the search path. This often results in an error. Attempting to combine S3 classes via an operator in this way is generally not recommended.

Lists vs. Attributes

Usually S3 classes are generated as lists (for example, the data.frame and lm classes). However, to create our modInt example, we used an attribute. This slightly simplifies numeric operations on objects of the modInt class and ensures that our numbers behave like regular integers in cases where we have not defined a method. However, it is just as easy to define the structure as a list, as the following example shows. Here, we create a modIntList class and a suitable print method:

```
> # Define a new modIntList class using a list structure
> modIntList <- function(x, modulus) {
+   # Define a list with two elements containing the number and modulus
```

```
+    object <- list(number = x %% modulus,
+                   modulus = modulus)
+    # Assign a class attribute to the object
+    class(object) <- "modIntList"
+    # Return the new object
+    object
+ }
>
> # Now define the print method
> print.modIntList <- function(aModIntListObject){
+    # Extract the relevant components from the object
+    theValue <- aModIntListObject$number
+    theModulus <- aModIntListObject$modulus
+    # Print the object in the desired form
+    cat(theValue, " (mod ", theModulus, ")\n", sep = "")
+ }
>
> # Examples
> modIntList(14, 6)
2 (mod 6)
```

The modInt and modIntList examples are relatively straightforward examples of using classes. Generally we recommend using lists to create S3 classes. A list enables us to easily store different types of objects within our class. The list approach is also more similar to the S4 "slot" approach that we will discuss in Hour 22.

Creating New Generics

When generating your own classes, you might find it sufficient to use existing generics such as print, plot, and summary. However, it can sometimes be useful to define new generic functions, particularly if you want others to build on your work.

We can use the UseMethod function to create our own generic functions. New generics should call the UseMethod function and do nothing else. The methods themselves should do all the work. Always define a default method using [genericFunction].[default]. The default method is invoked in the absence of any other methods. If there is no obvious "one size fits all" default, then a default method that returns a sensible error message should be defined.

Consider writing a generic version that mimics the mathematical square operation. For a numeric value x, this is just x^2. But what would such a function do for a character value or an object in our modInt class? In Listing 21.3 we define a new generic named square along with some methods for the cases we have just highlighted. Having very simply defined the generic in line 2, we proceed to define some methods starting with the default method. Some examples of the new generics are shown toward the end of the listing.

LISTING 21.3   Creating a New Generic

```
 1: > # Define a new generic
 2: > square <- function(x) { UseMethod("square", x) }
 3: >
 4: > # Define default method!
 5: > square.default <- function(x) x^2
 6: >
 7: > # Define some more methods
 8: > square.character <- function(x) paste(x, x, sep = "")
 9: >
10: > square.modInt <- function(x) {
11: +    # Standard square
12: +    simpleSquare <- as.numeric(x)^2
13: +    # Use correct modulus
14: +    modInt(simpleSquare, attr(x, "mod"))
15: + }
16: >
17: > # Check functionality
18: > square(2)
19: [1] 4
20: > square("A")
21: [1] "AA"
22: > x <- modInt(3, 4)
23: > square(x)
24: 1 (mod 4)
```

Inheritance in S3

One of the primary reasons for implementing a class structure is that it enables others to build upon it. Inheritance is a concept that allows us to take a class that has previously been defined and extend it. The benefit is that we need only define a handful of new generic functions. The rest are inherited from the base class. As we discussed earlier in the hour, a good example of this is the data.table class of object used by **data.table**. The data.table class extends/inherits from the data.frame class. We can see this inheritance when looking at the class of a data.table object:

```
> airDT <- data.table(airquality)
> class(airDT)
[1] "data.table" "data.frame"
```

As you saw in Hour 12, the data.table class changes the way a data frame prints. This is because the author has written a new print method specifically for the class. Other data.frame operations are unaffected by the extension. The summary and plot functions behave in exactly the same way for a data.table object as they do for a data.frame object.

When we query the class of a `data.table` object, a vector of classes is returned. To construct a new class that inherits from an existing class, we overwrite the class of our object with a vector of classes. For example, if we want to create a `clockTime` class representing integers as "mod 12" from our `modInt` class, we do so as follows:

```
> clockTime <- function(x){
+    # Fix x as mod 12
+    x <- modInt(x, 12)
+    # Define inheritance
+    class(x) <- c("clockTime", class(x))
+    x
+ }
> theTime <- clockTime(13)
> class(theTime)
[1] "clockTime" "modInt"
```

Earlier in the hour we defined a `print` method for our class. We also defined a method for the new `square` generic, the + operator. All of these are perfectly functional for our class, though for a `clockTime` class we expect a slightly different `print` method. In Listing 21.4 we define a new print method and add two instances of this class together. When we add them together, the `modInt` method is used because we haven't defined a `` `+.clockTime` ``. However, the result still prints in the `clockTime` format due to inheritance.

LISTING 21.4   Inheritance in Action

```
 1: > # Define a new print method for the clockTime class
 2: > print.clockTime <- function(aClockTimeObject){
 3: +    cat(as.numeric(aClockTimeObject), ":00\n", sep = "")
 4: + }
 5: >
 6: > # Examples
 7: > time1 <- clockTime(5)
 8: > time2 <- clockTime(42)
 9: > time1
10: 5:00
11: > time2
12: 6:00
13: >
14: > # Add together to demonstrate inheritance
15: > time1 + time2
16: 24: 11:00
```

The example on line 15 works because of a sensible step that we took earlier when defining the `` `+.modInt` `` method in Listing 21.2. In line 12 we overwrote the class of the return object with the original class of one of the two objects we started with. If we hadn't done so, then adding the two `clockTime` objects would return a `modInt` object, and we would lose one of the primary benefits of inheritance.

NOTE

Extending the Class Hierarchy

We can continue to extend classes indefinitely. However, it is rare to see S3 classes extended more than three or four times.

TIP

Checking Inheritance

Occasionally we may need to check that an object inherits from a particular class in order to ensure that a particular method will behave as expected.

Documenting S3

When building packages, it is important to document everything you can. You will see in Hour 22 that documenting more complex classes requires us to use new **roxygen2** tags; S3, on the other hand, is much more straightforward. To start with, the class itself has no formal definition, so the only things we can document are the class constructor function, the methods, and any generics that we define. Each of these is a regular R function, and so we use standard tags such as @param and the others listed in Table 19.1 of Hour 19.

Technically we don't have to generate help files for every method that we define, particularly if the method follows the argument-naming structure of the generic; you may notice that several of the methods in base R do not have help files (try ?print.lm, for example). However, it's always good practice to create documentation, and **roxygen2** makes it so easy, so why wouldn't you?! Though this may be obvious, it is also helpful to mention in the title and description that the method relates to a particular class of object.

Limitations of S3

One of the reasons that the S3 concept is not popular among software developers is that we cannot formally define a new class of object before instantiating the object, whereas in most class implementations it is common to check that the components of an object are of the expected structure for the class object. The lack of a formal class definition leaves S3 open to user error, unless we decide to go the extra mile and write checks for both the constructor function and the individual methods. Not only does this involve a lot of duplication, we may soon find that half our code base is dedicated to error handling. If the prevention of user error matters that much, it's time to step up to S4 classes or beyond.

The concept of inheritance is also fairly weak in S3; we have to be very careful to ensure that our methods allow for inheritance and do not force the creation of objects of one particular class. In class systems such as S4, inheritance is more formal, and type checking and validity are passed from the parent class through to the child class.

Summary

Following on from Hours 19 and 20, where you saw how to construct an R package, you have now seen how classes—and S3 classes in particular—can be used to improve package maintainability and add structure to our code base.

In Hour 22, we look at the more formal forms of object orientation available in R, starting with S4 classes. This will open the door to new concepts such as validity checking, multiple dispatch, and message-passing object orientation.

Q&A

Q. If S3 was the first implementation in S, isn't it time to move on to something more advanced?

A. Perhaps. Many people don't like S3, saying, "It's lazy," "It's not a proper class implementation," and so on. However, most of the good bits of R use S3 classes, and it's usually better to try to build on top of the good bits!

Q. I've heard that S3 isn't actually a class system at all. Is this true?

A. It's not a very strict system, but it is, nevertheless, a class system. Technically it is an informal form of generic function object-oriented programming.

Q. If an S3 method takes the form `[genericFunction].[class]`, what is going on with `data.frame`?

A. R has its quirks! It can be confusing to understand what is going on with functions such as `print.data.frame`. To confuse things even more, it is entirely possible to create a `frame` class and define a `print.data` method for that class, but I suggest you don't! The overall message here is that R is flexible, and though a period can indicate the presence of an S3 class implementation, it can also just be part of an object's name. That said, it's good practice not to use periods when naming variables.

Workshop

The workshop contains quiz questions and exercises to help you solidify your understanding of the material covered. Try to answer all questions before looking at the "Answers" section that follows.

Quiz

1. True or false? S3 and S4 classes were first introduced in S version 3 and S version 4, respectively.

2. Which of the following should be used to plot the object `myLm` of `lm` class?

   A. `plot`

   B. `plot.lm`

   C. `plot.myLm`

   D. `myLm.plot`

3. How do you find out what methods are available for an S3 class?

4. What is the name of the function used to define new generics?

5. True or false? You must document an S3 method when building an R package.

Answers

1. **True**. This is another case of R inheriting behavior from S.

2. **A**. Technically `plot.lm` can be used directly; however, directly invoking a method is generally discouraged.

3. You use the `methods` function and specify the `class=` option.

4. The `UseMethod` function enables us to create new generics. We define a generic by writing a function that calls `UseMethod`.

5. **False**. However, you really should document it, particularly if the method does anything sophisticated.

Activities

1. Define a new S3 class. The aim of the class is to store simulated data from various known statistical distributions. In order to construct the new class, create the following items:

   ▸ A constructor function that takes inputs `n` and `distribution`, representing the number of values to sample and the distribution to sample from. Ensure that the function has the option for other parameter arguments, as needed.

▶ A print method that displays a table of summary statistics for the simulated data (mean, median, standard deviation, min, and max).

▶ A plot method that draws a histogram of the random numbers, with a default title that states from which distribution the data has been simulated and how many values have been simulated.

Formal Class Systems

What You'll Learn in This Hour:

▶ S4 classes

▶ Reference classes

▶ R6 classes

▶ Other available class systems

In Hour 21, "Writing R Classes," you were introduced to the concept of classes, and we walked through the basic features of an S3 class in R. The S3 system provides a soft introduction to classes, allowing much of the flexibility that we have become accustomed to with R. In order to provide this flexibility, however, some of the main benefits of a more formal class system have been sacrificed. When developing S3 classes, we still need to be very careful to check that the input values are handled appropriately. Further, inheritance is not formally defined and we must be careful to write functions that allow for it.

During this hour, we look closely at two alternative class systems available in R: the S4 system and Reference Classes. Along the way, you will be introduced to new concepts such as validity checking, multiple dispatch, message-passing object orientation, and mutable objects.

S4

The S4 system was introduced in S version 4. Like S3, the S4 system is a form of generic function object-oriented programming. However, the system is much more formal and requires that we define the class structure before instantiating objects. This makes it easier to write methods because it is not possible to pass an object with the wrong structure to an S4 method.

The S4 system also benefits from a more formal form of inheritance that is specified when we define a class. When we extend an S4 class, all of the type and structure checking from the parent class is passed on to the child, thus reducing the need for duplicate code. Finally, S4 supports something called multiple dispatch, meaning that generic functions can operate based on multiple inputs.

Instances of S4 structures are rare in the base and recommended R packages, though the structure is used in several of the additional packages available on CRAN and throughout the BioConductor package repository. There is a tendency for S4 package names to end in 4, particularly where they implement something that has already been implemented in an S3 structure. This is not strictly adhered to, however.

Working with S4 Classes

It is slightly easier to find information about S4 classes and methods than it is with S3. To start with, we can find out if any object is an S4 object using the function isS4, to which we pass any R object. The isS4 function simply returns TRUE if an object is an S4 object and FALSE otherwise. Once we know that we have an S4 object and have ascertained the class (using the class function), we can call upon a number of other useful functions to find out more information about the class. Table 22.1 lists three functions that can be used to find out more information about a class. The table also describes their usage, with an example of usage for the merMod class contained within the **lme4** modeling package.

TABLE 22.1 Querying S4 Classes

Function	Description	Usage
getClass	Returns an object containing the definition of a specified class.	getClass("merMod")
getSlots	Returns a named character vector, where the names represent the class slots and the values represent the required object type for the slot.	getSlots("merMod")
findClass	Useful when working with class extensions. The function returns the package name and physical location on disk for which the class is defined.	findClass("merMod")

If we are working with a new package, we can find out what classes it contains using the getClasses function—for example, getClasses("package:lme4"). The same function can also be used to list all classes currently defined within in an R session. Similarly, the getGenerics function can be used to list all available generics within a package or an R session generally.

A list of all the methods available for a generic function may be obtained via the showMethods function. Here's an example:

```
> showMethods("tail")
Function: tail (package utils)
x="ANY"
```

```
x="Matrix"
x="sparseVector"
```

The `methods` function you saw in Hour 21 also works with S4 classes.

Help with S4

Constructors and generics are named R functions, and we can find help in the standard way, either via the RStudio GUI or by typing `?functionName`. Unlike S3 classes, S4 classes are formally defined and can therefore be documented. We use a special syntax of the form `class?className` in order to find out more about the class.

Defining an S4 Class

In the previous section, we stated that an S4 class must first be defined before we can instantiate objects. In other words, we cannot simply take an object and assign it a new class as we could with S3. This means that S4 classes can take longer to construct; however, the more formal definition provides us with benefits, such as the following:

- ▶ Type-checking
- ▶ Validity

Type-checking and validity ensure that when we define a class, objects within that class adhere to a particular structure and type. Unlike with S3, we can therefore assume that the structure is correct when we write methods for our class. This saves us from having to write additional error-handling steps within the methods and avoids duplication of code, thereby improving the maintainability of our code.

Setting the Class

To formally define an S4 class, we use the `setClass` function. The `setClass` function lives in the **methods** package, which is loaded by default when we start R interactively. Structurally, you can think of an S4 class as being a bit like an R list, where each element of the list is an R object with its own type and structure. In S4 terminology, we refer to these elements as "slots." The formal structure of an S4 class requires that we define the required structure for each slot—for example, `integer`, `numeric`, `character`, `matrix`, and so on. The two primary arguments to the `setClass` function are therefore the name of the class and a `slots` argument that defines the structure of the class. The `slots` argument expects either a list or a named character vector, where the names represent the names of the slots and the data represents the object type.

CAUTION

Loading the methods Package

When we start R in interactive mode, the **methods** package is loaded by default. However, R can also be executed in batch mode via Rscript, which does *not* load the **methods** package by default. When integrating an S4 structure into your own package, you should add a dependency on the **methods** package.

Let's start by looking back at the modInt structure that we defined in Hour 21. We take the basic concept of the structure and define it instead as an S4 class named modInt4. For any object in our class, we must store two important pieces of information: the base number and its modulus. Each of these is integer, so we specify their structure using the integer class. Note that although modular arithmetic only works with integer values, we don't actually need to store the data as integer, because numeric would suffice. However, we later use the data type to illustrate the impact of this formal definition.

```
> setClass("modInt4", slots=c(x = "integer", modulus = "integer"))
```

CAUTION

Change in Definition

Historically, S4 slots were defined via a representation argument within the setClass function. A representation function was then used to define both the slot structure and any inheritance. Although this functionality is now deprecated, representation is still the second argument to setClass for compatibility reasons. The S3methods, access, and version arguments are similarly deprecated. Further information is provided within the setClass help file.

We also use the setClass function to define inheritance, which we'll return to later in the hour.

Creating a New S4 Instance

Once we have formally defined a class, we can begin to create objects of that class. As with S3, it is good practice to do so via a class constructor function, though again it is not necessary. To generate an S4 object, the constructor function must include a call to the new function. The new function does the hard work of creating a prototype object from the class definition and populating the slots with any inputs we provide. The call to new ensures that our class has the required slots and that the information contained within each slot is of the correct type.

The first argument is the Class argument. This tells R what class is to be instantiated. Any slot names for the class are passed via an ellipsis (. . .). In the following example we create a constructor function for the modInt4 class that we previously defined. The final line contains the required call to the new function.

```
> modInt4 <- function(x, modulus){
+    # Divide by the modulus to get new number appropriate for that modulus
+    x <- x %% modulus
+    # Create a new instance
+    new("modInt4", x = x, modulus = modulus)
+ }
```

Having defined the constructor, we are now ready to create objects of our class. The following examples demonstrate the behavior of the type checking. In the first example, we pass the non-integer pi value and the integer 12L. We use L to ensure that the value is stored as integer as opposed to numeric.

Because pi is non-integer, the object cannot be created, and we receive an appropriate error message. In the second example, we pass two integer values that are actually stored as numeric in R. Again, the object cannot be created because both x and modulus must be of integer type. In the final example, we pass 4L and 12L. Both are integers, and our object is successfully created. Note that by default the name of the class is printed along with each of the slots.

```
> # Try to create some objects of our class
> modInt4(pi, 12L)
Error in validObject(.Object) :
  invalid class "modInt4" object: invalid object for slot "x" in class "modInt4":
  got class "numeric", should be or extend class "integer"

> modInt4(4, 12)
Error in validObject(.Object) :
  invalid class "modInt4" object: 1: invalid object for slot "x" in class
➥ "modInt4":
  got class "numeric", should be or extend class "integer"
invalid class "modInt4" object: 2: invalid object for slot "modulus" in class
➥ "modInt4":
  got class "numeric", should be or extend class "integer"

> modInt4(4L, 12L)
An object of class "modInt4"
Slot "x":
[1] 4

Slot "modulus":
[1] 12
```

Here we match the name of the constructor function to the name of the class as well as the names of the arguments to the names of the class slots. This is a very simple example of a class, and it makes sense to do so. However, the constructor function can take any arguments so long as the arguments that are eventually passed to new match those we defined using setClass. A good example of this is the lmer function in **lme4**, which takes arguments such as formula and data, fits a linear mixed-effects model, and generates an object of class merMod, which contains slots such as theta and beta.

Validity

As you have seen, the slot structure of an S4 class provides a handy mechanism for checking that the information provided is of the correct type. Occasionally we may need to provide some additional checks to ensure that an object conforms to expectations. Consider the data frame definition that we provided in Hour 21. A data frame consists of a list of vectors, but these vectors must also be of consistent length. In the S4 framework, we can provide such a check using a validity function.

A validity function is simply a function that contains all the checks we require in order to ensure that an object is of the correct structure. There are no naming restrictions on validity functions; however, it is standard practice to include the name of the class within the name. The "lowerCamelCase" convention is most commonly used, and periods should be avoided because they can falsely imply an S3 structure.

We now define a validity function for our modInt4 class. The check ensures that the two values are positive integers and that the base number is less than the modulus. Validity functions should return TRUE if the object is considered valid and FALSE if any of the checks are violated. The validity function should expect an S4 object as its only argument. It is good practice to name the argument object.

```
validModInt4Object <- function(object) {
  # Define checks
  # Note that the class definition already ensures that x and mod are integer
  xNonNeg                <- object@x >= 0
  modulusPositive        <- object@modulus > 0
  xLessThanEqualToModulus <- object@x <= object@modulus
  # Combine checks
  isObjectValid <- xNonNeg & modulusPositive & xLessThanEqualToModulus
  # Return TRUE or FALSE
  isObjectValid
}
```

Once we have defined the check, we need to link it to our class. We do so via the setValidity function. The setValidity function expects two main arguments:

- **Class**—The name of the class as a character string
- **method**—The name of the validity function

We can now link the `validModInt4Object` validity function to our `modInt4` class, like so:

```
> setValidity("modInt4", validModInt4Object)
Class "modInt4" [in ".GlobalEnv"]

Slots:

Name:      x modulus
Class: integer integer
```

NOTE

Defining Validity with `setClass`

In addition to `setValidity`, we can use the `validity` argument to the `setClass` function to link the function to the class that it checks.

Methods

As with S3, the S4 framework implements generic function object orientation. In order to define a method for our class, we must first define a generic. We then link the method back to the generic and our class using the `setMethod` function. Let's look first at the `setMethod` function. Table 22.2 lists the three required arguments to `setMethod`, along with a description of how they are used.

TABLE 22.2   The `setMethod` Function

Argument	Description
f	The name of the generic function for which we are setting the method.
signature	Typically a named vector or list of classes that are to be passed to the method. For simpler methods it can just be the name of the class to which the method applies.
definition	A function definition that describes what happens when the generic function is called with the objects specified in the signature.

As with S3, a number of generic functions are available "out of the box." In particular, S4 objects have a default `show` method, equivalent to `print` in S3. We can define a new `show` method to control how an object prints to screen. In the following example, we define a new show method for the `modInt4` class and then use the `setMethod` function to link the method to the class and generic function:

```
> showModInt4 <- function(object){
+   # Extract the relevant components from the object
+   theValue <- object@x
+   theModulus <- object@modulus
+   # Print the object in the desired form
+   cat(theValue, " (mod ", theModulus, ")\n", sep = "")
+ }
>
> # Link the previous function to the show generic and modInt4 class
> setMethod("show", signature = "modInt4", showModInt4)
[1] "show"
>
> # Display an object
> modInt4(3L, 12L)
3 (mod 12)
```

The more formal S4 framework and validity checking ensures that any object of `modInt4` class is of the correct structure and that any slots are of the correct type. The `show` method requires no additional checking. It is very clear and straightforward to follow.

CAUTION
___

Editing Methods

Methods must be linked to a generic and class via `setMethod`. If we redefine a method, we must then call `setMethod` again to relink the method to the generic and class.
___

Defining New Generics

In the previous example, we defined a new method for an existing generic, `show`. As with S3 classes, it is also possible to define new generics. We do so via the `setGeneric` function, which has two main arguments, as described in Table 22.3.

TABLE 22.3   Main Arguments to `setGeneric`

Function	Description
name	A character string representing the name of the generic function.
def	Leave blank if the function has already been defined. Alternatively, define the generic function with this argument.

In the following example, we first define a function called `square4`, an S4 equivalent of the `square` function we defined in Hour 21. We then turn the function into a generic with `setGeneric`.

```
> square4 <- function(x){
+     x^2
+ }
> setGeneric("square4")
[1] "square4"
```

Once the generic has been created, we can define new methods, which we link to classes via the `setMethod` function:

```
> squareModInt4 <- function(x) {
+     # Standard square
+     simpleSquare <- as.integer(x@x^2)    # Ensure value is valid
+     # Use correct modulus
+     modInt4(simpleSquare, x@modulus)
+ }
>
> # Link the modInt4 method to the square4 generic and modInt4 class
> setMethod("square4", signature = "modInt4", squareModInt4)
[1] "square4"
>
> # Test the method
> a <- modInt4(5L, 12L)
> a
5 (mod 12)
> square4(a)
1 (mod 12)
```

It is important to ensure that argument names match between the methods and the generic. If they don't, this is not only bad practice, but R throws a warning to tell you that it has changed the argument name in the method to match the generic.

Multiple Dispatch

In the following example, we create a new generic, `add`, and define what happens when we add two objects of class `modInt4`. This is an example of multiple dispatch, whereby a generic function can dispatch (pick a method) based on multiple arguments. Note that although we provide two objects of the same class, the multiple dispatch mechanism could be used to define what happens when we add objects of a different class. As in the previous example, we start by defining a function, `add`, and then turn it into a generic with `setGeneric`.

```
> add <- function(a, b){
+   a + b
+ }
> setGeneric("add")
[1] "add"
```

The add function we defined acts as the default method for the generic. Next, we define a method for our modInt4 object. Because the add function requires two objects, we must be careful to define an appropriate signature to ensure that the generic dispatches correctly.

```
> # Define a function that adds modInt4 objects
> addModInt4Objects <-  function(a, b){
+   # Sometimes we still need to define checks within the method
+   if(a@modulus != b@modulus){
+     stop("Cannot add numbers of differing modulus")
+   }
+   # Add the numbers together
+   totalNumber <- a@x + b@x
+   # Return the correct class
+   theResult <- modInt4(totalNumber, a@modulus)
+   theResult
+ }
>
> # Link the previous function to the add generic and modInt4 class
> setMethod("add", signature = c(a = "modInt4", b = "modInt4"),
+           addModInt4Objects)
[1] "add"
>
> # Test the function
> p <- modInt4(3L, 12L)
> q <- modInt4(7L, 12L)
> add(p, q)
10 (mod 12)
> add(q, q)
2 (mod 12)
```

Inheritance

You were introduced to the idea of inheritance in the previous hour. It is possible for S3 objects to inherit from one another, but as with much of S3 it is not formally defined. Inheritance is much better defined for S4 classes. We specify the inheritance when defining the class with setClass using the contains argument. Though the argument name may seem counterintuitive, we use contains to specify superclasses—in other words, classes that our class inherits from.

Consider the example of the 12-hour clock and the `clockTime` class we discussed in Hour 21. We define an S4 equivalent that inherits from `modInt4` as follows:

```
> setClass("clockTime4", contains = "modInt4")
```

At this point, our class is exactly the same as the `modInt4` class and contains slots x and modulus. It has also inherited all of the methods from the `modInt4` class without us having to think about inheritance when defining the `modInt4` methods.

```
> getSlots("clockTime4")
        x    modulus
"integer" "integer"
>
> methods(class = "clockTime4")
[1] add  show
see '?methods' for accessing help and source code
```

In Listing 22.1 we walk through a complete example, defining the class as we did earlier and then walking through some of the possible follow-on actions. In particular, we define a constructor function (lines 5 through 10) and a validity function (lines 14 through 17) to ensure that the modulus is equal to 12. We also define the `print` (`show`) method (lines 31 through 36). If we felt the need, we could define any additional methods specific to our `clockTime4` class.

LISTING 22.1 Building a `clockTime4` Class

```
 1: > # Define the class
 2: > setClass("clockTime4", contains = "modInt4")
 3: >
 4: > # Define constructor
 5: > clockTime4 <- function(x){
 6: +    # Ensure that x is in mod 12
 7: +    x <- x %% 12L
 8: +    # Create a new instance
 9: +    new("clockTime4", x = x, modulus = 12L)
10: + }
11: >
12: > # Define validity
13: > # Existing modInt4 validity is inherited
14: > validclockTime4Object <- function(object) {
15: +    isMod12 <- object@modulus == 12L
16: +    isMod12
17: + }
18: >
19: > # Link the validity function with the clockTime4 class
20: > setValidity("clockTime4", validclockTime4Object)
21: Class "clockTime4" [in ".GlobalEnv"]
22:
```

```
23: Slots:
24:
25: Name:        x modulus
26: Class: integer integer
27:
28: Extends: "modInt4"
29: >
30: > # Redefine show method
31: > showclockTime4 <- function(object){
32: +   # Print the object in the desired form
33: +   cat(object@x, ":00\n", sep = "")
34: + }
35: > setMethod("show", signature = "clockTime4", showclockTime4)
36: [1] "show"
37: >
38: > # Test the class
39: > clockTime4(5L)
30: 5:00
41: > clockTime4(13L)
42: 1:00
```

Listing 22.1 highlights another property of S4 inheritance, which is that validity is also inherited. This significantly cuts down on the amount of checking we have to do.

Documenting S4

The formal declaration of an S4 class requires some additional effort when it comes to documenting the class with **roxygen2**. The call to setClass should be documented with a standard title and description of the class. Each slot should be documented using the @slot tag.

```
#' An S4 Class that implements modular arithmetic
#'
#' @slot x An integer value in the specified \code{modulus}
#' @slot modulus An integer value representing the modulus for \code{x}
setClass("modInt4", slots=c(x = "integer", modulus = "integer"))
```

We must document S4 methods, but we have a choice as to whether to document in the class, in the generic, or separately within its own specific help file. Generally the decision as to where to document the method depends on how complicated the method is and how the method is to be used. Clearly we can only document the method via the generic if we created the generic ourselves, however.

We can control where the method is documented using either the @describeIn tag or @rdname tag. For example, to document the addModInt4Objects function within the help file for the add generic, we first create an **roxygen2** header for the generic add function and separately add a single **roxygen2** header line above the function definition for addModInt4Objects that contains a @describeIn tag.

```
#' @describeIn add Adds two modInt4 objects of the same modulus
addModInt4Objects <-  function(a, b){
  # Sometimes we still need to define checks within the method
  if(a@modulus != b@modulus){
    stop("Cannot add numbers of differing modulus")
  }
  # Add the numbers together
  totalNumber <- a@x + b@x
  # Return the correct class
  theResult <- modInt4(totalNumber, a@modulus)
  theResult
}
```

Reference Classes

Reference Classes were developed by John Chambers and have been available in the **methods** package since R version 2.12. Because they were the first new class implementation in R and because they followed S3 and S4, they are often referred to as "R5" classes. However, unlike with the S3 and S4 classes, the number 5 has nothing to do with the R version and is essentially meaningless.

Reference Classes are quite different from S3 and S4 and implement a much more common form of object-orientated programming known as message-passing object orientation. In message-passing object orientation, methods belong to the class and generic functions are not required. Message-passing object orientation is also used in Python, C++, and Java.

Creating a New Reference Class

Much like S4, we begin by defining the class. We do so via the function setRefClass. In terms of usage, the main difference between setClass and setRefClass is that with setRefClass we use the term "fields" instead of "slots." The similarity extends to inheritance, for which we use the contains argument.

One important difference with Reference Classes is that we save the output of the setRefClass function as an object. The object should have the same name as the class as defined by the first argument to setRefClass. We'll walk through Reference Classes using a variant on the modular arithmetic example that we used for S3 and S4 classes. However, message-passing object orientation is very different from generic function object orientation, and in practice message-passing object orientation is typically used to solve a different kind of problem. In particular, message-passing tends to be better suited to software development.

```
> modIntRef <- setRefClass("modIntRef",
+                           fields=c(x = "integer", modulus = "integer"))
```

This is the first time we have created a class as an object. Like with any R object, we can type its name to see what it looks like and query its class.

```
> class(modIntRef)
[1] "refObjectGenerator"
attr(,"package")
[1] "methods"
```

The object that we have created is a refObjectGenerator object. The refObjectGenerator object is a function that generates new objects from the class. The object that it generates is an environment much like a package environment or the global environment. The subject of environments is an advanced topic, but in essence an environment is a lot like a list, and we can access elements using the $ syntax *myEnvironmentName$ObjectName*. It can be very useful to think of Reference Classes and the objects we create from them as lists. We store all relevant information for the class in this list, including the fields, inheritance, and methods. There is no need for generic functions.

CAUTION

S4 or Reference Class?

Reference Classes are actually implemented as S4 classes with the data stored in an environment. Because the Reference Classes system is built on top of the S4 system, the isS4 function also returns TRUE for Reference Class objects.

Defining the class effectively creates our constructor function for us. We can instantiate new modIntRef objects using the modIntRef function that was created by the call to setRefClass.

```
> a <- modIntRef(x = 3L, modulus = 12L)
> a
Reference class object of class "modIntRef"
Field "x":
[1] 3
Field "modulus":
[1] 12
```

Because Reference Classes are based on S4 classes, we can use the new function to generate classes directly, though the practice is generally discouraged. The new function is also a method for our class, however, and can be invoked in the standard Reference Class manner.

```
> b <- modIntRef$new(x = 4L, modulus = 6L)
> b
Reference class object of class "modIntRef"
Field "x":
[1] 4
Field "modulus":
[1] 6
```

TIP

What Does a Reference Class Contain?

Because Reference Class objects are environments, we can use the `objects` function to see what they contain. Here's an example:

```
> objects(a)
[1] "copy"      "field"      "getClass" "modulus"   "show"      "x"
```

Defining Methods

With Reference Classes, methods are stored as part of the object that defines the class. They can be accessed and modified using *className*$methods syntax. We can also think of the methods element itself as another list, where each element is a defined method. Because there are no generic functions, we can generally name methods in any way we like, though some methods have a special meaning (for example, initialize).

TIP

Using setRefClass to Define Methods

Methods can also be defined directly when calling setRefClass.

In the following sections, we look at redefining our modular arithmetic class using a Reference Class context. We briefly revisit some of the key themes we have just seen with S4 classes.

Initialization

The initialize method is the Reference Class equivalent to a constructor function. However, instead of generating an object containing the required fields (slots), we generate each field separately using a special assignment operator, <<-. When we call the new function, the class structure does the rest for us, ensuring that new objects of our class contain the correct fields.

CAUTION

The <<- Operator

The <<- operator assigns directly to a function's parent environment. This can make it difficult to track what a function is doing; therefore, the use of <<- should generally be avoided.

In Listing 22.2 we create an `initialize` method for our `modIntRef` class based on the constructor function we defined earlier for `modInt4` objects. We must explicitly create both x and modulus using the <<- assignment operator, even though the `modulus` argument is unaltered by the function. This is due to scoping, but it is not something we will explore any further.

LISTING 22.2 Defining an `initialize` Method

```
 1: > modIntRef$methods(list(initialize = function(x, modulus){
 2: +    # Create the object from the starting number, x and modulus, modulus
 3: +    # Divide by the modulus to get new number appropriate for that modulus
 4: +    # Assign fields *if* they are provided (ensures we can copy the object)
 5: +    if (!missing(x)) {
 6: +      x <<- x %% modulus
 7: +    }
 8: +    if (!missing(modulus)) {
 9: +      modulus <<- modulus
10: +    }
11: + }))
```

Notice the syntax in the first line of Listing 22.2. We are updating the `methods` argument to `modIntRef` by defining a list. All methods are stored as a named list of method names. When creating new methods, however, we do not need to redefine old methods. Another important step here is to ensure that variables are only assigned if they are provided by the user. This enables us to create a template object if required but also enables us to copy the object later on.

Mutable Objects

Mutability is quite a common term in object-oriented programming; however, it may be unfamiliar if you come from an analytic background. Generally R is not mutable, meaning that we do not directly edit or change objects when we execute functions. Instead, we have to force R to overwrite an object. For example, suppose we define a vector, x, that we want to sort:

```
> x <- c(1, 3, 2)
```

We can use the `sort` function to sort x, but the operation does not actually update x:

```
> sort(x)
[1] 1 2 3
> x
[1] 1 3 2
```

To overwrite x, we need to assign the result back to x, like so:

```
> x <- sort(x)
> x
[1]  1  2  3
```

Because R stores values in memory, what we actually do here is copy the result to memory before overwriting x. Reference Classes are mutable, meaning that the methods we define directly update the object. This is a behavior you briefly saw in Hour 12, "Efficient Data Handling in R," when working with the **data.table** package. We referred to mutable behavior as "updating by reference."

The fact that Reference Classes are mutable changes the way in which we think about objects. Methods are applied directly to an object in order to change it. For that reason, the application of Reference Classes usually differs from standard S3 or S4 applications. We must therefore write methods in a similar vein to the `initialize` function defined in Listing 22.2 by updating fields directly.

Method Definition

When developing methods for a Reference Class, we are working within the class's environment. At the time the method is called, we can be sure that all the fields we require exist and are of the correct type and structure, as defined by the `initialize` function. We do not therefore need to pass field names to any methods we write. Arguments that are not available as fields in our class are passed in the standard way.

Let's look at an example of defining and calling a method. In Listing 22.3 we define an `addNumber` method that adds a number to an object of the `modIntRef` class. The number is provided by the user of our function, but the x and `modulus` values that we refer to in lines 3 and 5 come from the class fields. Note that we use the double-headed assignment arrow, `<<-`, to update x in the original object. From line 8 onward, we demonstrate the mutability of the object by adding 1 and then 10 to the object, which is updated directly.

CAUTION

Local Variables

As with any R function, we can create temporary objects within the body of our function. These objects are removed once the function has finished executing. Due to functional scoping, you should avoid naming dummy variables after field names because the function can be confusing. If you do, R throws a warning at the point at which the method is defined.

LISTING 22.3 Defining Methods

```
 1: > modIntRef$methods(list(addNumber = function(aNumber){
 2: +    # Add aNumber to x locally
 3: +    x <<- x + aNumber
 4: +    # Ensure x is correct for the modulus
 5: +    x <<- x %% modulus
 6: + }))
 7: >
 8: > a <- modIntRef$new(x = 3L, modulus = 12L)
 9: > a
10: Reference class object of class "modIntRef"
11: Field "x":
13: [1] 3
13: Field "modulus":
14: [1] 12
15: > a$addNumber(1L)
16: > a
17: Reference class object of class "modIntRef"
18: Field "x":
19: [1] 4
20: Field "modulus":
21: [1] 12
22: > a$addNumber(10L)
23: > a
24: Reference class object of class "modIntRef"
25: Field "x":
26: [1] 2
27: Field "modulus":
28: [1] 12
```

Copying Reference Class Objects

For the immutable objects we worked with in previous hours, copying an object was very straightforward. Once we have copied an object, all links between the new object and the original object are lost. For example, consider an object, y, that we clone from another object, x, in the following example:

```
> x <- 5
> y <- x
```

The object y is a clone of x, and at this point both objects have the same value, 5. However, there is no link between them. We can change the value of x to 6, but y still retains the value 5, as you can see here:

```
> x <- 6
> x
[1] 6
> y
[1] 5
```

Mutable objects do not behave like this. Consider the object a that we created and modified in Listing 22.3. The object has the `modIntRef` class and is therefore mutable. Now let's try to copy a in the traditional way to create a new object, b:

```
> # Remind ourselves of the value of a
> a
Reference class object of class "modIntRef"
Field "x":
[1] 2
Field "modulus":
[1] 12
> # Create b as a copy of a in the traditional way
> b <- a
> b
Reference class object of class "modIntRef"
Field "x":
[1] 2
Field "modulus":
[1] 12
```

Now we add 1 to a using our `addNumber` method:

```
> a$addNumber(1L)
> a
Reference class object of class "modIntRef"
Field "x":
[1] 3
Field "modulus":
[1] 12
> b
Reference class object of class "modIntRef"
Field "x":
[1] 3
Field "modulus":
[1] 12
```

The object b has also been updated! This is updating by reference and is a property of mutable objects. It can be extremely useful, but to those unfamiliar with the concept, it is also a potentially dangerous trap. Luckily all Reference Classes inherit from a base `envRefClass` object that has a `copy` method. The `copy` method enables us to copy in the traditional manner. Here's an example:

```
> a <- modIntRef$new(x = 3L, modulus = 12L)
> b <- a$copy()
> b
Reference class object of class "modIntRef"
Field "x":
[1] 3
Field "modulus":
[1] 12
```

Documenting Reference Classes

It is actually much simpler to document a Reference Class system than an S4 system. This is because methods are stored with the class as opposed to being linked via generic functions. We therefore need only document the class. A special @field tag is used for documenting class fields.

R6 Classes

The R6 class system was developed by Winston Chang and first released to CRAN in 2014. The name builds on the "R5" nickname given to R's standard Reference Class implementation. The R6 implementation is essentially a variant of the Reference Class implementation that does not rely on S4 classes.

The R6 system is not part of base R. It is contained within a package called **R6** that must be installed from CRAN. Once it is loaded, we can create a new instance of an R6 class by using the R6Class function. After that, the syntax of the R6 system is extremely similar to that of R's standard Reference Class system. We instantiate new objects using the new method and can define an initialize method to check inputs and construct the class.

Public and Private Members

One potential advantage of using the R6 implementation is that it contains the notion of public and private fields and methods, an object-oriented programming concept generally known as encapsulation. The terminology gets very confusing very quickly, but the basic idea is to distinguish between members (fields or methods) that are accessible from anywhere (public) and members that are only accessible from within the class itself (private).

The benefits of encapsulation are probably best described elsewhere, but the main aim is to provide control over what others have access to in your class. Because private methods are not generally available, no other classes can depend on them. This leaves you free to adjust or change the method at a later date. In contrast, a public method is one that you are happy for someone else to use and build upon.

An R6 Example

The example in Listing 22.4 walks through a brief but complete example of creating an R6 class with public and private methods. The example contains a complete definition of the class, modInt6, and three public methods: initialize, show, and square. To illustrate the concept of private methods, a private method, adjustForModulus, has also been defined. This method ensures that the value of x is always less than the modulus. The method is accessed by the public square method via private$adjustForModulus and updates by reference when called.

One of the main differences in terms of usage between R6 and standard Reference Classes is the use of self to refer to the object instead of the double-headed assignment arrow, <<-.

LISTING 22.4 Defining an R6 Class

```
 1: > library("R6")
 2: > modInt6 <- R6Class("modInt6",
 3: +            # Define public elements
 4: +            public = list(
 5: +              # Fields
 6: +              x = NA,
 7: +              modulus = NA,
 8: +              # Methods
 9: +              initialize = function(x, modulus){
10: +                if (!missing(x)) {
12: +                  self$x <- x %% modulus
13: +                }
14: +                if (!missing(modulus)) {
15: +                  self$modulus <- modulus
16: +                }
17: +              },
18: +              show = function(){
19: +                cat(self$x, " (mod ", self$modulus, ")", sep = "")
20: +              },
21: +              square = function(){
22: +                self$x <- self$x^2
23: +                # Use private method to ensure x < modulus
24: +                private$adjustForModulus()
25: +              }
26: +            ),
27: +            # Define private methods
28: +            private = list(
29: +              # Function to ensure correct modulus
30: +              adjustForModulus = function(){
31: +                self$x <- self$x %% self$modulus
32: +              }
33: +            )
34: + )
```

```
35: > a <- modInt6$new(3L, 12L)
36: > a$show()
37: 3 (mod 12)
38: > # Now square a
39: > a$square()
40: > a$show()
41: 9 (mod 12)
```

There is plenty more that R6 classes can offer; however, the usage is very similar to that of standard Reference Classes.

NOTE

Active Bindings

The notion of active bindings is also supported in R6. Active bindings look like fields but call a function each time they are accessed.

Other Class Systems

The object-oriented programming options available in R are by no means limited to the set you have seen in the past two hours. The **R.oo** package has been around since 2001 and provides convenience wrappers for setting up S3 classes as well as an Object class from which you are able to extend in order to create objects that can be modified by reference.

Another relatively popular alternative is the **proto** package. The **proto** package enables prototype programming, a form of object-oriented programming with no classes! Beyond that, there are a few more packages that implement forms of object-oriented programming, but we won't describe them all here. No doubt more will be written in the future.

Summary

Following on from Hour 21, where we were introduced you to the concept of writing an S3 class, we have now looked in greater detail at R's more formal class systems, S4 and Reference Classes, including a brief tour of the R6 implementation and some of the other options available. Each of the implementations has its advantages and disadvantages, and it is up to you to decide which, if any, is of most use to you. It's worth bearing in mind, however, that R has been written in order to be flexible and fast to type. It has not been written in order to facilitate object-oriented programming!

In the "Activities" section, you now have the opportunity to build your own S4 and Reference Classes and develop methods for these classes.

Q&A

Q. What's best for me? S3, S4, standard Reference Classes, or R6?

A. If you're starting out with classes, then S3 or S4 classes are a good place to start because they're not too dissimilar from standard R coding. If you're comfortable with the concepts of object-oriented programming, however, then one of the two forms of reference classes discussed in this hour will give you a lot more control. However, be aware that as the level of control increases, flexibility tends to be reduced.

Q. If S3 classes have the convention `[genericFunction].[class]`, what are the S4 and Reference Class naming conventions?

A. There is no required naming convention due to the different dispatch mechanism used by `setMethod` for S4 classes and the message-passing approach used in Reference Classes. The "`lowerCamelCase`" naming convention is extremely popular for classes and indeed any objects in R. There is also a growing trend of using underscores to separate words within an object name.

Workshop

The workshop contains quiz questions and exercises to help you solidify your understanding of the material covered. Try to answer all questions before looking at the "Answers" section that follows.

Quiz

1. True or false? An S4 object is a special type of list.

2. True or false? A Reference Class object is a special type of list.

3. What is multiple dispatch?

4. What is a mutable object?

5. What is the difference between a slot and a field?

Answers

1. **False.** It can be helpful to think of an S4 object as being like a list, but it is not. For one thing, we access elements using @ as opposed to $.

2. **False.** A Reference Class object may appear even more like a list than an S4 object due to the $ syntax we use. However, it is actually an environment, not a list.

3. In generic function object orientation, method dispatch controls which method is selected when a generic function is called. When the dispatch mechanism can depend on multiple arguments, we call this multiple dispatch.

4. A mutable object is simply one that can be changed. In R, we typically deal with immutable objects. Instead of changing an object, we overwrite it with a new value. Reference Class objects are mutable, however.

5. We say "slots" when working with S4 classes and "fields" when working with all forms of reference class, but they essentially refer to the same thing.

Activities

1. Define a new S4 class. The aim of the class is to store simulated data from various known statistical distributions. In order to construct the new class, you need to create the following:

   ▶ A constructor function that takes inputs n and distribution, representing the number of values to sample and the distribution to sample from. Ensure that the function has the option for other parameter arguments, as needed.

   ▶ A print method that displays a table of summary statistics for the simulated data (mean, median, standard deviation, min, and max).

   ▶ A new generic combine method that enables two objects (provided they are of the same distribution) to be combined to form a new set of samples, where the total number of samples is the sum of the number of samples from the original objects.

2. Define a new Reference Class. The aim of the class is to store financial account information:

   ▶ Define the class as standardAccount. The class should have a single field, balance, that defaults to $50 (a minimum initial deposit to set up the account).

   ▶ Write methods called deposit and withdraw that update the account balance field when called. The withdraw method should not allow the balance to go into the red (that is, fall below zero).

   ▶ Extend the class by creating a new class, goldAccount. The goldAccount class should allow an overdraft of $1,000.

Dynamic Reporting

What You'll Learn in This Hour:

▶ What dynamic reporting is

▶ How to create a report in R

▶ Including R code in reports

▶ The basics of markdown and LaTeX

Up to this point you have seen the fundamentals of the R language as well as aspects of R that allow us to ensure that we write high-quality, well-documented, and easily shareable code. In this hour, we are going to take a look at one of the ways you can extend your use of R, specifically for simplifying the generation of reports that rely heavily on R-generated output.

What Is Dynamic Reporting?

We all produce reports for a variety of reasons on a regular basis. If you have used R to manipulate data, perform analysis, or produce graphics, you are likely at some point to have copied results or inserted a graphic into a report. This usually means that you have all of your analysis saved in one place and your final report in another, and you need to ensure that you keep both up to date. This can be particularly challenging if your data changes on short notice and you need to quickly regenerate your report, or if you need to produce the same report on a regular basis.

Dynamic reporting, also commonly referred to as automated reporting or reproducible reporting, is a means by which we can generate a report entirely in R. The content of the report and the code to perform any manipulation or analysis are stored together. There are a number of advantages to writing reports in this way, including the following:

▶ No need to copy and paste into a separate report

▶ Easy to track what code was used for the analysis in a report

▶ Simple to re-run the report if the data changes

▶ Easy to run reports that need to be produced on a regular basis

Traditionally, we did this in R using Sweave. Sweave allows us to combine R code inside LaTeX documents. LaTeX is a markup language that is used commonly in scientific reporting. It was designed for writing technical documents and requires a TeX installation. Although a very powerful tool, it has quite a steep learning curve. More recently the package **knitr** was introduced to R. Although it still allows users to produce documents using LaTeX, it also allows us to use Markdown, which is another markup language. Markdown is much simpler to get started with, having a restricted syntax. Also, rather than only producing static PDF documents, it allows us to generate HTML or Microsoft Word files as well as PDF. This makes it very simple to embed any HTML content that we want into reports, and as you will see in the final hour of this book, this means we can generate interactive documents.

An Introduction to knitr

As just mentioned, the package **knitr** has been designed to simplify the way in which we generate documents in R. You already saw the package **knitr** in Hour 20, "Advanced Package Building," when we generated a user guide for a package.

Although we commonly think of reports as long documents that contain an analysis or summary of results that we can produce in Microsoft Word or similar software, we can also think about reports as being presentations that we typically produce using Microsoft PowerPoint or other similar software. We can use **knitr** to produce both types of documents, in either PDF or HTML format, primarily depending on whether we choose to use LaTeX or Markdown to write our documents (although Markdown is more flexible in the file type that can be produced).

Simple Reports with RMarkdown

You have already seen the basics of RMarkdown in Hour 20. Markdown itself is a simple, plain-text markup language that has a number of variants that are all very similar. RMarkdown is the variant that allows us to include chunks of R code inside a document to be rendered to HTML. Note that the RStudio options make it very simple to render an RMarkdown document as a PDF, which requires a Tex installation, or as a Microsoft Word document. In this hour, we will only work with HTML documents for simplicity.

A Basic RMarkdown Document

To create an RMarkdown document, we need to create a file with the extension .Rmd. Using RStudio, we can create a template RMarkdown document that includes sample RMarkdown content. We can create this file by selecting R Markdown from the "File > New File" menu. This presents an options window that allows us to select the type of document that we want to generate. An example of this options window is shown in Figure 23.1. As you can see, you can select the type of document you want to create as well as the output you want to generate. In this case, we will simply use the default document and create HTML output. You will also notice that this screen allows you to insert the title of the document and the author name. Adding these components on this screen will automatically insert them correctly into the document header. After you click OK, a template document will be opened.

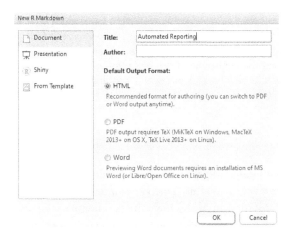

FIGURE 23.1
RMarkdown file creation options in RStudio

All RMarkdown documents begin with a header that defines certain components, such as the title, author, and date, as well as the output format and any options for the output format such as styling. An example of the header is shown in Listing 23.1, lines 1 to 5.

LISTING 23.1   RMarkdown Example

```
 1: ---
 2: title: "Automated Reporting"
 3: author: "Aimee Gott"
 4: output: html_document
 5: ---
 6:
 7: The following report contains an analysis of the data from 2015.
 8:
 9: ## Analysis
10: A simple linear model was fitted to the data to determine the main factors that
11: contribute to a change in the dependent variable. We can see below some simple
12: summaries of the data.
13:
```

After this header we can simply start writing our document. This could be plain text, but we can also format the text using the Markdown formatting options you saw in Table 20.1 in Hour 20. An example of how a Markdown document might look can be seen in Listing 23.1.

TIP

Creating Presentations

As you will have noticed from the options in Figure 23.1, you can also create a presentation using Markdown. Selecting the HTML presentation options will control all of the setup for you. The main difference to note is that new slides are started with a new Level 1 or Level 2 heading; otherwise, all markdown formatting and code chunks are the same.

Building an HTML File

Because we are writing our document in a markup language, we will need to build the RMarkdown file to generate the HTML. The easiest way to do this is using the interface in RStudio. You will notice that after opening an RMarkdown file you have the additional option at the top of your file viewer labelled "Knit HTML." Before generating the HTML, you will need to save the RMarkdown file with the extension .Rmd. Selecting the "Knit HTML" option will generate the corresponding HTML file and open a preview for you, as well as save the HTML file in the same location as the RMarkdown file. This HTML file can be opened by any web browser and can be shared in the same way as any other static file.

Including R Code and Output

We include sections of R code in documents inside code "chunks". These chunks in RMarkdown are indicated by three back ticks at the start and end of the chunk. We also use curly brackets to indicate that the code is R code and include any additional options we wish to set. Three examples of code chunks are shown in Listing 23.2.

LISTING 23.2   RMarkdown Code Chunks

```
 1: ```{r, collapse = TRUE}
 2: library(mangoTraining)
 3: summary(pkData$Conc)
 4: ```
 5:
 6: ```{r, echo = FALSE}
 7: library(ggplot2)
 8: qplot(Time, Conc, data = pkData)
 9: ```
10:
11: ```{r, echo = FALSE}
```

```
12: library(knitr)
13: kable(head(pkData))
14: ```
```

As you can see in these examples, we can include any executable R code inside these chunks, whether the code generates console output or graphics output. The final code chunk, in lines 11 to 14, even includes table output. The **knitr** function `kable` will convert data output to Markdown table code, resulting in an HTML table in your document.

You will also notice in these code chunks that we have set some options inside the curly brackets, called `collapse` and `echo`. The first of these, `collapse`, keeps the code and output in the same box in the output. This is useful if you have a number of lines of code and output that you want to group together. This is useful in vignettes, but in general you would not want to include the R code in a formal document. In this case, the `echo` option is particularly useful. The `echo` option controls whether the code is returned in the document as well as the output. You will notice that this has been set in the second two code chunks, on lines 6 and 11. In these cases, when the document is created you will see that only the output appears (in these cases, a graphic and a table).

TIP

Setting Up Your Document

You will notice that in the sample code chunks here, each chunk loads an R package that is then used. It is actually good practice to include all these components in a single code chunk at the start of the document, as you would any other R script. We would recommend that you also include in this chunk any sourcing of additional R scripts or reading of data. As you will see in Table 23.1, there are options you can set to ensure that this chunk is run but no output included in the report.

There are many more options you can set to control the behavior and output of code chunks, whether this is how or if the code is run or the look of graphics output. Some of the most commonly used options can be seen in Table 23.1.

TABLE 23.1   knitr Options for Code Chunks

Option	Arguments	Practical Use
echo	TRUE/FALSE	Controls whether the R code appears in the output. Generally used to generate the report content without including code that is not required.
eval	TRUE/FALSE	Controls whether or not a code chunk is evaluated. Useful for displaying code that you don't actually want to run.

Option	Arguments	Practical Use
include	TRUE/FALSE	Determines whether a chunk is included in the final report. When this is set to FALSE, the code chunk is run but no output is included in the report. This is useful for chunks that perform setup operations, such as loading packages.
comment	"##"/NA	The characters in front of each line of code output. Setting this to NA will prevent any characters from being printed before code output.
out.width	character string e.g. "10cm"	The width of output graphics in the final document. Note that the argument must include the units as well as the value.
out.height	character string e.g. "6cm"	The height of output graphics in the final document. Note that the argument must include the units as well as the value.

TIP

Additional Code Chunk Options

We can set many more options for a code chunk. The easiest way to see all these options is to take a look at the **knitr** webpage at http://yihui.name/knitr/. This site is maintained by the package author, Yihui Xie, and includes a complete listing of all the options that can be set. To see these options, navigate to the Options page.

The final thing to mention in relation to including R code is how to include code inline—that is, in the body of the text. This is again done inside back ticks, but this time just one at each end of the code. We need to indicate that this is R code that should be executed, but otherwise we can include a line of code that will be run when the document is built. For example, we may have the following line in our RMarkdown document:

```
The median concentration for dose group 25 was `r
➥median(pkData$Conc[pkData$Dose==25])`
```

In this instance, the median value would be inserted for us on creation of the document. This makes it very simple to reference values in the text and not have to worry about having to update the text if the data changes. An example of how the HTML for the content shown in this hour may look can be seen in Figure 23.2.

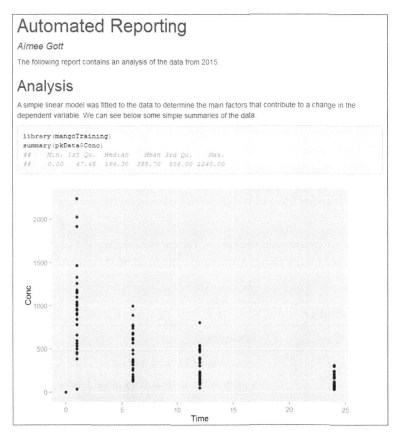

FIGURE 23.2
Extract of a rendered HTML file generated from RMarkdown

Reporting with LaTeX

When it comes to creating documents in LaTeX, you will need to ensure that you first have a TeX installation. This is separate software that is not supplied with R, and the exact require-ments will depend on your operating system. Windows users can install MiKTeX, OS X users will need to install MacTex, and Linux users TeX Live. For the remaining sections, it is assumed that you have been able to install the appropriate software for your operating system.

As previously mentioned, LaTeX is a markup language that is widely used in scientific reporting. One of its primary advantages is that it's very simple to incorporate scientific notation into docu-ments. A full introduction to LaTeX is beyond the scope of this book, but we will introduce some of the basics here. More specifically, we will focus on how to generate LaTeX documents from R and how to include R code and output, which will be new to those already familiar with LaTeX.

A Basic LaTeX Document

When we are generating documents using LaTeX in R, we create .Rnw files. These are Sweave files, but they can be converted to PDF using **knitr**, giving us all the options available in the **knitr** package. We can open a Sweave file from the RStudio New File menu by selecting R Sweave. In RStudio, this will open a document that contains some initial LaTeX tags for us to get started with. The whole document begins with the tag \documentclass, which identifies the type of document we will produce. The next tag in the template will be \begin{document}, followed by \end{document}. It is between these tags that we will contain all the content of our document.

To add content to our document, we must again use specific format options. Table 23.2 shows the main LaTeX tags required for the components equivalent to those we introduced in Markdown in Hour 20.

TABLE 23.2   Basic LaTeX Notation

Format	Code	Example
Level 1 heading	\section{}	\section{Introduction}
Level 2 heading	\subsection{}	\subsection{Loading the Package}
Level 3 heading	\subsubsection{}	\subsubsection{Main Functions}
Italic	\emph{}	This is \emph{really} important!
Bold	\textbf{}	The \textbf{devtools} package
Superscript	$text^superscript$	Multiply by 4^2
Bulleted list	\begin{itemize} \item \end{itemize}	\begin{itemize} \item Load package \item Run sampleFromData \end{itemize}
Numbered list	\begin{enumerate} \item \end{enumerate}	\begin{enumerate} \item Load package \item Run sampleFromData \end{enumerate}

As an example of how a LaTeX document might look, Listing 23.3 shows the LaTeX equivalent of Listing 23.1.

LISTING 23.3 A Basic LaTeX Document

```
 1: \documentclass{article}
 2:
 3: \title{Automated Reporting with LaTeX}
 4: \author{Aimee Gott}
 5: \date{}
 6:
 7: \begin{document}
 8:
 9: \maketitle
10:
11: The following report contains an analysis of the data from 2015.
12:
13: \section{Analysis}
14: A simple linear model was fitted to the data to determine the main factors that
15: contribute to a change in the dependent variable. We can see below some simple
16: summaries of the data.
17: \end{document}
```

You will notice that just like the Markdown document, we have a header that gives the document type, the title, and the author. It is also worth noting that to have the header appear in your document, you will need to include the \maketitle tag, shown on line 9.

TIP

Creating the PDF

Just like for Markdown documents, much functionality has been incorporated into RStudio, and this includes compiling the PDF. Rather than any knit option, however, you will see the option "Compile PDF." This will require the TeX installation we mentioned. To ensure that you are using **knitr**, and therefore have all **knitr** options available, you will need to check the Sweave global options. From the Tools menu select "Global Options", and then select the "Sweave" tab. You will notice in this menu system the option for how to weave the files (that is, Weave Rnw files using). Ensure that this is set to **knitr**. If you created the file before changing these options, you will need to remove the concordance line that will have been inserted by RStudio.

Including Code in a LaTeX Document

Just as with Markdown, we can include R code in our documents by incorporating code chunks. When we are using **knitr**, we have all the same chunk options, but in terms of the code the only difference is the way in which a code chunk is identified. Listing 23.4 gives the same code chunks as we included for Markdown in Listing 23.2.

LISTING 23.4 Sweave Code Chunks

```
 1: <<collapse = TRUE>>=
 2: library(mangoTraining)
 3: summary(pkData$Conc)
 4: @
 5:
 6: <<echo = FALSE>>=
 7: library(ggplot2)
 8: qplot(Time, Conc, data = pkData)
 9: @
10:
11: <<echo = FALSE>>=
12: library(knitr)
13: kable(head(pkData))
14: @
```

As you can see, the code chunks when we are writing Sweave documents start with << >>=, with any options being set inside the inner < >. We can use all the same **knitr** code chunk options listed in Table 23.1. The code chunks end with the @ symbol. We can include in the code chunks any executable R code that generates any form of output, including graphics, and using the `kable` function again we can generate a table, this time in LaTeX format.

As with Markdown, we can also include inline code. The Sweave equivalent is \Sexpr. As an example, we might have the following line in our document:

```
The median concentration for dose group 25 was
\Sexpr{median(pkData$Conc[pkData$Dose==25])}
```

Anything inside the `Sexpr` will be executed as a single line of code and the output inserted into the text when the PDF is compiled. An example of the PDF that would be generated from the examples in this hour can be seen in Figure 23.3.

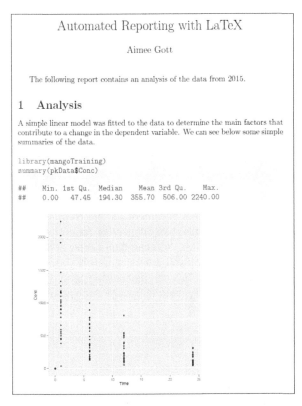

FIGURE 23.3
Extract of the output PDF file created from the Sweave content shown

Summary

You have now seen the basics of how to generate a static report in R. There are many more things you can do to these reports, such as including styles to ensure that the reports look well presented and, where necessary, follow a required company or institution template. However, here we have introduced the basics of what can be done. In the final hour, we are going to see how to extend some of these ideas to generate interactive web applications and interactive reports.

Q&A

Q. **I am just starting out creating reports in R. Which should I learn, Markdown or LaTeX?**

A. If you have never used LaTeX before, I would recommend starting with Markdown. Its limited syntax means that it is much easier to get started with, but allows the flexibility to create documents in a number of formats. However, if you need to include a large number of mathematical formulas or a more sophisticated layout in your documents, you may find that it is more beneficial to learn LaTeX. You can include formulas in a Markdown document, but this requires an additional component, mathjax, that allows you to write LaTeX inside a Markdown document.

Q. **Can I customize the style of my documents?**

A. The styling or template you use will depend on the type of document you are creating, but it is straightforward to do. If you are creating an HTML file, you will need to have or create a CSS file that defines the styles for components of HTML. You can then simply add this information to the header of your Markdown document. If you are using LaTeX, you will need to create a LaTeX-style file to apply to your documents. This can be challenging to do initially, but if the style already exists, you will typically only need to change the type of document that is created in the `documentclass` option.

Workshop

The workshop contains quiz questions and exercises to help you solidify your understanding of the material covered. Try to answer all questions before looking at the "Answers" section that follows.

Quiz

1. What are the two markup languages you have seen for creating documents from R?

2. How do you refer to blocks of R code in a document?

3. Do you have to include R code in your final document?

4. What file extension do you give to Markdown files and Sweave files, respectively?

Answers

1. The two markup languages are Markdown (or more specifically, RMarkdown) and LaTeX.

2. Blocks of R code are referred to as "code chunks."

3. No, you can set the option `echo` to be `FALSE`, and this will prevent the code from appearing in the final document.

4. You give the extension .Rmd to RMarkdown files and .Rnw to Sweave files.

Activities

1. Create a simple RMarkdown document that has the following attributes:

   ▶ Has a title, your name, and today's date

   ▶ Has three sections—introduction, analysis, and conclusion—each containing a paragraph of simple text

   ▶ Includes a code chunk that generates a plot of `Ozone` against `Wind` from the `airquality` data

   ▶ Fits a simple linear model of `Ozone` against `Wind`, returning the coefficients of the model in a table

   ▶ Ensures that none of the R code or any warnings or messages are displayed in the final document

2. Generate the HTML file for the RMarkdown document you have just created.

3. Try creating this same document using LaTeX.

Building Web Applications with Shiny

In this final hour, we are going to look at another of the tools that allows you to extend your R code, in particular giving you the ability to interactively share your analysis and results. Although you might initially be put off by the idea of building a web application, we are going to introduce a package that allows you to generate web applications entirely in R, writing only R code. This is currently one of the most popular packages available in R, with more and more packages being added to CRAN that use this framework.

A Simple Shiny Application

The package we are going to use to generate web applications is **shiny**. This package has been available through CRAN for almost three years, but its widespread usage has grown rapidly over the last year. One of the main reasons it has become so popular is that it makes the power of a web application available to R users without the need to learn HTML or JavaScript. In this section, we look at the basics of creating an application.

Structure of a Shiny Application

Before we get started with writing code, it is worth getting familiar with the components that make up a Shiny application. During development we need to think about two main components: First of all, the user interface. What will the application look like? How will components be arranged on the page? Second of all, we need to think about what is called "the server." What will the application do? When an option is changed, what needs to happen?

It is possible—and for bigger applications, recommended—to build a Shiny application in two scripts named ui.R and server.R, but here we will work in just a single file. Throughout this hour, we are simply going to create a ui object and a `server` object that will be passed to the function `shinyApp`. We are going to contain all these components in a single script. If we save this script as app.R, we will obtain some shortcuts in RStudio that allow us to run the application at the click of a button.

You can see an example of how the file will look in RStudio in Figure 24.1. In the script app.R, you can see the overall structure of the script and the outlines for the ui and `server` components, which we will return to in the next sections, along with the call to the `shinyApp` function. Also, you can see the Run App button at the top of the script window. By selecting the drop-down menu, you can see the options available in this graphic. This controls whether the app is opened in a separate window, in the viewer pane, or in your default web browser. As you can see in the example in Figure 24.1, this particular application, which at this point is empty, will open in the viewer pane.

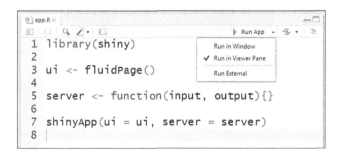

FIGURE 24.1
Example of the app.R file in RStudio and the additional Run App options

Having seen the empty components of a Shiny application, we now need to think about what will go into them. We start off by looking at the user interface, which is controlled by the ui object.

The ui Component

As stated earlier, the ui object is where we define how our application is going to look. It is here that we specify the input components, the type of outputs, and how they will all be arranged.

As a very simple example, let's consider an application that has a simple text input and uses it as the title for a histogram, which we will also output in the application. The code for this application can be seen in Listing 24.1.

LISTING 24.1 A Simple User Interface

```
 1: library(shiny)
 2:
 3: ui <- fluidPage(
 4:
 5:   textInput(inputId = "title", label = "Enter title text:"),
 6:
 7:   plotOutput(outputId = "histogram")
 8:
 9: )
10:
11: server <- function(input, output){}
12:
13: shinyApp(ui = ui, server = server)
```

You will notice that the only component we have changed here is the `ui` object. We will return to the `server` object in the next section. The `ui` object is created initially by a call to the function `fluidPage`. This is a function that controls the layout of the application. There are many more layout options that are beyond the scope of this hour.

Let's consider the elements we have contained in our `ui` object. The first element we have provided is the `textInput` function, which creates a text input box in the application. This is one of many input functions that includes check boxes, numeric selectors and sliders, and drop-down selections, to name a few. All of these input functions follow the same structure, with the first two arguments always being the same, as shown in line 5 of Listing 24.1. The first argument is `inputId`. This is the name we are going to use to refer to this element in the code for our application. Each input object needs to have a unique name so that it can be identified, and you will see how this name is used in the next section. The next argument is `label`. This is a character string that appears in the user interface to tell the user what the purpose of the component is. If this is not included, the user won't know what they are supposed to put into this text box or what it will do.

NOTE

Input Functions and Shiny Documentation

The **shiny** package is maintained by RStudio, who provides extensive documentation both in the **shiny** package and online. For more information on all the available input functions, as well as outputs and layouts, see the documentation available on the Shiny web pages at shiny.rstudio.com.

Before we consider the next component, notice that on line 5 of Listing 24.1 there is a comma to end the line. This is because we are about to provide another argument to the function `fluidPage`. Although it is easy to forget to include commas and brackets in the correct places, when we start creating the Shiny application, it does get much easier. A good indicator of a missed comma is the error message Unexpected symbol, although the latest versions of RStudio now includes in-editor error checking to help you identify a missed component a little easier.

The final component in the user interface object is an output function. In this case, we are returning a plot, so we are using the plotOutput function. Just as with inputs, there are a variety of output objects we can create, and the output function we will use depends on the object we are creating. Outputs can include text, tables, and images as well as HTML. Just like with the input object, we need to give an output object a name. Here, we have used the argument outputId to give a unique name to this component. You will see how this is used in the next section.

At this point we can run the application, but you will notice that the only thing you see is the text entry. Entering text will not do anything because we haven't told the application what to do with that text. We don't have a plot at the moment because we haven't told the application to create one. We will do all of this with the server component.

The `server` Component

The server element of a Shiny application is the part that controls what the application does. In our simple example it would control what output is generated and what happens when we change the plot title. The server component is actually a function with two arguments: input and output. We must always use these exact arguments. You can see this in both Figure 24.1 and Listing 24.1, line 11. Inside the function we then create the output objects that will be rendered in the user interface. Let's continue the example we started in the last section. Listing 24.2 shows the extended code with the server function now completed.

LISTING 24.2   Adding the `server` Function

```
 1: library(shiny)
 2:
 3: ui <- fluidPage(
 4:
 5:    textInput(inputId = "title", label = "Enter title text:"),
 6:
 7:    plotOutput(outputId = "histogram")
 8:
 9: )
10:
11: server <- function(input, output){
12:
13:    output$histogram <- renderPlot({
14:
15:       hist(rnorm(100), main = input$title, xlab = "Simulated Data")
```

```
16:
17:    })
18: }
19:
20: shinyApp(ui = ui, server = server)
```

You can see on line 13 that we have created an element in the output list called `histogram`. This is going to be an output object that is passed to an output function—in this case, it is being passed to the `plotOutput` function in the `ui` object. The name of the element that we create in the server needs to match the name we have given to the output function in the user interface so that the object will be displayed.

We create the objects themselves by using "render" functions. There is a corresponding render function for each output function we use in the user interface. Inside of the render function we put all of the code that we need to create the output object. In this case we have included a call to the function `hist`, which generates some random normal data to plot. Included in this function call is the reference to `input$title`. Here, we are asking Shiny to get the input object named `title` that we created in the user interface. Again, notice that the name matches the `inputId` element that we gave in the `ui` object (line 5 of Listing 24.2). This means that when the plot is created, it will take the value of the `input$title` element and pass it to the `main` argument of `hist`. As you will see when you run this application, whenever we change the title, the plot will update to have the new value of `input$title`.

This is now a complete application with inputs and reactive outputs. If you run this application, you will see something similar to Figure 24.2; note that the layout may be slightly different depending on window size. You will notice that as you change the text in the text input box, the application updates the graphic to include this new text.

Although this is just a simple application, we can extend the number of inputs and outputs to generate much more complex applications, with multiple inputs contributing to multiple outputs. One of the great advantages of **shiny** is that it is based entirely in R, so we have access to all the manipulation, visualization, and analysis tools we have seen throughout this book. All of them can be run from a Shiny application, with their outputs returned and updated as inputs change. An example of a more extensive application built on **shiny** is shown in Figure 24.3. This application has been extended further with the package **shinydashboard** and contains a number of pages that allow the user to interact with their data in different ways. To get to an application of this kind, we need to look at another concept that is going to help us a lot as we build bigger and more complex applications.

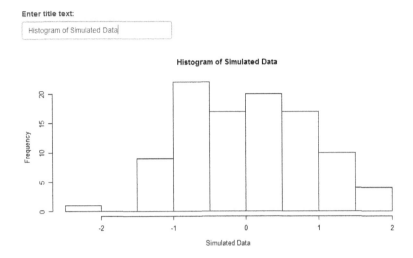

FIGURE 24.2
Complete application generated from code in Listing 24.2

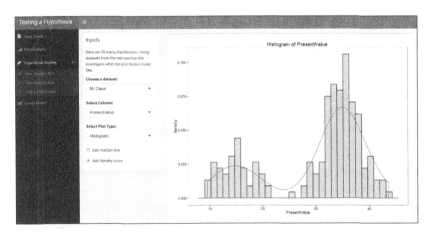

FIGURE 24.3
Example of a more extensive Shiny application

Reactive Functions

You might have noticed when running the application in Listing 24.2 that every time you changed the title, the plot was regenerated, and this caused the data to be resampled. This was because both the simulation of the data and the updating of the plot were contained within the same "reactive" function, in this case a "render" function. Therefore, when the input element changed, **shiny** knew to update the plot, but this also re-simulated the data. If you look back at the code, you will notice that in line 15 we have both the `rnorm` function and the `input$title` object. We can actually change this behavior by working with multiple reactive functions.

Why Do We Need Reactive Functions?

Hopefully at this point you can see that a reactive function is useful. In this example, it may be undesirable to the end user that the data re-simulates just because we want to change the title. But suppose that the simulation was very large, or we wanted to read in a large dataset, or even perform a complex analysis before generating a graphic. We don't want changing the title to be connected to re-running all of these components. Reactive functions therefore allow us to separate out each of the components of our application so that we can run the code as few times as possible.

When we start to develop larger applications, it is vital that we think about what is being run and how often. It's so important, in fact, that we should start to practice this with small applications that we create. When it comes to a Shiny application, we want to run code as little as possible. For any application, you need to consider, how often do I want to run this section of code? Do I really want to run it each time I change any option?

It is important to be aware that any element that is contained within the input list (for example, `input$title`) is a reactive value. A reactive value must be contained inside a reactive function in a Shiny application. We didn't mention this earlier, but the render functions are actually reactive functions, which is why they can appear here. There are, however, a number of other reactive functions that we can use to aid the development of our applications and to reduce how often code is run.

Creating a Simple Reactive Function

As mentioned earlier, all of the render functions are reactive functions, but it is often the case that there is some action we want to perform separately to generating the output. This could be reading in data, manipulating data, fitting a model, or all of these components. The simplest and most versatile function for performing these actions is the function `reactive`.

This function allows us to create a function that will only be called again when any of the inputs inside the function are changed. Consider the example we have been working with, but let's add in an extra component that tells our application how many random normal values to simulate. Instead of putting this simulation inside the `renderPlot` function, we are going to contain it inside a `reactive` function. The code we would use to do this can be seen in Listing 24.3.

LISTING 24.3   Incorporating Reactive Functions

```
 1: library(shiny)
 2:
 3: ui <- fluidPage(
 4:
 5:    numericInput(inputId = "num", label = "Number of Simulations:", value = 100),
 6:
 7:    textInput(inputId = "title", label = "Enter title text:"),
 8:
 9:    plotOutput(outputId = "histogram")
10:
11: )
12:
13: server <- function(input, output){
14:
15:    data <- reactive(rnorm(input$num))
16:
17:    output$histogram <- renderPlot({
18:
19:      hist(data(), main = input$title, xlab = "Simulated Data")
20:
21:    })
22: }
23:
24: shinyApp(ui = ui, server = server)
```

The main thing to notice here is how we have incorporated the `reactive` function. You will notice on line 15 that we have created an object called `data`. This is in fact a function object that we will call later. We have then included the call to `rnorm` inside the `reactive` function. At the point that we want to use this data, in the call to `hist` on line 19, we now call this `data` function. The difference now is that the `data` function will only regenerate the simulated data when the `input$num` value changes, rather than each time the `hist` function is called. You will be able to see this behavior if you run this code and try changing both the numeric value and the title.

You can have as many `reactive` functions as you want in an application, and you can even have nested `reactive` functions. For instance, you may have a `renderPlot` function that plots the output from a model. This `renderPlot` may call a `reactive` function that fits the model, which in turn calls a `reactive` function that reads in or simulates your data. In addition, some other reactive functions are available in the **shiny** package that will handle reactive values differently. For more information, take a look at the help files for the functions `isolate`, `observeEvent`, and `eventReactive`.

Interactive Documents

In the last hour, you saw how to create dynamic documents that allow you to generate a report or even a presentation entirely from R, mixing both the document content and the R code. Here, you have now seen another means of sharing analysis, in the form of Shiny applications. However, we can in fact combine the two. We are able to create a document that includes Shiny components. We can quickly open a template document of the correct format from RStudio using the New R Markdown menu you saw in Hour 23, "Dyanmic Reporting." Instead of selecting the Document option, we can instead choose Shiny. You will notice that this gives you the additional "runtime" option in the document header.

We include Shiny components inside an R code chunk in the same way we would include any other code. When it comes to the Shiny component, we include inputs in exactly the same way. We can use an `inputPanel` function to group together all of the inputs. In a Shiny document, we don't need to include the usual output functions; we simple include the render functions that would usually be in the `server` function. So if we wanted to include the same inputs and outputs as we have seen in this hour, but inside a markdown document, our code chunk would look like the following:

```
```{r, echo=FALSE}
inputPanel(
  numericInput(inputId = "num", label = "Number of Simulations:", value = 100),

  textInput(inputId = "title", label = "Enter title text:")
)

data <- reactive(rnorm(input$num))

renderPlot({

    hist(data(), main = input$title, xlab = "Simulated Data")

    })
```
```

An example of how this would render in the document can be seen in Figure 24.4. The important thing to note is that this is no longer a static file. Because we have a Shiny element in the document, we need to have an R session available to run it. You will notice that the options in RStudio are no longer "Knit," but "Run Document."

If you have an existing Shiny application and you simply want to embed it into a document, you can do so by using the `shinyAppDir` function, pointing to the location of your Shiny application and setting elements such as the width and height of the application in the document.

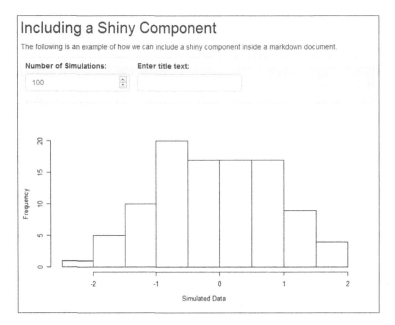

FIGURE 24.4
A Shiny element inside a reactive document

Sharing Shiny Applications

Creating a Shiny application that will allow you to share your work is very simple and flexible, but an important thing to consider is how you are going to share your application. Up to this point you have probably just run your examples on your own machine with your own version of R. If you want to allow others to work with you and run analysis or investigate outcomes, you need to be able to provide your application. You can of course simply send the files to other users or incorporate the application into an R package, but this requires the users to have R installed and all of the correct packages. However, often the reason you want to create a Shiny application is to share what you are doing with non-R users.

The best way to share your application in this case is to have your application hosted on a server that allows you to send a single URL to the end users. There are a couple of ways you can do this. First of all, you can have your application hosted by RStudio with shinyapps.io. This is a service for which you can sign up, with one of a range of packages that allows you to have RStudio host your application for you. Alternatively, you can host your application on your own server using Shiny Server. There is both a free and a pro version available, with the pro version adding features such as authentication. Much more information about all of these services is available from the RStudio website, which will allow you to determine the best approach for you.

Summary

In this final hour, we introduced the basics of the package **shiny**, giving you enough tools to get started. There is much, much more that you can do with a Shiny application that is beyond the scope of this hour. The **shiny** package is maintained by RStudio, which offers extensive material describing some of the features not covered here, including controlling the layout of an application, many more of the input and output options, how you can work with data, and how you can customize your application with CSS components, just to name a few. Everything you have seen in this book has given you the foundations to go on and learn more about what can be done with R and understand for yourself the corresponding documentation. In the final two hours, we have introduced just two of the popular means of sharing R with non-R users, but what can be achieved goes far beyond our coverage. Hopefully this has given you a taste of what is possible so that you can jump in and try it out for yourself.

Q&A

Q. Can I open my Shiny application in my web browser?

A. Yes, you can. You can do this by changing the default option in the Run App drop-down menu, or you can use the Open in New Window button in the viewer window/pane.

Q. Why can't I run any other code while my Shiny app is running?

A. While you are running your Shiny application, your R session will be blocked. This is because while the app is active, R code is being run and re-run. Because you can't run multiple processes at the same time in R, you cannot run any other code while you run your Shiny application.

Workshop

The workshop contains quiz questions and exercises to help you solidify your understanding of the material covered. Try to answer all questions before looking at the "Answers" section that follows.

Quiz

1. Which component controls what the application will look like?

2. What two arguments do you need to give to all input functions?

3. There are two arguments you must give to a `server` function. Which of the following options is not required?

   A. `input`

   B. `output`

   C. `session`

4. What are the main benefits of using a `reactive` function?

Answers

1. The `ui` component controls how the application will look to the end user.

2. All of the input functions, whether text, a number, or a drop-down menu, start with the arguments `inputId` and `label`. The argument `inputId` is used by the application to reference the objects, whereas the `label` argument is used in the user interface to tell the user the purpose of the element.

3. Both the `input` and `output` arguments are required arguments to the `server` function that you need to give in exactly this format. You can optionally use the `session` argument to pass session information to the Shiny application `server` function.

4. One of the main benefits of using a `reactive` function is that you can break up the running of the application. Rather than tasks being re-run when they do not need to be, you can use `reactive` functions to ensure that they are only re-run when an input option is changed.

Activities

1. Create an application that takes three inputs:

   ▶ A numeric slider of values between 1 and 500

   ▶ A drop-down menu to select color values

   ▶ A text string to give the plot title

2. Update the application to return a histogram of simulated values using all of the preceding options.

3. Extend the application to include a check box that adds a vertical reference line at the median value of the data.

4. Ensure that the data is not re-simulated each time an option is changed.

5. Use the available documentation to update the layout of the application to ensure that all the inputs are in a column on the left and outputs in a column to the right.

Installation

This appendix provides some details for installing R on Windows, OS X, and Linux distributions. Instructions for installing the Rtools component required for building R packages on Windows are also provided. Up-to-date instructions are maintained on the book's website, http://www. mango-solutions.com/wp/teach-yourself-r-in-24-hours-book/.

Installing R

R is installed from a central repository named CRAN. Most users typically navigate to CRAN via www.r-project.org, although you can also navigate directly to CRAN.

1. Click the "download R" link on the R Project main page.

2. Choose the most local CRAN mirror. Each mirror is exactly the same, so it does not actually matter which one you choose, although it helps reduce traffic if you choose a local mirror.

3. From the main home page of CRAN, there are three options, depending on your operating system. Click the appropriate link.

Installing R on Windows

The following steps describe the process of installing R on Windows:

1. There are three available "subdirectories." Click the link to "base."

2. At the top of the page the most recent R release on Windows is available for download via a link—for example, "Download R 3.2.2 for Windows." Click the link to download the installer to a temporary location (or choose "run" if presented with the option).

3. Choose your language and follow the instructions in the wizard.

   ▶ When presented with the option to configure startup options, as shown in Figure A.1, it is advised that you select No and accept the defaults.

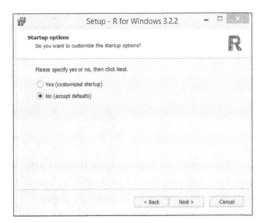

FIGURE A.1
Startup Options

▶ Keep clicking Next through all the options, assuming you are happy with what the wizard is going to do.

▶ When you are ready, click the Finish button.

Installing R on Mac OS X

Carefully read the notes at the top of the page before downloading R on OS X.

The first link under the Files heading contains a link to the most recent version of R available on OS X—for example, R-3.2.2.pkg. Select this link and run the installer.

1. Once the file has downloaded, run the .pkg file.

2. Choose your language and follow the instructions in the wizard.

▶ Keep clicking Next through all the options, assuming you are happy with what the wizard is going to do.

▶ When you are ready, click the Finish button.

Installing R on Linux

Choose the appropriate link for your Linux distribution. Each distribution contains its own instructions and/or README file for installing R. For Debian and Ubuntu, the latest stable version of R is available in official repositories. An example of the help for Ubuntu is shown in Figure A.2. Detailed instructions for downloading and installing R are provided on the home page.

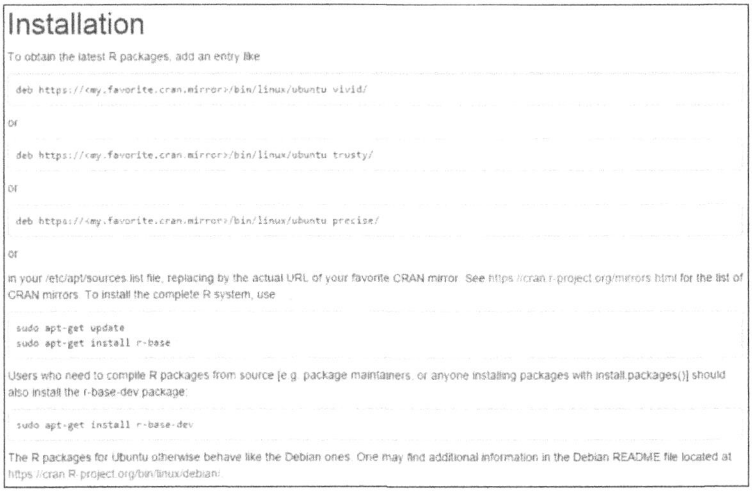

Installation

To obtain the latest R packages, add an entry like

```
deb https://<my.favorite.cran.mirror>/bin/linux/ubuntu vivid/
```

or

```
deb https://<my.favorite.cran.mirror>/bin/linux/ubuntu trusty/
```

or

```
deb https://<my.favorite.cran.mirror>/bin/linux/ubuntu precise/
```

or

in your /etc/apt/sources.list file, replacing by the actual URL of your favorite CRAN mirror. See https://cran.r-project.org/mirrors.html for the list of CRAN mirrors. To install the complete R system, use

```
sudo apt-get update
sudo apt-get install r-base
```

Users who need to compile R packages from source (e.g. package maintainers, or anyone installing packages with install.packages()) should also install the r-base-dev package.

```
sudo apt-get install r-base-dev
```

The R packages for Ubuntu otherwise behave like the Debian ones. One may find additional information in the Debian README file located at https://cran.R-project.org/bin/linux/debian/

FIGURE A.2
Installing R on Ubuntu

Installing Rtools for Windows

Building packages requires a number of additional command-line tools that are not available by default on Windows. You can access them by installing Rtools, a set of development utilities available on CRAN. Linux users will typically install r-base-dev (Debian) or similar in the same way you would install R. OS X users will typically need to install XCode, available via the AppStore, and then install Command Line Tools from within XCode. Up-to-date instructions for installing these additional components are maintained on the book's website, http://www.mango-solutions.com/wp/teach-yourself-r-in-24-hours-book/.

You can navigate directly to CRAN. Otherwise, start by navigating to the R-Project website.

1. Click the "download R" link.

2. Choose the most local CRAN mirror.

From the main home page of CRAN:

1. Click the Download R for Windows link.

2. Click the Rtools link (https://cran.rstudio.com/bin/windows/Rtools/).

3. There is a table of Rtools versions available for download. You must install the correct version of Rtools for the version of R you are using. The "R Compatibility" column lists which versions of R are appropriate for each Rtools release. See Figure A.3 for an example.

Download	R compatibility	Frozen?
Rtools33.exe	R 3.2.x and later	No
Rtools32.exe	R 3.1.x to 3.2.x	Yes
Rtools31.exe	R 3.0.x to 3.1.x	Yes
Rtools30.exe	R >2.15.1 to R 3.0.x	Yes
Rtools215.exe	R >2.14.1 to R 2.15.1	Yes
Rtools214.exe	R 2.13.x or R 2.14.x	Yes
Rtools213.exe	R 2.13.x	Yes
Rtools212.exe	R 2.12.x	Yes
Rtools211.exe	R 2.10.x or R 2.11.x	Yes
Rtools210.exe	R 2.9.x or 2.10.x	Yes
Rtools29.exe	R 2.8.x or R 2.9.x	Yes
Rtools28.exe	R 2.7.x or R 2.8.x	Yes
Rtools27.exe	R 2.6.x or R 2.7.x	Yes
Rtools26.exe	R 2.6.x, R 2.5.x or (untested) earlier	Yes

FIGURE A.3
Rtools download table

As an example of which version to download, if you are using R 3.1.2, you will need to install Rtools31.

4. Click the appropriate version of Rtools.

5. If you are asked whether you wish to run or save the .exe file, choose "run."

6. Once the file has downloaded, click Run.

7. Choose your language and follow the instructions in the wizard. Pay attention to the following:

   ▶ When you are asked to choose a location for the installation, as shown in Figure A.4, Rtools typically downloads directly to C:\. If you wish to change this, do so at this point. It is good practice to include the version number (excluding the period) in the name of the destination directory. For example, save Rtools 3.3 to Rtools33. This will help keep track of Rtools versions when you are working with multiple versions of R.

   ▶ In order to build C .dll files, ensure that all components are selected when you are presented with this option. Do not install the "Extras to Build 32 bit R: TCL/TK" or "Extras to Build 64 bit R: TCL/TK" unless you actually intend to do so (it is not advised that you do).

   ▶ During the install process, you will be asked if you want to update your system path (see Figure A.5). This is important to be able to build packages; if you choose not to let the install process handle this, you will need to add it manually. Check the box to save the version information to the registry.

8. When you are ready, click the Install button.

FIGURE A.4
The Select Destination Location screen

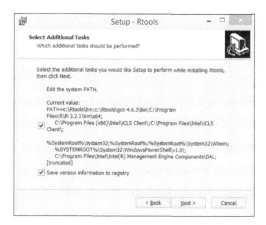

FIGURE A.5
The Select Additional Tasks screen

Installing the RStudio IDE

RStudio is installed from RStudio's own website, www.rstudio.com. Please be aware that these instructions may change as RStudio changes its website. Specifically, buttons may be moved or their names changed.

1. The RStudio home page has traditionally contained one or more obvious links in order install the RStudio IDE. The IDE is currently available via a link that states "Powerful IDE for R." Select the link to take you to the RStudio IDE download page.

2. You are presented with the option of installing the Desktop or Server version of the IDE. Select the "Desktop" link (see Figure A.6).

FIGURE A.6
Install RStudio Desktop button

3. The "Desktop" link takes you to the appropriate section of the page, where you are presented with the option to download the Open Source edition or the Commercial License version. Assuming you do not wish to purchase the commercial version at this time, click the DOWNLOAD RSTUDIO DESKTOP button.

4. Clicking the DOWNLOAD RSTUDIO DESKTOP button takes you to a page with a number of links to installers for the open-source version of RStudio Desktop. Scroll down through the page until you see an installer that is appropriate for your operating system (for example, RStudio 0.99.484 – Windows Vista/7/8/10). Click the link to download the installer.

5. Run the installer. If you are on Mac OS X, you are presented with an install wizard:

   ▶ Navigate through the wizard, clicking Next to accept the default options.

   ▶ When you are ready, click the Finish button to install RStudio.

Index

H

I

X

Y-Z

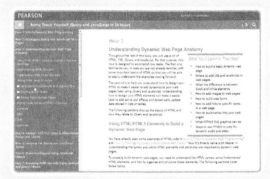
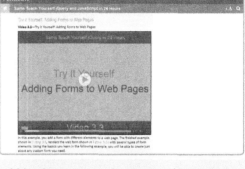
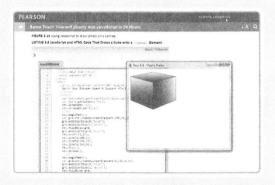
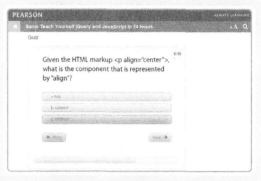